Energy Economics and Policy

Second Edition

SECOND EDITION

ENERGY
ECONOMICS
and
POLICY

JAMES M. GRIFFIN
Texas A & M University

HENRY B. STEELE
University of Houston

ACADEMIC PRESS COLLEGE DIVISION

(Harcourt Brace Jovanovich, Publishers)
Orlando   San Diego   San Francisco   New York   London
Toronto   Montreal   Sydney   Tokyo   São Paulo

Academic Press, Inc.
Orlando, Florida 32887

United Kingdom Edition Published by Academic Press, Inc.
(London) Ltd., 24/28 Oval Road, London NW1 7DX

ISBN: 0-12-303952-5
Library of Congress Catalog Card Number: 85-48013

Printed in the United States of America

To Richard, Stuart, John,
Julie, Nelson, and Justin
and others of their generation
with the hope that the word "crisis"
will never again be applicable to energy matters

CONTENTS

PREFACE

Because economics has attempted to address the important issues of its day, it has the reputation of being an exciting field of study. In Adam Smith's time, the question was whether economic self-interest could provide the basis for a viable and progressive economic and political system. In the early ninteenth century, as Ricardo and others attempted to understand the benefits and problems raised by the rapidly expanding trade among nations, the field of international economics was first systematically formulated. As a field of study, macroeconomics originated only in the 1930s, as Keynes and others attempted to understand the Great Depression. The Arab Oil Embargo of October 1973 emphasized the importance of energy to the operations of an industrialized economy. Since then, the proliferation of economic research in the area has signaled the emergence of energy economics as a specialty field within the domain of economics.

Until the appearance of the first edition of this book, numerous books and articles had been written concerning various analytical and policy aspects of the energy "crisis." Most of this discussion centered around questions of social and political policy. Very little systematic attention was given to the economic analysis of the policy problems presented by the changing role of energy in modern economies. The established techniques of microeconomics had not been intensively applied to the analysis of energy resources as scarce inputs to production processes. While several edited monographs appeared composed of selected articles on economic aspects of energy issues, there was no single textbook providing a unified analysis of energy economics and energy policy. This book was written to fill that gap. Since the appearance of the first edition of this text in 1980, we have witnessed a proliferation of edited conference proceedings, technical monographs, and books. The study of energy economics has become a legitimate specialty in economics, occupying the interests of many of the profession's most gifted researchers and policy analysts. Precisely because of these developments, a need exists for the comprehensive overview offered in the second edition of this book. Again, our emphasis is on policy. We believe that policy analysts will find this a particularly useful book. The application of a microanalytic approach to complex policy problems offers the prospect of markedly improving policy decisions.

Since 1973, the number of courses in energy economics has grown at a rapid rate. Our goal is to facilitate that growth by significantly reducing the cost of preparing and offering such a course by providing the microeconomic constructs, factual material, institutional descriptions, and discussion questions in a self-contained book. Our hope is that anyone who enjoys teaching microeconomic theory will be quite comfortable with the text. Student response to the first edition has been most encouraging.

Energy Economics and Policy will serve as a text for an undergraduate course in energy economics that presumes as a prerequisite a course in the principles of economics. In addition to the introduction and conclusion, this book contains eight chapters. Two of these chapters (Chapters 2 and 3) form the theoretical backbone of the book and are concerned with the microeconomic analysis of the allocation of depletable energy resources. Each of the other six chapters (Chapters 4 through 9) is addressed to a particular major energy policy issue: OPEC, the environment, conservation, national security, price regulation, and the economic potential of new energy sources. The analysis in Chapters 2 and 3 should be presented in class at some length. While accessible to students who have had only a single principles of economics course, these chapters can be more readily comprehended by students who have also had intermediate microeconomics. This book could also be used as a unifying text to accompany other more specialized readings in a graduate course in energy economics, in which case it would be logical to give relatively less stress to the materials in Chapters 2 and 3. Finally, for courses that may be taught to students with an interest in energy policy but with little background in economics, it is possible to bypass Chapters 2 and 3. Most of the analysis and virtually all of the policy issues can be grasped even by students who lack a mastery over the theoretical material in Chapters 2 and 3.

The second edition represents a thorough revision, with virtually all chapters undergoing substantial changes. In addition to the updating of factual material since 1979, considerable effort was made to simplify and better unify the text. Chapter 3 on dynamic resource allocation has been greatly simplified with a new emphasis on price paths over time and the role of expectations in determining them. Results of Chapter 3 involving backstop fuels are now integrated with the discussion of new technologies in Chapter 9. New topics in the second edition include prorationing regulation and the failure of voluntary unitization, the Windfall Profit Tax, natural gas deregulation, a new model of OPEC behavior, the Strategic Petrolum Reserve and optimal rules for its use, and an emphasis on long-term environmental issues such as carbon dioxide build-up and acid rain.

It is perhaps the duty of those who deal extensively with policy analysis to clarify their own policy orientations. We share the professional biases of most economists, who are in favor of efficiency and are opposed to waste. Our stance is thus in favor of competition and against monopoly. This professional bias, while by no means unusual, may at times make our analysis seem a bit one-sided. For example, as economists we find nothing whatsoever to approve of when we examine OPEC's record of unparalleled success in exploiting its oil export monopoly power between 1973 and 1983. On the other hand, we find much that is competitive in appraising the performance of energy industries in the last two decades, particularly in contrast with OPEC behavior. And in appraising the performance of governmental policymakers we, unfortunately, find more to criticize then to praise, since public policy, even on economic matters, tends to be guided largely by criteria other than those of economic efficiency.

Professional judgments need not be identical with personal views. As human beings we do not necessarily subscribe exclusively to the rather narrow organizational goals pursued by private companies. We are not necessarily condemning OPEC for seizing upon the historically unequalled opportunities afforded it in the early 1970s to strive after a broad range of political as well as economic goals. Neither are we condemning governmental policymakers for being understandably responsive to the desires of the numerous noneconomists among their constituencies. To do any of these things would betray a lack of balanced judgment.

Nevertheless, the primary purpose of this book is to instruct students in the economic aspects of energy issues, and we would be neglecting our duty if we failed to point out the ways in which certain policies or practices followed by energy companies, by OPEC, or by importing governments may act counter to the goal of economic efficiency. Economists must insist upon placing policy issues in a cost-benefit framework, and it is regrettably true that the actions taken by those who make decisions on economic matters may impose unnecessary costs upon society if those actions are not guided by the criterion of efficiency. What is most important is that the decision maker act so as to minimize the economic cost of achieving the goals that he or she is empowered to pursue.

We wish to thank a number of people who have offered comments and suggestions. We are particularly indebted to Morris A. Adelman of the Massachusetts Institute of Technology, Stephen L. McDonald and Allen Jacobs of the University of Texas, W. Michael Hanemann and David J. Teece of the University of California at Berkeley, Duane Chapman of Cornell University, F. Gerard Adams of the University of Pennsylvania, Douglas Greenly of Moorhead State University, Jane Hall of California State University at Fullerton, David P. Manuel of the University of Southwest Louisiana, Clifton Jones of the University of Richmond, Joy Dunkerly of Resources for the Future, and John Boatwright of the Exxon Corporation for useful comments on particular parts of the manuscript. The authors retain sole responsibility for all views expressed, all conclusions reached, and of course for all errors which may be present.

Energy Economics and Policy

Second Edition

THE DIMENSIONS OF THE ENERGY PROBLEM

To those who have lived through it, the energy crisis of the 1970s is like a bad dream—something to be forgotten and relegated to the past. People have a natural tendency to discard unpleasant experiences, assuming conveniently (1) that they were isolated events, which (2) resulted from forces beyond one's control and (3) are therefore best forgotten. After all, if the experience is truly a unique event beyond one's control, its likelihood of being repeated is negligible and there is consequently nothing to be learned from it that might apply to the future. To most Americans, the energy crisis of the 1970s meant a variety of things: gasoline lines, lowered thermostats, sharply higher fuel bills, unprecedented inflation rates, high unemployment levels, and the fear that greater catastrophes lay ahead. Of these effects, perhaps the worst was the fear of even worse future catastrophes as a widespread feeling permeated society that the industrialized nations of the world were powerless before the whims of the leaders of small kingdoms in the Middle East. Should such leaders elect to sever the umbilical cord tying the oil fields to the industrialized nations, we might well freeze in the dark, as the great western industrial machines slowed to a halt.

Although thoughts of such possibilities are unpleasant, is the energy crisis best forgotten as a bad dream? The theme of this book is that the energy crisis of the 1970s was neither an isolated event nor beyond the control of astute policy makers. Simply stated: the energy crisis can reoccur, but through well formulated policy, it can be largely avoided or at least attenuated. There is much to be learned from the events precipitating the energy crisis of the 1970s and the often misguided policies that were hastily concocted. The policy emphasis was on expediency, dealing in a piecemeal fashion with the symptoms rather than the cause of the disease. The result was a set of policies that were inconsistent and that frequently, when combined with other policies, had an effect opposite to their intended purpose. Even though the Energy Crisis of the 1970s is now history, important policy choices remain that will shape the energy future of the twenty-first century.

What do we wish to accomplish in this survey of the dimensions of the energy problem? This chapter begins by sketching in the role of energy in economic development, noting the sequence of the three energy eras to date: wood, coal, and petroleum. The next section develops a brief summary of past and present world patterns of energy consumption, illustrating the evolution of energy sources from wood through coal and petroleum fuels. A third section traces the pattern of past and present energy supply networks, highlighting the transition of industrial economies from domestic to imported fuels and the changing importance of various geographic regions in the supply of energy resources. Subsequently, we examine the long term price trends and their effects on macroeconomic activity. Exactly what is the energy problem we face in the last part of the twentieth century? The energy problem is examined from three currently popular perspectives: (1) The real energy crisis is yet to come, as the energy crisis of the 1970s was only a preview; (2) the energy crisis is a thing of the past, having disappeared along with monopoly power of OPEC; or (3) the energy problem is one of supply uncertainty and how best to adapt to highly uncertain future prices and fuel availability.

ENERGY: ITS ROLE IN ECONOMIC DEVELOPMENT

Humanity has employed a variety of energy sources in its continuing pursuit of greater comfort, enhanced security from want, and the satisfaction of wants through increasingly elaborate artifacts. Animals were eventually domesticated, and human muscular efforts, at first applied to hunting and scavenging, were later channeled into cultivation and artisanship. Captives and the disfavored could be converted into an energy source through the institutions of servanthood and slavery. But inanimate energy sources proved more productive in an increasing variety of applications. Wood, while always important as a fuel for heating and illumination, became for some time the most important industrial fuel source. Wind power had long been the source of energy for sea transportation, supplementing the efforts of rowers. Water was also an important source of mechanical energy even before industrialization, with grain mills and other energy users being located at waterfalls or dams along major rivers, using the kinetic energy of falling water to turn waterwheels and associated machinery.

History reveals three primary energy eras: wood, coal, and petroleum fuels. There was no sharp discontinuity between adjacent eras. The use of wood as a fuel for space heating can be traced back to prehistoric times, but its employment as a fuel for manufacturing or industrial purposes probably dates back less than 50,000 years, when artisans in Asia Minor and northern Europe used heat energy from wood in the preparation of weapons and ornaments. Coal began to be employed on a large scale in Europe only after the elimination of forest cover from areas of intensive fuel use. Coal was first mined on a large scale in the British Isles in the period of Queen Elizabeth I (1558–1603) replacing the diminishing forests as a fuel source. The use of coal spread gradually across Europe and slowly into Asia, and the coastal areas of the Far East and the Southern Hemisphere were also affected by the availability of exported coal.

By the 1780s, the Industrial Revolution began a new age in which energy was intensively used to produce artifacts. Coal, which at first had supplemented wood supplies, now came to supplant them as demands for steam power increased rapidly in the industrializing areas. By the mid-1850s, England had no choice but to rely upon coal almost exclusively for steam power, or face the prospect of converting all of its remaining forests into ashes and cinders. Coal's higher heating value per unit of weight and volume greatly reduced energy transportation costs, helping it to gain market acceptance.

Wood and coal, coupled with the development of steam generation technology, enabled a massive substitution of human labor by inanimate labor. A distinguishing feature of the Industrial Revolution compared to previous times was the unprecedented increase in output per worker. With the substitution of steam power for physical labor, output was no longer constrained by the size of the labor force.

When crude oil was first marketed on a large scale in the 1860s, it did not immediately begin to crowd coal out of the market. Instead, petroleum began by creating new markets for itself. The lubricants derived from petroleum were uniquely suitable to the needs of high-speed machinery, and many advances in mechanical engineering would have been impossible without the improved lubricants derived from crude oil. Kerosene did replace whale oil as an illuminant, and none too soon from the standpoint of preserving whales from extinction. Eventually oil began to compete more effectively with coal when its value as a boiler fuel was recognized and its costs became competitive with those of coal. However, it was not until the development of the internal combustion engine that crude oil displaced coal, in the first part of the twentieth century. Natural gas began to compete with crude oil as a source of nation-wide energy supplies in the 1930s when the technology of long-distance low-cost gas pipelines was developed. For a number of years gas consumption grew more rapidly than that of oil, and gas displaced oil in some markets because of its superior convenience, cleanliness, and economy. At present oil and gas still account for about three fourths of the energy consumed in the United States, and similarly high percentages in other developed countries.

These three energy eras played vital roles in economic development, suggesting that the next energy era will also have pronounced effects on the magnitude and type of economic development. As an economy develops, it demands more energy in more convenient forms, available on a wider geographic basis. In general, the more rapid the rate of economic growth, the more rapid the replacement of solid fuels by fluid fuels.

In earlier years petroleum products made considerable contributions to economic growth in indirect as well as direct ways. Kerosene, as an illuminating oil, satisfied a great preexisting demand for a reasonably priced source of light for industrial uses, for public lighting in urbanized areas, and for home lighting, which permitted more widespread literacy and self-education. With the advent of electric lighting in the 1880s, the market for kerosene illuminants began to decline and more of this market was captured by coal-fired central power stations.

Perhaps no two inventions transformed society more fundamentally than electric power circuitry and the internal combustion engine. Automobiles gave the entire population an enhanced mobility, and this mobility in turn made for an increasing flexibility in the location of industry and of the population itself, increasing the efficiency of geographic resource allocation. On the farm, the internal combustion engine made it possible for fewer farm workers to turn out more foodstuffs. Farm trucks and tractors rapidly replaced livestock as sources of motive power, enhancing agricultural productivity.

Electrification in turn spurred the development of new industrial processes which greatly enhanced labor productivity. But such advances were even more evident in the home, with the advent of the electric refrigerator, stove, dishwasher, radio, and many other home appliances.

Before turning to examine the historical data for these three energy eras, let us pause to consider what common denominator should be used to measure energy. The most common solution proposed by scientists and engineers is that energy should be measured by the heat content of the fuel, or the amount of heat energy the fuel could provide if all of its inherent heat content were to be converted into thermal energy. The unit most commonly used in economic applications is the British thermal unit (Btu), which is the amount of energy necessary to raise the temperature of one pound of water by one degree Fahrenheit. The Btu content of a fuel is thus related to its heat of combustion. One barrel of crude oil has an energy content of about 5.8 million Btu; 1000 cubic feet of natural gas contains only 1.035 million Btu. Thus one barrel of oil is equivalent in Btu terms to about 5600 cubic feet of natural gas. This ratio is not unacceptable as a means of comparison, but it has some shortcomings.

First, the ratio might seem to imply that if the heat content ratio is 5.6 to 1, then the price ratio should be 5.6 to 1. But fuels are valued for other attributes than Btu content alone. The form of the fuel (solid, liquid, or gaseous) is quite important in most applications. So also are the costs of using the fuel, including expenditures on boilers and other facilities, the cost of fuel preparation, storage expenses, safety precau-

Key Energy Conversion Relationships

Energy Source	Unit	Btu Equivalents
Electricity	Kilowatt hour (kwh)	3412 Btu/kwh
Natural Gas	Cubic foot (cf)	1026 Btu/cf
Coal	Ton	22.14 MMBtu
Crude Oil	Barrel (b) or 42 gallons	5.5 MMBtu/b
Wood	Cord	22.5 MMBtu cord
Uranium-235	Gram	75,000 MMBtu/gram

Where MM = millions, k = thousands.

SOURCE: D. Chapman, Energy Resources and Corporations *(Ithaca, New York: Cornell University Press, 1983) p. 15.*

tions needed, pollution potential, and other factors. Rather rarely, in fact, do two or more fuels compete directly in a given market on a strict Btu content basis. The best example in previous years was the choice of coal, oil, or gas by utilities with facilities for using all three fuels.

Different conversion efficiencies among fuels also cause problems in using the Btu as a common denominator. While coal, oil, and gas can be compared reasonably well, hydroelectric power and nuclear energy cannot. What is the Btu content of the water used to generate hydroelectric power? One approach would be to convert the kilowatt-hours generated directly into their Btu equivalent. Since water can be heated by electricity, the conversion merely requires computing the number of pounds of water that can be raised one degree Fahrenheit by the application of one kilowatt-hour of electric power. It is generally felt that the use of this purely physical conversion factor would underestimate the share of total energy provided by hydroelectric power, since fossil fuel energy sources are measured in terms of their inherent energy content without adjustment for thermal efficiencies when utilized in combustion equipment. Hence one usually measures hydroelectric power by computing the number of Btu's of fuel that would have been required to generate a kilowatt-hour in a fossil fuel plant. This number would vary somewhat, depending upon whether oil, gas, or coal was used for generation, but the statistical practice has been to use the average value for all fossil fuel plants during a given year.

A similar problem arises in connection with nuclear power. The Btu's of heat energy given off by the uranium fuel in the reactor could be measured directly, but the usual practice is to measure nuclear electricity in terms of the Btu's of fossil fuel required in conventional steam-electric plants to generate a kilowatt-hour. Since the conversion efficiency of uranium fuel into usable process heat is considerably less than that of fossil fuels, an inconsistency is introduced that actually underestimates the number of Btu's required to generate electricity from nuclear fission.

Even after we admit these shortcomings, the use of the Btu as a common denominator in comparing energy sources is probably the best simple measure available. But for a comprehensive economic analysis of the costs and benefits of using different fuels, one must also look at engineering considerations, including conversion losses at various stages in the process of going from the energy content of the raw fuels to the useful work performed for the final consumer. In addition, economists emphasize that demand factors are also important and stress that consumer preferences for certain types of goods and services are such as to make them willing to pay higher prices for a Btu of energy in one form than in another.

PAST AND PRESENT WORLD ENERGY CONSUMPTION PATTERNS

Table 1.1 presents data on the percentage of world energy consumption by regions and energy sources for the years 1925, 1950, and 1980. The regions include the three major industrial areas (United States and Canada; Western Europe; Japan), the communist bloc, and the rest of the world. The energy sources include coal, oil, gas, and primary electricity, covering both hydroelectric power and nuclear energy. The regional analysis indicates that growth rates in energy consumption have been greater outside North America and Western Europe since 1925 than in these traditionally highly industrialized countries. Specifically, the share of world energy consumed by the United States and Canada has declined from 50 percent in 1925 to 48 percent in 1950 to 30 percent in 1980. Western Europe lost out between 1925 and 1950, largely as a result of wartime devastation, falling from 35 percent of world energy consumption to 22 percent, and declining modestly to 19 percent by 1980. Japan's energy growth rate has been very rapid, its share of world energy consumption increasing from 2 percent in 1925 to 3 percent in 1950 and 5 percent in 1980. Communist areas, however, have shown the greatest relative growth. Communist countries increased their share from 7 percent in 1925 to 18 percent in 1950 and to 32 percent in 1980. Other areas have accounted for only small amounts of total consumption, but their growth rates have been appreciable, resulting in an increase in their share of energy demand from 6 percent in 1925 to 9 percent in 1950 and to 14 percent in 1980.

Table 1.1 very clearly shows the decline in the importance of coal. In 1925, coal accounted for 83 percent of world energy consumption,

TABLE 1.1 Percentage of World Energy Consumption by Regions and Energy Sources, 1925, 1950, and 1980

	Share of World Energy Consumption			% Energy from Coal			% Energy from Oil			% Energy from Gas			% Energy From Primary Electricity		
	1925	1950	1980	1925	1950	1980	1925	1950	1980	1925	1950	1980	1925	1950	1980
U.S. and Canada	50	48	30	75	38	21	19	39	43	6	17	26	1	6	10
Western Europe	35	22	19	96	78	21	3	14	53	—	—	14	1	8	12
Japan	2	3	5	92	83	16	4	6	67	—	—	6	4	11	11
Communist areas	7	18	32	87	82	48	11	14	29	2	2	19	—	2	4
Other areas	6	9	14	83	47	24	12	40	55	2	5	12	3	8	6
Total world	100	100	100	83	56	29	13	29	44	3	9	19	1	6	8

SOURCES: *1925, 1950:* J. Darmstadter, P. Teitelbaum, and J. Polach, *Energy in the World Economy (Baltimore: The Johns Hopkins Press, 1971),* pp. 14, 85; *1980:* "BP Statistical Review of the World Oil Industry," 1980, p. 16.

but declined to 56 percent in 1950 and to only 29 percent by 1980. Regionally, coal's share decreased in the United States and Canada from 75 percent in 1925 to 38 percent in 1950 and 21 percent in 1980. An even greater shift away from coal has occurred in Western Europe since the Second World War, where a 78 percent dependence in 1950 fell to 21 percent in 1980. Japan's shift out of coal was similarly pronounced: from 92 percent in 1925 to 83 percent in 1950 but only 16 percent in 1980. Of all the areas considered, the communist bloc has been slowest to abandon coal, even though this movement is well in progress. Dependence in 1925 was lower than in Western Europe and Japan—87 percent—but had declined only to 82 percent in 1950 and still stood at 48 percent by 1980.

By and large, coal was replaced by oil imports in Western Europe, Japan, and other noncommunist areas. Gas also replaced coal in the United States, Canada, and the Soviet Union, while the share of primary electricity generation increased in all areas during this period. In the United States, oil's share of energy consumption increased from 19 percent in 1925 to 39 percent in 1950 and 43 percent in 1980. In Western Europe the increase was much more dramatic: from 3 percent to 14 percent to 53 percent over the same period. In Japan, the rate of increase was less between 1925 and 1950—from 4 percent to 6 percent—but much greater between 1950 and 1980, when the increase was from 6 percent to no less than 67 percent. Oil consumption in the communist bloc increased from 11 to 14 to 29 percent during this period, while in the rest of the world the increase was from 12 to 40 to 55 percent. In the world as a whole, oil's share of energy consumption increased from 13 percent in 1925 to 29 percent in 1950 and 44 percent in 1980.

The share of gas in world energy consumption increased from 3 percent in 1925 to 9 percent in 1950 and 19 percent in 1980. Initially, gas became a major energy source only in the United States and Canada, where economical overland transportation to markets was available. Unlike oil, gas usually cannot be economically exported for long distances by water, owing to high costs and risks in gas liquefaction. Gas consumption in the United States and Canada increased briskly, from 6 percent of energy consumption in 1925 to 17 percent in 1950 and 26 percent in 1980. Western Europe consumed virtually no natural gas until after the discovery of large fields in Holland in the 1950s and in the North Sea a decade or more later. By 1980, European gas consumption had grown to 14 percent of total energy use, and this trend is accelerating today with increased supplies from the Soviet Union and the North Sea. The gas fields of the Soviet Union were increasingly exploited in the postwar period, so that gas consumption in the communist bloc increased from 2 percent of energy use in 1925 and 1950 to 19 percent in 1980. Finally, gas consumption in other areas of the world increased appreciably, rising from 2 percent of energy consumption in 1925 to 5 percent in 1950 and 12 percent in 1980.

Table 1.1 understates the importance of electricity as a final fuel form because it measures only that electricity generated by hydropower or nuclear fuel. Fossil fuels used for the generation of electricity are already included in the other columns. Energy from the generation of primary electricity increased from 1 percent of energy consumption in 1925 to 6 percent in 1950 and then to 8 percent by 1980. While all of this electricity was from hydropower in 1925 and 1950, by 1980 approximately half was being generated from nuclear energy, particularly in Western Europe. In addition, minute amounts of power were being generated from geothermal sources.

Table 1.2 shows the same sort of information for the United States, for the longer period from 1850 to 1984. Two breakdowns are presented, inclusive and exclusive of firewood. The former table is valuable in that it shows total energy consumption in the economy by all sectors; the latter, by excluding firewood, focuses on industrial sector uses but even excludes some of these, since wood was used for purposes other than domestic heating during the nineteenth century, including the fueling of steam locomotives on many routes.

The inclusion of wood shows that on a Btu energy content basis, 91 percent of all energy consumption was supplied by wood in 1850, 73 percent in 1870, and 56 percent in 1880. The share of wood declined rapidly thereafter, falling to 10 percent by 1910 and to about 1 percent by 1970. Paradoxically, the total consumption of energy has increased so greatly that the amount of wood consumed in 1984 was almost half as large as was consumed in 1850, despite the fact that it accounts for less than 1 percent of today's consumption!

Coal increased from 9 percent of energy consumption in 1850 to 76 percent in 1910, declined steadily to 18 percent in 1975, and has since increased to 23 percent by 1984. Coal did not exceed 50 percent of energy consumption until 1884. Again, although the share of coal in total energy consumption has steadily declined, the absolute amounts consumed have generally increased owing to the large growth in total energy consumption.

One of the surprises of Table 1.2 is the relatively slow growth of oil consumption before about 1910. One major reason for the failure of oil to displace coal earlier as a source of industrial fuel was the tendency of those inside as well as outside the oil industry to underestimate the magnitude of oil reserves. Industries were reluctant to make large investments in oil-burning equipment if they considered it likely that oil reserves would be depleted in 10 to 15 years. Also, demand for oil was relatively limited before the advent of the automobile. Petroleum was first sold as a patent medicine, a use with limited sales volume potential. There was a ready market for kerosene for illumination, but the

TABLE 1.2 Percentage Energy Consumption in the United States by Energy Sources (Including and Excluding Wood), 1850–1984

	Including Wood Consumption						Excluding Wood Consumption				
	Wood	Coal	Oil	Gas	Hydro-electric Power	Nuclear Power	Coal	Oil	Gas	Hydro-electric Power	Nuclear Power
1850	91	9					100				
1860	84	16					100				
1870	73	26	1				96	4			
1880	56	41	3	4			91	9			
1890	35	57	4	3			88	6	6		
1900	20	71	4	3	3		87	5	4	4	
1910	10	76	7	3	3		84	8	4	4	
1920	7	75	11	4	3		80	12	5	3	
1930	6	59	22	9	3		62	24	10	3	
1940	5	51	30	11	3		53	32	12	3	
1950	3	41	32	19	4		42	22	20	4	
1955	3	32	36	25	4		33	27	26	4	
1960	2	23	40	31	4		23	41	32	4	
1965	2	22	40	33	4	0.1	22	41	34	4	0.1
1970	1	19	39	37	4	0.3	19	40	37	4	0.3
1975	1	18	41	34	4	2.0	18	42	34	4	2.0
1980	1	23	24	42	5	5	20	27	45	4	4
1984	1	23	24	42	5	5	23	24	42	5	5

SOURCES: *1850–1955: S. Schurr and B. Netschert, Energy and the American Economy, 1850–1975 (Baltimore: The Johns Hopkins Press, 1960); 1960–1984: U.S. Bureau of Mines, Mineral Yearbook, annually.*

market for gasoline was quite limited before internal combustion engines using refined fuels were developed. Not much gasoline could be sold to dry-cleaning establishments, since not much was needed to remove stains. There was a ready market for petroleum lubricants to improve the operating performance of machinery—but here too the size of the total market was limited.

Oil consumption amounted to only 1 percent of total U.S. energy consumption in 1870, and had increased to only 4 percent by 1900. But with the growing popularity of the automobile, its share rose to 11 percent in 1940, and 40 percent by 1960, at which point further market share growth was halted by competition from natural gas. Since 1975 rising prices of oil, relative to those of other fuels, have led to widespread substitution of other fuels for oil.

Gas was insignificant in 1880 but increased to 4 percent of energy consumption by 1890, at which rate it held roughly constant until after 1920, owing to the high cost of transporting natural gas long distances before pipeline innovations were made in the 1930s. Gas consumption then increased rapidly, from 11 percent in 1940 to 19 percent in 1950, 31 percent in 1960, 37 percent in 1970, and 42 percent in 1980.

Hydroelectric power has remained fairly constant as a percentage of total energy consumption, developing in the 1890s and reaching a share of 3 percent by 1900. Since 1950 this share has been roughly 4 percent, but hydroelectric power will have a hard time keeping up with the growth of total energy demand in the future, since the availability of good unused hydroelectric sites is very limited. Nuclear power began to be commercially produced in 1957, but not until the early 1960s was as much as one tenth of 1 percent of total energy thus generated. This share increased to 2 percent by 1975 and to 5 percent by 1984.

If we exclude firewood from consideration in Table 1.2, the energy consumption picture looks quite different, particularly in the nineteenth century. Among fossil fuels, coal had great predominance until the 1920s, accounting for as much as 80 percent of energy consumption in 1920. After this time, however, coal's steady relative decline is quite evident. After 1910 the exclusion of wood makes little difference since firewood had declined so much in importance; hence the columns for the other energy sources do not differ greatly in the two tables.

It should be noted that while wood fuel is included in Table 1.2 for the United States, where it has been of little importance in recent years, it is excluded (for lack of data) from Table 1.1, which covers the world. This is unfortunate since wood is an important fuel in many nonindustrialized areas of the world, and has become more important in such areas since the increased price of oil has forced many countries to turn back to domestic wood supplies for reasons of economy.

PAST AND PRESENT WORLD
ENERGY SUPPLY PATTERNS

Before about 1700, energy consumption typically took place near the energy sources themselves. Plants and animals were harvested on site, and wind and water power also had to be used on location. Storage of mechanical energy was not yet possible, and the only sort of storage of any importance was that of food between harvests and firewood cut in expectation of winter. It was uneconomical to haul firewood long distances, so early energy-intensive industries such as iron mills tended to locate in wooded areas, and over long periods of time these areas lost their forest cover. At this time, energy-using processes tended to flourish only in proximity to water power, wood, or coal, and the coal fields of Europe, particularly those in England, Germany, France, Poland, and western Russia, were the scene of much early industrial activity. After the innovation of modern methods of iron and steel making, the best situated industrial regions were those having close access to iron ore, coal, and limestone. The geographic scarcity of such areas tended to limit the spread of industrialization until fuels with greater transportability were discovered.

Coal shipments by water were not prohibitively expensive, and there were some well-established coal transport routes in the 1800s. Western Europe shipped coal to South America and Africa, China exported to Japan, and the United States sold coal to Canada. There was also considerable coal traffic between adjoining European countries. But on the whole, significant industrial coal consumption occurred only within reasonable proximity to the coal fields themselves. With the advent of petroleum, however, geographical imbalances between oil-producing regions and energy-consuming regions prompted the rapid development of extensive transportation networks. As early as 1900, many oil fields were found relatively close to seacoasts, and since water transportation of oil was relatively inexpensive, petroleum became an important international industry. Early trade, however, was in refined products rather than in crude oil, and it was not until after 1945 that international movements of crude oil predominated.

Table 1.3 shows the percentage of world crude oil production by major producing countries for the period 1860–1984. It is obvious that the United States and Russia divided more than 90 percent of world output between them until after 1910. The United States produced over 90 percent of the world output until about 1878, but the opening of large Russian fields in the 1880s and 1890s made for a closer approach to parity in output. Russian output exceeded American production in 1900, but United States output spurted ahead after 1900, while Russian production fluctuated, and was eventually seriously disrupted by the disorders of the 1917 revolution. Although total world oil output increased substantially after the First World War, United

TABLE 1.3 Percentage of World Crude Oil Production by Country, 1850–1984

	United States	Russia	Indonesia	Mexico	Venezuela	Middle East	Africa	Other
1860	98							2
1865	92	2						6
1870	91	3						6
1875	91	5						4
1880	88	10						2
1885	60	34						6
1890	60	37						3
1895	51	44	1					4
1900	43	52	2					3
1905	63	25	4					8
1910	64	27	4	1				4
1915	65	14	3	8				10
1920	64	4	3	23				6
1925	71	5	2	12	2	3		5
1930	64	8	2	3	10	3		10
1935	60	9	2	2	9	4		14
1940	63	10	3	2	10	4		8
1945	66	6	1	2	12	7		6
1950	52	7	1	2	15	15		8
1955	45	9	2	2	14	19		9
1960	35	14	2	1	14	23	1	10
1965	27	16	2	1	12	25	6	11
1970	22	17	2	1	8	30	13	7
1975	16	18	2	1	4	36	16	7
1980	14	20	3	3	4	30	16	10
1984	16	22	3	5	3	20	6	25

SOURCES: *1860–1920: U.S. Bureau of Mines; 1925–1965:* Energy in the World Economy; *1970–1984: Monthly Energy Review.*

States production was 71 percent of the global total by 1925. The United States share still stood at 66 percent by 1945, but the development of Middle Eastern and North African reserves during the post-war period reduced the United States share of total output steadily, from 52 percent in 1950 to 35 percent in 1960 and 16 percent in 1984. Russian output, on the other hand, recovered from damage during the Second World War to rise from 6 percent of world output in 1945 to 14 percent in 1960 and 22 percent in 1984, exceeding United States output after the early 1970s.

In the nineteenth century both United States and Russian crude oil was refined domestically and the products—chiefly illuminating oils— were exported by water to consuming areas. It was not until the 1890s that a petroleum industry devoted to exporting crude oil developed, and then it was on a small scale in Indonesia. Still, the first important regular shipments of crude oil as such originated in the Indonesian fields. Indonesian output never accounted for a large share of world production, but it has been important in world trade for almost a century. Between 1 and 4 percent of world crude oil has been produced in Indonesia, the market share rising to about 4 percent in 1905–1910 and declining to about 3 percent in 1984. Mexico became the next important producing and exporting center, with an output volume equal to 23 percent of world production by 1920. Mexican output dropped rapidly in the early 1920s, however, and had fallen to 3 percent by 1930 and to 1 percent by 1960. With the large new reserves found in Mexico since the Arab embargo of 1973 however, Mexican production has risen sharply to 5 percent by 1984. Mexico has become the fourth largest producer and could well expand its market share further.

Venezuela was the next important export source for crude oil. By 1930, Venezuelan output was 10 percent of world output, and Venezuela succeeded Mexico as the world's largest oil exporter. Venezuelan output rose to 15 percent of the world total by 1950, but then declined to 10 percent by 1968 and to only 3 percent by 1984, despite relatively large reserves potential. The beginning of large scale permanent oil export trade was launched with Venezuelan field developments in the 1920s and 1930s. The Middle East became a significant exporting area at about the same time as Venezuela, although production in Iran had begun as early as 1909. Because of the disruptions occasioned by the Second World War, production did not increase as rapidly as existing reserves justified, but by 1950 exports reached 15 percent of total world production, increased to 23 percent by 1960 and to 36 percent by 1975. The sharp decline in market share held by the Middle East to 20 percent in 1984 is the result of production cutbacks by these countries to sustain prices and not the result of diminished reserves. Middle East countries possessed about 55 percent of world oil reserves in 1984, despite their 20 percent share of production.

African output became significant by 1960 with the expansion of Algerian production, and increased to 16 percent of world production in 1975 with the addition of Libyan and Nigerian oil production. The sharp decline in market share over the period 1980 to 1984 is attributable to reduced production by these three key producers, who are also OPEC members. Other regions of the world, notably Rumania in the nineteenth century and Canada after 1945, accounted for the remaining 2 to 25 percent of world output.

The market share statistics of Table 1.3 attribute greater importance to the United States and Russia than they deserve and less importance to the Middle East, Africa, and Mexico. In the future, the marginal sources of oil will come almost entirely from the latter group as Soviet export volumes have declined to low levels and the United States has become a substantial oil importer. The chief oil export routes extend from the Persian Gulf to Western Europe, Japan, North America, and Australia. Other major oil exports flow from North Africa to Europe and North America, from Indonesia to Japan, and from Venezuela to other parts of the Western Hemisphere. With increasing reliance upon Middle Eastern, African, and Mexican oil exports, the importing countries have become heavily dependent upon imported energy. As of 1983 about 33 percent of United States oil consumption was imported, compared with 64 percent in Europe and virtually 100 percent in Japan. This degree of import dependence had left these major oil-consuming economies highly vulnerable to supply interruptions.

PRICE DEVELOPMENTS: PRE- AND POST-OPEC

Energy prices, like raw materials prices, tend to fluctuate more widely than the prices of finished consumer goods and services. In the past this has been due more to fluctuations in supply than in demand. When English forests were on the point of disappearing, firewood prices skyrocketed. When whaling activities had greatly reduced the number of whales, the price of whale oil surged upward. Economists are not surprised to learn that coal came along to supplement firewood, and kerosene arrived just in time to supplant whale oil. In the past, output rates from oil fields have fluctuated, making prices highly unstable. Labor problems in the coal fields have interrupted production with consequent price escalations.

The energy market has been a very important market in every industrializing country since the beginning of the Industrial Revolution. Coal deposits are usually sufficiently widespread and capable of being mined by numerous small operators that problems of monopoly pricing should not arise in the absence of governmentally supported programs of price control. But in Europe each industrializing country was more or less in competition with the others, and the most progressive governments adopted a policy, not always effectively implemented, of keeping down the price of coal in order to speed industrialization. Price pressure on coal in the United States was quite strong in those areas where essentially free firewood could be gathered. After the advent of petroleum, coal had another competitor. Oil from relatively large flowing fields had lower costs than coal, which needed to be mined, and early oil producers would undersell coal in many markets and still make very good profits.

Since oil is a close substitute for coal, price trends in oil definitely affected the rate at which oil replaced coal. Table 1.4 presents a summary of data on current and real United States and world crude oil

TABLE 1.4 Current and Real U.S. and World Crude Oil Prices, 1880–1984

Year	Current U.S. Price[a] ($/bbl) (Average Price)	U.S. Consumer Price Index (1957–59 = 100)	Real U.S. Price in 1957–59 ($/bbl)	World Price: Estimated Actual Transactions Price	Real World Price in 1957–59 ($/bbl)
1880	$ .94	34	$ 2.76		
1890	.77	32	2.41		
1900	1.19	39	4.10		
1905	.62	31	2.00		
1910	.61	33	1.85		
1915	.64	35	1.83		
1920	3.07	70	4.40		
1925	1.68	61	2.75		
1930	1.19	58	2.04		
1933	.67	45	1.49		
1940	1.02	49	2.09		
1945	1.22	63	1.95		
1950	2.51	84	3.01	$ 1.71	$ 2.04
1955	2.77	93	2.97	1.63	1.75
1960	2.88	107	2.70	1.53	1.43
1965	2.86	110	2.50	1.33	1.21
1970	3.18	134	2.37	1.26	.94
1971	3.39	145	2.34	1.66	1.14
1972	3.39	150	2.26	1.84	1.23
1973	3.89	154	2.53	2.91	1.89
1974	6.74	175	3.85	10.77	6.15
1975	7.67	187	4.10	10.72	5.73
1976	8.19	202	4.05	12.17	6.02
1977	8.57	211	4.06	13.24	6.27
1978	9.00	227	3.96	13.30	5.85
1979	12.64	253	5.00	20.19	7.98
1980	21.59	287	7.52	32.20	11.22
1981	31.77	317	10.02	35.10	11.07
1982	28.52	336	8.48	32.11	9.55
1983	26.19	346	7.56	27.73	8.01
1984	26.00	357	7.28	27.20	7.62

[a]Average Price received by Domestic Sellers, which is the weighted average of the prices of old oil and new oil.

SOURCES: *American Petroleum Institute*, Petroleum Fact and Figures, *U.S. Bureau of Mines; since 1976, Monthly Energy Review.*

prices for the period 1880–1984. Comparison of nominal price trends over time is very misleading in inflationary times. Consequently, Table 1.4 includes a measure of general inflation, the consumer price index. For example, a market bundle costing $100 in 1957–59 would have cost $34 in 1880 or $357 in 1984. For purposes of long term comparison, the real oil prices properly measure the price of crude oil relative to this hypothetical bundle of consumer goods. It is apparent that the real price of oil has fluctuated widely in the United States. During the period 1880 to 1933, the price fluctuated almost yearly depending on the occurrence of supply schedule shifts from new large field discoveries. Paradoxically, in 1920, the real price of oil stood at $4.40 per barrel (a value not exceeded until 1979) and reports predicted future shortages as reserves sufficient to meet only 15 years' production appeared to be available. The forecasts changed rapidly as the large fields in Texas and Oklahoma were discovered in the late 1920s and early 1930s. In 1933, flush production from the newly discovered East Texas field—the largest field in the United States—sent the real price per barrel plummeting to $1.49 (only $.67 in current dollars). With the erection of a maze of state and federal regulations, oil prices were stabilized and even rose moderately following World War II. For the period from 1950 to 1973, real United States crude prices trended slowly downward, being largely insulated by import controls from the lower world oil prices. Between 1973 and 1981 United States crude prices rose fourfold (or, in current dollars, eightfold). This price move generally lagged the increase in world oil prices, because in 1973 United States crude prices came under price controls that were not lifted until 1981. Over this period, regulation allowed United States prices to increase but at a rate considerably slower than world oil prices. For example, in 1979, domestic producers received an average price of $12.64 per barrel in current dollars, despite world prices of $20.19 per barrel. Since 1981, the lifting of price controls has meant that domestic prices fluctuate with world crude prices, varying only by quality and location differentials.

To better understand United States price patterns since 1973, one must look at world oil prices. Real world oil prices fell precipitously during the period from 1950 to 1970, so much that many economists criticized the protectionist trade policy of the United States government, which insulated the domestic crude market from cheap imported oil. Suddenly, following the Arab Oil Embargo and OPEC's muscle flexing, this all changed. Compared to the 1970 real price of $.94 per barrel, the 1974 price involved a sixfold real price increase. From 1974 through 1978, the real price of world oil was reasonably constant. In 1979, events surrounding the Iranian Revolution triggered a second energy price shock, sending current oil prices from $13.30 to $35.10 by 1981. In real terms, the price increased from $5.85 per barrel in 1978 to $11.22 per barrel in 1981. Thus in only 11 years, the real price of world oil had increased by over 11 times, explaining pointedly why the term "energy crisis" was born.

Since 1981, world oil prices have declined in real terms from $11.22 per barrel to $7.62—a 32% decrease. Nevertheless, the real price of $7.62 per barrel is still eight times the 1970 real world oil price, reminding us that we still live in a world of high-priced oil.

Energy/Macroeconomic Linkages: The Fable of the Elephant and the Rabbit

What effects, if any, do rising energy prices have on overall output and the general level of prices? Given the conventional separation between microeconomics and macroeconomics, there is a tendency to reply "not much." After all, energy-producing industries composed in 1980 only 4 percent of GNP—hardly a dominant percentage. On the other hand, casual empiricism would suggest that the energy crisis of the 1970s was closely correlated with the severe macroeconomic dislocations of that decade. Coincidentally, the term "stagflation" was coined in the same decade that the term "energy crisis" emerged. For example, the decade of the 1970s was the first decade since the 1930s in which real per-capita personal income actually declined. The annual average United States inflation rate was 7.6 percent per year as contrasted with 2.2 percent for the decade of the 1960s. The unemployment rate averaged 8.8 percent for the decade as contrasted with 4.5 percent for the 1960s. These general conclusions apply not only to the United States but to virtually all of the industrialized countries. The two most severe postwar recessions followed directly on the heels of the 1973–74 price increases and the 1979–80 increases. Are such events merely coincidences or indicative of a strong linkage running from energy to the macroeconomy?

Professors William Hogan and Alan Manne posed the problem by reference to the colorful fable of the elephant and the rabbit.[1] They ask whether a stew (total macroeconomic output) containing one rabbit (the energy sector) and one elephant (the nonenergy sector) can be expected to taste more like an elephant stew or a rabbit stew! Following the metaphor, our question becomes whether a reduction in the size of the rabbit will have a significant impact on the taste of the stew.

One possibility might be that a doubling of energy costs would reduce GNP in direct proportion to its value share, if energy inputs are required in fixed proportions to nonenergy inputs. Twice as much GNP would have to be allocated to energy inputs as before, doubling their value share. However, if the input mix were more flexible, a doubling of energy costs could lead to a reduction in energy usage sufficient to leave its value share unaffected, so that GNP would be reduced only by half as much as in the previous case. Obviously the key consideration here is the ease with which nonenergy inputs can be substituted for energy inputs in the production of GNP, and this ability is represented by the concept of the elasticity of substitution designated by the Greek letter σ.

The shapes of the isoquants associated with given values of the elasticity of substitution are represented for three distinct cases in Figure

1.1a. The first case, when σ equals zero, is that of fixed-proportions technology (alluded to above) which requires that the input mix be maintained in a constant ratio, and corresponds to isoquants shaped like I_1. Since a reduction in the energy input cannot be replaced by an increase in the nonenergy input, output will fall and the value share of energy inputs will rise.

The intermediate case allows for some flexibility in the input mix at a constant level of output, and is exemplified by isoquant I_2 from a Cobb-Douglas production process, implying that σ = 1. Under a Cobb-Douglas technology a reduction in energy inputs can be just matched by an increase in nonenergy inputs that will keep the value share of the former constant.

The last case assumes that the technology is completely flexible, so that nonenergy inputs are perfectly substitutable for energy inputs; this is represented by isoquant I_3. Here the elasticity of substitution is infinite (σ = ∞), with the possibility that energy inputs could be completely eliminated without any reduction in output being necessary.

The importance of the energy sector in the macroeconomy can now be determined in this framework by examining the possibilities for substitution between energy and nonenergy inputs. It is important to distinguish short-run from long-run substitution relationships. Energy use in the short run is tied directly to the existing stock of energy-using equipment such as generators, automobiles, and current housing facilities. Therefore in the short run there is little ability to substitute

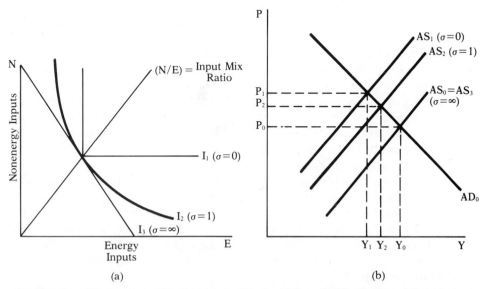

FIGURE 1.1 The relationship between the elasticity of substitution (σ) and aggregate macroeconomic output (Y).

energy for nonenergy inputs. If the elasticity of substitution is low, then reductions in energy input availability will have significant negative feedback effects on the overall economy and the adverse energy-macroeconomy linkage must be taken into account by policy analysts. In the long run, the capital stock of energy-using equipment can be redesigned to provide more fuel-efficient engines, automobiles, and houses. The elasticity of substitution is therefore likely to be much greater in the long run than in the short run. If the elasticity of substitution is high, reduced energy availability will be less damaging to the macroeconomy, and the weaker feedback effect might be sufficiently small to be ignored. This relationship between the microeconomic concept of the elasticity of substitution and macroeconomic conditions can be more clearly demonstrated.

Figure 1.1b provides a very simple model of the macroeconomy as described by conventional aggregate demand and aggregate supply curves. Initially the economy is in long-run equilibrium at national product level Y_0 and price level P_0, being characterized by aggregate demand AD_0. An increase in relative energy prices would be expected to affect the costs of producing a given level of output at each price. The shift of the aggregate supply curve away from AS_0 that would be produced by a given energy supply "shock" will be seen to depend crucially upon the value of the elasticity of substitution between energy and nonenergy inputs.

Recalling Figure 1.1, consider the supply response in the case where $\sigma = 0$, so that substitution of nonenergy inputs for energy inputs is not technologically possible. The resultant upward shift of the aggregate supply curve would be a significant one, possibly all the way to curve AS_1. Prices in the aggregate would rise from P_0 to P_1, while national product would fall from Y_0 to Y_1.

For the intermediate case we have $\sigma = 1$ under the Cobb-Douglas technology that allows enough substitution of nonenergy inputs for energy inputs to maintain a constant value share for energy. Here the aggregate supply curve would also be shifted upward as a result of an increase in relative energy prices, but not nearly as much as in the previous case, perhaps moving only to curve AS_2. Prices would still be increased, but only from P_0 to P_2, and national product would fall less dramatically from Y_0 to Y_2.

The third case of Figure 1.1b entails perfect substitutability between energy and nonenergy inputs, so that $\sigma = \infty$. The aggregate supply curve would *not* be shifted *at all* by the energy shock, since the same level of output could be produced at the same prices as before, using all nonenergy inputs. Therefore the aggregate supply curve AS_3 coincides with the initial curve AS_0, and prices and national product remain unchanged.

In the short run, intuition would suggest that the elasticity of substitution is quite low, as energy usage is closely tied to the stock of energy-using equipment, which cannot be redesigned and replaced over night. Consequently, most evidence shows that the energy shocks contributed significantly to the stagflation of the 1980s. In the long run, energy-consuming equipment can be redesigned and substitution possibilities become much greater. The available evidence, as discussed in Chapter 7, suggests that the long-term effects of an energy shock are not nearly so great as their short run macroeconomic dislocations.

CHANGING PUBLIC PERCEPTIONS OF THE "ENERGY PROBLEM"

Public perceptions of the nature of "the energy problem" have proven to be highly changeable, fluctuating within a few short years from the view that it is a problem of the greatest gravity to the opinion that it is a nonproblem. From the vantage point of the mid-1980s, the most popular view is that there is no energy problem. According to this view, the energy crisis of the 1970s was precipitated by OPEC's contrived shortage of oil. But during the 1980s, OPEC's monopoly power was checked by falling world oil demand and by increasing non-OPEC production, resulting in falling real prices of crude oil.

In contrast, a popular viewpoint of the 1970s was that the world faced a real physical shortage of oil and that OPEC price increases merely reflected an increase in the true economic cost of supplying crude oil. According to this view, despite these price increases, the world is heading toward a severe and prolonged energy crisis, as future oil production will be inadequate to meet demand and other energy forms would be insufficient to fill the void. The events of the 1970s are seen as merely a brief preview of the catastrophe forthcoming within the next 15 to 25 years.

A third view focuses on the security aspects of the distribution of noncommunist world oil reserves. This view holds that the real problem facing the Western industrialized nations is their heavy long-term dependence on imported oil, the bulk of which must originate from the strife-torn Middle East. Nations in this region can easily manipulate the flow of oil to the West to achieve a variety of economic or political objectives inimical to the interest of oil importers. Thus future supply disruptions from this region seem likely, with the result being severe short-run macroeconomic effects and potential political upheavals, which could lead to armed conflict.

One's policy prescriptions would vary, depending upon which one (if any) of the above three views one subscribes to. If the energy problem is now history, the policy posture might range from doing nothing to adopting a few actions to encourage further decreases in OPEC's remaining monopoly power. On the other hand, if the real energy crisis is yet to come, OPEC is to be applauded rather than execrated. The objective becomes achieving the transition to nonoil energy resources as soon as possible, and high oil prices help to accelerate the process. But if the problem is supply uncertainty, means must be found that will deter Middle East countries from engaging in embargoes and supply disruptions, while at the same time reducing our short-run vulnerability to supply disruptions by programs of oil storage, emergency conservation procedures, and so forth. Let us now turn to a closer look at each of these three conceptions of the energy problem.

Viewpoint of the 1970s: The Real Energy Crisis Is Yet to Come

A popular view of the 1970s was that OPEC has done importers a favor by raising oil prices because the real energy crisis is yet to come; oil supplies will be largely depleted in the next decade or two, forcing massive rapid transitions to other fuels. This view is prominently put forth by the report of the Workshop on Alternative Energy Strategies (WAES) involving participants from numerous countries and individuals from academics, business, and government. This 1977 report shows that under a variety of scenarios, a severe shortage of world oil will result before the year 2000. Even assuming considerably higher prices and slow economic growth, their scenarios indicate the shortage will occur before 2000. With more likely price and economic growth rates the shortage could occur in the late 1980s.

Such a conclusion might at first glance appear improbable in view of the physical reserves of oil at the time. As shown in Table 1.5, noncommunist world oil reserves in 1975 stood at 555 billion barrels, contrasted against the 1975 production rate of only 15.5 billion barrels per year.

It would appear that the ratio of reserves to production in 1975 was about 36 to 1, if we divide 555 billion barrels of reserves by the 15.5 billion barrels of oil produced outside the communist areas in 1975. Hence if no more oil were ever discovered, it seems that we would still be able to consume at the 1975 rate for 36 years.

But there are several additional factors that alter this conclusion. First, oil cannot be withdrawn from underground reservoirs at an absolutely constant rate. Second, future demand is likely to continue to increase at some rate, even with much higher prices. We cannot assume that demand levels in 1975 will remain constant through 2011. Third, additional volumes of oil reserves are likely to be found throughout the world during the next 50 or more years. Oil reserves measure only the existing inventory of known deposits capable of

TABLE 1.5 Total World Crude Oil Reserves by Region in 1975 and 1984, in Billions of Barrels of Proved Reserves

	1975	1984
OPEC areas:		
Saudi Arabia	152	169
Other Middle East	208	201
Other OPEC	90	81
Total OPEC	450	451
North America	40	82
Western Europe	25	23
Rest of Noncommunist World	40	29
Total Non-OPEC	105	134
Total, All Noncommunist Areas	555	585
Communist Areas	103	85
Total World	658	670

SOURCE: *Oil and Gas Journal, Year-end Summary Issues, 1975 and 1984.*

being extracted, and need not necessarily decline, as illustrated by comparing 1984 reserve levels with 1975 levels.

In order to deal with the first problem, we must recognize that oil cannot be produced from underground reservoirs at too rapid a rate without great sacrifice of ultimate recovery. Overly rapid production dissipates natural reservoir pressures, leaving oil trapped in the source rock. Consequently, the minimum ratio between reserves and production is about 10 to 1, implying that in order to produce the 15.5 billion barrels of oil in 1975, there must have been at least 155 billion barrels of reserves at the beginning of 1975. For some types of reservoirs the minimum ratio may be as high as 15 to 1. Hence even if we impose an average ratio as low as 12 to 1, we can count on only 24 years of production at the rate of 15.5 billion barrels per year (the 1975 rate). After the twenty-fourth year, total reserves will be less than the 186 billion required to yield 15.5 billion barrels at the minimum ratio of reserves to production of 12 to 1, and the last 183 billion barrels must be produced more slowly over a period of many years. The remaining reserves are not lost, but must be produced more slowly in lesser volumes over a longer period of time.

Second, if demand increases at several percent per year, this naturally reduces the life expectancy of a given volume of reserves. If, for example, the rate of production increases by 1 percent per year, reserve life is reduced from 36 years to 31; if the rate of increase is 3 percent per year, reserve life is only 25 years; for a 5 percent rate of increase, 21 years, and so on. Furthermore, the life-shortening effects of increases in demand and the minimum ratio of reserves to production are additive. If the rate of demand increase is 3 percent per year, not only is the reserve life cut from 36 to 25 years, but the ratio of reserves to production falls below the necessary 12 to 1 ratio during the fifteenth year of production. Thus only a 15-year interval exists before demand has to be constrained by limitations of productive capacity.

Third, let us assume, as does the WAES Report, that new discoveries continue to be made and proved reserves are augmented by new reserves. If demand is constant from year to year, then as long as the existing reserves to production ratio is greater than minimal, there is no problem in regard to productive capacity. But if demand is increasing at a certain rate, then reserve additions must be sufficient to keep the ratio of reserves to production above the minimum level for an indefinite time. If demand increases at 3 percent per year, then at some point before the fifteenth year, in our earlier example, reserves must begin to increase by more than 3 percent per year, or production will eventually be constrained by capacity limitations.

How many barrels of new discoveries can be made every year? During the period 1950–1975 the annual average was about 27 billion barrels in the world outside communist areas. There have been considerable fluctuations, however. During the period 1965–1970, an average of 52 billion barrels per year was achieved. The assumption has been that during the next few decades average annual new discoveries will probably decline rather than increase. However, this is not certain, since prices now are much higher than they were during prior years when discovery activities were limited by lower price horizons. The WAES Report considers two cases: of 20 billion barrels per year in the high-discovery case and of 10 billion barrels per year in the low-discovery case. If the rate of reserve additions is 20 billion barrels per year as assumed in the WAES "high case," then consumption can increase for 29 years at the rate of 3 percent per year before the ratio of reserves to production drops below 12. Even if the discovery rate falls as low as 10 billion barrels per year, the low case assumed by WAES, it will be possible to supply a production increase at the rate of 3 percent per year for 20 years. Thus, even under reasonably conservative estimates of discovery rates and relatively liberal estimates of growth rates (2.6% per year), it appears that oil supply expansion is unlikely to be constrained by reservoir engineering considerations before 1995. However, the WAES Report notes that for "conservation" reasons, rulers of barren desert areas unable to invest large sums of money domestically with adequate efficiency might well limit production to rates at which the reserves to production ratio could never fall to the 12 to 1 limit suggested by reservoir engineering considerations. Thus the real energy crisis could arrive well before 1995, depending on the production limits imposed by the key Middle East producers.

According to the WAES Report, not only is future oil production likely to be constrained, but other energy forms have only modest expansion possibilities, leaving a substantial shortage. With regard to natural gas supplies, the WAES Report suggests that the future supply picture is not favorable. Despite large reserves, transportation costs will probably remain too high to permit imported gas to replace declining domestic gas reserves in the industrialized countries, except in those few cases where overland transport is economical. Total natural gas reserves in 1975, in billion barrels of oil equivalent heat content, are about half as large as total oil reserves—242 billion barrels oil equivalent in the noncommunist world, with another 144 billion barrels oil equivalent in communist areas.

Since the noncommunist world production of natural gas was 6 billion barrels of oil equivalent in 1975, the ratio of reserves to production in 1975 was 40.3 years. Unfortunately, the bulk of noncommunist reserves are in the Middle East, and it is not possible to build pipelines from the Persian Gulf to Chicago, Tokyo, or similar major industrial consuming centers. Transportation alternatives for ocean shipment include liquefaction and conversion to methanol, but these are very expensive.

According to some experts, coal may once again become the major source of world energy, since this is a relatively abundant and widespread energy source, capable of production at tolerable cost levels, and with total reserves adequate to supply expanding energy needs for several centuries or more. While world oil reserves in the proved category amount to about 550 billion barrels, economically recoverable world reserves of coal total at least 3 trillion barrels oil equivalent, or almost six times as much. The same relationship prevails between estimated ultimately recoverable oil reserves, currently assessed at about 2 trillion barrels, and potentially recoverable coal reserves, estimated in the range of 12 trillion barrels oil equivalent. At current rates of world coal consumption, known economically recoverable reserves would be adequate for 230 years, while the inclusion of potentially recoverable reserves would increase the supply to about 1150 years.

The present military superpowers are also the superpowers in coal reserves. The Soviet Union and its Eastern European dependencies possess about 39 percent of the world's economically recoverable reserves, followed by the United States with 33 percent. China accounts for another 14 percent, leaving the rest of the world with only about 14 percent, primarily in Western Europe, Oceania, Africa, and India. Middle Eastern coal reserves are negligible.

The market evolution from coal into oil and gas was dictated not only by the lower cost of petroleum fuels but also by their superior convenience, versatility, and cleanliness in combustion. Any large-scale retreat into coal can be accomplished only against the resistance of those opposing the environmental impacts of coal mining and coal-fired combustion. It will indeed be difficult to convert back to coal if there are many laws that prevent or economically penalize both its mining and its burning. But even if coal were given the green light environmentally, there are few new uses into which it would be welcomed. Apart from trains using coal-generated electricity, coal has no current sales in the transportation sector, although—over time and at great cost—diesel locomotives could conceivably be replaced by coal-fired units. Residential users will resist coal consumption because of its adverse impact on the microenvironment of the home. There is some scope for increasing use of coal as a boiler fuel for heavy industry, and of course coal use can be expanded in the electric utility sector, but the expansion potential is somewhat limited here since half of electricity is already generated by use of coal fuel, with nuclear power currently supplying the incremental growth in this market. Coal's greatest chance to become a dominent energy source again lies in the devising of technology to convert this solid fuel into liquid and gaseous forms. Given the long lead times in constructing such plants and the relatively high costs, the WAES Report is not optimistic that synthetic fuels could make an appreciable contribution before the year 2000.

Nuclear power has some of the disadvantages of coal without sharing in coal's major advantage of plentiful reserves available at tolerable mining costs. Power from nuclear fission depends on the use of enriched uranium, which is a relatively expensive input and must be extracted from uranium ores that may or may not prove to be in relatively short supply. Uranium ores do not currently appear to be abundant in the earth's crust. Even though the energy content of a pound of uranium reactor fuel is about as great as that of 10 tons of coal, there are many more tons of coal than there are pounds of uranium-235.

The major disadvantages to the rapid increase of nuclear power have to do with environmental risks and impacts and with the limited scope for use of nuclear power in the energy market. Although nuclear power does not give rise to the conventional types of air and water pollution, its potential for thermal and radioactive pollution is considered so great by so many that strong opposition exists to any expansion of nuclear capacity in a number of industrial countries. The major risks concern not only the chance of a reactor accident, but also the hazards associated with the transportation, storage, and possible illegal diversion of high level nuclear fuels and wastes.

Furthermore, the overall market penetration of nuclear power will be limited since it cannot be used in the residential, industrial, or transportation sectors. Nuclear power essentially competes with fossil fuels as an input in electricity generation; owing to the size of reactors, it cannot economically be used in mobile power plants smaller than those employed in large marine vessels. Nevertheless, according to the WAES Report, the demand for electricity will continue to grow and much of the growth will be fueled by nuclear power. Although only about 2 percent of all energy consumed in noncommunist areas in 1975 was in the form of nuclear power, it is estimated that this share will increase to a range of between 6 to 9 percent by 1985, and to between 14 to 21 percent by 2000, according to the WAES Report. Thus nuclear power will account for at most about one-fifth of energy consumption in noncommunist areas by 2000.

Hydroelectric power, the other source of primary electrical power generation, is unlikely to expand very much in industrialized areas, since almost all the best sites have been exploited. The only likely future trend is the possible use of numerous smaller sites that may become economical at higher prices for fossil fuels. And although there are many suitable but unused sites in nonindustrialized countries, the effect on world energy supply will be quite small.

Even though the hope of the distant future is focused upon renewable energy systems relying upon solar energy in its various forms, WAES concluded that solar energy will not make a major contribution to world energy supplies by 2000.

In sum, the viewpoint of the 1970s, characterized in the WAES Report, is that the world is rapidly running out of oil and that other energy sources seem unlikely to fill the gap. Without strong immediate action to set energy priorities and facilitate development of new energy technologies, a genuine shortage of energy supplies will occur in the late 1980s or 1990s. And once the energy capacity shortage arrives, it will not be easily dispelled. Other energy forms will not suddenly materialize to save the day, because they have long lead times.

Viewpoint of the 1980s: OPEC and the Energy Crisis Are Now History

The prevailing opinion in the mid-1980s is that the energy crisis is now history. According to this view, the energy crisis of the 1970s was precipitated by OPEC's monopoly power, but now the cartel's monopoly power has been severely if not fatally curtailed. As indicated in Table 1.4, the real world price of oil has fallen significantly from a high in 1981 and prospects are that this trend should continue. Up until 1981, OPEC appeared to be an extremely successful cartel, having raised the real price of oil over 11-fold in an 11 year period. But suddenly OPEC's hold over the world oil market slipped markedly. Figure 1.2 shows the trends in noncommunist world oil demand and production by non-OPEC sources. Over the period from 1973 to 1980,

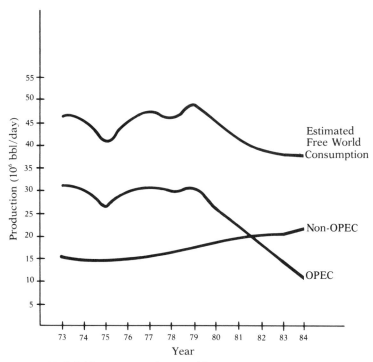

FIGURE 1.2 Noncommunist world consumption together with OPEC and non-OPEC supply.

oil demand remained rather stable despite the enormous price increase, convincing OPEC that demand was very price inelastic. Similarly, production from non-OPEC sources expanded only modestly, enabling OPEC to produce as much oil in 1980 as it did in 1973, prior to the embargo. But the proceeds from such production in real dollars in 1980 were almost ten times the 1973 collections. In a world of relatively stable exports, OPEC was a very cohesive cartel. Indeed, OPEC appeared immune to the fate of most cartels.

But Figure 1.2 shows that after 1980, OPEC no longer looked so invincible. Oil demand suddenly began to plunge and non-OPEC production continued its slow but steady expansion. To a cartel intent on holding the line on price, the choice was clear that OPEC would have to reduce production. But even with production cuts that by 1984 sent OPEC production to 17 million barrels per day, this was insufficient to prevent declining crude prices.

Efforts to establish production quotas in 1984 met with only mixed success. Allegations of widespread cheating suggested that a number of OPEC producers were now acting independently rather than jointly coordinating output. In 1985, many authorities thought that cheating would continue and even become intensified, putting further downward pressure on prices.

To summarize the implications of this viewpoint, four major points deserve emphasis. First, according to this view, the energy crisis is over. In the mid-1980s, energy was abundantly available at declining real prices; moreover, strong economic growth and insignificant inflation characterized the macroeconomies of this period. Second, OPEC was the culprit behind the energy crisis of the 1970s; consequently, the decline of OPEC means the end of the energy crisis. Third, if the energy crisis of the 1970s was due to scarcity artificially imposed by OPEC, lower oil prices and the resulting greater oil consumption are desirable. Stated another way, further oil price decreases should be viewed positively and any corresponding increase in oil consumption is a healthy response to lower prices. Thus the problem is not that the world has been consuming too much oil; rather, the problem is that artificially imposed scarcity has prevented consumption from growing at a faster, more socially desirable rate. Finally, the policy implications of this viewpoint range from doing nothing on the assumption that cartels are inherently unstable, to pursuing policies that would further undermine OPEC and prevent its revitalization.

A Third Viewpoint: The Energy Problem Is Essentially a Supply Uncertainty Problem

The third viewpoint, popularized in the 1970s and still held today by many, puts almost exclusive stress on the supply disruption aspects of oil imports from politically unstable areas with perceived national interests that may not harmonize with those of oil importers. In crude terms, the industrialized importers have money and need oil; the exporters have oil but also have plenty of money, and may feel from time to time that their need to achieve political goals is more important than their need for money. This view of the energy problem foresees a series of future oil embargoes or supply disruptions, each potentially more devastating than the last. Even though Table 1.3 indicates that in 1984 only 20 percent of world crude oil production came from the Middle East, such a statistic greatly understates the present and future importance of this region to oil consuming nations. Table 1.5 indicates that in 1984 the Middle East, including Saudi Arabia, held 370 billion of the 585 billion barrels of the noncommunist world's oil reserves—or 63 percent. The magnitude of Middle East oil reserves implies that marginal supplies will increasingly come from this strife-torn area. Currently, supplies to Western Europe come largely from North Sea production, with a reserve base of only 23 billion barrels. Likewise, the United States benefits from its own production and adjacent oil production in Canada and Mexico, but here again the North American reserve base appears small compared to the Middle East. Thus over time, the United States and Western Europe will become increasingly dependent on Middle East oil. Already, Japan is 100 percent dependent on imported oil, the bulk of which comes from the Middle East.

For a variety of reasons, the Middle East is an extremely volatile part of the world. Figure 1.3 shows a map of the Middle East and surrounding regions. Note first the location of the key Middle East producers (Saudi Arabia, Iran, Iraq, Kuwait, United Arab Emirates) adjacent to the Persian Gulf. With the exception of a few pipelines, oil supplies must move by tankers through the Straits of Hormuz at the mouth of the Persian Gulf. Merely by blocking this narrow 45 mile passageway, oil shipments could be cut off.

FIGURE 1.3 Map of the Middle East. Major oil pipelines are shown as broken lines. Major oil fields are indicated by small black spots of irregular shape.

Other attributes also contribute to the instability of the region. Hostilities, both real and latent, between the revolutionary Iranian government and Iraq, Kuwait, and Saudi Arabia are but one example. Then, too, Arab-Israeli tensions are capable of igniting events similar to those associated with the 1973 Yom Kippur War.

According to this view, past experience has shown that Arab members of OPEC do not limit their decisions to that set which maximizes their money profits. To accomplish political goals, such as achieving Arab supremacy in the long struggle with Israel, the tactics of economic warfare are acceptable. Oil may be withheld during an embargo if the Arabs can thereby inflict greater economic harm than they sustain, while achieving political aims.

There is much to be said in support of this viewpoint. The Middle East is a most unstable area politically, owing not only to the Arab-Israeli conflicts, but also to Islamic fundamentalism, to the split between radical and conservative regimes, and to the possibility of Soviet naval intervention in the Persian Gulf. The Soviet Union has long coveted the oil fields of the Middle East, and if its own expensive plans to supply itself by expanding high-cost Siberian oil production fail, it will need Arab and Iranian oil that it lacks the hard currencies to purchase. If Persian Gulf oil fields come to be placed under Soviet sponsorship, regardless of the means used, the security problem of the industrialized oil importer is intensified.

Sorting Out Facts from Fiction

Our problem as students of energy issues is to sort out the facts from fictions in these and other viewpoints. Does energy cost too much, as in the viewpoint of the 1980s? Or, following the 1970s viewpoint, is it still priced too low to avoid large supply shortages in the future? How can we plan our energy future to achieve (1) adequate supplies of each energy source, which (2) are obtained from secure regions and (3) are competitively priced? In the last section of this introductory chapter we make an anticipatory survey of the major policy problems that are considered at length in the following chapters of this book. We highlight each of these policy areas from the standpoint of prospective energy supply availability, security, and price, to the extent that each of these categories is applicable.

RECENT ENERGY POLICY PROBLEMS

Six major energy policy problem areas are explored in Chapters 4 through 9. These are (1) the influence of the OPEC cartel on crude oil exports; (2) environmental aspects of energy industries; (3) coping with energy supply disruptions; (4) conservation issues in energy consumption and production; (5) governmental policies, price controls and taxation on oil and natural gas; and (6) energy research and development, particularly that which is directed to new energy sources. Each is briefly summarized below with respect to the three viewpoints in the preceding section.

Chapter 4 examines the validity of the 1980s viewpoint that the energy crisis was due to OPEC's monopoly power and is now history. This chapter considers the origins of OPEC, its evolution, and its role in the 1973 Arab oil embargo. The activities of the international oil companies during this period are also studied. A number of microeconomic models of cartel behavior are analyzed to provide insights into the future strength and viability of the OPEC cartel.

Chapter 5 analyzes the role of energy as a source of air and water pollution and other types of environmental degradation. Environmental restrictions aimed at preventing pollution may also prevent the development of energy sources needed to forestall an energy shortage. A critical question is whether energy production and consumption can be reconciled with legitimate environmental concerns. We examine the efficiency of several economic and regulatory approaches to ameliorating conflicts between energy supply and environmental enhancement.

Chapter 6 considers the dimensions of the supply disruption problem, examining the macroeconomic effects of past and possible future embargoes. How a country chooses to insure against or cope with an embargo differs widely from one energy importer to another. A number of alternative policies are analyzed and an economic methodology for choosing among them is set forth.

Proponents of the 1970s viewpoint that the real crisis is still to come emphasize the necessity of conservation to forestall the disaster. Chapter 7 considers the feasibility, the desirability, and the appropriate mechanisms for promoting conservation.

A prominent aspect of United States energy policy has been a system of governmental regulations on oil and natural gas, which included price controls and the windfall profits tax. Chapter 8 considers the effect of these policies on United States oil consumption, production, and import dependence.

Chapter 9 investigates the current status of energy research and development in expanding supplies and reducing costs of producing fuels from new sources of energy. If we can find ways of economically substituting non-oil-based energy for that derived from crude oil, then the future energy supply crisis, which (under the 1970s viewpoint) will arrive when crude oil supplies are exhausted, may not even occur. If non-oil-based energy sources are provided from domestic resources, the supply disruption problem is eliminated as a major focus of concern. Chapter 9 examines these issues, focusing upon existing technological and other obstacles that must be overcome by energy research and development in order to provide new supplies of energy at economical costs.

Chapter 10 recognizes that, in order to deal with complex energy problems, a variety of policies must be adopted. But how can we be assured that policies adopted to solve one problem will not create secondary problems of equal gravity? There are no simple answers, but economic analysis does provide a framework by which the trade-offs between competing goals can be reconciled.

Before embarking on the study of these fascinating issues, however, we must prescribe a medicinal tonic for the student—a substantial dose of microeconomic theory. In order to analyze the energy problem from an economic perspective, we must first acquire the necessary tools. Chapters 2 and 3 consider the static and dynamic criteria for optimal allocation of nonrenewable energy forms over time. But the use of such tools does not, of course, assure that all economists will recommend the same policies. The theory tonic is prescribed only to immunize the student against the contagion of advocating simplistic and emotionally biased solutions—a contagion prevalent in energy policy discussions.

The apparatus of economic theory, requiring clarity in one's assumptions, consistency in one's hypotheses, and rigor in one's analysis, aids immeasurably in providing a higher plane for policy formulation. Our goal in writing this book is to raise the plane of analysis and to aid in the identification of sources of disagreement—not to seek uniformity of opinion on specific policies. We have not hesitated to reveal our own policy positions in many instances, but the theoretical framework employed is positive rather than normative.

Note

1. William W. Hogan and Alan S. Manne, "Energy-Economy Interactions: The Fable of the Elephant and the Rabbit?" in *Advances in the Economics of Energy and Resources*, Robert Pindyck, editor (Greenwich, CT: J.A.I. Press, 1979).

STATIC CRITERIA FOR EFFICIENT ENERGY RESOURCE ALLOCATION

The policy importance of energy requires that effective economic analysis be *prescriptive* as well as *descriptive*. If the analysis is to lead to useful policy recommendations, a methodology must be devised both for identifying and for quantifying energy market distortions that lead to inefficient resource allocation. Since some market distortions are far more serious than others, their effects must be quantified so that policy can be focused on the more important problems. For such purposes, economists have devised applied welfare analysis or cost–benefit analysis to measure quantitatively the welfare loss to society of a given market distortion. A primary concern of this chapter is the introduction of this applied welfare methodology. Since it will be employed extensively throughout the text, this material should be studied carefully.

In addition to requiring quantification of market distortions, energy economics obliges the student to acquire understanding of a second dimension of theoretical analysis. Current patterns of energy consumptions rely on nonrenewable energy forms. The coal, oil, and natural gas content of the earth's crust is fixed. As the current stewards of these resources, present generations owe to future generations the efficient allocation of these resources *over time*. The problem of optimal energy use over time adds a new perspective to the energy allocation problem. Not only do we want to allocate energy efficiently among competing uses *at a point in time*, but we must also allocate energy between competing uses *over time*. Thus the resource allocation problem has both static and dynamic aspects. This chapter is concerned with static resource allocation, while Chapter 3 explores the criteria for efficient dynamic resource allocation.

A REVIEW OF STATIC RESOURCE ALLOCATION CRITERIA

THE THEORETICAL IDEAL

In order to understand why market distortions occur, it is important to have firmly in mind the criteria for efficient resource allocation.

Therefore, we turn to a review of the standard *Pareto optimality criteria* presented in most introductory and intermediate microeconomics texts. Consider an economy consisting of two goods: air conditioning and gasoline. Residents of warm climates are assumed to choose between consuming air conditioning in one's home or consuming gasoline on an auto trip to the beach or a local lake. In this hypothetical economy, for an overall optimum resource allocation to occur, optimization must occur at three stages. Optimization must occur *among* consumers, *between* producers of gasoline and air conditioning, and *between* producers *and* consumers.[1]

Optimization Among Consumers

For consumers to optimize their well-being, they must select that combination of gasoline and air conditioning for which the last dollar spent on the two items brings equivalent satisfaction. Let us define the marginal utility of gasoline (MU_G) as the incremental satisfaction gained from consuming the last gallon of gasoline, and MU_A as the marginal utility of the last unit of air conditioning consumed. The market prices of gasoline and air conditioning are P_G and P_A, respectively. The marginal utility of the last dollar spent on gasoline is obtained by simply dividing the marginal utility of the last unit of gasoline by its price (MU_G/P_G). Thus for each person to maximize consumer satisfaction given the market prices of gasoline and air conditioning, we require

$$(2.1) \qquad \frac{MU_A}{P_A} = \frac{MU_G}{P_G}$$

If for some person the ratio for air conditioning is 3 ($MU_A/P_A = 3$) and the ratio for gasoline is 2 ($MU_G/P_G = 2$), then the consumer can improve his lot by reducing gasoline consumption and raising air conditioning consumption until the equality of equation (2.1) holds. Thus the first necessary condition for efficient resource allocation is that each consumer optimizes by selecting the combinations of gasoline and air conditioning that maximize his or her well-being.

Optimization Between Producers

At a second stage, optimization must occur among producers of gasoline and air conditioning. If firms are to maximize profits, they must necessarily minimize the costs of producing the desired output of gasoline and air conditioning. If cost-minimizing behavior prevails, inputs of capital, labor, and energy are used in the most efficient manner. Therefore, for any combination of gasoline and air conditioning output, resources cannot be reallocated to provide greater outputs of one good, holding constant the output of the other. In fact, Figure 2.1 depicts the locus of such optimal output combinations of gasoline and air conditioning. The curve labelled *PPF* for production possibility frontier shows, for any level of air conditioning output, the maximum gasoline production possible, given society's limited capital, labor, and energy resources. If firms minimize costs, the combination of goods offered will fall on the production possibility frontier.

The student will recognize the curves labelled I_0, I_1, and I_2 as being social indifference curves. Along each of these curves, the total social welfare of the people in the economy is constant. The downward slope to each social indifference curve indicates that if the economy must give up a unit of one commodity, such as air conditioning, then it must be compensated by receiving an increased level of the other commodity, such as gasoline. Since consumers place a positive evaluation on both air conditioning and gasoline, total social welfare increases as the quantities of either or both of the goods consumed increases. Hence the total social welfare enjoyed by the economy at any point along social indifference curve I_1 is greater than that which it enjoys at any point along curve I_0. Similarly, social welfare is greater at any point on I_2 than it is at any point along I_1, and so on. The tangency between the production possibility frontier and the social indifference curve at point Z indicates that the economy is obtaining the maximum social welfare possible, given the limitations on the production capabilities of the society.

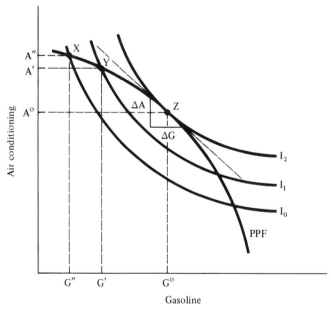

FIGURE 2.1 A competitive equilibrium.

The negative slope of the production possibility frontier is referred to as the marginal rate of transformation (MRT). The marginal rate of transformation shows that to increase gasoline production by ΔG, air conditioning production must be reduced by ΔA in order to divert the resources needed for the increased gasoline production. We want to show that the marginal rate of transformation is simply equal to the ratio of the marginal cost of gasoline (MC_G) to the marginal cost of air conditioning (MC_A) as follows[2]:

$$(2.2) \qquad MRT \equiv -\frac{\Delta A}{\Delta G} = \frac{MC_G}{MC_A}$$

Intuitively, equation (2.2) follows, since if 3 units of air conditioning must be given up to get 1 unit of gasoline, then the marginal cost of gasoline is 3 times the marginal cost of air conditioning.

A more rigorous proof follows from the process of cost minimization implicit in the production possibility frontier. If firms minimize costs, then the last dollar spent on labor and capital inputs must make the same contribution to increased output. Defining the marginal product of an input (MP_i) as the incremental output occurring as a consequence of the use of an additional unit of input i, we see that the incremental output for the last dollar spent on input i is the marginal product of i divided by its price, MP_i/P_i. For capital (K), labor inputs (L), and energy inputs (E), in the production of gasoline, we obtain the cost-minimizing condition

$$(2.3) \qquad \frac{MP_L{}^G}{P_L} = \frac{MP_K{}^G}{P_K} = \frac{MP_E{}^G}{P_E}$$

If the ratio $MP_i{}^G/P_i$ expresses the incremental output for the last dollar spent, then $P_i/MP_i{}^G$ expresses the marginal cost of gasoline, that is, the dollar cost of the last increment to output.

It follows then that the marginal rate of transformation can be expressed as the ratio of the marginal costs of gasoline to air conditioning[3]:

$$(2.4) \qquad MRT \equiv -\frac{\Delta A}{\Delta G} = \frac{\Delta A/\Delta L}{\Delta G/\Delta L} = \frac{(P_L/MP_L{}^G)}{(P_L/MP_L{}^A)} = \frac{MC_G}{MC_A}$$

The first equality follows by definition of the marginal rate of transformation. The second equality must hold since the same amount of labor (ΔL) is being transferred from one industry to the other. The third equality follows by multiplying both the numerator and denominator by P_L and recognizing that $\Delta A/\Delta L$ is by definition the marginal product of labor in air conditioning production. Similarly, $\Delta G/\Delta L$ is equivalent to $MP_L{}^G$. The final equality follows from the above rationale that the marginal cost of gasoline can be expressed as $P_L/MP_L{}^G$, and so on.

Cost minimization assures that the gasoline and air conditioning industries operate on the production possibility frontier, but it does not guarantee the production of the optimal combination of gasoline and air conditioning. For simplicity, assume there is only one consumer, whose indifference curves are given in Figure 2.1. Each indifference curve shows different combinations of air conditioning and gasoline to which the individual is indifferent. Since more is preferred to less, greater consumer satisfaction is associated with indifference curve I_2 than I_1 or I_0. For example, combination $A'G'$ at point Y is inferior to A^0G^0 at point Z, where the marginal rate of transformation equals the slope of the indifference curve.

Optimization Between Consumers and Producers

Let us consider how an optimization process *between* consumers and producers could bring about the optimal production–consumption combination A^0G^0. Suppose that initially production is at point X with A'' air conditioning and G'' gasoline. As evidenced by the indifference curve (I_0) passing through X, the consumer is willing to give up $A'' - A'$ air conditioning for only a slight increase in gasoline production. Yet the marginal rate of transformation shows gasoline production could be expanded by much more: $G' - G''$. Thus if the consumer could somehow return air conditioning of $A'' - A'$, resources could be diverted to gasoline production which would enable increased production of $G' - G''$ gasoline. Our only consumer clearly benefits as he moves to point Y on the higher indifference curve I_1. Similarly, the move from Y to Z leads to improved consumer well-being. In return for giving up air conditioning of $A' - A^0$, consumers receive incremental gasoline output of $G^0 - G'$, which leads to the welfare optimum at point Z.

If the markets for gasoline and air conditioning are perfectly competitive, then the optimum quantity A^0G^0 will result. Note that the slope of the indifference curve, the marginal rate of substitution (MRS), shows the amount of air conditioning (ΔA) an individual is willing to forego to obtain another unit of gasoline (ΔG), holding constant the level of well-being. Since the level of utility or well-being is unchanged, we can express the following relationship:

$$(2.5) \qquad MRS \equiv -\frac{\Delta A}{\Delta G} = \frac{(\Delta U/\Delta G)}{(\Delta U/\Delta A)} = \frac{MU_G}{MU_A}$$

Equation (2.5) simply says that if MRS is 3, society is willing to trade 3 units of air conditioning for 1 unit of gasoline. If so, the marginal utility of gasoline must be 3 times the marginal utility of air conditioning. From the first stage of optimization between consumers, it follows from equation (2.1) that the marginal rate of substitution equals the relative price of gasoline to air conditioning:

$$(2.6) \qquad \text{MRS} = \frac{MU_G}{MU_A} = \frac{P_G}{P_A}$$

If markets are purely competitive, then price equals marginal cost ($P_A = MC_A$ and $P_G = MC_G$). Assuming pure competition and using equations (2.1) and (2.4), we find:

$$(2.7) \qquad \text{MRS} = \underbrace{\frac{P_G}{P_A}}_{\substack{\text{Consumer} \\ \text{optimization}}} = \underbrace{\frac{MC_G}{MC_A}}_{\substack{\text{Producer} \\ \text{optimization}}} = \text{MRT}$$

Consumer/producer optimization
(Pure competition)

Since the marginal rate of substitution equals the marginal rate of transformation at the point $A^0 G^0$, competition assures the optimal combination $A^0 G^0$ is produced.

Equation (2.7) summarizes the three stages of optimization. Consumer optimization assures that the rate at which people are willing to substitute air conditioning for gasoline is inversely proportional to their prices. At the second stage, cost minimization by producers assures that the rate at which air conditioning can be substituted for gasoline is inversely proportional to their marginal costs. Finally, pure competition forces the price of the good to equal its marginal cost. Pure competition then assures a welfare optimum, where the marginal rate of transformation equals the marginal rate of substitution. The output combination $A^0 G^0$ in Figure 2.1 is said to represent a Pareto optimum, since it is not possible to improve welfare by making at least one person better off and no one worse off. Note that if the distribution of income were altered, the shape of the indifference curve in Figure 2.1 would change, leading to an alternative Pareto optimum.

In sum, the criteria for efficient resource allocation are met when the price of a good equals its marginal cost. However, these results are subject to an important caveat. It is assumed that there are no externalities, which occur when the social and private valuations of price and marginal cost differ. The market price, which reflects the individual's marginal valuation of the benefits from the last unit consumed, must also reflect the marginal valuation of the benefits received by society from the last unit. Similarly, the marginal cost, which measures the private cost to the firm of producing the last unit, must also coincide with the marginal cost to society of producing the last unit.

It should also be noted that the assumptions employed here imply that consumers always seek more of every positively evaluated commodity, and that a dollar spent on furs and European travel is worth as much to society as a dollar spent by a retired couple on their fuel bill.

FOUR TYPES OF MARKET FAILURE

The preceding section emphasizes that to achieve efficient resource allocation, the marginal social benefit, as reflected in a good's price, must equal the marginal social cost of its production. Market distortions are said to occur whenever these conditions are not met. Distortions can arise either through inappropriate government policies or through market failures. In this section, let us consider under what conditions an unregulated market economy will fail to attain these efficiency conditions. By identifying the sources of market failure, we can identify those situations where government intervention is justifiable for promoting economic efficiency.

Externalities

Even if markets are purely competitive, optimal resource allocation may not occur because of deviations between social and private valuations of costs and benefits. Externalities are defined as situations in which the private calculation of benefits or costs differs from society's valuation of benefits or costs. Since in a market economy private costs and market prices determine the output of the good in question, nonoptimal output levels will result.

Externalities can occur in both production and consumption. Examples of production externalities typically focus on pollution. An excellent energy-related example is the electric utility plant burning high-sulfur coal near a major metropolitan city. While the private cost of the electricity, as measured by the firm's cost, may be 6¢ per kilowatt-hour (kwh), the social cost of the electricity production may be much higher, perhaps 9¢/kwh. Included in the social cost are the health costs imposed on the city's inhabitants due to increased sulfur oxide concentrations in the air. As shown in Figure 2.2(a), the socially optimal output is Q_s, where marginal social benefit equals the marginal social cost of electricity. Unfortunately, since the private cost of electricity is 6¢/kwh, this leads to a 6¢ price and consumption of Q_p.

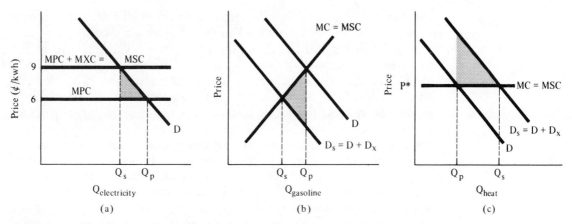

FIGURE 2.2 Examples of externalities. (a) External production diseconomy. (b) External consumption diseconomy. (c) External consumption economy.

There are situations where production externalities confer positive attributes as well. The marginal social cost schedule may actually be less than the marginal private cost schedule due to residual employment effects of a plant moving to a small community, for example.

Consumption externalities arise when in the process of consuming a good privately, additional positive or negative benefits accrue to others. Consider the case of gasoline consumption. Can we argue that the price paid for the last gallon of gasoline reflects its marginal social benefit? To the gasoline consumer paying the price, the last gallon of gasoline undoubtedly confers benefits equal to its price; otherwise, the individual would have purchased something else. To the inhabitants of office buildings and apartments in congested areas, the value to them of the last gallon of gasoline consumed by someone else is negative because of the resulting auto emissions. Figure 2.2(b) depicts a situation where the social demand schedule D_s lies vertically below the private demand schedule D, the difference D_x reflecting the amount the residents would be willing to pay motorists to reduce gasoline consumption. In this case, the socially optimal level of gasoline consumption is Q_s, since at that output the marginal social benefit of the last unit of gasoline equals its marginal social cost. In contrast, the market result (output Q_p) leads to an overconsumption of gasoline of amount $Q_p - Q_s$.

Consumption externalities also occur in which marginal social benefits exceed private benefits. Consider the case of the exotic dancer who, preferring scant clothing, chooses to heat her high-rise apartment to 75°F in the winter. Apartment dwellers living on higher floors find that since heat rises, they need to purchase less fuel to heat their apartments. In view of these external economies, the socially optimal solution is for the lascivious bachelors living above the dancer to subsidize her heating bill, encouraging her to wear even less and to further raise the thermostat, consequently further reducing their heating bill. Figure 2.2(c) graphically describes the situation. The demand curve D reflects the private benefits to the exotic dancer. The demand schedule D_s reflects the social benefits of consumption, which include the sum of private benefits to the exotic dancer plus the benefits to her neighbors upstairs. In the absence of any compensation by the bachelors upstairs, the dancer will pay price P^* and choose heat consumption of Q_p, since at this level marginal private benefits equal the marginal cost of heat. However, if the neighbors upstairs collectively compensated the dancer for the heat savings they enjoyed, she would raise her thermostat to the socially optimal temperature (e.g., 80°F) and purchase Q_s units of heat. When side payments of this nature do not occur, her fuel consumption falls below the socially optimal quantity and a misallocation of resources occurs.

Public Goods

Public goods are in fact a special case of a consumption externality in which one person's consumption of the public good does not preclude others from enjoying similar benefits. Once produced, a public good can be made available to additional consumers at zero cost. Examples of public goods include television signals, lighthouses, and national defense. A new television watcher can tune into channel 8 without weakening the signal received by other viewers of channel 8. Similarly, ships entering a dark harbor can all benefit from the light beams from the lighthouse. Too, new immigrants to a country can benefit from the level of national defense at effectively zero cost.

If public goods are purchased individually, their production will either be zero or very small compared to the optimal level where marginal social benefits equal the marginal social cost of production. Since the private benefits accruing to any one individual are small compared to the cost of the item, the public good will be severely underproduced. Suppose national defense was supplied privately. Some might acquire handguns, others might hire bodyguards, but no one would have the resources to outfit an army capable of defending the country from external attack. Graphically, the case of a public good is merely an extreme example of an external consumption economy as in Figure 2.2(c), except that the private demand schedule D will lie very close to the price axis. This implies that the privately supplied quantity will be very small compared to Q_s, the socially optimal production.

Recall from the earlier discussion of Pareto optimality that perfect competition is also necessary to assure that the optimal combination of gasoline and air conditioning is produced. Let us consider the effect of a monopoly in the production of gasoline. The gasoline monopolist faces the market demand curve in Figure 2.3 and a horizontal long-run average cost curve (LRAC) and marginal cost curve (LRMC). The profit-maximizing monopolist will produce only that output level where the marginal cost of gasoline production equals its marginal revenue (MR). Contrasted to the competitive outcome where price equals marginal cost (output Q_c and price P_c), the monopolistic outcome is lower production Q_m and a higher price P_m. This outcome depicts a long-run equilibrium with a corresponding misallocation of resources, since for the Q_mth output, marginal social benefits exceed marginal social costs.

The effect of monopoly on resource allocation can be seen in Figure 2.1 by the production at point Y on the production possibility frontier. The gasoline monopolist has succeeded in raising the price of gasoline above its marginal cost. Assuming air conditioning is supplied competitively, the price of gasoline relative to air conditioning has risen. Consumers react by choosing combination Y entailing less gasoline and more air conditioning. Thus even though point Y is on the production possibility frontier, resources are misallocated since resources

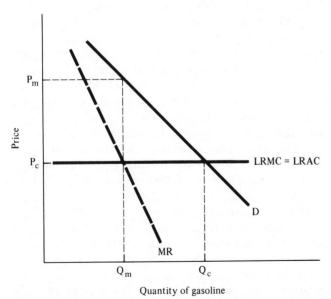

FIGURE 2.3 The effects of monopoly on resource allocation.

could have been diverted from air conditioning to gasoline production, thereby raising consumer welfare.[4]

Oligopoly describes the situation where there is more than one producer, yet the number of producers is small enough that they recognize their mutual interdependence. Pricing and output decisions by any one firm are likely to have repercussions on the pricing and output decisions of other firms, leading to possible marketwide adjustments. Unlike pure competition and monopoly, oligopoly theory does not lead to well-defined predictions as to market prices and quantities. In practice, the behavior of oligopolies varies dramatically from one industry to the next, depending on entry conditions, the number and size of the firms, and so on. In some cases with high barriers to entry and only a few firms, oligopoly can lead to the same price–quantity outcome as monopoly. On the other hand, where entry is relatively easy and the number of firms is larger, the industry may be "workably competitive" as over the long run, price will equal long-run marginal costs, and profit levels will be normal. Finally, there is the oligopoly situation resulting in an output greater than Q_m but less than Q_c and a price less than P_m but greater than P_c.[5] In this situation, the loss in economic efficiency is not as great as monopoly, but nevertheless of policy concern.

Decreasing Cost Production

If the firm's long-run average cost function declines continuously, the firm is considered to be a natural monopoly.[6] With economies of scale persisting over the complete output range, perfect competition is neither feasible nor efficient. One firm can displace other small competitors by simply increasing production and at the same time lowering price and average costs. Production from a single plant confers efficiency benefits since economies of scale allow it to produce at lower real resource costs to society. To avoid the inefficiencies of underproduction by monopolists as outlined in the previous section, regulatory bodies have been established to set price equal to the firm's average costs.

Figure 2.4 illustrates the case of an electric utility or natural gas pipeline where scale economies persist over the relevant output range so that long-run marginal costs (LRMC) are declining, thus producing decreasing long-run average costs (LRAC). Although for efficiency purposes it is desirable that only one firm serve the market, the unregulated monopoly outcome of output Q_m and price P_m would result in output well below the socially optimal output Q_s where the marginal social cost of the last unit equals the marginal social benefit. Public utility regulation was devised to solve the problem, at least partially. Regulators immediately realized that the socially optimal output Q_s was not possible because if the regulated firm charged price P_s it would not recoup its full costs and would soon face bankruptcy. Furthermore, local taxing authorities were unwilling to subsidize the lo-

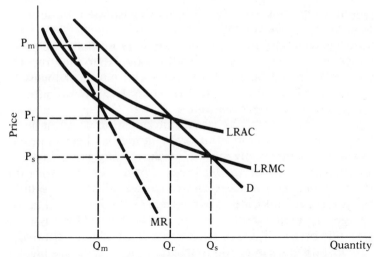

FIGURE 2.4 Natural monopoly and its regulatory outcome.

cal utility. The solution was "rate of return" regulation which allowed firms to charge a price sufficient to cover all costs and provide investors with a fair rate of return. Effectively, this price sets average costs equal to average revenue, which occurs at the intersection of the demand schedule and the long-run average cost curve. Under public utility regulation, the regulated price P_r results in an output of Q_r. Although output Q_r is preferable to the outcome in unregulated monopoly, it is still less than the socially optimal output Q_s. Another criticism of the regulatory approach is the tendency of regulated firms not to minimize costs over time.

1. List several energy-related examples of externalities both in production and consumption.
2. List energy-related examples of monopoly power and decreasing cost production.
3. Could one argue that making an economy less subject to an oil embargo has public goods aspects?
4. Prove that public utility regulation that sets price equal to LRAC fails to achieve the socially optimal output level in the case of decreasing cost production.

A METHODOLOGY FOR QUANTIFYING WELFARE EFFECTS

The previous four types of market failures provide a guideline for government intervention in energy markets. To the extent that observed phenomena fit into one of these four classifications, there is an economic justification for government intervention in the market. Our sole criterion for government intervention in energy markets is to improve the efficiency with which energy is allocated. Noneconomic criteria for intervention based on political and social equity considerations fall into the range of value judgments where there is little basis for agreement or scientific determination.

It is not sufficient merely to observe a market failure and call for government intervention. Market failures are numerous because even if one cannot point to monopoly power or decreasing costs, clearly most firms or industries impose at least some minor externalities on society. In the vast majority of cases these market failures have only trivial effects on resource allocation. Moreover, as the history of regulation reveals, government intervention is not costless. Therefore, in policy analysis, our first problem is to devise a methodology that will allow us to quantitatively assess the magnitude or seriousness of any given market failure. After identifying and quantifying the more serious market failures, we can then begin to devise specific corrective policies.

In order to quantify these effects, we must measure economic welfare under alternative market conditions. Since welfare is defined as the difference between social benefits and social costs, obtaining empirical measures of social costs and social benefits is critical. At the outset, it must be recognized that they are difficult to measure precisely. At best, we can hope for reasonable empirical approximations, the data requirements of which are both feasible and cost-effective. The subsequent sections outline an empirically practical procedure for approximating social benefits and social costs.

Measuring Social Benefits

Social benefits are defined as the total amount society is willing to pay for a given quantity of goods, holding constant society's level of well-being. Graphically, this is seen in Figure 2.5. The indifference curve (I_0) for the typical consumer shows the combinations of gasoline and other goods for which the individual is indifferent. Instead of plotting the quantity of other goods on the vertical axis, we plot the expenditures on these items. Therefore, the marginal rate of substitution shows the price the consumer is willing to pay for each unit of gasoline. For example, δ_1 is the dollar amount of spending on other goods the buyer is willing to forego for the first unit of gasoline, while δ_2 is the dollar amount the consumer is willing to give up of other goods for the second unit of gasoline. For the sixth unit, the consumer is willing to forsake δ_6 expenditure on other goods to obtain the sixth unit of gasoline.

By reading off the prices the consumer is willing to pay for each

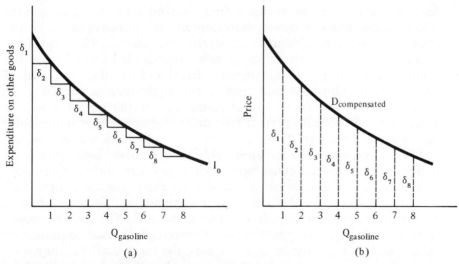

FIGURE 2.5 (a) Determining the value of incremental gasoline consumption. (b) Derivation of the marginal social benefit schedule.

additional unit, it is possible to construct a marginal social benefits schedule, which shows the marginal social benefits derived for each unit of gasoline. Students of intermediate price theory will recognize the marginal social benefits schedule as nothing more than the compensated demand schedule, which shows the consumer response to price changes holding consumer well-being constant.[7]

The area under the compensated demand curve indicates the aggregate social benefits of a given output level, since it shows the summation of the amounts willing to be paid for each unit. The social benefits of four units of gasoline consumption are obtained by adding the area under the compensated demand schedule corresponding to the first units of gasoline, which is $\delta_1 + \delta_2 + \delta_3 + \delta_4$. Similarly, if given the option to purchase six units of gasoline, the consumer is willing to pay $\delta_1 + \delta_2 + \delta_3 + \delta_4 + \delta_5 + \delta_6$. Suppose we wanted to calculate the change in social benefits from raising gasoline production from four to six units. The change in social benefits is $\delta_5 + \delta_6$ since this represents the amount the consumer is willing to pay for the fifth and sixth units.

Conventional demand curves estimated by econometric techniques show the consumer response to price; however, they do not hold the individual on a given indifference curve. The market price and quantity data used to estimate conventional demand schedules do not hold consumer satisfaction constant. The shape of the conventional demand schedule depends on the sum of substitution and income effects. Recall that the substitution effect measures the change in consumption due to the price change while holding utility or consumer well-being constant.[8] The substitution effects are, of course, what are measured in Figure 2.5(b) by the compensated demand schedule. The income effects show the change in consumption as a consequence of the change in real income resulting from the price change. The total effect of a price change is thus to change relative prices holding constant the level of well-being (the substitution effect) and to affect the level of real income holding constant relative prices (the income effect).

Figure 2.6(a) depicts an initial consumer equilibrium at A with a price at δ_4 and consumption of four units of gasoline. Let us consider the effect of reducing the price to δ_5. The substitution effect, which holds the consumer on the same indifference curve, leads to a shift from A to B. Gasoline consumption increases from four to five units. Additionally, the decrease in gasoline price raises the consumer's real income, enabling the movement to the higher indifference curve I_1 with the new equilibrium combination at point C. (The student should note that the reduced gasoline price permits increased spending on other goods.) As drawn in Figure 2.6(a), the income effect (shown by the shift from point B to point C) shows the effect of higher real income on the purchases of gasoline and other items. In this example, the income effect did not alter gasoline consumption. If the income effect on gasoline consumption is zero, leaving only the substitution effects to determine the shape of the demand schedule for gasoline, then the compensated and conventional demand schedules for gasoline are identical. Figure 2.6(a) shows that for a price reduction from δ_4 to δ_5, gasoline consumption rose from four to five units. This is precisely the result given by a compensated demand curve! Figure 2.6(b)

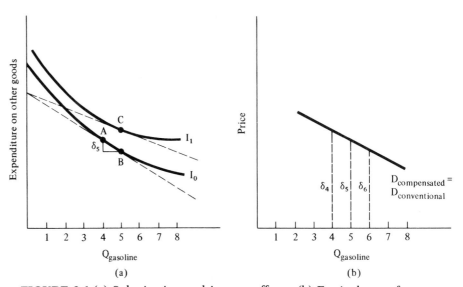

FIGURE 2.6 (a) Substitution and income effects. (b) Equivalence of compensated and conventional demand schedules.

shows that the compensated and conventional demand schedules are identical if the income effects are zero.

In Figure 2.6(a), the use of conventional demand functions to approximate the theoretically correct compensated demand function poses no problem. The two are identical because of the absence of income effects. But in real world examples income effects may not be zero. For example, a price reduction from δ_4 to δ_5 may increase gasoline consumption from 4 gallons to 5.2 gallons. While the substitution effect may by itself have increased consumption to 5 gallons, the income effect of higher real income may account for the increase from 5 to 5.2 gallons. Are there any guidelines to suggest when income effects are likely to produce appreciable divergencies between conventional and compensated demand schedules? In general, the extent of the bias varies depending on three factors. First, if the substitution responses are large compared to the income effects, the percentage bias will be small. Second, the extent of bias depends on the commodity's importance in the consumer's budget. For example, if gasoline had cost only 1 percent of the budget, the effect of a price change for gasoline would have little effect on real income. For this reason, the bias caused by using a conventional demand schedule tends to be small. A third factor influencing the bias is the extent to which the income elasticity differs from zero. Clearly, the bias for items such as luxury goods with large income elasticities will be much greater than the bias associated with necessities.

In practice, the bias resulting from using a conventional demand schedule is probably negligible. However, there are situations where the bias is appreciable. Providing reasonable econometric estimates of the relevant income elasticities are available, some adjustments can and should be made.[9]

QUESTIONS

1. Why is it that even if a good may be strongly income-elastic, the conventional and compensated price elasticities of demand will be similar, providing the good in question forms only a small fraction of one's budget?

2. What fraction of your expenditures is made on gasoline, electricity, and natural gas?

3. Suppose gasoline is an inferior good. Is the compensated price elasticity more or less elastic than the conventional price elasticity? For a given quantity reduction, can you show that the conventional demand schedule will lead to an overestimate of the loss in social benefits? For a quantity increase, can you show the opposite?

Measuring Social Costs

The key to understanding the notion of social costs is to remember that we are concerned only with the *real resource costs* associated with the production of a given output. The real resource costs can differ appreciably from the costs on an accounting statement. In addition to the costs of capital, labor, and materials, other factors must be considered in determining real resource costs. User costs, which are simply the opportunity cost of using a nonrenewable resource, reflect a real opportunity cost even though they do not show up as a cost on the firm's balance sheet. Similarly, if the production of the good imposes production externalities on society in the form of air or water pollution, these costs are real in that they represent impairment of health and damage to property. Thus externally borne costs must be added to the firm's private costs of production to arrive at social costs.

The importance of measuring only real resource costs cannot be overemphasized as there is a natural tendency to assume that the price of a good reflects its social costs. Even assuming externalities are negligible, the relationship between the price and social cost of a good can differ because of monopoly profits and government taxes and subsidies. For example, suppose a tax is placed on air conditioning, causing its price to double. Can we conclude that the real resource costs involved in producing air conditioning have doubled? The capital, labor, and material inputs are the same as before the price increases; therefore, the social costs are unchanged.

For applied welfare analysis it is necessary to construct a marginal social cost schedule (S) that reflects the cost of real resources needed to bring forth the next unit of output. For applications at the firm level, the firm's long-run marginal cost curve (excluding all nonreal resource payments) is entirely analogous to the marginal social cost schedule. For industry applications, the marginal social cost schedule is nothing more than the long-run supply schedule for a competitive industry free of externalities. It should be noted that all taxes or subsidies should be netted out of the long-run supply schedule in order to measure real resource costs. Recall that an upward-sloping long-run supply schedule denotes an increasing cost industry. For example, crude oil exploration and production is an increasing-cost industry as new reserves are found at greater depths, offshore, and in smaller pool sizes. Figure 2.7 depicts such an increasing cost industry. Note that the marginal cost of producing the Q^*th unit is shown by the vertical line Q^*B. The total social cost of output Q^* is given by the area OBQ^*.

Even though social costs are easier to conceptualize than social benefits, their measurement is subject to error that emanates from three problem areas. First, in situations where production externalities are nonnegligible, some measure of these external damages must be added to private costs to obtain social costs. A second difficulty arises from the pervasive effects that taxes and subsidies exert on the competitive industry's long-run supply schedule. While sales or excise taxes are

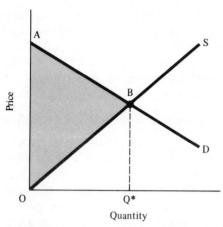

FIGURE 2.7 The welfare optimum.

easily subtracted from gross proceeds, other taxes such as the firm's contribution to Social Security taxes and the corporate income tax are less obvious.[10] A third measurement problem is illustrated by Figure 2.7. In order to estimate the added social cost of production in excess of Q^*, one must know the slope of the supply schedule, which is sometimes quite difficult to measure empirically. Fortunately, many industries are constant-cost industries so that the marginal social cost schedule is horizontal, thus alleviating the problem.

QUESTION

1. Distinguish which of the following should be included as a real resource cost: *(a)* a 5 percent sales tax, *(b)* a $1.00 per unit subsidy on the item, *(c)* a 5 percent employment tax, *(d)* monopoly profits, *(e)* historical capital costs, *(f)* rental payment for land, *(g)* opportunity costs of capital inputs, *(h)* materials costs, and *(i)* pollution costs imposed on third parties.

Graphical Depiction of Welfare Losses and Gains

The maximum level of welfare occurs when the marginal social benefit of the last unit of output equals its marginal social cost. In Figure 2.7, welfare is maximized where output is Q^*. At any output below Q^*, the marginal social benefit of the last unit exceeds its marginal social cost, implying that welfare can be increased by raising output. At any output above Q^*, the marginal social cost of the last unit exceeds its marginal social benefit. Therefore, welfare can be increased by cutting output back toward Q^*. The shaded area *OAB*, obtained by the difference between total social benefits and total social costs, represents the level of welfare from output of Q^*. The reader can verify that the shaded area representing welfare (the difference between social benefits and social costs) is maximized when output is Q^*.

For most purposes, we are not as much interested in measuring total welfare as the *change* in welfare resulting from a policy change. As a practical matter, we are only concerned with showing that the welfare gain is, for example, $10 billion for a policy change. Whether total welfare has increased from $1000 billion to $1010 billion or from $30 to $40 billion is irrelevant. Starting from any given resource allocation with a variety of distortions, it is possible to determine whether a proposed policy change will raise or lower economic welfare. We can measure the welfare loss or gain associated with any given policy change by simply taking the change in social benefits less the change in social costs.

To illustrate this approach, consider the following example. Figure 2.8 provides a graphic depiction of a market exhibiting a negative production externality. Society's supply schedule, reflecting the marginal social cost of production, exceeds the industry's supply schedule by the amount of the external damage costs borne by third parties. The critical equilibrium occurs at price P_0 and output Q_0. The proposed policy change is to institute a flat pollution tax of t per unit of production. The effect of such a tax is to raise the industry supply schedule

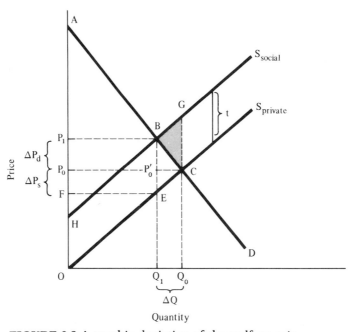

FIGURE 2.8 A graphic depiction of the welfare gain.

to equal society's supply schedule (S_{social}). By internalizing the externality, the price of the product will rise to P_1 and output will fall to Q_1, the welfare optimum output.

The formal method of calculating the welfare loss or gain is to solve for total social benefits and costs prior to and after the policy change—the difference being the welfare loss or gain. Following this procedure, we know that *after* the pollution tax:

$$(2.8) \qquad \begin{array}{ccccc} \text{Welfare} & = & \text{Social benefits} & - & \text{Social costs} \\ ABH & = & OABQ_1 & - & OHBQ_1 \end{array}$$

The level of welfare *before* the policy change is given by

$$(2.9) \qquad \begin{array}{ccccc} \text{Welfare} & = & \text{Social benefits} & - & \text{Social costs} \\ ABH - BCG & = & OACQ_0 & - & OHGQ_0 \end{array}$$

The change in welfare is simply the difference between equations (2.8) and (2.9):

$$(2.10) \qquad \begin{array}{ccccc} \Delta\text{Welfare} & = & \Delta\text{Social benefits} & - & \Delta\text{Social costs} \\ BCG & = & -BCQ_0Q_1 & + & BGQ_0Q_1 \end{array}$$

Thus the gain in welfare is the shaded area BCG.

The short-cut method of calculating the welfare gain or loss is to recognize that all the net changes in social benefits and costs must occur in the output region between Q_0 and Q_1, since this is the region over which output is affected. This method involves the direct use of equation (2.10). Since output does not fall below Q_1 in either case, welfare over these regions is unaffected. Similarly, output does not rise above Q_0. By looking only at the affected output range, that is, that lying between Q_1 and Q_0, we can see that the tax will reduce output and reduce social benefits by BCQ_0Q_1. Since less of the output is available to satisfy consumer needs, social benefits will fall. Social costs decline by an even greater amount, BGQ_0Q_1, leading to a net welfare gain BCG. Thus, one subtracts the area representing losses from the area representing gains.

Researchers experienced in the applied welfare analysis frequently rely on a still shorter shortcut, which makes use of the fact that welfare is affected only over the interval Q_1 to Q_0. Suppose one defines the distortion at each output level as the difference between marginal social benefits and marginal social costs.[11] At Q_0, the distortion is a negative number equal to the length of the line segment CG. At Q_1, there is no distortion, since marginal social costs and benefits are equal. By summing the distortions over the output interval Q_1 to Q_0, one obtains the welfare gain BCG. Thus, one looks only at net gains (or net losses) on each transaction in the affected area.

1. Suppose in Figure 2.8 that instead of taxing the polluting industry, a subsidy of *t* were paid. Calculate the welfare loss. Prove using both the formal and shortcut methods. (*Hint:* A subsidy reduces the firm's production costs.)

2. Suppose in Figure 2.8 that the government overreacted and levied a tax of 2*t* per unit of output. Show the effect on welfare. (*Hint:* Focus only on the affected output range, dividing it into two ranges.)

3. Suppose that in Figure 2.8, the private supply schedule correctly reflects social costs, that is, there are no externalities. Show that a welfare loss of *BCE* would occur from a tax of *t*. Prove by both the formal and shortcut methods.

4. In Figure 2.2(a), (b), and (c), pencil in letters and solve for the welfare gains from correcting the externalities by moving from Q_p to Q_s. The welfare gains should coincide with the shaded areas.

Quantifying the Welfare Loss or Gain

In Figure 2.8, it is clear that the welfare gain from the pollution tax is area *BCG*, but what does area *BCG* imply in terms of dollars? If we know the exact shape of the demand and the social supply schedule, we could employ integral calculus to solve for the difference between the two functions over the range Q_1 to Q_0 to obtain a dollar estimate of the welfare loss. There is a much simpler method of approximating the welfare gain that requires only three pieces of information: the dollar sales of the good in question, the percentage change in price, and the relevant elasticities of supply and demand. Dollar sales data for any product are merely the product of price times quantity. The percentage change in price depends, of course, on the existing price level and the tax rate. Data on the price elasticities of supply and demand are not as readily available, but nevertheless, econometric and engineering analysis studies are frequently available to provide these estimates.

Let us consider how these data would be used to calculate the welfare gain *BCG*. First note that, geometrically, area *BCG* is equivalent to area *BCE*. Note that in Figure 2.8, if the P_0 price line is extended through the triangle *BCE*, the triangle *BCE* is divided into two right triangles, BCP_0' and CEP_0'. We then use the fact that the area of each right triangle can be represented as follows:

(2.11) $$\text{Welfare gain} = \text{Triangle } CEP_0' + \text{Triangle } BCP_0'$$
$$= \tfrac{1}{2}\Delta P_s \Delta Q + \tfrac{1}{2}\Delta P_d \Delta Q$$

Equation (2.11) utilizes the fact that the area of a right triangle is one-half the base times the height. In this case, the base ΔQ is the same for each triangle. The heights differ, however, as ΔP_s and ΔP_d are generally not equal. We do know, however, they sum to equal the tax rate t ($t = \Delta P_s + \Delta P_d$).

The reader can verify by simple division that the following equation is equivalent to equation (2.11):

(2.12)
$$\text{Welfare gain} = \frac{1}{2}\left(\frac{\Delta P_s}{P_0}\right)^2 (P_0 Q_0)\left(\frac{\Delta Q}{\Delta P_s}\frac{P_0}{Q_0}\right)$$
$$+ \frac{1}{2}\left(\frac{\Delta P_d}{P_0}\right)^2 (P_0 Q_0)\left(\frac{\Delta Q}{\Delta P_d}\frac{P_0}{Q_0}\right)$$

But the terms in parentheses are nothing more than

(2.13)
$$\text{Welfare gain} = \frac{1}{2}\left(\frac{\Delta P_s}{P_0}\right)^2 \times \text{sales} \times E_s$$
$$+ \frac{1}{2}\left(\frac{\Delta P_d}{P_0}\right)^2 \times \text{sales} \times E_d$$

where E_s and E_d are elasticities of supply and demand.

As an example, suppose sales are $1000. The market price P_0 equals $1.00 and the proposed tax is 50¢. Let us depart from the strict mathematical implications of Figure 2.8 and assume for simplicity that the elasticity of demand (E_d) is unity and the elasticity of supply (E_s) is 2. First, we must solve for ΔP_s and ΔP_d. Note that ΔP_s is that portion of the per unit tax borne by producers and ΔP_d is that portion of the per unit tax shifted forward to consumers. It is easy to show that the ratio of the two price changes equals the inverse ratio of the elasticities:

(2.14)
$$\frac{E_d}{E_s} = \left(\frac{\Delta Q_d}{\Delta P_d}\frac{P}{Q}\right) \Big/ \left(\frac{\Delta Q_s}{\Delta P_s}\frac{P}{Q}\right) = \frac{\Delta P_s}{\Delta P_d}$$

since

$$\Delta Q_s = \Delta Q_d = \Delta Q$$

If the ratio of E_d to E_s is 0.5 ($E_d/E_s = \frac{1}{2}$), then by equation (2.14), $\Delta P_s = \frac{1}{2}\Delta P_d$. Now since ΔP_s plus ΔP_d equals a tax of 50¢, it follows that $\Delta P_d = 33\frac{1}{3}$¢ and $\Delta P_s = 16\frac{2}{3}$¢.

Substituting those values into equation (2.13), we obtain a welfare gain of $83.50:

(2.15)
$$\text{Welfare gain} = \frac{1}{2}\left(\frac{0.166}{1}\right)^2(1000)(2) + \frac{1}{2}\left(\frac{0.333}{1}\right)^2(1000)(1)$$
$$= 0.5(0.028)(1000)(2) + 0.5(0.11)(1000)(1)$$
$$= 28.00 + 55.50$$
$$= \$83.50$$

In sum, given data on the percentage price increase, dollar sales, and estimates of the price elasticities of supply and demand, we can quantify the welfare loss or gain. By attaching a dollar value to the various market failures, we can distinguish between the important and the trivial market failures for policy purposes.

QUESTIONS

1. Suppose the long-run social and private supply schedule is horizontal. Can you show that the triangle $\frac{1}{2}\Delta P_s \Delta Q$ is zero and that the welfare loss from $\Delta P_d \Delta Q$ will be $125? What does this suggest about the role of a less than perfectly elastic E_s in reducing the welfare loss?

2. Suppose that in the problem in equation (2.15), authorities imposed only a tax of 25¢ instead of the 50¢ tax. Will the welfare gain be one-half of $83.50, or less? Why?

3. Rework equation (2.13) assuming $E_s = 8$ and $E_d = 4$. Show that the welfare loss is $334. What can you conclude about the magnitude of the elasticities in affecting the welfare loss?

4. Prove that a vertical demand schedule implies a zero welfare loss.

The Measurement of Income Distribution Effects: Consumer and Producer Surplus

Aggregate welfare must accrue to consumers in the form of consumer surplus, to producers in the form of producer surplus, or to the government in the form of government tax revenues. This follows from the fact that the standard analysis involves these three economic agents. Figure 2.9 depicts the situation of a competitive industry free of externalities. A welfare optimum occurs at output Q^* and price P^*. After a unit tax is levied, the higher prices P_T lead to reduced consumption of Q_T. The effect of this policy is to reduce welfare by BCD, since over the output interval Q_T to Q^* social benefits exceed social costs by the triangle BCD.

Even though the welfare loss is the triangle BCD, we shall see that the income distribution effects of the tax are much larger. Consumer surplus is found by taking the difference between the amount consumers are willing to pay for a given production level and the amount actually paid. In Figure 2.9, for output of Q^*, consumers are willing to pay $OABQ^*$. Since the price is P^* per unit, the amount actually paid is only OP^*BQ^*. The difference between the amount buyers are willing to pay and the amount they actually pay is P^*AB, the consumers' surplus. After the tax, the level of consumer surplus has fallen to $P_T AC$, which for output Q_T is the difference between the amount consumers are willing to pay (area $OACQ_T$) and the amount paid (rectangle $OP_T CQ_T$).

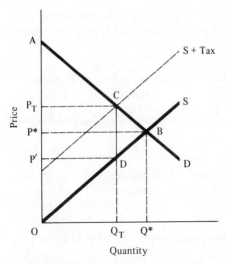

FIGURE 2.9 Measuring the distributional effects.

Producer surplus is defined as the difference between the amount actually received by producers and the minimum amount necessary to bring forth the relevant output. In the standard case of constant cost industries, the competitive industry's long-run supply schedule is horizontal. In this case, there are no excess profits and thus no producers' surplus. However, in an increasing-cost industry with a rising schedule, competitive firms can earn producers' surplus on the sale of inframarginal units. In increasing-cost industries such as petroleum extraction, the tendency is for each new oil field to exhibit higher marginal costs due to greater drilling depths, poor locations, and declining field size. Producers of fields that were found 30 years ago at low costs can earn producers' surplus, while at the same time investors in the new field discoveries earn no excess profits. Note that for the last unit produced, there is no producers' surplus in a competitive industry.

In the example, the initial output Q^* reveals that producers received revenue of OP^*BQ^*, yet only compensation of OBQ^* would have paid the incremental costs of each unit between output zero and Q^*. Therefore, initially producer surplus is OP^*B. Following the tax, producer surplus decreases to area $OP'D$, since the net price actually received by producers is P'. The amount received by producers is $OP'DQ_T$, while the minimum cost to produce output Q_T is area ODQ_T.

With a price of P^* and output Q^*, taxes are zero, leaving government revenue initially at zero. After imposing the fixed unit tax, the price rose to P_T and output fell to Q_T. Tax revenues are given by the rectangle $P'P_TCD$, which measures government revenue.

Let us combine these results to examine the income distribution resulting from the tax change. Recalling the fact that welfare must accrue to the various economic agents, which in this case consist of consumers, producers, governments, and parties affected by externalities, after the tax increase, we find:

(2.16)

$$\text{Welfare } (Q_T) = \underset{\text{surplus}}{\text{Consumer}} + \underset{\text{surplus}}{\text{Producer}} + \underset{\text{revenue}}{\text{Government}} + \underset{\text{effects}}{\text{External}}$$

$$OACD \quad = \quad P_TAC \quad + \quad OP'D \quad + \quad P'P_TCD \quad + \quad 0$$

Prior to the tax, welfare is divided as follows:

(2.17)

$$\text{Welfare } (Q^*) = \underset{\text{surplus}}{\text{Consumer}} + \underset{\text{surplus}}{\text{Producer}} + \underset{\text{revenue}}{\text{Government}} + \underset{\text{effects}}{\text{External}}$$

$$OAB \quad = \quad P^*AB \quad + \quad OP^*B \quad + \quad 0 \quad + \quad 0$$

The changes in the respective surpluses are obtained by subtracting (2.17) from (2.16):

(2.18)

$$\Delta\text{Welfare} = \underset{\text{surplus}}{\Delta\text{Consumer}} + \underset{\text{surplus}}{\Delta\text{Producer}} + \underset{\text{revenue}}{\Delta\text{Government}} + \underset{\text{effects}}{\Delta\text{External}}$$

$$-BCD \quad = \quad -P^*P_TCB \quad - \quad P'P^*BD \quad + \quad P'P_TCD \quad + \quad 0$$

In cases not involving externalities, it is customary to exclude the external effects term, leaving only consumers' and producers' surplus and government revenue.

The welfare loss of BCD is small contrasted to the effects on income distribution. Government is an unambiguous winner with increased revenues of $P'P_TCD$. Consumers lose consumer surplus of P^*P_TCB, while producers lose surplus of $P'P^*BD$. The size of the income distribution effects relative to the effects on welfare helps explain why many policy changes may never be acceptable politically. The difficulties are particularly great if the loss in consumer surplus falls on lower income groups or if the tax is imposed on an industry with a powerful congressional lobby. In these situations, the tax would never be approved, regardless of whether it led to a welfare loss or gain.

QUESTIONS

1. Suppose in Figure 2.9 that instead of a tax, a subsidy of t per unit were introduced. Show the areas of changes in consumer, producer, and government surplus.

2. Suppose in Figure 2.9, the industry was monopolized. Solve for the welfare loss and the effects on income distribution.

3. Solve for the income distributional effects in Figure 2.8, showing that the welfare gain (BCG) consists of a loss in consumers' surplus ($-P_0P_1BC$), a loss in producers' surplus ($-P_0CEF$), a gain in government revenue (P_1BEF), and a gain in external effects ($BGCE$).

INCOME DISTRIBUTIONAL
ASPECTS OF WELFARE ANALYSIS

Policies that promote economic efficiency by increasing total welfare frequently alter the distribution of economic welfare between groups, leaving some groups worse off than before. For example, suppose that a given policy change leads to a large welfare gain but has the effect of significantly lowering the standard of living of poor people. Since many would be opposed to lowering the poor's standard of living, there is an apparent conflict between equity and efficiency.

To many, the choice might appear to be either equity or efficiency. The more socially concerned citizenry will opt for equity, rejecting any policy which disadvantages some particular group. The difficulty with this position is that society in the aggregate may pay a high price in terms of foregone welfare to assure that one particular group is not disadvantaged. Since everyone's conception of equity differs, rigorous adherence to such notions leads to a nihilistic attitude toward economic policies. It becomes a justification for the status quo.

At the opposite end of the spectrum is the proponent of economic efficiency, concerned only with maximizing aggregate economic welfare. The identities of the gainers and losers of a given policy change are irrelevant. The apparent disregard for equity considerations can stem either from the feeling that equity is a subjective criterion or from the belief that over the long run the positive and negative distributional effects on any one group average out.

While many economists are sympathetic to this latter view, in a democracy there is no tenure for policymakers. A congressman from Detroit would find it difficult to persuade his constituency that his vote to eliminate a tariff on imported cars can be justified by the long-run benefits of free trade. If economics is to play a prominent role in shaping policy, it must be aware of the conflict between equity and efficiency and be prepared to offer solutions to mitigate the conflict.

Our approach is to recognize that in many cases equity and efficiency considerations can be separated and, at the same time, dealt with simultaneously. By treating equity and efficiency as separable, separate policies can be designed to deal with each. In the first step, the policy needed to improve resource allocation is enacted. In the second step, policies designed to correct the income distribution effects of the efficiency-promoting policy are enacted. Such legislation can be considered simultaneously even though logically it constitutes two distinct steps. For example, if people with an income of $5000 per year or less were substantially impacted in a negative manner by an efficiency-promoting policy, the income tax rates for families in this category could be reduced so as to offset the effects of the efficiency-creating policy.

It is important that the policy to correct the income distribution consequences of the initial policy not lead to additional welfare losses. For example, suppose that the good in Figure 2.8 constitutes a large portion of the budgets of the poor. The pollution tax t raises the price from P_0 to P_1, thereby reducing the typical poor person's real standard of living by $50 per year. The appropriate income distribution policy would be to reduce their tax burden by $50, minus the money value to them of the reduced pollution they encounter. Too often policymakers choose an alternative policy of allowing the poor to continue paying the original price P_0. Such a policy reduces welfare because this encourages overconsumption by the poor. The poor family, facing a price of P_0, will consume up to the point where the marginal social benefit of the last unit of product is well below the marginal social cost of production. No one, rich or poor, is entitled to the special privilege of consuming at a rate where the social costs of production exceed the benefits.

QUESTIONS
1. Assume the social cost of a good is $5 per unit, yet a local politician claims society can only afford to pay $1 per unit. Does the imposition of a $1 price actually benefit society? Supposing the income elasticity of the good is unity for all income groups, are the poor relatively disadvantaged if the price is allowed to rise to $5?

2. Contrast the efficiency implications of the following two statements:
   a. Energy policy should promote aggregate economic welfare, and the Internal Revenue Service and welfare programs should correct for any large income distributional effects.
   b. Energy policies must be fair to all parties, allowing any benefits or sacrifices to be shared equally.

FROM A PARTIAL TO A GENERAL EQUILIBRIUM APPROACH

One objection to the type of welfare gain calculation outlined above is that it represents a partial equilibrium in that it focuses only on one market. It does not consider secondary welfare effects resulting in markets related to the one directly impacted by the policy change. The traditional wisdom has been to disregard these secondary welfare effects because it was felt that policies that lead to welfare gains in a partial equilibrium analysis will also lead to welfare gains in a general equilibrium setting. Beginning in the 1960s, this assumption has been challenged by the theory of "second best."[12]

The theory of second best argues that if there are certain preexisting market distortions that are not subject to change, the application of partial equilibrium criteria for efficient resource allocation in those areas where market failures are amenable to policy change may generate welfare losses rather than gains. Theoretically, it can be shown that programs promoting the "best" policy based on what is efficient in a partial equilibrium sense inflict more than offsetting welfare losses on the markets with preexisting distortions. Consequently, it may be optimal to devise policies of a second-best nature in terms of partial equilibrium analysis, which nevertheless turn out to offer a higher level of welfare in a general equilibrium framework.

To illustrate the possibility that second-best problems may arise, consider the market for fuel inputs into electricity generation. Suppose that the nuclear fuel market has a preexisting distortion not easily amenable to policy change. Due to limited liability for a nuclear accident, electricity generation plants do not pay the full social cost of nuclear power, leading to excessive use, beyond the level where marginal social benefits equal marginal social cost. Now suppose that congressional concern over air pollution leads to a tax on fossil fuels used to generate electricity. The tax would surely reduce fossil fuel consumption. Since the social costs of the fuel (including the air pollution damages) exceed the social benefits, a welfare gain in the fossil fuel market would result from the lower fuel consumption. On the other hand, lower fossil fuel consumption implies greater nuclear generation. By raising the price of fossil fuel relative to nuclear fuel, the demand for nuclear fuel shifts outward because nuclear and fossil fuels are substitutes. The increased consumption of nuclear fuel only exacerbates the situation, leading to an offsetting welfare loss, since for each additional unit of nuclear generation the social costs exceed the social benefits. Depending on how large the gap is between marginal social costs and marginal social benefits, the welfare loss in the nuclear fuel market might even exceed the welfare gain in the fossil fuel market!

Professor Harberger has provided a mechanism to include second-best phenomena in our conventional partial equilibrium framework.[13] Rather than measuring welfare losses and gains in only one market, we can calculate the secondary welfare effects in other markets as well.

Let us consider the case of an economy with three products. Market A is characterized by pure monopoly. Market B is perfectly competitive with no externalities. Market C is perfectly competitive but involves a production externality arising from water pollution. Let us assume that while the antitrust authorities have the power to correct the monopoly situation, the environmental protection agency is unable to prosecute producers of C, under existing laws and political realities. Thus market *C* is characterized by a distortion not amenable to policy change. Furthermore, assume goods *A* and *B* are substitutes and goods *A* and *C* are complements.

Figure 2.10 describes an initial equilibrium for three markets. To simplify the diagrams, each industry is assumed to exhibit constant costs, implying that the marginal social cost schedule for each industry is horizontal. Initially, the monopoly selected that output where marginal revenue equals marginal cost, leading to an output of A_0 and the price of P_0. In market *B*, the distortion-free market, output is B_0. In market *C*, which has the implacable production externality, producers supply output C_0, since at that output, price equals marginal private costs.

The effect of antitrust action in market *A* has three effects. First, in market *A*, competition leads to a lower price P_1 and greater output A_1. Second, if we assume good *B* is a substitute for good *A*, the lower price of good *A* causes the demand for good *B* to shift inward, leading to a smaller output B_1. The third effect occurs in market *C*. If good *C* is a complement to good *A*, the lower price of *A* will shift the demand schedule for *C* to the right, leading to increased consumption of C_1.

Let us now examine the welfare gains and losses in the respective markets. For good *A*, the increase in output from A_0 to A_1 leads to a welfare gain of triangle *FGH* since the change in social benefits is A_0FHA_1 and the change in social costs is only A_0GHA_1. The easier method of calculating the welfare effects in markets *B* and *C* is to think of the price of *A* being gradually reduced to the competitive level. As the price of *A* gradually falls, the demand for good *B* moves slightly to the left. For each unit of output reduction we see that there

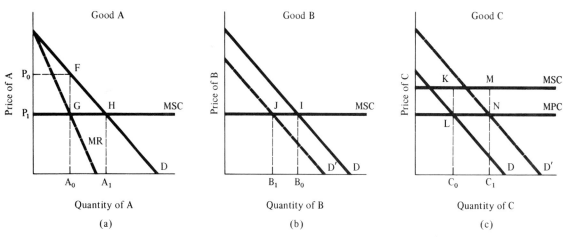

FIGURE 2.10 The introduction of general equilibrium phenomena. (a) Pure monopoly. (b) Competitive industry with no externalities. (c) Competitive industry with production externality.

is no *distortion*.[14] For each unit, the marginal social benefit just equals the marginal social cost. The reader should visualize shifting the demand curve for good B from D to D' by small increments. For each unit of production cut back, the marginal social benefit just equals the marginal social cost. Ultimately, output is reduced from B_0 to B_1. The important result is that since for each output level between B_0 and B_1 there are no distortions, the welfare effects must be zero. This is indeed a powerful result, because it means that even though many markets may be affected by a policy change, if they are relatively free of distortions, we need not worry about secondary welfare effects!

Market C is a different story. Since goods A and C are complements, as the price of A gradually fell, the demand schedule for C gradually shifted to the right. For each minor reduction in the price, we can calculate the distortions associated with that incremental output. For each additional unit of output the distortion is given by the line segment KL in Figure 2.10. After all, KL shows the difference between the marginal social costs of the additional output and its marginal social benefits. Since output increases from C_0 to C_1, the welfare loss is the rectangle KLMN.

By combining the welfare gain in market A (triangle FGH) with the welfare loss in market C (rectangle KLMN), we can determine if indeed it is socially optimal to eliminate the monopoly in market A. In this case, the answer would appear negative. In any event, Harberger has provided us with a methodology to measure such effects.

Is Harberger's solution practicable? After all, there are thousands of goods in the economy, not three. Must we analyze distortions in 999 secondary markets if we are only interested in one market? Does what appears simple for a three-good economy become a Pandora's box in practice?

We think the Harberger approach is simple and manageable. The secondary effects generally require analysis only in a few markets. First, one must separate those goods that are strong substitutes or complements to good A from those that are largely independent. It is only the former that we are concerned with, since it is only their demand schedules that will shift to the right or left, generating a possible welfare loss or gain. If good A is Swiss cheese and good C is tennis shoes, we would not expect the demand curve for tennis shoes to shift due to lower prices for Swiss cheese. Since the set of goods that are either strong substitutes or complements is small, the number of markets involving secondary welfare effects is small.

Next, one must distinguish between those complement and substitute goods with and without distortions. Those goods without appreciable distortions can be omitted since there are neither welfare losses nor gains resulting from shifts in their demand schedules, as shown by good B in our previous example. This leaves the complement and substitute goods that have distortions. Even among these, one should distinguish between those likely to be remedied by future policy changes and those implacable distortions, such as good C.

In sum, secondary welfare effects are important only when both *(a)* the good is a strong complement or substitute to the good subject to the policy change and *(b)* the market for the good contains an implacable distortion. In many situations, both conditions *(a)* and *(b)* are not met, thus allowing us to proceed with a partial equilibrium analysis of welfare. Nevertheless, as we shall see, there are situations where these conditions hold and it is important to incorporate these secondary welfare effects into the analysis.

QUESTIONS
1. Show that if all sectors of the economy were free of distortions, a policy applying partial equilibrium criteria to correct a single existing market failure would be unambiguously appropriate.
2. Suppose in Figure 2.10 that good C is independent of good A (i.e., neither substitute nor complement). Show that the welfare effects on good A are the only welfare effects.
3. Suppose in Figure 2.10 that good C is a strong substitute for good A. Show the welfare effects in all markets.

CONCLUSIONS

The previous discussions of static criteria for efficient resource allocation emphasize that the key to efficient resource allocation occurs in the way energy is priced. At any time, the price of the energy resource should reflect its marginal social costs. This implies that any divergence between social and private costs arising as a consequence of public goods or externalities should be corrected by internalizing such external costs. To assure the equivalence of price and marginal costs, a competitive market framework is required. Monopoly elements must be eliminated if prices are to equal marginal costs.

Applied welfare analysis allows the policy analyst to quantify the welfare loss associated with any given market failure. This enables policies to focus on the market distortions that, if remedied, have the largest payoff for increased efficiency. Policy changes to improve energy resource allocation will not be easily won. Even though a policy change leads to an aggregate welfare gain, certain groups may suffer deleterious income distribution effects. Our position is that efficiency and equity considerations are separable; however, they must be considered simultaneously using the income tax or welfare system to redress burdens imposed on the poor as a consequence of an efficiency-generating policy change.

1. For a detailed review, see Edwin Mansfield, *Microeconomics* (New
York: Norton, 1985), Chaps. 13 and 14.

2. In equation (2.2), MRT is a positive number obtained by affixing a
negative sign to the ratio $\Delta A/\Delta G$. The slope $\Delta A/\Delta G$ is negative,
since G must be given up to get additional A.

3. The negative sign is omitted since labor is being transferred between air conditioning and gasoline production; ΔL is positive in
one case and negative in the other.

4. For a review of monopoly, see Mansfield, op. cit., Chap. 10.

5. For a review of oligopoly models, see F. M. Scherer, *Industrial Market Structure and Economic Performance* (Chicago: Rand McNally,
1980).

6. See Mansfield, op. cit., p. 278.

7. See Mansfield, op. cit., pp. 94–98.

8. See Mansfield, op. cit., pp. 90–93.

9. The extent of the bias can be determined by the following formula
relating the price elasticities for the compensated (e_i) demand
schedule and the uncompensated (E_i) demand schedule. The difference between the compensated and uncompensated price elasticity
is equal to expenditure share (S_i) for the ith good (the expenditures
on good i divided by total expenditures on all goods) times the
income elasticity of demand (n_{iy}) for good i:

$$e_i - E_i = S_i n_{iy}$$

This equation is provided in J. M. Henderson and R. E. Quandt,
Microeconomic Theory (New York: McGraw Hill, 1971), pp. 31–37.
What do these three factors mean in terms of measuring social
benefits from energy consumption? The three factors work in different directions. The expenditure shares and income elasticities
for energy are generally relatively small. On the other hand, the
price elasticity indicates an inelastic demand schedule. To give the
reader some idea of the potential bias, let us assume the following
"ballpark" estimates. Assume the typical consumer spends 5 percent of his income on energy and the income elasticity of energy is
$+1$. Furthermore, assume the uncompensated price elasticity is
-0.5. In this case, the bias is determined by the equation [$e_i -
(-0.5) = 0.05(1)$]. Solving for e_i, we see the bias is -0.05, the true
elasticity is -0.45, and the percentage bias is about 11 percent.
Changes in social benefits calculated with the -0.5 elasticity
will indicate greater price responsiveness, implying that to entice
the consumer to consume one less unit requires a smaller increase
in price than would be needed with the price elasticity of -0.45.

For this example, the change in marginal social benefits of the last unit will be understated by using the uncompensated demand schedule. Just the opposite occurs in the case of an inferior good.

10. Based on assumptions of tax incidence, we might attempt to eliminate their effects. However, given the uncertainty surrounding the incidence question, no attempt is made to eliminate these taxes in most studies.

11. The literature of applied welfare analysis expresses a similar approach mathematically to the shortcut method but uses integral calculus. If we define the distortion $Z(Q)$ as the difference between social benefits and social costs, then the welfare gain is obtained by integrating the function $Z(Q)$ over the affected interval Q_1 to Q_0.

$$\text{Welfare gain} = \int_{Q_0}^{Q_1} Z(Q)\, dQ = -\int_{Q_1}^{Q_0} Z(Q)\, dQ$$

Since in this example Z is negative for each dQ, the negatives cancel out, leaving a welfare gain. It may be helpful to use actual equations to illustrate welfare changes. Let us assume the following:

Demand is given by $P_D = 2 - 0.001Q$
Market supply is given by $P_S = 0.0005Q + 0.5$
Social cost is given by $P_S{}^* = 0.0005Q + 1.0$

Thus the welfare gain is

$$\int_{Q_0}^{Q_1} (P_D - P_S{}^*)\, dQ \approx 83.50$$

since

$$Q_0 = 1000; \qquad\qquad Q_1 = 666.67$$
$$P_{D0} = P_{S0} = \$1; \qquad P_{S0}{}^* = \$1.50$$
$$P_{S1}{}^* = P_{D1} = \$1.33; \qquad P_{S1}{}^* = \$0.83$$

The Z function is useful in that it focuses only on the distortion corresponding to a specific output level. Note that at Q_0, the distortion is equal to the tax rate. At Q_{0-1}, the distortion is slightly less than the tax rate. Continuing to reduce output, we see that for the Q_1th unit, the distortion is exactly zero. Integrating equation (2.15) is equivalent to summing the welfare gains for each unit of output reduced between Q_0 and Q_1. For many applications this is the simplest way of calculating the welfare loss or gain, that is, by summing the distortions (the difference between social benefits and social costs) for each unit of output over the affected range Q_0 to Q_1. For additional readings, see Arnold Harberger, "Three Basic Postulates of Applied Welfare Analysis," *Journal of Economic Literature*, Vol. IX(3) September 1972, pp. 785–797.

For a comprehensive source, see Richard E. Just, Darrell L. Hueth, and Andrew Schmitz, *Applied Welfare Economics and Public Policy* (Englewood Cliffs, NJ: Prentice-Hall, 1982).

12. See R. G. Lipsey and K. Lancaster, "The General Theory of Second Best," *Review of Economic Studies*, 1956–1957, Vol. XXIV(1), pp. 11–32.

13. See Harberger, op. cit.

14. There is a tendency to use the new demand schedule D' as a measure of social benefits. This would be incorrect because the demand curve D' is derived from different indifference curves, implying consumer satisfaction is not held constant. For small shifts in the demand schedule, the marginal social benefits just equal the marginal social cost for the incremental unit.

CRITERIA FOR EFFICIENT DYNAMIC RESOURCE ALLOCATION

INTRODUCTION

The analysis in Chapter 2 is purely static; that is, production and consumption are assumed to occur in one particular time period. In many cases, there is no reason to introduce dynamic considerations except to recognize that policies which would generate welfare gains or losses during the current period would also generate welfare gains or losses in future periods, thus providing an even stronger rationale for or against the policy change. For example, static analysis is more than adequate to analyze the welfare effects of a tax on hot dog vendors. Each week the vendor purchases new supplies of mustard, hot dogs, and buns and rents his equipment. Moreover, the effects of one week's purchases on next week's prices are likely to be minimal. Thus each week can be viewed as a separate event, independent from past or future market periods.

In the case of nonrenewable natural resources, each period is not independent of the other. With a nonrenewable resource base, today's consumption reduces the resource base available for tomorrow. Consequently, both the firm and society must attempt to optimize production over many periods, recognizing that actions in one period affect opportunities in future periods. Since our dominant energy forms—oil, natural gas, coal, and uranium—fit into this category, we must be concerned that energy consumption is efficient not only in a static sense, but also over time, that is, in a dynamic sense.

Intertemporal Profit Maximization

The first and most fundamental assumption underlying the economics of nonrenewable resources is that firms attempt to maximize long-run profits over time, or intertemporally. The profit maximization motive that is so essential to static economic analysis is equally important in the dynamic case. In static analysis, the production decisions in one period do not affect profits in other periods, so that firms simply proceed to equate marginal cost with marginal revenue in each period, obtaining the maximum profit (Π_i) for any period i. The result is a production plan resulting in an optimal stream of profits (Π_i) over time (Π_0, Π_1, Π_2, . . ., Π_n), which maximizes the firms' long-run profits over time.

However, with production using nonrenewable resources, the decision to produce and earn profits of Π_0 today necessarily precludes the ability to produce and earn profits in future time periods. How then can the firm select the optimal tradeoff between current and future profits? Basically, the firm must apply a discount rate to future profits, since a dollar today is worth more than a dollar in the future. Normally, the firm's discount rate will closely approximate the market rate of interest, differing only by an adjustment for risk. Thus, the rate of interest provides the firm with guidance as to the value of one dollar's profit today in comparison, for example, with a profit of $1.50 in 5 years. In effect, if the market rate of interest is 10 percent per year ($r = 0.1$), then a profit of $1.10 next year has a present value of $1.00. In fact, it is possible to calculate the present value of the profit stream (Π_i) beginning in the current period 0 and terminating at some distant period n in the future:

$$(3.1) \qquad \text{Present value} = \Pi_0 + \frac{\Pi_1}{1 + r} + \frac{\Pi_2}{(1 + r)^2} + \frac{\Pi_3}{(1 + r)^3} + \cdots + \frac{\Pi_n}{(1 + r)^n}$$

Equation (3.1) provides the firm with guidance as to what is meant by long-run profit maximization. By choosing a profile of profits (Π_0, Π_1, Π_2, . . ., Π_n), the present value of future profits can be maximized. By maximizing the present value of future profits, one maximizes the value of the firm, since stockholders' perception of the value of existing shares is based on the anticipated stream of profits over the future n periods plus the salvage value of the firm in the last period.[1] Any other alternative stream of profits (Π_0^a, Π_1^a, Π_2^a, . . ., Π_n^a) will lead to a lower present value.

What forces are at work to compel the firm to maximize the present value of future profits? The answer is market forces. If the firm finds itself in a competitive market, its very corporate survival depends on its ability to maximize profits. Even in markets insulated from competitive forces, factors are at work promoting profit maximization. Normally, managers will seek to maximize the value of the firm's shares since they typically receive stock options and/or profit-related bonuses. If the firm does not select the optimal stream of profits (Π_0, Π_1, Π_2, . . ., Π_n), it becomes a candidate for corporate takeover. The existence of suboptimal profits provides an incentive for an acquiring firm to rectify the profit performance. By restoring the firm to a production time path that maximizes long-run profits, the value of the firm's shares can be raised, providing an above normal return to the acquiring firm.

QUESTIONS 1. Suppose you own a shut-in gas well with reserves of 1 billion cubic feet. You know with certainty that natural gas will be much more valuable in 10 years and will sell for $10 per thousand cubic feet. Assuming the market rate of interest is 10 percent, what price would you sell the gas reserves for today? (Hint: $3.85 million.)

2. Suppose in question 1 that you do not know future gas prices with certainty. To compensate for the risk attached to natural gas as an asset, you adopt a discount rate of 12 percent. In effect, if the risk-free return on treasury bonds is 10 percent, you add a 2 percent risk premium. Now what is the present value of the gas well, applying a 12 percent discount rate? (Hint: $3.22 million.)

USER COSTS

While equation (3.1) correctly describes the present value calculation, it lacks the economic insight provided by static analysis. For example, in static analysis, profit maximization automatically implies selecting the production level where marginal cost equals marginal revenue. In the nonrenewable resource case, can the firm arrive at Π_0, Π_1, Π_2, . . ., Π_n in equation (3.1) by simply setting marginal cost equal to marginal revenue in each period? If so, we arrive at a surprising result. Knowing that price equals marginal cost in a competitive market, one might be tempted to reason that the competitive world price of oil should be about $.25 per barrel since the marginal cost of producing oil is approximately $.25 per barrel in most Persian Gulf countries. This fallacy arises from an inadequate understanding of marginal costs. In the static case of a firm using renewable resource inputs, the decision to produce today in no way affects the costs of producing in the future. Thus marginal cost (MC) consists entirely of the marginal production cost (MC^p), that is, the capital, labor, and material costs of producing the last unit of output. In cases involving the use of nonrenewable products, the decision to produce a barrel of oil today precludes the possibility of producing it at some time in the future. The resource owner must trade off the opportunity value of selling the resource today versus the opportunity value of selling it at some future time. This is precisely the notion captured by the user value, or as it is most commonly called, the user cost. The user cost in period i reflects the opportunity value of producing a unit of output in that period. While there is no tax collector present to collect these user costs, the firm clearly foregoes the current opportunity value of the resource when it chooses to leave it for later production. Thus, in the nonrenewable case, marginal cost (MC) in period i is modified to include both the conventional marginal production cost (MC_i^P) and the user cost (U_i):

(3.2) $$MC_i = MC_i^P + U_i$$

The method of calculating the user cost is predicated on long-run profit maximization (i.e., setting marginal revenue, MR_i, equal to marginal cost, MC_i). The user cost, which shows the opportunity value of producing a marginal unit today, is calculated by simply subtracting marginal production costs (MC_i^P) from marginal revenue (MR_i):

(3.3) $$U_i = MR_i - MC_i^P$$

Combining equations (3.2) and (3.3) we reaffirm the standard price theory result that marginal costs (including user costs) equal marginal revenue even for nonrenewable resources.

Since U_i represents the opportunity value of selling a barrel in period i, the producer may elect to switch part of his production in period i to some other period i' where user costs are higher. In fact, if the producer is to maximize his long run profit, he should be indifferent between producing the last barrel in any given time period. That is, user costs should be equated across all production periods, so that:

(3.4) $$U_0 = U_1 = U_2 = U_3 = \cdots = U_n$$

But equation (3.4) overlooks the fact that a dollar received today is worth far more today than is a dollar received ten years from now. Thus, wealth-maximizing producing agents must in reality discount future user costs at the market rate of interest (r), implying that *discounted* user costs must be equated over time:

(3.5) $$U_0 = \frac{U_1}{1 + r} = \frac{U_2}{(1 + r)^2} = \frac{U_3}{(1 + r)^3} = \cdots = \frac{U_n}{(1 + r)^n}$$

This means that the user costs must rise at the rate of interest if the net present value of the resource is to be maximized, that is:

(3.5a)
$$U_1 = U_0 (1 + r)$$
$$U_2 = U_1 (1 + r)$$
$$U_n = U_{n-1} (1 + r)$$

As an example, if the interest rate is 10 percent ($r = .10$) and $U_0 = \$1$, the user cost (U_i) must be \$1.10 in period 1, \$1.21 in period 2, \$1.33 in period 3 and so forth, in order for the discounted user costs to be equal over time. If, for example, $U_3 = \$2$, the producer has not chosen an optimal production strategy since the discounted value of oil produced in period 3 would be $1.50 ($U_3/(1.1)^3$) and yet the discounted value for all other periods is $1. The producer can increase the present value of its reserves by allocating more production to period 3 and reducing production in the other periods. Thus, the problem facing the wealth-maximizing producer is to schedule production over time such that equation (3.5) holds for the last barrel produced in any period.

A more formal proof of the result that equality of discounted user costs (equation (3.5)) follows from maximization of the present value of the resource (equation (3.1)) can be shown as follows. For simplicity, consider a model with two periods rather than n periods. According to equation (3.1),

$$
(3.6) \qquad PV = \Pi_0 + \frac{1}{1+r} \Pi_1
$$

Now consider the effect of moving one unit of production from period 0 to 1 (i.e., $-\Delta Q_0 = \Delta Q_1$):

$$
(3.7) \qquad \Delta PV = \Delta\Pi_0(\Delta Q_0) + \frac{1}{1+r} \Delta\Pi_1(\Delta Q_1)
$$

But the change in profit ($\Delta\Pi_0$) resulting from rescheduling production of the last barrel is simply the difference between marginal revenue and marginal production cost ($MR_0 - MC_0^P$). Thus equation (3.7) can be written equivalently as:

$$
(3.8) \quad \Delta PV = (MR_0 - MC_0^P)(\Delta Q_0) + \frac{1}{1+r}(MR_1 - MC_1^P)(\Delta Q_1)
$$

By definition [see equation (3.2)], we can replace the difference between marginal revenue and marginal production cost with the appropriate user cost:

$$
(3.9) \qquad \Delta PV = U_0(\Delta Q_0) + \frac{1}{1+r} U_1(\Delta Q_1)
$$

But if PV is truly at a maximum, a small change of ΔQ_0 will not affect PV. Setting $\Delta PV = 0$ in equation (3.9) and utilizing the fact that the production increase in one period equals the decrease in the other period ($-\Delta Q_0 = \Delta Q_1$), we obtain the familiar result.

$$
(3.10) \qquad U_0 = \frac{U_1}{1+r}
$$

Thus, equating the present value of user costs necessarily implies that the firm has selected a production strategy that maximizes the present value of the resource.[2]

QUESTIONS

1. Can you explain why you cannot use equation (3.2) to compute the user cost? You must first compute user cost from equation (3.3) and then, knowing the user cost, it is possible to compute marginal cost in equation (3.2).
2. Explain why a profit-maximizing producer must reorder production until the present values of the user costs are equated over time. If $U_1/(1 + r) > U_0$, what must happen to production in Q_0 and Q_1?
3. Suppose you have 3 grades of coal, with respective user costs per ton of $-\$5$, $\$1$, and $\$10$. Will coal grade 1 be mined? How about grades 2 and 3? Explain why the low-cost mines will be exploited first.

USER COSTS AND EXPECTATIONS ABOUT THE FUTURE

The notion of user costs is extremely complex because they are not easily identified and calculated as marginal production cost might be. But it is precisely their complexity that makes user costs so fascinating. In understanding user costs, there are a few key points to keep in mind. First, a set of user costs $(U_0, U_1, U_2, \ldots, U_n)$ is conditional on a given set of expectations about the future. As long as the "old expectations" (that set of expectations under which the profit-maximizing production schedule was originally made) are fulfilled, the user costs will rise at rate r over time as seen in equation (3.5a). For example, in Figure 3.1, over the time period 0 to t_0 user costs rise along a given path at rate r. Suddenly, at time period t_0, producers revise their original expectations, probably due to new information about the future, and form "new expectations." User costs shift upward, rising along a new path, as producers judge that the opportunity value of the reserves has become much greater. Second, these expectations depend on demand as well as supply conditions, and future as well as present conditions. Remember from equation (3.8) that it is necessary to form expectations about future marginal revenues and thus future demand conditions as well as production costs. These expectations are no doubt further influenced by the expected size of the resource base. Large additions to resource supplies will drive down both current and expected future market prices and marginal revenues. Curiously, even when present demand conditions develop exactly as expected, if pro-

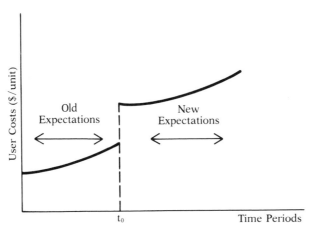

FIGURE 3.1 User costs and producer expectations.

ducers become convinced that future demand will be much greater than previously expected, user costs will be revised upward as in Figure 3.1, switching user costs onto a new path. The mechanism is simple—at time period t_0 producers revised upward their expectation of user costs in some future period. Thus based on the old production plan, the discounted future user cost now exceeds the user cost of today's production, leading to a reduction in current production and a planned increase in future production. As current production is reduced, user costs rise to the new user cost path.

Implications for the Pricing of Nonrenewable Resources

The previous section establishes the key result that the user cost will tend to rise with the rate of interest *for a given set of expectations*. But our concern is more with the implications for the pricing of nonrenewable energy sources than with the change in user costs. As we shall see in the subsequent section, the linkage between user costs and prices can differ widely, depending on the set of assumptions made.

HOTELLING'S *r* PERCENT PRICE PATH

According to Harold Hotelling, the linkage between user costs and prices is direct. Prices, like user costs, would also tend to rise at the rate of interest. In his famous 1931 article in the *Journal of Political Economy*, Hotelling set forth this provocative idea.[3] In view of the trivial marginal production cost of most Persian Gulf oil, it is remarkable that Hotelling chose to simplify his analysis to a case where marginal production costs are zero ($MC^p = 0$), even though these reserves were at that time undiscovered. Together with the assumption of perfect competition (i.e., the firm's marginal revenue equals the market price), one can substitute prices (P_i) for user costs (U_i) in equation (3.5) as follows:

$$(3.11) \qquad P_0 = \frac{P_1}{1 + r} = \frac{P_2}{(1 + r)^2} = \cdots = \frac{P_n}{(1 + r)^n}$$

Equivalently, prices will rise at the rate of interest:

$$P_1 = P_0(1 + r)$$
$$P_2 = P_1(1 + r)$$

(3.11a)
$$\cdot$$
$$\cdot$$
$$\cdot$$

$$P_n = P_{n-1}(1 + r)$$

Hotelling's result is captivating because of both its simplicity and its underlying economic sophistication. By making just three key assumptions—(1) long-run profit maximization, (2) zero marginal production costs, and (3) perfect competition—we arrive at the result that prices will tend to rise in a smooth predictable manner with the rate of interest. Hotelling's r percent rule seems sensible because deposits of oil, coal, or natural gas are irreplaceable assets of value, and in order to entice producers to hold oil for future periods, they must receive a return of exactly r percent per year. Prices cannot systematically rise faster than r percent per year, since current production would cease in anticipation of a return greater than r percent, driving up current prices, which would induce shifting of production toward the current period and restore the rule. Conversely, systematic price increases of less than r percent per year would lead producers to raise current production, thereby lowering the present price, which would induce shifting of production to future periods, again restoring the equilibrium implied by the rule.

While prices must rise at r percent per year to establish a market equilibrium, there are an infinite number of price paths that will rise at r percent per year. For example, at $r = .10$, oil prices could move along a path of 1.00, 1.10, 1.21, 1.33 . . . or another path of $30.00, $33.00, $36.30, $39.93 and so forth. How can we establish the market-clearing price path? Or, put another way, what is the optimal initial price?

Mathematically, the solution can become quite complicated with n time periods. But if we restrict the number of time periods to two (the present and the future), a graphical solution is possible. Let us consider the case in which 60 barrels of oil are to be consumed between the current period 0 and the future period 1. Assume for illustrative purposes that the expected demand curves in the two periods are $P_0 = 50 - .5Q_0$ in period 0 and $P_1 = 50 - .33Q_1$ in period 1. Furthermore, the rate of interest is taken to be $r = .10$. To preserve the zero marginal production cost assumption, we assume that the oil is being stored in the backyard swimming pools of our competitive oil producers.

Figure 3.2 provides a graphical description of how the optimal price path is determined. Beginning on the left-hand vertical axis, we measure price in the current period; the price is $50 per barrel when current output is zero. We draw the demand curve, D_0, emanating from $P_0 = \$50$ and sloping downward to the right with a slope of $-.5$.

Similarly, the demand schedule for the future period emanates from $P_1 = \$50$ on the right-hand vertical axis and slopes downward to the left with a slope of $-.33$. The prices of oil in the two periods can be determined by inspection of the two demand curves for any particular output division between the two periods. For example, if $Q_0 = 40$ and $Q_1 = 20$, the two demand curves imply prices of $P_0 = \$30$ and $P_1 = \$43.34$.

The next step is to determine the user cost schedules U_0 and U_1 for the two periods. Recall from equation (3.11) that the user cost is identical to price in Hotelling's case. Thus for the current period, U_0 is identical to the demand schedule. Similarly, for the future period, $U_1 = P_1$; thus the user cost and demand schedule are identical. But since U_0 is equated with the discounted future period's user cost, we

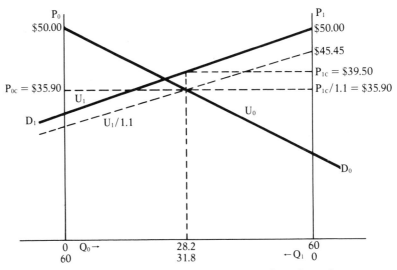

FIGURE 3.2 Solution of the Hotelling price path and production rates.

must consider the dashed line, labelled $U_1/1.1$. The discounted user cost schedule is obtained by discounting the intercept of $50 to give a $45.45 intercept. Likewise the slope is discounted by 1.1, giving a slope of $-.3$. As a consequence, $U_1/1.1$ shows, for any output level, the original market price in period 1 divided by 1.1, the discount factor.

According to equation (3.5), the intersection of U_0 and $U_1/1.1$ shows the optimal output allocation between the two periods which equates the discounted user costs. Furthermore, by reference to the demand schedules for these output levels, we obtain the solution for the prices in the two periods. According to Figure 3.2, 28.2 barrels will be produced in the first period and 31.8 barrels will be produced in the future. Corresponding to 28.2 barrels in the current period is a market price of $35.90. Corresponding to the 31.8 barrels produced in the future period is a market price of $39.50 per barrel—a price exactly 10 percent higher than the $35.90 price in the current period.[4]

It is easy to see that no other output combination and price path will bring about a long-run profit maximizing equilibrium. Consider an output level of less than 28.2 barrels in the current period. At that output combination, U_0 exceeds $U_1/1.1$, which will encourage producers to increase current production and reduce future consumption. But the increase in current production only lowers U_0 and raises $U_1/1.1$. Nevertheless, producers will find it profitable to expand current production until $U_0 = U_1/1.1$. Similarly, one can show that if current production were greater than 28.2 barrels, market forces would drive current production down to the optimal level.

The graphical analysis in Figure 3.2 serves to emphasize the numerous determinants of the user costs and price path. As noted earlier, both future and current demand expectations are important. Marginal production costs are also potentially important. Also, if oil reserves had been 100 instead of 60, the user costs would have been much smaller, and the price path would have started from a lower initial price.

QUESTIONS

1. What three assumptions give rise to equation (3.11a)? Explain the role of each.

2. Would you think that Hotelling's rule would apply to coal mining? Why or why not?

3. Suppose in Figure 3.2 that expectations about future demand implied a $10 higher price at every output level. Show graphically how you would solve for the new optimal output levels and price path.

4. Using Figure 3.2, and assuming instead that reserves were 100 barrels, how would you solve for the new optimal output levels and the price path?

5. Assuming a constant demand schedule over time, what would the output price path look like, that corresponds to the rising price path? Draw the output path.

THE PREDICTIVE POWER OF HOTELLING'S MODEL

Critics of Hotelling's model are quick to point out that observed oil prices do not move along a smooth price path, rising with the rate of interest. Table 1.4 and Figure 4.1 show that the path of oil prices bears little resemblance to Hotelling's predictions.

Before discarding Hotelling's simple model, let us first recall the three critical assumptions: (1) long-run profit maximization, (2) zero marginal production cost, and (3) perfect competition. Finally, there is the hidden caveat that any one price path is conditional upon a unique set of expectations about future and present supply and demand conditions. This last caveat alone might explain why prices failed to move along a smooth path. For example, if producers were continually revising their expectations, one might observe frequent jumping from one price path to another. Still other explanations will result from relaxing the assumptions of zero production costs or perfect competition. Let us proceed to extend Hotelling's simple model by considering the effects on the observed oil price path of: (1) a monopolistic market, (2) the size of the resource base, (3) the presence of a backstop fuel, (4) the rate of discount, (5) the magnitude of the long-run price elasticity of oil demand, (6) the rate of world economic growth, and (7) increasing marginal production costs.

A Monopolistic Market Structure

For the monopolist facing zero production costs, user costs will be identical to marginal revenue, which then must rise with the rate of interest:

$$(3.12) \quad MR_0 = \frac{MR_1}{1 + r} = \frac{MR_2}{(1 + r)^2} = \frac{MR_3}{(1 + r)^3} = \cdots = \frac{MR_n}{(1 + r)^n}$$

This result follows directly from equation (3.3) when $MC^p = 0$. Obviously, with marginal revenues rising, prices will also rise, but the rate of increase depends on the nature of the demand curve. In the usual textbook case of a linear demand curve, the initial price will be higher under monopoly and will rise at a slower rate relative to perfect competition. The reason why the price of the monopolist lies above that of the competitive market, and grows more slowly, may not be apparent. Remember that with zero extraction costs under monopoly, user costs equal marginal revenue, not price, and thus marginal revenues must grow at rate r as in equation (3.12). With a linear demand schedule, an r percent increase in marginal revenue yields a less than r percent increase in price. Thus if prices are to increase at a slower rate than under competition, they must be initially higher. Figure 3.3 contrasts the competitive price path with the monopolist's price path when facing a linear demand schedule. Thus, the monopolist's higher initial price will promote more conservation in earlier periods, allowing for relatively greater production and lower prices in the later periods, extending the economic life of the resource. This example supports the claim, "the monopolist is the conservationist's best friend." While this may be true, we simply note that the monopolist exacts a huge fee for performing this rationing function and that the monopolist's price path distorts the optimal intertemporal resource allocation of perfect competition. From society's perspective, the present value of lower prices over period 0 to t_0 in Figure 3.3 far outweighs the present value of the monopolist's lower prices after time t_0. But of course this explains precisely why the monopolist chose an initially higher but more slowly increasing price path.

Still another intriguing aspect of Hotelling's 1931 paper was that he explicitly considered the case of the monopolist facing a demand curve that had a constant price elasticity at every price. Hotelling demonstrated that under such conditions, the monopolist's price path will be identical to that of the competitive market! Some scholars have accepted Hotelling's result as if it were a prophecy. To them, the question of whether OPEC is a cartel is moot—the price of oil would be the same under either regime!

To reach this conclusion based on Hotelling's simplistic model would be to commit an egregious error, for two reasons. The demand for oil is not a static function with a constant price elasticity. As dis-

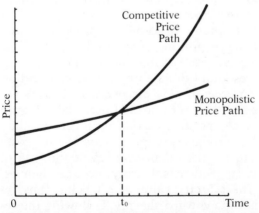

FIGURE 3.3 Possible monopolistic versus competitive price paths.

cussed in Chapter 7, the long-run demand schedule is much more price elastic than its short-run counterpart. Since it may take twenty years to achieve the full long-run price adjustment, a monopolist can exploit the short-run inelasticity of oil demand by initially charging a higher price. Thereafter, prices may even decline for a substantial period as consumers react to the price jump. Thus, the nature of the demand for oil suggests that the monopolist's price path is likely to be more like Figure 3.3, with a higher price initially and a slower rate of price increase thereafter than would occur under competition.[5]

Notwithstanding these objections, some may argue that even if the two price paths are not identical, the period of time t_0 in Figure 3.3 during which the monopolist's price exceeds the competitive level is relatively short and the period thereafter of lower prices under monopoly is relatively long. Applying this logic to today's situation, one might argue that OPEC's prices may exceed that of a competitive market, but within ten years we will reach a time when the price of oil will be actually lower, thanks to OPEC. Obviously, it matters greatly whether t_0 is 10 years or 50 years. Unfortunately, our ability to pinpoint t_0 is poor. Furthermore, it matters greatly whether some "backstop" fuel will be present to place a ceiling on future price increases. (A backstop fuel is a fuel available in effectively unlimited quantities at a constant extraction cost per unit.) If a backstop fuel exists, the high future prices that would occur under competition would not materialize. We will explore in more detail later the price implications of a backstop fuel.

The Size of the Resource Base

Irrespective of whether one posits monopoly or competition, user costs play an influential role in oil price determination. Since user costs are based on expectations of present and future supply and demand conditions, it is instructive to look in greater detail at factors that influence producers' perceptions of user costs.

In order to attribute a scarcity premium to oil, oil producers must first form expectations about the magnitude of the underlying oil reserve base. The size of existing oil reserves may be a poor indicator, since these are only the reserves found to date and future exploration will surely result in new discoveries. If new discoveries occur as expected, producers need not revise their estimates of user costs. Figure 3.4 illustrates a Hotelling-type competitive market with zero production costs. Over the period that producers' expectations of user costs remain unchanged (period 0 to t_0), the oil price rises at the rate of interest. Suppose that at time t_0, geologists sharply increase their estimate of the reserve base. The scarcity value of oil being thus reduced, user costs will be revised downward sharply. Following the revision, as long as expectations are unchanged (period t_0 to t_1), prices

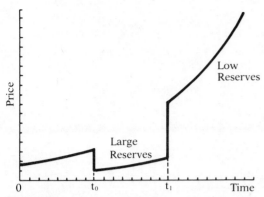

FIGURE 3.4 Price paths under alternative resource base assumptions.

again rise at the rate of interest. Now assume that in period t_1, oil producers become convinced that the ultimate resource base is much smaller than they had ever thought. Prices will immediately shoot upward and thereafter rise with the rate of interest until expectations are revised again. Figure 3.4 illustrates the interesting point that prices need not follow a smooth price path since changing expectations will cause switching to alternate price paths. Thus Hotelling's model may be correct, but have only limited predictive power because prices are continually jumping from one price path to another due to changing expectations.

The Presence of a Backstop Fuel

In view of the vast potential supplies of unconventional crude oil from tar sands, oil shales, and coal, economists have been prompted to consider the impact their development will have on the price of petroleum. For simplicity, let us assume that the reserves of these oil substitutes become infinitely elastic at some price P^*. Obviously, these resources are also nonrenewable, but the reserve base may be so large that their user costs are effectively zero. Alternatively, the backstop fuel may be a renewable energy source such as solar energy. In either case, at price P^*, virtually unlimited supplies will be available. As Figure 3.5 indicates, the time path of oil price is substantially altered. No longer does the price continue to rise indefinitely at the rate of interest. The solid line price path depicts a world of perfect foresight. The price increases at rate r until it reaches P^*, at which time the backstop fuel would enter the market to meet all demand at the price P^*. Presumably, backstop fuel producers watch the price rise and correctly anticipate that the backstop fuel plants should be ready in year t_0 with sufficient capacity to meet expected demand. Also, according to this view, oil producers would want to dispose of all of their oil before t_0,

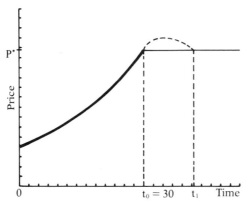

FIGURE 3.5 Oil prices with a backstop fuel.

since after t_0 the user cost would become constant. In reality, conventional oil production will continue past t_0 because oil fields cannot be exhausted instantaneously. Also, it seems plausible to conjecture that oil prices might even overshoot the price of the backstop fuel, P^*, if at t_0 the introduction of the backstop fuel is initially insufficient to meet market demand. The dotted line occurring after t_0 shows how prices might temporarily overshoot while the backstop fuel industry is adjusting to meet demand (period t_0 to t_1). After t_1, oil prices would be constrained to P^*.

What implications do backstop fuels have for the pricing of oil today? Assume for argument's sake that shale oil and coal liquefaction exist as backstop fuels for crude oil at a constant cost of $70 per barrel (i.e., suppose $P^* = \$70$). Let us further assume that existing crude oil reserves are sufficient for 30 years ($t_0 = 30$). What is the appropriate price of oil today? Applying Hotelling's model with $P_{30} = \$70$, we arrive at a current price in period 0 in Figure 3.5 of $4.01 for a 10 percent discount rate.

$$(3.13) \qquad P_0 = \cdots = \frac{P_{30}}{(1.1)^{30}}$$

$$P_0 = \frac{\$70}{17.45} = \$4.01$$

For a discount rate of 5 percent, the current price would be $16.20. Calculations such as these are obviously highly subjective and inexact, but even with highly conservative assumptions about the backstop fuel price and years of available oil reserves, world oil prices appear to be well above the levels implied by a competitive market.

To Hotelling, the choice of the appropriate discount rate was obvious—use the market rate of interest. Since inflation was not a problem in 1931, Hotelling was content to state his results in nominal terms, not adjusted for inflation. Today, future inflation rates are perhaps more uncertain than oil prices, causing practitioners to favor oil price forecasts expressed in dollars of constant purchasing power. Thus, the preference is to forecast the real price of oil, that is, the future price of oil deflated by the future general price index. The real rate of interest (r^*) is simply the nominal rate of interest (r) less the expected inflation rate (i), as shown below:

$$(3.14) \qquad\qquad\qquad r^* = r - i$$

Hotelling's framework, nevertheless, remains valid. We simply substitute the real rate of interest for the nominal rate of interest and interpret oil prices in dollars of constant purchasing power.

Having resolved the inflation confusion, one must ask whether the real rate of interest, usually estimated at 2 to 3 percent per annum, is the appropriate real discount rate. If oil reserves were a riskless asset, private investors would utilize the real rate of interest since it reflects the real, long-run return on a risk-free asset. Oil producers usually argue that geological and political risks of oil exploitation require using a much higher real discount rate to reflect the elements of uncertainty and guarantee a normal real return on the average. Professor Adelman points out that the political risks are so large in the Middle East that a real discount rate of 9 percent may be conservative.[6]

To illustrate the effects of changes in the real discount rate, Figure 3.6 depicts price paths under three alternative discount rates. From

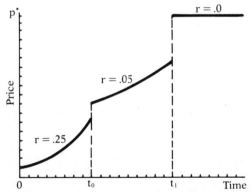

FIGURE 3.6 Price paths under alternative discount rates.

period 0 to t_0, producers employ a very high real discount rate of 25 percent in anticipation of nationalization. Now suppose the risk of nationalization abates and the real discount rate is reduced to 5 percent. Finally, in period t_1 the state obtains control of production and adopts a zero real discount rate. With a zero real discount rate, the user costs are constant over time. If a backstop fuel were available at P^*, the competitive price would jump to P^* and remain forever at that real price level. After all, a zero discount rate implies indifference between a dollar today and a dollar in 30 years, when the backstop fuel would be available.

The Magnitude of the Long-Run Price Elasticity of Oil Demand

Since demand conditions affect marginal revenues and thereby the user costs, the price path even in a competitive market depends on the price elasticity of demand. In the short run, the price elasticity for crude oil is generally known to be quite inelastic. The magnitude of the long-run elasticity is known with much less certainty. The problem is exacerbated by the fact that a substantial adjustment period is required to alter the energy efficiency of the existing capital stock. Long lags, combined with unprecedentedly high price levels, make for a great deal of uncertainty regarding the value of the long-run price elasticity. Figure 3.7 contrasts two price paths, one under high elasticity expectations and one under low price elasticity expectations. With expectations of a low price elasticity, the price path begins at price P_0 and rises thereafter at the discount rate as usual. Suppose that in period t_0 producers come to believe that long-run demand is much more price elastic than previously believed. Clearly, at the prices projected

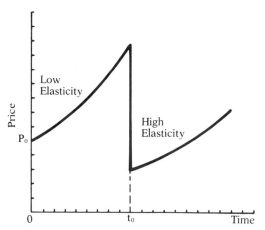

FIGURE 3.7 The importance of the price elasticity of demand.

for the future, consumers will not demand the previously projected production. This revision in expectations about future price elasticities of demand forces an abrupt downward adjustment in the user cost. Even though the price rises at the discount rate after t_0, the base from which it rises is much lower and the price path lies below the original price path.

The Rate of World Economic Growth

Still another factor influencing the calculation of user costs is the growth in oil demand resulting from world economic growth. Besides price, the major determinant of oil consumption is the level of economic activity. As discussed in Chapter 7, there is a strong positive correlation between the standard of living and energy consumption. The point is that if producers expect rapid long-run growth rates, ceteris paribus, user costs will be higher. Although Figure 3.7 illustrated the case of low and high price elasticity expectations, it could have just as easily represented the effects of different expectations about economic growth rates. The period from 0 to t_0 would be representative of expectations assuming high economic growth rates, while the period from t_0 into the future would signal a period in which economic growth projections had been scaled downward.

Increasing Marginal Production Costs

Even though Hotelling's assumption of zero marginal production cost seems quite applicable to oil produced in the Persian Gulf, a close look at oil production elsewhere reveals that marginal production costs increase over a broad output range. In a given oil province, the lower cost deposits are exploited first, leaving additional reserves to be found at higher prices. As the production from stripper wells across Illinois and Kansas proves, at higher prices it is always possible to wring additional oil from the earth's coffers.

A confusing aspect of existing oil reserve estimates is that they are classified as "known" reserves capable of being extracted at present prices and technology. They provide no estimate of the reserve base available from additional exploration at existing prices and technology, nor any measure of the size of uneconomic reserves that may become economic with higher prices or improved technology.

Suppose we assume that additional reserves and production will be forthcoming at higher prices. What effect will this have on the price path? Figure 3.8a assumes for pedagogical purposes that reserves are of three types. Type 1 reserves are limited to quantity Q_1^*, and, like Persian Gulf reserves, are available at a negligible extraction cost. Type 2 reserves are available in quantity $Q_2^* - Q_1^*$ at a marginal extraction cost of C_2^* per unit. Finally, we assume a renewable re-

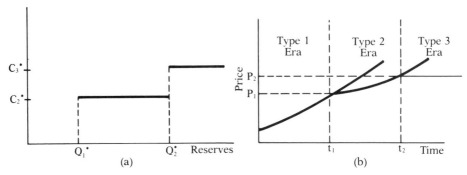

FIGURE 3.8 Effects of a heterogeneous resource base. (a) Reserves available at various extraction costs. (b) Price path with rising extraction costs.

source (type 3 reserves) that offers a backstop fuel available at cost C_3^* per unit.

As in Figure 3.5, will the price path rise at r percent until it hits the backstop? No. As shown in Figure 3.8b, prices rise at a relatively much faster rate during the period from 0 to t_1 (when the lowest cost reserves are depleted). Over this period extraction costs are zero, user costs are equivalent to price, and therefore price will rise relatively quickly. The new price path beginning at t_1 and ending at t_2 rises at a much slower rate than the price path over the period 0 to t_0. The backstop fuel price is reached in period t_2 just as type 2 reserves are ultimately depleted, and backstop fuel production commences. Prices escalate at a slower rate in each subsequent era because extraction costs become a bigger part of marginal costs. For the period from t_1 to t_2, user costs are only a portion of total marginal costs, and prices rise only to reflect the increase in user costs. Even though the user cost for type 2 reserves will escalate at r percent per year, prices will rise only at a fraction of that rate because extraction costs, which are constant at C_2^*, make up such a big fraction of overall marginal costs and hence, price in a competitive market. Of course, after t_2 the backstop is reached and user cost for reserve type 3 is zero. Thus without any user costs, prices will be constant over time at $P_2 = C_3^*$.

How can we generalize the results of Figure 3.8b? Suppose that instead of three types of reserves, there were numerous reserve types. Prices would be expected to rise at a rate well below the rate of interest as, over time, extraction costs make up increasing fractions of the price. Furthermore, if technological change reduces the marginal production costs over time, it is even possible that the reduction in MC_i^p could exceed the rise in U_i so that total marginal costs and price might actually decline. Thus user costs may not be a large portion of overall marginal costs and thereby not greatly affect resource price patterns. Many energy economists feel that it was this zero extraction cost assumption that led Hotelling so far astray.[7]

1. Why will prices jump to the backstop fuel cost if $r = .0$?

2. Explain why $P_0 = \$16.20$ if $r = .05$ in equation (3.13). If production was sufficient for 30 years along the price path beginning at $4.01 per barrel, why will it take longer to reach the backstop moving along a higher price path? Supposing that at a 5 percent discount rate it takes 40 years, show that $P_0 = \$9.94$.

3. Using Figure 3.8b, explain why the lowest cost reserves will always be exploited first. Also explain why no one owning type 1 reserves would choose to hold them past period t_1.

MARKET FAILURES IN A DYNAMIC CONTEXT

The previous discussion sets forth the criteria for efficient resource allocation over time, regardless of whether this goal is to be achieved by market forces or by central planning. Given the primary reliance on market forces in Western countries, it is appropriate to outline the conditions under which intertemporal market failures could occur, opening the door for possible inefficient or nonoptimal intertemporal resource allocation. Once having isolated these conditions, policymakers have a basis from which to argue for public intervention to correct any such failures.

The standard types of static market failures outlined earlier, such as monopoly and externalities, may also occur in a dynamic framework. Since their resource allocation effects are similar, there is no reason to restate them here and provide dynamic illustrations. The question is whether the dynamic framework of analysis provides additional possibilities for market failures. These possibilities center on the question of the social rate of discount. Here there are two possibilities for market failure. First, market rates of interest, which guide firms' calculation of values, may differ from the social discount rate, leading to an inefficient allocation of resources over time. The second possibility is that social and market interest rates may be equivalent and yet the firm may select its own private discount rate that exceeds the social rate of discount.

If Market Interest Rates Differ from the Social Rate of Discount

One potential source of dynamic market failure arises when firms discount future user costs at market interest rates that differ from the social rate of discount. Typically, the assertion is that market rates of interest exceed the social rate of discount, implying that future user costs are lower than they would otherwise be, thus causing overproduction of resources in the current period, and correspondingly, underproduction in future periods.

On the face of it, it would seem that the market rate of interest must reflect the social discount rate because the market rate of interest reflects society's rate of time preference. A common result from most principles textbooks is that the rate of interest is determined by the intersection of the savings schedule and the marginal efficiency of investment schedule. The marginal efficiency of investment schedule is obtained by ranking the investment possibilities according to the rate of interest that yields a zero present value. On the savings side, consumers compare current consumption with future consumption, concluding that the ratio of the marginal utility of current consumption to the marginal utility of future consumption is $1 + r$, where r is the social rate of time preference.[8] The problem is that while the rate of interest will reflect the existing society's social rate of discount, it makes no allowance for future generations, who are not present to express their social rate of time preferences.

Noneconomists tend to be particularly critical of the discounting of future consumption because it places a greater value on present consumption than future consumption. To illustrate the small weight given future generations by the discount process, the present value of one dollar 50 years from today is worth less than 1 cent today, assuming a 10 percent discount rate. Examples such as these prompted the well-known British economist A.C. Pigou to conclude that the whole process of discounting is morally indefensible.[9] To Professor Pigou, the appropriate rate of social discount is zero. The value of one unit of a nonrenewable resource to persons living in a future age when the resource has been physically exhausted may well be infinite, if no substitutes are then available; even if its value is finite (and possibly quite large), it should not be discounted by current consumers at *any* rate.

Basically, three separate arguments have been set forth in defense of using market interest rates as the appropriate rate of social discount. First, the example of a dollar in 50 years being worth less than 1 cent today overstates the degree to which future generations are disregarded. In the usual case, the appropriate discount rate is a real discount rate, which for a riskless asset is around 3 percent. Thus, applying a 3 percent rate instead of a 10 percent discount rate, the value of $1 in 50 years is $.23 rather than $.01. Thus, when performed properly, discounting may be a bit nearsighted, but it is not blind.

The second argument in favor of utilizing market rates of interest is based on past experience. Presumably, one consequence of using the market rate of interest to discount future consumption is that future generations will eventually be left with a world of increasing resource scarcity and associated falling per capita incomes. If discounting is morally indefensible, it must be because of its deleterious effects on future generations. Is the present generation the inheritor of an empty resource vault caused by the profligate ways of past generations?

It is likely that the highest grade ores, the largest oil fields, and the lowest cost coal deposits have already been exploited, as theory would predict. In terms of productive factors other than raw materials, previous generations have bequeathed to us more knowledge, better educational facilities, and high-technology capital equipment. Paradoxically, even in terms of nonrenewable resources, technology seems to have provided economic abundance in the face of increasing physical depletion. Even though the quality of the in-situ resources exploited today is far poorer than those of a century ago, the cost of producing the associated resource-using final goods has declined over time. Barnett and Morse[10] conducted a study of 29 important nonrenewable resources over the period 1870–1957. They found that, when corrected for inflation, the prices of all but a few of these resources have actually fallen over this period. Data for more recent periods analyzed by V. Kerry Smith indicate there is no strong evidence supporting either secularly rising or declining relative resource prices.[11] Margaret Slade found that for 11 nonrenewable commodities the former tendency for prices to decline seems to hold no longer as prices have stabilized and in some cases increased.[12] It seems clear that technology has for some time run depletion a strong race. In sum, as long as each generation provides future generations with the technology to produce energy-intensive goods at current or even moderately higher real prices, there would appear to be no compelling argument against the current practice of discounting future consumption by the market rate of interest.

The third argument is more a defense of the status quo method of allocating resources than one which argues that the social rate of discount equals the market rate. In most countries, the rights to subsurface minerals belong to the government rather than to private interests. As a consequence, a part of the resource base is not necessarily subject to the use of market rates of discount. To the extent that the rate of discount applied by the governments in developing their natural resources is less than the market interest rate, production is deferred for future generations. There is the danger that the government may select such a low social rate of discount that when the resources are ultimately developed, technology will have provided a cheaper substitute. However, if the government rate of discount is only slightly below the market rate of interest, this may indicate a desirable negative risk premium, particularly if society is risk-averse with respect to future unanticipated shortages. Since firms maximize the expected present value of a resource, the market rate of interest may not reflect this risk aversion. A system of private ownership of part of the resource base together with government ownership of the remainder may lead to some average rate of discount between the market rate of interest and the government rate of discount. The resulting average rate may be more appropriate, especially to the degree that it more properly reflects the risk aversion phenomenon.

Perhaps the greatest threat to efficient resource allocation is governmental decisions based neither on market rates of interest nor on a legitimate measure of the social rate of discount. Political exigencies may dictate either premature development of resources or underexploitation of resources. History suggests that bad decisions are not restricted to dictators and ill-informed bureaucrats. For example, in the late nineteenth century, there was much concern in Britain that the continued exploitation of British coal would leave the country without any coal reserves, facing much higher future energy costs. The famous British economist William Stanley Jevons had this to say on the coal question in 1866.[13]

> It is shown that we owe almost all our arts to continental nations, except those great arts which have been called into use here by the cheapness and excellence of our coal. It is shown that the constant tendency of discovery is to render coal a more and more efficient agent, while there is no probability that when our coal is used up any more powerful substitute will be forthcoming . . . If we lavishly and boldly push forward in the creation and distribution of our riches, it is hard to overestimate the pitch of beneficial influence to which we may attain in the present. But the maintenance of such a position is physically impossible. We have to make the momentous choice between brief greatness and longer continued mediocrity.

Had Britain opted to conserve its coal at that time, would it have been better off? History suggests quite the opposite. Those in Jevons' generation would have faced much higher prices for imported coal and/or a slower rate of economic development. Even future generations would probably not have benefitted. It is likely that even today the cost of delivered coal from the technically progressive U.S. mines would be less than that of the "low" cost British reserves of the nineteenth century. In addition, British oil from the North Sea probably dominates both of these alternatives.

If Private Discount Rates Exceed the Market Rate

Assuming that the social rate of discount is approximated by the market rate of interest, let us examine the possibility that the firm's private rate of discount exceeds the market rate of interest. One might conclude this is impossible, since another firm would acquire the resource because it would be willing to pay a higher price. Because the acquiring firm is using the market rate of interest to discount future profits rather than the higher discount rate of the firm owning the resource, the present value of the resource is higher to the acquiring firm. Therefore, can we dismiss this situation as an impossibility? Yes, assuming the costs of transferring the resource do not exceed the value differential.

The question is, under what circumstances would *all* firms be unwilling to apply the market rate of interest as a discount factor? The answer pertains to any risk premium that may be inherent in the peculiar nature of the resource. To the extent that the private and social risk premiums are equivalent, it is entirely appropriate to adopt a discount rate in excess of the market interest rate. Such a risk premium might arise if future technological change might make the resource worthless. Thus, whether the resource is owned privately or publicly, the same risk premium would be appropriate.

There are situations where there is a private risk premium, but no corresponding social risk premium. Consider the case of an oil company operating in a country subject to revolutions. Recognizing that a change in government could mean nationalization, the firm is likely to adopt a private rate of discount well above the market rate of interest. From that firm's perspective, or any other firm's perspective, not to make some allowance for such eventualities would display very poor business acumen. Nevertheless, from the perspective of the inhabitants of the country in question, the effect is to accelerate current production in excess of the socially optimal level. Over the longer term, the total amount of foreign and/or private investment is reduced, so that there is an underexploitation in the long run. Curiously enough, the dilemma would not necessarily be solved by transferring the development of the resource base to the government in power. To the extent that each successive and typically short-lived government maximizes its own wealth, similar short-run overproduction and long-run underinvestment occurs. Regardless of the solution, it is clear that the citizens of countries subject to such political instabilities pay a high price in the short-run overexploitation of the country's resource base and long-term underdevelopment of its resources.

Myopic exploitation of resources in which user costs are effectively disregarded is not limited to politically unstable countries. The institutions determining property rights are vital. In the United States, subsurface mineral rights are generally privately owned. Therefore, it is common to find many oil producers operating in one oil field. Furthermore, with a legal system determining ownership by the rule of capture, producers are entitled to all the oil their wells can produce. Thus, unrestrained competitive behavior in the 1930s led producers to disregard user costs. After all, a barrel not produced today might not be available for capture by the same producer tomorrow. The results were massive overdrilling and overproduction, often permanently damaging the oil reservoir. Later, in Chapter 7, we return to this fascinating form of market failure.

AN ECONOMIST'S PRESCRIPTION FOR EFFICIENT ENERGY RESOURCE ALLOCATION: A PRICING PROBLEM

The previous discussions of static and dynamic criteria for efficient resource allocation emphasize that the key to efficient resource allocation is the way in which energy is priced over time. At any point in time, the price of the energy resource should reflect its marginal social costs. This implies that any divergence between social and private costs arising as a consequence of public goods or other externalities should be corrected by internalizing such external costs. In terms of market structure, the equivalence of price, reflecting marginal social benefits, and marginal social costs requires a competitive market framework. Monopoly elements must be eliminated if prices are to equal marginal social costs.

In order for resources to be allocated efficiently over time, it is furthermore necessary that the user cost or opportunity cost of selling a resource in some future period must also be included in the marginal social cost. Even though this user cost does not involve an out-of-pocket payment such as production costs, it does reflect a real resource cost in that the resource could be used alternatively in the future.

We saw that the economic definition of conservation, rather than implying a simple reduction in the current rate of resource exploitation, implies that the user costs of a resource should rise over time at the social rate of discount. Therefore, over time, prices should rise to reflect these user cost changes. If they do not, resource allocation is not efficient over time. Based on currently available evidence, the market rate of interest offers a sufficiently close approximation to the social rate of discount. To the extent that nondiversifiable risks are present, the rate of discount should be adjusted to reflect these differences.

At first it might seem strange to tell the student to examine whether energy prices are efficient. There is, after all, a tendency to focus on the quantity of energy production, arguing that some fuels are being overproduced while others are underproduced. By focusing on quantities, we too often forget that we are trying to achieve that output combination where the marginal social benefit of the last unit produced equals its marginal social cost. By first looking at prices we are obliged to measure marginal social costs and benefits. Therefore, we view efficient energy allocation as a pricing problem. If energy is priced such that the marginal social benefits equal the marginal social costs both statically and dynamically, we need not be concerned with actual consumption and production levels. The socially optimal quantities of energy production and consumption are the byproducts of efficient prices. This interpretation is followed subsequently throughout this book.

1. One can assume that the salvage value of the firm is included in <u>Notes</u> profits in period n.

2. A more elegant proof involves the solution to a constrained optimization problem assuming that there are only 60 barrels available:

$$\max_{Q_0, Q_1} \Lambda = P_0Q_0 - C(Q_0) + \frac{1}{1 + r}[P_1Q_1 - C(Q_1)]$$

subject to $Q_0 + Q_1 = 60$, or equivalently, maximize the Lagrangian expression,

$$L = P_0Q_0 - C(Q_0) + \frac{1}{1 + r}[P_1Q_1 - C(Q_1)] - \lambda(Q_0 + Q_1 - 60)$$

The first-order conditions are:

(i) $\quad \dfrac{\partial L}{\partial Q_0} = U_0 - \lambda = 0 \left[\text{where } U_0 = \dfrac{\partial[P_0Q_0 - C(Q_0)]}{\partial Q_0} \right]$

(ii) $\quad \dfrac{\partial L}{\partial Q_1} = \dfrac{1}{1 + r} U_1 - \lambda = 0$

(iii) $\quad \dfrac{\partial L}{\partial \lambda} = -Q_0 - Q_1 + 60 = 0$

By setting (i) equal to (ii), we can prove that

$$U_0 = \frac{1}{1 + r} U_1$$

Note also that this formula combined with equation (iii) gives a two-equation system with two unknowns, Q_0 and Q_1, that can be solved to obtain optimal production rates and prices. Another interesting point is that the Lagrange multiplier λ represents the present value of the user cost in each period (i) and (ii).

3. See H. Hotelling, "The Economics of Exhaustible Resources," *Journal of Political Economy*, April 1931. For an excellent recent discussion, see P.S. Dasgupta and G.M. Heal, *Economic Theory and Exhaustible Resources* (Cambridge: Cambridge University Press, 1979).

4. In solving mathematically for the optimal output levels, we use the following two facts: (1) The present value of user costs must be equal in both periods, and (2) only 60 barrels will be produced in the two periods. (See Note 2, above.) These facts yield two equations with two unknowns:

$$U_0 = \frac{1}{1 + r} U_1$$

$$MR_0 - MC_0 = \frac{1}{1.1} (MR_1 - MC_1)$$

$$50 - .5Q_0 = \frac{1}{1.1} (50 - .33Q_1)$$

(i) $\quad -.55Q_0 + .33Q_1 = -5$

(ii) $\quad Q_0 + Q_1 = 60$

Solving (i) and (ii) simultaneously, one obtains the optimal output levels Q_0^* and Q_1^* as follows:

$$Q_0^* = 28.2 \quad \text{and} \quad Q_1^* = 31.8$$

Then substituting Q_0^* and Q_1^* into the demand equations, optimal prices P_0^* and P_1^* can be solved for:

$$P_0^* = 50 - .5(Q_0^* = 28.2) = 35.90$$
$$P_1^* = 5 - .33(Q_1^* = 31.8) = 39.50$$

5. In fact, this result is demonstrated in R.S. Pindyck, "Gains to Producers from the Cartelization of Exhaustible Resources," *Review of Economics and Statistics*, May 1978.

6. See M.A. Adelman, "OPEC as a Cartel" in J.M. Griffin and D.J. Teece (eds.), *OPEC Behavior and World Oil Prices* (London: Allen & Unwin, 1982).

7. See William A. Vogeley, "Issues in Mineral Supply Modeling" in R. Amit and M. Avriel (eds.), *Perspectives on Resource Policy Modeling* (Cambridge, Mass.: Ballinger, 1982).

8. For example, see Paul Samuelson, *Economics* (New York: McGraw-Hill, 1973), pp. 334–335.

9. A.C. Pigou, *The Economics of Welfare*, 4th edition (London: Macmillan Co., Ltd., 1932).

10. Chandler Morse and Harold Barnett, *Scarcity and Growth: The Economics of Natural Resource Availability* (Baltimore: Johns Hopkins Press, 1963).

11. See Robert S. Manthy, *Natural Resource Commodities: Century of Statistics* (Baltimore: Johns Hopkins Press, 1979). Also, see V. Kerry Smith, "Measuring Natural Resource Scarcity: Theory and

Review," *Journal of Environmental Economics and Management,* Vol. 5, 1978, pp. 150–171.

12. See Margaret Slade, "Trends in Natural Resource Commodity Prices: An Analysis of the Time Domain," *Journal of Environmental Economics and Management,* 1982. Also, see D.C. Hall and J.V. Hall, "Concepts and Measures of Natural Resource Scarcity with a Summary of Recent Trends," in *Journal of Environmental Economics and Management,* December 1984, pp. 363–379.

13. W.S. Jevons, in *The Coal Question* (1866), A.W. Flux, ed. (New York: A.M. Kelly, 1965).

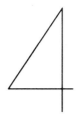

OPEC BEHAVIOR AND WORLD OIL PRICES

INTRODUCTION

Just as the Great Depression left an indelible mark on the 1930s, the "energy crisis" left its mark on the 1970s. As we look back on the 1970s, we pause to ask: "What role did the Organization of Petroleum Exporting Countries (OPEC) play in precipitating this crisis?" This question in turn prompts the next question: "If, indeed, OPEC played a significant role, what are the chances that OPEC may once again play such a role?" The answers to these two questions are to preoccupy us for the remainder of this chapter.

As illustrated in Figure 4.1, after two decades of falling oil prices, the 1970s ushered in a new era in the history of the world petroleum industry. The price of oil at the end of the decade was about twenty times higher than it was at the beginning, resulting in profound economic, political, and social consequences for consumers and producers. History tells us that the magnitude of the price increases in the 1970s can be traced to the Arab Oil Embargo of October 1973 and later the Iranian Revolution of 1978–79. On the face of it, it would appear that oil prices are determined by political events, not underlying economic forces. Consequently, a large contingent of political scientists and OPEC observers tend to view oil prices as the result of the interplay of political forces. Economists watched with amusement in 1974 as Henry Kissinger, then Secretary of State and a distinguished Harvard political scientist, dispatched a special envoy to Riyadh, Saudi Arabia, to negotiate an oil price rollback. The presumption was that prices which had been politically manipulated upward could similarly be manipulated downward. Implicit in Kissinger's actions is the assumption that the profit or wealth maximization paradigm is inapplicable when the economic actors are sovereign nation states rather than individual firms. Many would argue that the economic models are inapplicable, as nation states are much more concerned with achieving political and security objectives than wealth maximization.

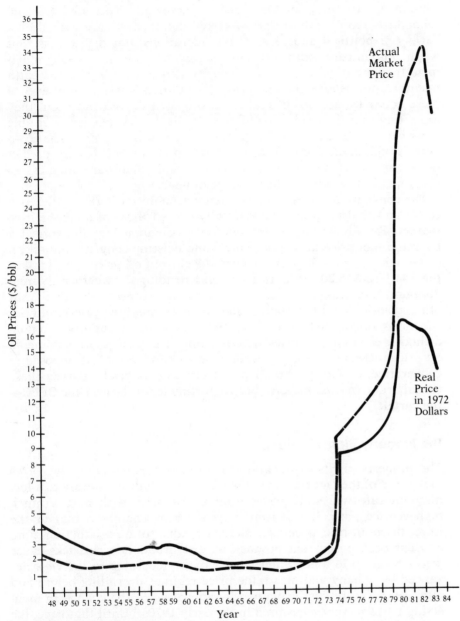

FIGURE 4.1 Actual market price and real price in 1972 dollars, per barrel of Saudi Arabian light crude oil, 1947–1983.

SOURCE: See Table 1.4.

The economist's answer to these challenges is threefold. First, while political events may have triggered the oil price increases of the 1970s, a closer look at these events shows that the price increases would not have been sustained without the deliberate actions of key OPEC members. Moreover, these actions appear economically motivated. Second, economists readily admit that sovereign nation states are guided by a variety of political and security considerations, but the actions that would maximize wealth also closely match those that would maximize their political objectives—security and power. In effect, wealth maximization is a reasonable proxy for political goals, so that even if these countries are not in reality seeking wealth maximization, they are acting as if they did. After all, with more money, one is better able to assist one's friends and to defend oneself against enemies. The economist's final point is that most economic models yield clearcut predictions, capable of refutation, whereas political models are often essentially qualitative without testable hypotheses.

The conventional view among energy economists is that OPEC is a cartel and that oil prices substantially exceed those of a competitive market. Recall the simple calculation in Chapter 3 that assumed a backstop fuel price at $70 per barrel and existing conventional oil reserves adequate for 30 years. Today, the current oil price would fall in the $4.01 to $16.20 per barrel range, depending on whether the real discount rate was 10 percent or 5 percent, respectively. But what other theories might explain higher than competitive prices without the monopolizing influence of a cartel? There are essentially two nonorthodox economic theories that attempt to explain the phenomenal oil price increases of the 1970s. Both rely on individual, as opposed to cooperative, action by the oil producers. Let us briefly survey these two alternative explanations, before putting forth the case for OPEC—the cartel.

The Property Rights Explanation

The property rights explanation for oil price increases in the 1970s makes use of the fact that switching from a high discount rate to a low discount rate will shift prices from a low price path onto a much higher price path. Recall from Figure 3.6 in Chapter 3 that at the lower discount rate, producers suddenly value future production more and cut back on current production. The production cutbacks cause prices to jump to a new higher price path. According to the view advanced by Johany and Mead, the price regimes prevailing before and after 1973–74 are best explained by appealing to the change in ownership patterns that transpired in the early 1970s.[1] Until that time, the concessions granted by the producing countries to the oil companies permitted the companies, in essence, to make unilateral production decisions. Accordingly, since production policies were essentially the prerogative of the companies, discount rate assumptions were made on the basis of the companies' perceptions of the future. Since expropriation risk was nontrivial in many countries in the 1960s, the wealth maximizing strategy for the companies involved a high discount rate and rapid depletion. This was fueled by forever-escalating royalty and tax demands by producer countries, which further served to reinforce expectations that profits would decline in the future. The result, according to Johany, was that the companies "produced as if there were no tomorrow," depressing world crude oil prices in the process.

According to this view, the events of 1973–74 marked a watershed in the world oil market, principally because of the transfer of control over production policies that occurred at that time. As Johany explains it,

> the oil producers decided to determine the price of their oil unilaterally rather than through negotiations with the oil companies as had been done in the past. Once the host countries became the ones who decide the rate of oil output and its price, the role of the companies had been essentially reduced to that of contractors. That amounted to a de facto nationalization of the crude oil deposits.[2]

This reassignment of property rights was significant because the companies and the host countries have different discount rates and that implies different rates of output. These differences can be traced to intrinsic differences in the discount rate as well as to differences in risk evaluation. With lower discount rates, current production will fall, thereby driving up the world price. At the time of the transition, production will drop sharply, causing a switch to the higher price path. According to this line of reasoning, 1973–74 represented such a transition period with a switching to a higher price path.

Table 4.1 shows, for various OPEC countries, the percentage of oil production owned by the national governments as opposed to the concessionaires. The period 1970–74 reflected sharp increases in govern-

TABLE 4.1 Percentage of Government Owned Oil Production for Selected Years in OPEC Countries

Country	1970	1972	1974	1976	1978	1980
Saudi Arabia	.9	.7	58.5	58.7	58.7	97.7
Iran	4.5	5.0	96.2	96.2	94.6	100
Kuwait	1.2	1.2	55.1	90.6	94.1	90.6
Iraq	0	53.8	77.2	100	100	100
Libya	0	3.6	60.7	64.2	65.7	67.5
U.A.E.	0	0	49.5	62.1	64.4	64.4
Venezuela	1.2	1.9	2.5	100	100	100
Qatar	0	0	60.0	78.5	99.4	100
Nigeria	0	0	54.9	55.1	54.9	71.1
Indonesia	11.7	16.2	30.5	36.6	44.6	45.7
Algeria	14.6	76.9	88.2	90.5	89.1	93.7
Ecuador	—	1.3	25.4	25.5	62.9	62.7
Gabon	0	0	0	0	0	0

SOURCE: OPEC Annual Statistical Yearbook.

ment ownership and the announcement of plans for future relinquishment of concessionaire production.

Even though this theory apparently explains the price increase of 1973–74 without any reference to OPEC or collusion, this theory has several deficiencies. First, it is unclear whether the production increases of the 1950s and 1960s were the desires of the companies or of the countries. The Shah of Iran pushed especially hard on the companies to expand production. This is completely at odds with the property rights model. However, Iran might be considered an exception, as the Shah's lust for current revenues was legend. Still another objection is that it offers no obvious interpretation of the doubling of prices in 1978–79. As is clear from Table 4.1, the transfer of ownership had long since taken place, so that further reductions in the discount rate could not have occurred. Similarly, the rationale for changed expectations of other factors affecting user costs, which could allow competitive prices to double, is not apparent. There is no evidence that producers altered their long-run expectations in 1978–79 regarding future reserves, future demand growth, the price of the backstop fuel, and so forth. Furthermore, following the rationale of a competitive model, one would expect that after the 1978–79 price rise due to short-run supply constraints, the price would return to the earlier price path with an easing of these constraints. But as Figure 4.1 clearly indicates, prices did not return to the post-Embargo 1974 price path.

The Target Revenue Explanation

Still another noncartel explanation for the price increases of the 1970s relies upon a combination of behavior that does not maximize wealth with independent behavior to yield a backward-bending supply curve for the major oil producers. A backward-bending supply curve yields the pathologic result that a price increase leads to a production decrease. According to this model, the 1973–74 price increase was triggered by political events, but at the higher prices individual countries consulted their backward-bending supply schedules and cut back production, enabling prices to stick at their post-Embargo levels. But how does one justify a backward-bending supply schedule?

The target revenue model depicts OPEC as a collection of nation states whose oil production decisions are made with reference to the requirements of their national budgets. Their budgetary needs are in turn a function of their economy's capacity to absorb productive investments. Absorptive capacity can be quite limited where the economy is small in relation to oil revenues, or where the infrastructure is inadequate to support rapid escalation in consumption and investment levels.

More formally, oil revenues can be considered as the source of funding for potential investment projects, which can be arrayed along a representative marginal efficiency of investment schedule (see Figure 4.2a). If a country is unwilling to invest for returns less than r^*, then investment needs are limited to I^*. In Figure 4.2b, if oil production decisions are made in order to meet the investment objective represented by I^* (which is their target revenue), then increases in the world price (from P_0 to P') in the current period will tend to result in reduced production (Q_0 to Q') in the current period. Conversely, if prices fall, producers will increase production to meet their revenue target I^*. The supply schedule thereby generated will have the "wrong" slope; that is, it will be backward-bending, at least over the relevant range.

An intertemporal dimension can readily be added. Economic development can be viewed as expanding investment opportunities and thereby raising the target revenue. Consequently, any specific backward-bending supply curve is dependent upon a given level of infrastructure. Given time for adjustment, the target revenue can rise substantially, so the target revenue model might be thought of as a more adequate description of OPEC behavior in the short run than in the long run. But at least during the 1970s this theory would suggest that oil revenue "needs" were quite limited, due to the limited ability of many of these economies to absorb domestic investment. Thus oil production was restrained by domestic investment as oil production was set to meet target revenues.

A key element in this theory is that it rejects wealth maximization. Foreign investment is not viewed as a substitute for domestic investment. After all, a wealth-maximizing asset portfolio would entail foreign investment as well as domestic investment and oil reserves. Proponents of the target revenue model, such as Teece,[3] argue that OPEC producers have perceived foreign investment to be unattractive, not only on account of the perceived low returns (generally when the dollar was depreciating in relation to other key currencies and producers

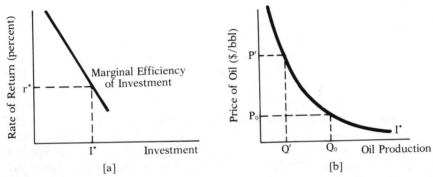

FIGURE 4.2 Target revenue model. (a) Investment determination. (b) Oil output determination.

held dollar denominated assets), but also because of political risks. These risks are of several kinds. One is the risk that the nation in which the funds were deposited might confiscate, freeze, or otherwise manipulate financial assets for political reasons. The other is that the existence of huge external liquid assets may facilitate the survival of revolutionary regimes, which, if successful in displacing existing governments, would have command over liquid assets that could be used to placate friends and buy off enemies. While admittedly such risks exist, it seems highly implausible that wealth maximizing agents, in selecting a portfolio of assets, would limit those portfolios to oil in the ground and domestic investments.

The target revenue model offers some interesting predictions that reveal its shortcomings. As we noted above, in the short run, a price increase will lead to a proportionate production cutback; this potentially explains how, following the price increases of 1973–74 and 1978–79, prices stabilized at the higher level. But another prediction of the model is that a price decrease will call forth greater production, thereby pushing prices still lower. In effect, prices are unstable downward as well as upward.

Objections to the target revenue approach center on the price decrease of $5 per barrel in 1983 (see Figure 4.1). The price decrease of 1983 did not lead to a production increase and a further price spiral downward. Instead, as Figure 4.3 shows, during this period the major OPEC producers cut oil production. Likewise, newspaper accounts were full of announcements that domestic investment projects had been cancelled or postponed. Rather than domestic revenue targets dictating oil production policy, the pattern appears just the reverse— the decline in oil revenues dictated a cutback in domestic investment. More formal statistical tests of this theory found that there was only one OPEC country, Algeria, for which the target revenue model appeared suitable.[4]

OPEC, The Cartel

If the two noncollusive theories just presented are inadequate to explain higher than competitive oil prices, does a cartel model perform any better? Before answering this question, some explanation of the term "cartel" is in order. The history of cartels reveals that they can take on many different forms, each with a separate personality and life expectancy. Too often, economists make the mistake of postulating a stylized cartel model, and upon finding that the facts do not fit the model, concluding that OPEC is not a cartel. So keep in mind that every cartel is unique. We have the rest of the chapter to describe the attributes unique to OPEC, but for now let us briefly review three key pieces of evidence to justify our treatment of OPEC as a cartel. First, even though the price increases of 1973–74 and 1978–79 were tied to

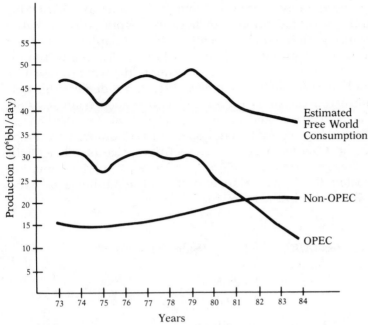

FIGURE 4.3 Non-communist world consumption together with OPEC and non-OPEC supply.

political events, the historical record we will soon examine clearly shows that deliberate production restraints were taken following these increases, allowing prices to stabilize at the lower output level. Second, OPEC has all the trappings of a cartel. Periodic meetings in Vienna and other lovely spots are not called for purposes of discussing horticulture. Rather, the OPEC ministers openly discuss and debate the appropriate pricing of the Saudi marker crude, against which all other OPEC crudes are priced. Furthermore, since 1983, OPEC ministers have set "voluntary" production levels, and carefully monitor their compliance. While one might argue that these meetings do not necessarily imply that these countries are bound by the decisions made there, the participation in such meetings provides strong circumstantial evidence. Third, formal statistical tests for the 11 largest OPEC producers compared to the 11 most important non-OPEC oil producers demonstrate quite convincingly that OPEC producers behave differently than do the non-OPEC producers. Stated simply, the test for cartelization asked whether a given country varied its production in step with other OPEC countries or selected its output independently. For 10 of the 11 OPEC countries tested, the cartel hypothesis could not be rejected. In contrast, for the 11 non-OPEC producers, the cartel hypothesis was rejected for all but one country.[5]

These three pieces of evidence convincingly demonstrate that OPEC has emerged as an organization with both monopoly power and the penchant for using that power. Recalling from Chapter 2 that we should concern ourselves only with market failures leading to significant welfare losses, we now need to approximate the welfare loss as a consequence of OPEC's monopoly power. Figure 4.4 depicts the welfare loss from cartelization as the sum of two shaded triangles ABC and ACD. The 1984 prices and quantities are known, but it is necessary to estimate the price that would occur under competition. From the discussion in Chapter 3 on the competitive price of oil, we will assume a midrange estimate of $7.50 per barrel. Applying equation (2.13) to measure the larger triangle ABC and assuming a demand elasticity of .7, we obtain the following

$$\text{Welfare Loss } (ABC) = \frac{1}{2}\left(\frac{\Delta P}{P}\right)^2 (\text{Sales})\,(E_d)$$

$$(4.1) \qquad\qquad = \frac{1}{2}\left(\frac{21.50}{29.00}\right)^2 (29 \times 14.6 \times 10^9 \text{ bbl})\,(.7)$$

$$= \$81 \text{ billion}$$

Thus, the welfare loss is on the order of $81 billion annually without even including the area ACD. Unfortunately, it is not possible to observe the marginal cost at the monopoly level (point D), leaving us

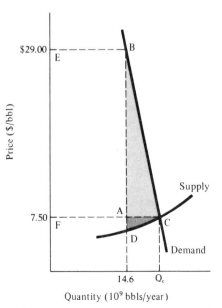

FIGURE 4.4 Measuring the welfare loss due to OPEC in 1984.

without a good measure of triangle *ACD*. The estimate of $81 billion annually is only a rough estimate, but it may even be a conservative estimate—for two reasons. The true price elasticity may well be larger than .7. Also, the welfare loss from the triangle *ACD* is omitted in the calculation.

In addition to the huge welfare losses, OPEC has had major effects on income distribution. Consuming nations have suffered major losses in consumer surplus. In Figure 4.4, the loss in consumer surplus is rectangle *ABEF* plus the triangle *ABC*. Combined, the two imply a loss in consumer surplus of $395 billion (314 + 81). Conversely, OPEC nations have experienced a major increase in producers' surplus. To the extent that this monopoly power can be neutralized or reduced, energy resource allocation can be improved. A primary purpose of this chapter is to explore the critical determinants of OPEC's monopoly power and to devise policies to minimize this power.

THE WORLD OIL INDUSTRY BEFORE 1960: OPEC AS AN EMBRYO

How did OPEC come to control over 90 percent of world crude oil export capacity on the eve of the Arab Oil Embargo in 1973? To answer this question we must first develop some historical perspective in order to appreciate the nature of the world oil market within which OPEC had its humble birth in 1960. Only against this background can we explain why in October 1973 the exporter cartel's monopoly power could have manifested itself so dramatically.

Oil has been an important commodity in international trade since the 1860s. Before the First World War, the most important participants in this world oil market were the major international companies: Standard Oil (today Exxon), Shell, and two Russian concerns, Nobel and Rothschild. During the First World War a new major international company, Anglo-Persian (today British Petroleum), was formed with British government ownership and backing. On the other hand, the Russian companies were destroyed as a result of the Russian Revolution. After the war, the governments of the oil-importing countries began to play a more significant role in encouraging their own national companies to search for oil throughout the world. But major company dominance of the world oil market was not to be permanent. Standard, Shell, and Anglo-Persian tried to stabilize world oil marketing in the 1920s, but the entrance of several other firms into world oil production in the 1930s increased the degree of competition present and limited the ability of a small group of companies to dictate prices and output.[6] With these new entrants (Gulf, Texaco, Standard of California [today Chevron], and Mobil) the number of international oil firms increased from three to seven—the "seven sisters." At the end of World War II, the "seven sisters" controlled virtually all crude oil involved in international trade. Table 4.2 shows the market shares of the "seven sisters" in 1950. These data exclude production from North America and communist areas, as import policies and the relative self-sufficiency of these countries excluded them from world oil markets.

Not only was the world market highly concentrated, but the companies' overlapping interests in the various concessions limited the extent of independent behavior by any one of the sisters. For example, the Aramco concession in Saudi Arabia was jointly owned and operated by Exxon (30%), Mobil (10%), Texaco (30%), and Chevron (30%). Likewise, the Kuwaiti concession was jointly owned by Gulf (50%) and British Petroleum (50%). This pattern of overlapping interests reduced the incentive and ability for any one company to increase production, as the output decision was made jointly by all the concession owners.[7]

Although the profits of the "seven sisters" pale to insignificance compared to modern-day OPEC profits, the international oil market was quite profitable following World War II. Figure 4.5 shows the market price of oil, the taxes paid to the exporter country, and the difference—company costs and profit margins. Costs were in the range of $.10 to $.20 per barrel, so the "seven sisters" were enjoying consid-

TABLE 4.2 Percentage Market Shares of International Oil Companies in World Oil Market

	1950	1957	1969[a]
Exxon	30.4	22.8	16.6
British Petroleum	26.3	14.4	16.1
Shell	13.8	17.5	13.3
Gulf	12.1	14.8	9.8
Largest four	82.6	69.5	55.8
Standard Oil of California	6.1	7.6	7.5
Texaco	5.7	6.9	8.0
Mobil	3.9	5.0	4.8
Largest seven	98.3	89.0	76.1
All others	1.7	11.1	23.9
TOTAL	100.0	100.0	100.0

[a]First half of 1969.

SOURCE: M. A. Adelman, The World Petroleum Market (Baltimore: Johns Hopkins University Press, 1972) pp. 80–1. Note that this excludes production from North America and communist countries.

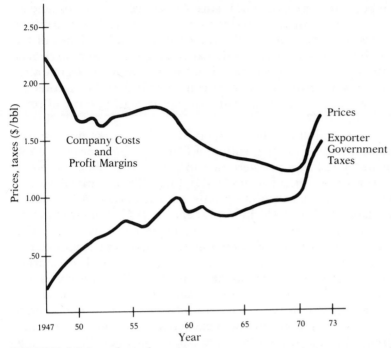

FIGURE 4.5 Actual market prices, exporter government taxes, and oil company profit margins per barrel of Saudi Arabian light crude oil (1947–1972). *SOURCE:* Vertical Divestiture and OPEC, *Petroleum Industry Research Foundation, New York, 1977, p. 9.*

erable economic rents. As expected, these oligopoly profits attracted new entrants. Consequently, several hundred smaller oil companies entered the world petroleum market to provide increasingly effective competition for the existing majors. Paradoxically, as we shall see later, the declining market power of the "seven sisters" provided a major stimulus for the creation of OPEC.

Throughout the post-Second World War period, the major oil companies—faced with increasing competition from their many new price-competitive rivals—were steadily losing the substantial market power they had possessed at the end of the war. As shown in Table 4.2, by 1957 the output of the four largest companies had fallen from 82.6 to 69.5 percent of the market. All other producers, who in 1947 held only 1.7 percent of the market, had grown to 11.0 percent. By 1960 the major international producers had lost much of their market power and were unable to keep world oil prices from falling significantly. Even the birth of OPEC in 1960 was unable to prevent the further loss of market power by the major oil companies during the 1960s, and by 1970 an essentially competitive world oil price level had been established. By 1969, Table 4.2 shows that other companies produced 23.9 percent of production. Figure 4.5 shows in a dramatic way the impact on oil company per-barrel net profits of the increasing market competition between 1947 and 1970, as crude oil prices fell from $2.22 to $1.26 per barrel while exporter government taxes rose from 22 cents to 94 cents per barrel. Company profit margins after production costs fell from $1.79 to 22 cents per barrel during this period—perhaps the best single measure of the increasing force of price competition after 1947.

The declining profitability of the international oil companies proved to be a major stimulus to the creation of OPEC, because prior to 1960, exporter country tax receipts were tied to company profits. Since taxing conventions are critical to understanding OPEC, a bit of history on the precedents for a corporate profits tax is in order. A 50 percent profits tax dates back to 1943 in Venezuela. In 1943, Venezuela repudiated existing oil concession tax arrangements and raised the effective tax rate to 50 percent of company earnings. Venezuelan export revenues had declined sharply during the Second World War, when sinkings by submarines reduced tanker exports to the lower levels that could be protected by convoys. The revision of the terms of the concession was weathered with the aid of the U.S. Treasury, which applied preexisting tax regulations to the Venezuelan situation. Companies paying foreign income taxes were permitted to deduct those taxes as a credit against domestic income tax liabilities, provided foreign tax rates did not exceed domestic tax rates. The oil companies acceded to such changes, since a 50 percent profits tax meant only that U.S. tax liabilities were reduced by an amount equal to the increase in Venezuelan taxes. The Venezuelan tax system later became the model for other concessions. By 1950, Saudi Arabia was complaining about the situation, and Saudi Arabian oil was obviously of great future importance for all importers. Accommodating Saudi Arabia proved relatively simple. All the Saudis had to do was pass a national income tax law applying to all businesses, and Aramco (jointly owned by Exxon, Mobil, Texaco, and Chevron) would be able to shift its tax payments from Washington to Riyadh. After this was done in 1950, the other exporters clamored for the same 50–50 treatment.

But London, the Hague, and Paris were apparently not as generous as Washington in tax matters affecting foreign income. Only U.S. companies could be assured of automatically crediting foreign income taxes (if assessed at rates no greater than domestic rates) in full against domestic income tax liabilities. The most important single reason for the Iranian nationalization in 1951 was the reluctance of BP to agree to a 50–50 tax regime because this would cost a British company more after taxes than an American company. Still, despite company reluctance, the 50–50 scheme became universal for oil exporters.

Although exporter tax revenues soared, considerable resentment existed against both the oil companies and the importing countries. Even though the 50–50 sharing formula allowed the producing countries to capture a portion of the oil company's rents, the producing countries recognized that the consuming countries levied heavier taxes against their oil than they did. Particularly in Europe, retail gasoline prices exceeded $30 per barrel in the 1950s, owing to the large gasoline excise taxes collected by the consuming countries. Economic rents were spread unevenly between the consuming countries' treasuries, the international oil companies, and the oil producing countries. Furthermore, the lesson of Iran served as a constant reminder of where the economic power resided. Iran in 1951 had nationalized the properties of British Petroleum (BP) but was unable to sell oil, since BP simply increased its output in Iraq and Kuwait to make up for the Iranian losses, and one exporter gained at the expense of another. Iran tried to sell oil at bargain prices but found very few customers. BP stood ready to prosecute any buyers of Iranian oil in British courts under the doctrine of purchasing stolen property. BP was successful in winning at least one such case, but the main point was that Iranian oil was not needed in the world market in the early 1950s; there was sufficient excess productive capacity elsewhere, relative to demand, to make it easy to replace Iranian oil by oil produced in countries that did not nationalize. Eventually Iran was reopened to the world oil market in 1954, under a new consortium agreement, but this was done more for political reasons than for economic ones.

In the 1950s, exporter solidarity was at best shaky. Non-Arabs felt no broad community of interest with the Arabs; producers with large ratios of reserves to production sought rapid output increases, while those with lower ratios, like Venezuela, urged output moderation in the interest of price enhancement. Not until the end of the 1950s did circumstances conspire to create somewhat greater unity among the major exporters. In 1956–57, the Suez Canal had been closed by the renewal of Arab-Israeli hostilities; oil then had to be shipped to Europe and other west-of-Suez destinations by much lengthier routes, increasing the demand for tankers in the short run. However, the supply of tankers is extremely inelastic in the short run; hence not only were tanker rates greatly increased, but an "absolute" shortage of oil shipment capacity developed. Although shipments from the United States and Venezuela prevented undue hardship in Europe, oil prices went up quite considerably during this period, in response to short supplies and higher transport costs. But after the Suez Canal was reopened, prices declined. Oil company earnings per barrel declined, and it appeared that the producing countries' revenues would also decline.

There was such a revenue effect, but it was delayed. For tax computation purposes it is necessary to distinguish between the actual transaction price of oil as in Figure 4.1 and the posted price of oil on which host government tax revenues were computed. While prices for refined products had been posted in the exporting regions since the 1930s, crude oil prices were not officially posted in the Middle East until 1950, when the 50–50 tax split went into effect in Saudi Arabia and rulers were given a financial interest in oil prices. At that time concessionaires had to employ posted prices for crude oil tax purposes, so the posted price became a "tax reference price" as well as an indicator of market prices.[7] During the period 1950–57, available evidence suggests that actual transaction prices and posted prices were quite similar, but after 1957, the two diverged as transaction prices dropped sharply. (See Figure 4.5.) Initially, the companies were particularly cautious about lowering posted prices, since exporter governments would object fiercely. Hence even though transactions prices fell from the peak levels obtained during the Suez closure, companies did not in 1957 reduce posted prices. Thus exporter governments received more than 50 percent of oil company earnings, since taxes were computed on posted prices that were higher than those actually received.

Transaction prices fell further in 1958 when a sharp recession reduced oil demand in Europe for the first time in a number of years. Even so, companies were reluctant to cut posted prices, hoping that demand growth would quickly resume. But when the market failed to recover by February 1959, posted prices were cut despite exporter protest. Although demand ceased to decline, the increase in supply from both new and old companies was considerable, and transaction prices continued to decline slowly from month to month. In August 1960, another reduction took place in the posted price, and the exporters were finally given the stimulus they needed to unite. All exporters could agree upon the desirability of higher posted prices, and in particular upon the need to prevent any further declines in these tax reference prices. Only one month after the 1960 posted price cut, OPEC was formed. Ironically, the birth of OPEC was viewed as an unimportant event, given only a four-inch, single-column account on one of the back pages of the *New York Times*.[8]

THE WORLD OIL MARKET 1960–73: OPEC'S FORMATIVE YEARS

It has been said that OPEC is a four-letter word for monopoly, but one cannot capture the vivid turbulence of the cartel simply by selecting a label from the rather colorless categories of price theory. OPEC is only a loose cartel because of the continuing actual and potential divergence of interest among its members, but it nevertheless works since there are strong common forces uniting this diverse group. Pausing in search of a metaphor, we might liken OPEC to an extended polygamous family (it has been called worse names) containing able patriarchs, propertied wives, a shrewd uncle or two, and a sprinkling of indolent brothers-in-law and other arrogant, elegant idlers.

The original OPEC wedding took place on September 14, 1960, uniting five major oil exporters—Iran, Iraq, Kuwait, Saudi Arabia, and Venezuela—in the bonds of the pursuit of collusive restraint of producer competition in the world oil market. The family grew rapidly at first; Qatar was added in 1961, and Indonesia and Libya joined in 1962. The larger the group became, the greater the attractive force it exerted on other exporters. As attraction ripened into affinity, other countries became allied with the cartel. Abu Dhabi came on board in 1967, Algeria in 1969, and Nigeria in 1971. By that time all the major oil exporters then in existence were included. The development of new productive capacity in Ecuador and Gabon permitted these two exporters to enter the OPEC family in 1973, bringing the total number of members to an ominous thirteen. (Abu Dhabi allied itself with Dubai and Sharja in 1974 to form the United Arab Emirates, which supplanted the Abu Dhabi membership.)

OPEC in 1960 lacked the strength to act as a truly effective cartel. This disappointed some of its founders, such as Perez Alfonso of Venezuela, who had hoped OPEC could in a businesslike way proceed to set a world monopoly price and allocate production quotas among members, enforcing compliance through rewards and penalties. OPEC instead had to content itself with the achievement of lesser goals during the first decade of its existence. Monopoly became a long-term goal, while the short-term goals consisted of devising expedients by which individual members could wrest away as much as possible of the revenues of the oil companies operating within their own boundaries. Achieving the long-term goal required close cooperation among all members, while the shorter-term goals could be pursued country by country with no more coordination than that supplied by the OPEC organization itself as a forum for collusion. Achieving the first goal required control of prices and output; achieving the second required the use of taxation and regulation to transfer income from companies to governments.

The decade of the 1960s was highly favorable to OPEC. Internally, the cartel organization proceeded cautiously, achieving moderate gains, making no real mistakes, and avoiding temptations to overreach itself. Externally, events outside OPEC borders developed in ways that greatly strengthened OPEC's hand. In 1960, oil prices were low, exporters were disunited on many issues, excess production capacity existed outside the cartel, and oil transportation networks were becoming cheaper and more efficient, increasing competition among members. Active Arab-Israeli hostilities had ceased for several years. If any single OPEC member held out for higher prices or larger output levels, oil companies could turn to other members, or could for some period of time rely upon excess capacity in the United States. Ample transport facilities were available, and there were many small as well as large companies ready to perform the necessary logistics work to satisfy demand with an altered supply pattern.

But by 1970 conditions had changed radically. The most important single factor was the virtual disappearance of excess productive capacity outside the cartel. As shown in Figure 4.6, noncommunist world oil consumption doubled over the decade, with the strong growth in oil demand caused by rising income levels. Furthermore, with production peaking in the U.S. and Canada in the late 1960s, additional demand was created for OPEC crude. By 1973, even though the OPEC nations possessed huge untapped reserves, actual installed productive capacity was barely adequate to meet the surging demand. If OPEC members were to unite in restricting supplies, there would be no alternative source. And, OPEC members were becoming more united. A series of modest but cumulative negotiating successes by OPEC in the 1960s had given rise to hopes that united cartel action could achieve much more in the future. These hopes were inflamed by the success of Libya in 1970 in forcing its oil prices upward, and by the end of 1970 plans were afoot to transfer ownership of oil reserves from the companies to the exporter regimes. Arab-Israeli hostilities had resumed in 1967, and the continued occupation by Israel of conquered Arab lands made the renewed outbreak of war at literally any moment a real possibility. Oil transportation was less secure in 1970 since the Suez Canal had been closed after 1967, and the precedent had been set that oil pipeline shipments through Arab countries could be subject to prolonged interruption by sabotage.

Hence there was a very real danger that OPEC members might (1)

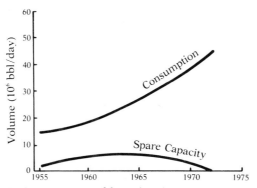

FIGURE 4.6 World crude oil spare capacity and consumption (excluding communist countries).

SOURCE: Statement of G. T. Piercy, Exxon Corporation, before the Senate Foreign Relations Subcommittee on Multinational Companies Hearing, Washington, D.C., February 1, 1974.

take advantage of any temporary disruptions arising in the flow of world oil to raise tax reference prices of oil in the short run, and insist on maintaining the price hike in the long run; (2) threaten to create disruptions in world oil flow unless importers recognized OPEC demands for higher and increasing prices; or (3) create such disruptions directly by united OPEC action and dictate prices and other terms accordingly on the basis of accomplished total cartelization. The period since 1969 has witnessed three instances of opportunistic activity of the first type: Libya in 1970, the Arab Embargo in 1973, and the Iranian revolution in 1978–79. The most important example of the second type is provided by the pressures employed to obtain the five-year price agreements between OPEC and the oil companies in Teheran and Tripoli in 1971.

Let us now look at what OPEC actually did between 1960 and 1973. There were three areas of activity: (1) tax system changes; (2) production control; and (3) steps toward nationalization of concessions. The two latter areas bore little fruit in the 1960s. Attempts to "program" production by setting a maximum annual growth rate in each member's exports were cautiously undertaken in 1965, only to be abandoned in 1967. Efforts aimed at the long-run nationalization of concessions took concrete form in 1968, when OPEC issued a declaration of goals including not only the maximization of tax revenues, but also the ultimate achievement of effective control of oil company operations through the replacement of present concessionaires on any pretext that could be justified under the very flexible doctrine of "changing circumstances." Under this doctrine long-standing concession agreements could be canceled, tax reference prices unilaterally determined by rulers, company profit rates controlled, accelerated relinquishment schedules provided for unexploited concession areas, and so on. This 1968 document provided the blueprint for exporter takeover of oil operations; all that was lacking was a timetable and other specifics of implementation. Neither oil companies nor importers paid too much attention to the OPEC manifesto at that time; the goals that were announced seemed too far beyond the grasp of the cartel at the time. Yet much of what has happened since 1970 has followed the guidelines of the 1968 declaration, including the nationalization of concessions.

On the tax front, OPEC moved with deliberation to achieve minor but significant increases in taxes per barrel. Although the tax rates were regarded as fixed (at least for the time being) under existing laws, tax revenues per barrel could still be increased by (1) reducing tax deductions or (2) increasing the tax reference price at which the oil was presumably sold. OPEC thus investigated ways of disallowing or otherwise minimizing expenses and other items reducing tax liabilities, and toyed with the idea of unilaterally imposing higher tax reference prices. Certain expenses were disallowed, such as marketing allowances, but the impact of these changes was very minor. More important was the separation of the government royalty from the other categories of company contributions to the exporter's treasury. Under tax agreements in effect as of 1960, rulers were to obtain 50 percent of company earnings in the form of taxes. Of this 50 percent, perhaps one-fourth would be a per-barrel royalty and the other three-fourths would be an income tax. Thus in a simple case, suppose the price of a barrel of oil is $2.00 (actual and tax reference prices will be presumed to coincide for the sake of the example) and its production costs are 20 cents. There is a one-eighth royalty and an income tax rate of 50 percent. Under existing tax laws, the income would be $1.80 per barrel, so that 90 cents would go to the ruler. But the royalty would be 25 cents, so that the income tax per se would be 65 cents.

OPEC convinced its members that if every country insisted upon the "expensing" of royalties, tax receipts would increase in such a way that no member would be differentially favored or slighted; hence there would be no effect on competition among members for output and concessionaires. Under this scheme the royalty would be deducted from the sales price as an expense item, lowering the taxable profit. But 50 percent of this taxable profit would be paid to the ruler, in addition to all of the royalty. Thus, in the above example, profit subject to the tax would be reduced to $1.55 ($2.00 − 0.20 − 0.25), of which one-half or 77.5 cents would be paid to the government as income taxes. But since the government also collects the 25 cents royalty, its income per barrel increases to $1.025, up by 12.5 cents from the previous treatment. The so-called expensing of royalties would make sense in a situation in which the royalty recipient and the government are two different parties; where they share the same pockets it is evident that fiscal opportunism rather than accounting theory was the reason for the change in treatment.

What about tinkering with tax reference prices? In theory, each country could keep its 50 percent tax rate and yet by legislation (whether or not in violation of earlier agreements) decree higher tax reference prices, so that at a fictitiously high price, a 50 percent rate might take 95 percent or more of actual profit. The problem with this approach was that each country would have to agree on the same tax reference price, and there was insufficient unanimity to achieve agreement. While the expensing of royalties was not divisive, since all members were affected in the same way, members wishing to expand output rapidly would not happily acquiesce in increases in tax reference prices, which would hamper the achievement of that goal. Furthermore, the successful setting of very high tax reference prices by all OPEC members would mean increases in OPEC prices relative to non-OPEC prices, and some diversion of exports to non-OPEC areas.

Although OPEC was unable to raise tax reference prices, it did succeed in preventing the companies from further lowering posted prices after August 1960. OPEC could achieve absolute solidarity on that point: no member would recognize prices below those of August 1960 for tax purposes. But competition continued to increase in the world oil market after 1960: new firms entered, OPEC members encouraged higher production in various ways such as granting new concessions or their equivalents, the national oil companies of both the importing and exporting countries increased supply through new discoveries, and so on. Potential supply continued to outrace demand at going prices, and at least some of the downward price pressure was actually translated into price reductions in crude oil transactions. Thus the OPEC governments did get more than 50 percent of company profits actually realized from market prices. The rate increased from 50 to between 65 and 70 percent in most OPEC countries, while OPEC ministers asserted that the "fair" share of profits between ruler and company would be about 80 to 20. Thus OPEC had decided that four-fifths of the producer surplus could safely be confiscated before there was real danger that supplies might decline due to reduction of company returns below the level consistent with the risks of foreign operation. OPEC members were not quite clear as to how the tax rate was to be effectively raised to 80 percent, but the 1968 OPEC manifesto mentioned above included some hints: control of company profit rates, participation in concessions, and so on. The details of these arrangements are too complex to enter into in this brief discussion, but one can be assured that at no time was OPEC not actively considering every feasible way to increase member oil tax revenues.

But one should not depict OPEC as anxious to bleed the companies to death—on the contrary, OPEC would have been delighted had world market conditions in the 1960s been such as to permit oil companies to raise actual prices and thus earn for both OPEC and themselves larger total producer surpluses. OPEC officials and consultants thought long and hard about ways in which members could alter their tax systems so as to force companies to increase the actual transactions price of oil, rather than just face a higher tax reference price from the exporter government. The difficulty was that true income taxes do not permit themselves to be used (or misused) in this way. Taxes based on actual taxpayer net income are efficient in that regardless of the tax rate (ruling out rates in excess of 100 percent) the company still maximizes profits after taxes at the same price and output level that would prevail in the absence of the income tax. The income tax does not affect marginal cost and hence does not affect the supply schedule of a competitive industry.

But as actual market prices continued to fall while OPEC tax reference prices remained constant, the income tax ceased to be based on income and became a flat excise tax per barrel. A per-barrel excise tax does affect marginal cost and hence the supply function of a competitive industry. Figure 4.7 shows that the market price of the oil pro-

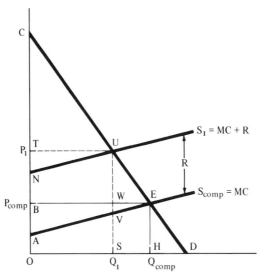

FIGURE 4.7 Effect of successful imposition by OPEC of a flat excise tax per barrel on producing companies.

duced by a given OPEC member could in fact be increased by raising the excise tax charged by the ruler. If a per-barrel excise tax R is added to the marginal cost of production (MC = S_{comp}), then the competitive supply function is raised to MC + R, and price is increased to P_1 while output falls to Q_1. Because oil demand is price-inelastic, the OPEC member gains since total royalties received now amount to the area *ANUV*, while producer surplus of *NTU* still remains to be taxed.

The problem with this kind of price-fixing is that each country would have to charge the same excise tax so that the cartel would achieve the monopoly price and an appropriate division of output among the members at that price. Given divergence among the goals of OPEC members, this would be very difficult to achieve. But fortunately for OPEC, as circumstances changed, persistence in the old tax system inherited from pre-OPEC days created more rather than less stability among members on pricing policy. All members had the same tax rates and roughly the same posted prices (after adjustment for oil quality differentials), and all treated royalties and other items in the same way. All members faced declines in the actual prices at which their oil was being sold. All sought insulation from market forces by refusing to recognize these price declines for tax purposes. But the net result of applying the same tax rate to the same posted price in the same way from country to country was to impose the same per-barrel excise tax on all oil produced by OPEC. During the period of declining market prices, OPEC members feared that prices might drop as low as $1.00 per barrel, and took some consolation from the fact that the "tax-paid cost" of oil in most countries was very close to $1.00 per barrel by the late 1960s so that OPEC taxes (plus a small marginal production cost) provided an effective price "floor" against further decline. Had taxes instead been based on the actual transaction prices, as oil company profits were eroded by competitive forces, prices could have fallen all the way to marginal costs.

At this juncture we must try to weave in two other OPEC-sponsored projects, which interacted with the tax system to affect the evolution of OPEC member control over oil exports. In the 1968 OPEC manifesto, there was encouragement for both national company development of OPEC member reserves and national "participation" in the concessions granted the companies. Both measures aimed at increasing local control over the exporter's oil operations. The doctrine of participation mixed well with the desire to promote the fortunes of the national oil company. If such a company could not find oil, let it be given the oil by the concessionaires. Participation was usually obtained at the same price at which compensation for nationalization would be paid: on the basis of the net depreciated asset value of the properties. Such values were typically quite low relative to the true market value of the reserves. But the national oil company had few if any customers at the outset. To whom did it sell? Initially, the national oil companies of the OPEC countries competed not only against their concessionaires but against each other; thus, they increased their nation's exports but often at the cost of reduced average price.

Even with discounted prices, the national oil companies of OPEC lacked the marketing outlets to sell all the oil they could acquire under participation deals. Thus it became necessary to have the concessionaires "buy back" OPEC's participation share of the oil produced. Hence there was a continuing dispute over how high the buy-back price would be.

Let us now turn to the political events that strengthened OPEC's unity during the 1960s. The Israeli victory in the 1967 war left the Arabs with lingering bitterness toward any activity that they perceived to be in any way related to supporters of Israel, such as the Western oil companies. An oil embargo was organized during this war, but not used. Following the victory of the Algerians in their long war against the French, the status of foreign oil companies in Algeria became increasingly tenuous. The 1965 Algerian agreement with the companies was continually abridged with special extensions and other demands that worked to the detriment of the foreigners. In 1969 the rich but feeble Libyan monarchy was overthrown by Arab radicals, whose first target was the oil companies. Libya took advantage of several factors that in 1970 gave its easily accessible Mediterranean oil a demand advantage, and hence potentially a price advantage, over other oils: (1) the sabotage of the trans-Arabian pipeline by Syria, preventing the delivery of Persian Gulf oil by pipeline to the eastern Mediterranean; (2) the continued closure of the Suez Canal since the 1967 war; (3) the unexpectedly great increase in demand for oil in Europe and elsewhere in 1970; and (4) the continuing shortage of oil transport facilities, persisting since the Suez closure but aggravated by the unexpected demand increase. All these factors increased the demand for Libyan oil, so the Libyan leadership found it expedient to resort to several measures to force through a price increase: intimidation, threats to nationalize the companies, and discriminatory reductions in output allowables, allegedly for "conservation" purposes. While it appears that there was no initial conspiracy between Libya and Syria regarding the pipeline sabotage, it is likely that collusion played a part in postponing repairs, permission for which was not granted for nine months. (The actual repairs took less than 24 hours.) Collusion did take place between Libya and Algeria, with the Algerian nationalization of certain foreign oil company properties during the Tripoli negotiations certainly strengthening Libya's hand.

What could the oil companies have done? As business organizations faced with a military and diplomatic threat, they would lose out unless backed up by other military and diplomatic organizations—their home governments. Support by the latter need not have meant war. All that was needed in 1970 was the assurance by home governments (especially American) that the companies could cooperate with each other during the emergency, with those companies suffering production cutbacks in Libya being allowed to obtain supplies from other companies or other areas at cost. OPEC was not yet sufficiently strong or united in 1970 to have withstood this threat, and Libya, as the smallest member in terms of population and GNP, could not have been the tail that wagged the OPEC dog. However, Libyan leadership excelled in fanaticism, and this won the day. Given the complete lack of importer government support, the companies acceded to the demands.

OPEC members were jubilant. If Libya, standing alone, could force an increase in oil prices, what might the entire cartel accomplish if it acted in unison? The Libyan agreement had been signed in September 1970. By December 1970, OPEC was meeting in Caracas to draw up an accelerated timetable for implementing the 1968 plan for cartel control of the oil export industry. Negotiations opened in both Teheran and Tripoli in early 1971, the aim being a five-year price pact that would provide for higher and increasing posted prices for oil during the period 1971–76.

The parties included the oil companies and the exporters; importer delegations were conspicuously absent. Threatening to embargo any company that did not accede to its demand, OPEC forced through a posted price increase of about 21 percent (from $1.80 to $2.18 per barrel for Saudi Arabian light crude oil, the standard reference oil price) and also a tax rate increase from 50 to 55 percent. Further increases of 2.5 percent per year would be imposed to allow for expected inflation. Finally, just before the agreement was signed, the Iranian ruler insisted on another escalation of 5 cents per barrel per year—the anomalous "Shah's nickel." Thus over the five-year life of the agreement, crude oil posted prices were to increase until they reached a 1976 level some 52 percent above the level of late 1970.

Crude oil prices had in fact increased by almost 1000 percent by the time the January 1976 expiration date of these five-year agreements rolled around. What went wrong? It is clear that both companies and OPEC members were unable to forecast the future in 1971. They underestimated inflation rates, overestimated the stability of the dollar, underestimated future market price trends, and underestimated political factors strengthening Arab solidarity.

Let us begin by stressing that OPEC was interested in tax revenues per barrel and not in actual prices received per barrel. OPEC and the companies both assumed that oil prices would remain weak in actual markets, so that posted or tax reference prices would remain above actual prices. OPEC was accordingly setting posted prices at a level that it estimated would be sufficiently above realized prices that the nominal 55 percent tax rate would in actuality give OPEC members 80 percent of oil company earnings. Thus OPEC primarily intended to enrich its own members, but more at the expense of the oil companies than that of final consumers. OPEC was not averse to increases in actual crude oil prices, but neither its members nor the companies felt that market conditions would permit permanently passing forward the per-barrel tax increases represented by the OPEC levies. As shown in Figure 4.6, the early 1970s were characterized by rapid demand growth and the virtual disappearance of spare productive capacity. Demand grew because economies were expanding and oil was an energy bargain even at slightly higher prices. Supply failed to grow as rapidly as anticipated for various reasons, many of them induced by OPEC actions: clamping ceilings on production in several countries and in general increasing risks to the point where new oil investment in OPEC countries declined. The point is that OPEC continued to base taxes on tax reference prices rather than actual prices, gambling that the former would remain above the latter. As events developed, actual prices surprisingly rose above posted prices, cutting the effective tax rate and generating OPEC demands for a still further increase in the tax reference price.

The Teheran Agreement was abrogated before the ink dried. The initial excuse was the devaluation of the dollar. OPEC members quoted prices in terms of U.S. dollars, but did not foresee devaluations of the dollar. The first devaluation in December 1971 cut the gold value of the dollar by 7.9 percent, and OPEC members insisted upon an oil price increase of 8.6 percent in compensation. The second devaluation took place in February 1975 and was for 10 percent, which OPEC translated into a 12.1 percent price increase. Both increases were in violation of the original agreements, which had no provision for price escalation in response to dollar devaluation.

World price inflation proceeded at a rate greater than the 2.5 percent provided for in the Teheran-Tripoli agreements (effectively 5 percent per year, inclusive of the "Shah's nickel"), but OPEC could not agree as to when, how, and by how much an upward adjustment should be achieved. By the summer of 1973 problems of both inflation and high market prices were causing OPEC members mental anguish, and were leading to demands for a new conference to amend the five-year agreements substantially. Market prices had by that time risen above posted prices. The desired 80–20 split between governments and companies had been reduced to about 65–35. On October 8, 1973 the Persian Gulf OPEC members met with oil companies to proclaim the necessity of raising tax reference prices from $3.01 to $5.12. The motivation behind this demand was not to raise the actual cost to consumers by 70 percent, but to raise tax reference prices sufficiently above current market prices to once again give OPEC members 80 percent of company earnings. (This required a tax reference price about 40 percent above actual prices.)

The companies were disconcerted by this price demand and requested a recess in the OPEC meetings so that they could consult with their headquarters offices. During this recess the Arab OPEC members involved decided to raise the tax reference price unilaterally, disavowing any necessity for negotiation. The timing of the price hike was ideal for OPEC, since coupling the price hike with the Arab Embargo stimulated buyer fears. Small and independent buyers who had no other source of oil than that which was subject to embargo responded by panic buying behavior, which raised prices well above the OPEC level in many transactions. Demand would in any event have been high—this was during the beginning of the winter heating season when purchases for inventory build-up would be underway—but all buyers bid more frantically when there was the likelihood that during the embargo total supplies might be cut by more than 20 percent. It was also feared that unforeseeable events in the developing Arab-Israeli conflict itself might increase the scope of hostilities and reduce shipments even below the level of announced production curtailments.

OPEC members watched rising market prices with great interest, and some of them conducted auctions to see just how high a price the market would support. When prices bid in these auctions exceeded $15 (and in some cases even $20) per barrel, some OPEC rulers thought they had at last found the "true value" of oil to the importers, and were enraged that they had been selling it for so little for so long. Within OPEC ranks, Iran insisted on high prices while Saudi Arabia argued the economic case for a smaller price increase. Although there was some compromise, Iran's position tended to prevail as the official tax reference price for OPEC oil was increased to $11.65 per barrel as of January 1, 1974. This price would mean a tax payment of some $7 per barrel to OPEC rulers; but the companies could not sell the OPEC oil at the full posted price, since competition and price regulation in the importing countries usually limited company netbacks on such oil to $7.25 to $7.50 per barrel, so that only 25 cents to 50 cents per barrel was left over to cover operating costs and profits after payment of taxes.

THE WORLD OIL MARKET SINCE 1973: OPEC REACHES MATURITY

The ease with which an unexpectedly high price increase was achieved by united OPEC action made the cartel thoughtful. United action had been possible due to Arab solidarity on the embargo, and opportunistic behavior on the part of non-Arab cartel members. In effect, the cartel's first stab at monopoly pricing had achieved the transition from "milking your own concessionaires" to "gouging the importers." The critical question continually facing OPEC is whether the price selected is the appropriate long-run wealth maximizing price path or whether it is too high or too low. Unfortunately for OPEC, this is an extremely complex problem with no precise answer.[9]

Initially, the Saudis had raised the tax floor to $7.40 per barrel, but they soon began to ask whether this was enough. Due to panic buying, oil prices had settled in the $10 per barrel range, conferring large windfall profits on the concessionaires and various middlemen. Saudi Arabia in November 1974 hit upon a brilliant solution. It would simultaneously (1) reduce the tax reference price of its oil by 40 cents, (2) increase the royalty charged from 12.5 to 20 percent, and (3) increase the income tax to 85 percent. These changes had the net effect of raising the tax floor in Figure 4.7 from $7 to more than $10 per barrel. Thus, under the deceptive tax structure, a 40-cent decline in tax reference prices could actually lead to a $3 per barrel increase in tax revenues, and thereby add $3 to the price the company had to charge in order to recover its outlays. This tax increase brought tax reference prices and actual prices much closer together. Instead of a gap between $11.65 and $7.40, the range was now between $11.25 and about $10.50.

OPEC soon simplified its price and tax system still further, doing away with the complicated fictions of tax reference prices, separate income tax and royalty rates, and so on, in favor of a straight levy that the companies had to pay. The national oil company would own all the oil produced by the company, but would supply oil to its former concessionaires at a discount of perhaps 15 cents to 25 cents per barrel, as a payment for the services of these companies in finding, developing, and producing the oil, and also for marketing it through their own facilities. Other purchasers from the national oil company had to pay the full market price.

After 1973 OPEC members moved rapidly toward de facto nationalization of the properties of their companies. Participation agreements were worked out in the major exporting regions—Saudi Arabia, Kuwait, Iran, Venezuela, and so on—under the terms of which the former concessionaires received payment for their properties and remained, at least for a limited period, as service contractors or the equivalent. Currently, OPEC members typically control all oil operations within their own national jurisdictions, hiring oil companies, large and small, to provide the necessary services to produce and market their oil.

Following the upheaval of 1973–74, the period from 1975 to 1978 was one of relative tranquility in terms of price and output.[10] As shown in Figure 4.1, price increases were rather mild over this period. Likewise, OPEC production, which had been rising sharply up until 1973, flattened out but did not drop sharply. As shown in Figure 4.3, by 1976 demand had apparently recovered from the 1973–74 price increase and the recession of 1975. Nominal price increases of 10 percent were recorded in September 1975, 5 percent in December 1976, and 5 percent in June 1977. When measured relative to inflation, crude prices declined in real terms over this period. But "tranquility" cannot be used to describe the sometimes acrimonious OPEC meetings at which the members' diverse price preferences were revealed. OPEC production had declined sharply in 1975 and recovered gradually in 1976–77. Particularly in 1975, this was a period of substantial production cutbacks by the Saudis. Saudi production for the first three quarters of 7.1 million barrels per day (hereafter MMB/D) represented a 17 percent cut, compared to the same period in 1974. At the same time that the Saudis were making unprecedented production cutbacks, the Iraqis increased production significantly. Also, there was widespread price discounting by Abu Dhabi, Libya, Iraq, Algeria, and Ecuador. Interestingly, in the face of these conditions, there was considerable disagreement over the extent of price "increase" that was preferred.

As the September 1975 meeting approached, Saudi Arabia favored a price freeze or "small increase" to help "assist the emerging signs of recovery" from the worldwide recession. In contrast, the Shah of Iran was among the more hawkish, calling for a 35 percent price increase. At the Vienna meeting, Sheik Yamani of Saudi Arabia proposed a 5 percent increase while Iran insisted on a 15 percent increase. Yamani warned that if the majority backed the Iranian plan, Saudi Arabia would freeze prices and let production rise to the limits of its capacity. Ultimately, a compromise of a 10 percent increase was reached.

The December 1976 OPEC meeting in Doha was even more entertaining. In the fall of 1976 there was a general expectation that oil prices would rise substantially. Industrial activity was up sharply, translating into rising OPEC demand (30.5 MMB/D). Furthermore, the persistence of U.S. inflation—then at 11 percent—called for a sizeable increase just to maintain a constant real oil price. Iraq, Qatar, and Venezuela called for a 25 percent increase; the Shah preferred a "very reasonable" 15 percent. Curiously, the Saudis proposed a zero increase. One explanation for their actions is that they were eager to gain favor with the newly elected President of the U.S., Jimmy Carter. The Doha meeting was filled with tension; Yamani left in the midst of the session, flying to Jiddah for consultations with Crown Prince Fahd. Yamani returned and offered to raise the price by 5 percent, which the other members rejected, choosing instead to raise it by 10 percent. Yamani refused to negotiate further, lifted the 8.5 MMB/D production ceiling, and announced that production would soon reach the 11.8 MMB/D maximum capacity. While Saudi production never reached its limit, Iran's and Iraq's exports were reduced sharply by 2.1 MMB/D and .7 MMB/D, respectively. Finally, in June 1977, the Saudis agreed to raise their price another 5 percent to reunify OPEC.

The Doha price split ushered in a brief period of conciliation. In the December 1977 meeting in Caracas, both the Saudis and the Iranians supported a price freeze. Political observers note that the price freeze coincided with the U.S. approval of the sale of F-15 fighter planes to Saudi Arabia and a separate arms package for the Shah of Iran.

By March 1978, OPEC countries were well aware that oil consumption had eclipsed the levels set in 1973, that economic expansion in the West was being sustained, and furthermore that persistent inflation was lowering the real price of oil by about 10 percent per year. The result was a 14.5 percent increase for the year, to take effect immediately.

Later in 1978, the "second oil crisis" began to unfold. While most newspaper accounts link the crisis to the Iranian Revolution, the precipitating event and the actions that sustained the panic buying came from the opposite side of the Persian Gulf. In September 1978, political unrest surfaced in Iran, which soon spread to Iran's oil production. Iranian production dropped from 6 MMB/D in September to 2.4 MMB/D by December 1978. The reduction in Iranian production came at a time when OPEC was producing at high historical levels, with only limited spare capacity (see Figure 4.3). Initially, the Saudis with 11.8 MMB/D capacity stepped in to supply an appreciable portion of the Iranian shortfall. Saudi production rose from 8.4 MMB/D in September to 10.4 MMB/D in December. Other countries such as Nigeria, Venezuela, and Iraq upped production by an additional .5 MMB/D. In effect, the bulk of the Iranian production shortfall had been made up by the other cartel members, so that prices should have increased only moderately.

On January 20, 1979, a day to remember, Saudi authorities suddenly imposed a January production ceiling of 9.5 MMB/D. To meet that production ceiling, production was cut from 10.4 to 8 MMB/D for the remaining 10 days of January. The effect was predictable. Spot prices of crude (crude sold in single cargo lots) soared, jumping from $18.50 in January to $27.38 in mid-February. Spot prices continued to rise in March as Saudi Arabia cut its output from 9.5 MMB/D to 8.5 MMB/D. By July 1979, when the Saudis raised output back to 9.5 MMB/D, spot prices had effectively doubled. Rather than raising production sufficiently to force the spot price down to the official Saudi marker price, the Saudis adjusted their official price upward. This continued leapfrogging of prices created expectations of ever-increasing prices. Whereas rising prices normally reduce overall consumption, demand remained strong (see Figure 4.3). Much of the increase in demand came from inventory speculation motives. As long as speculators expected still higher prices in the future, oil purchases for inventory accumulation at current levels were perceived as good investments.

The remainder of 1979 and 1980 were characterized by a pattern of rising spot prices followed by upward adjustments in the official prices. No longer were the official prices of the various OPEC countries closely tied to the official Saudi price. The sizeable differences that existed between spot prices and the official Saudi price created incentives for individual OPEC countries to price their crude at or near the spot price. Pricing over this period clearly indicates why Adelman and others describe OPEC as a "loose" cartel.[11]

On the eve of the Iran-Iraq War in the fall of 1980, the official Saudi price stood at $30 per barrel. Iranian production had "recovered" to about one-fourth of its prerevolutionary levels and Iraqi production stood at 3 MMB/D. Would the loss of Iraqi production and what remained of Iranian production cause prices to double yet once again? By the fall of 1980, conditions had changed dramatically from two years earlier. As shown in Figure 4.3, oil demand was beginning to drop sharply. Oil production from noncommunist areas responded to the drop in demand, falling from the record level of 48.9 MMB/D in 1979 to 45.6 MMB/D in 1980. Together with rising production from non-OPEC areas, this had the effect of substantially reducing OPEC's potential market. OPEC production in 1980 fell to a surprisingly low level—26.9 MMB/D in contrast to the 1979 level of 30.9 MMB/D. Thus even though Iraqi production declined by 2.7 MMB/D and Iranian production dropped another .6 MMB/D, the reduction in output by these two producers was no doubt welcomed by other OPEC producers. The spot price reached $43 per barrel in November 1980, but declined sharply thereafter.

Again the question facing the cartel was what the appropriate wealth-maximizing price should be. The tremendous uncertainties about the long-run elasticities of demand and non-OPEC supply meant there was no neat solution,[11] and OPEC was once again confronted with doubts over whether it had gone too far. The Saudis correctly perceived that with oil consumption dropping, a sizeable price increase would not be sustainable. But other OPEC members were not as realistic. In November 1981, a compromise was reached, and with the Saudis raising production and threatening further production increases, the official Saudi price was raised from \$32 to \$34 per barrel. In return, other OPEC countries agreed to bring their prices down into line with the new Saudi price.

The period from 1981 through 1984 provided OPEC with its first major test. Cartel cohesion was rather simple to attain in the period 1973–80, with prices having increased tenfold and OPEC production holding relatively stable. In such a situation, everyone is well aware of the benefits of collusion and intercountry rivalries tend to be muted. But the period 1981–84 brought home to OPEC the truth behind the laws of demand and supply. Simply put, the law of demand would hold that as a consequence of the phenomenal rise in the price of oil during the 1970s, world consumption of oil would decrease, particularly after consumers were given sufficient time to adjust to the higher prices. The law of supply would suggest that competitive suppliers, represented by the non-OPEC countries, would after some period expand production in response to higher prices. The predictions of the economic model in Figure 4.8 are obvious. The effects of OPEC raising the price from P^0 to P' are clearcut. World oil demand (D_{WORLD}) will decrease from Q^0 to Q'. Non-OPEC supply (analogous to the competitive fringe producers) responds by increasing non-OPEC production from Q_{NO}^0 to Q_{NO}'. The difference between the world demand and non-OPEC supply is the demand curve facing OPEC. Clearly, at higher prices OPEC's volumes are cut from $Q^0 - Q_{NO}^0$ to $Q' - Q_{NO}'$.

The consumption and non-OPEC production statistics in Figure 4.3 confirm the relevance of these simple economic principles. But why did the sharp decline in consumption wait until the 1980s to begin? Recall from the principles of economics the distinction between the short-run and long-run demand schedules. Oil demand is much more elastic in the long run than in the short run, because in the short run we were captives to a stock of energy using equipment that was designed for a world of cheap energy. Ultimately, that capital stock is replaced by one designed for today's energy prices and the effects of higher prices are fully realized. The early and mid-1980s were a period in which new, more energy-efficient autos, air conditioners, heaters, and factory equipment replaced their old, less energy-efficient counterparts. Also, with time, it becomes feasible to substitute other energy forms for oil.

The short-run/long-run explanation is also important in explaining the rise in non-OPEC production over this period. Again, oil fields cannot be discovered and brought into production instantaneously. Non-

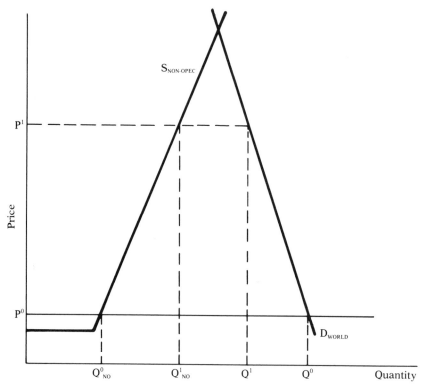

FIGURE 4.8 Determination of OPEC's production.

OPEC production began increasing in 1977, and has expanded steadily since.

By 1982, the effect of declining consumption coupled with rising non-OPEC production left OPEC producing less oil than its non-OPEC counterparts. For 1983, OPEC production averaged 17.6 MMB/D—a sharp contrast to the 30.9 MMB/D recorded in 1979. As a share of the noncommunist world's oil production, OPEC's market share had fallen to 46 percent as opposed to 68 percent in 1974.

How did this loose confederation of countries weather this first great test of cartel stability? Suddenly, with oil revenues declining sharply, OPEC countries had strong incentives to resist further production decreases. But if most OPEC countries were unwilling to absorb any of the reduction in production necessary to stabilize prices, Saudi Arabia and other key producers would have to sustain the brunt of the cutback. It is precisely in situations such as these that cartel coordination dissolves and rampant cheating ensues. Fears such as these prompted Iran's oil minister in August 1981 to propose setting up a formal cartel agency to market OPEC's oil collectively. But OPEC nations have traditionally eschewed any production controls, viewing their production decisions as sovereign national matters. By the following March (1982), conditions had necessitated a reevaluation. A market-sharing formula was approved. The plan stipulated a total OPEC production limit of 17.5 MMB/D as well as individual country limits. Adherence to these limits was apparently less than scrupulous, since by July 1982, reports indicated that both Nigeria and Libya were producing beyond their assigned limits.

Conditions deteriorated further as OPEC demand continued to drop. In the first quarter of 1983, Saudi production averaged less than 4 MMB/D. The spot price of oil had fallen below $30 despite an official Saudi price of $34. In March 1983, Saudi Arabia, with the support of Kuwait, Qatar, and the United Arab Emirates, lowered the official price of Saudi crude to $29 per barrel. This action sent a clear message to cheaters. The Saudis and others key producers would not maintain an official price by cutting production only to let other producers expand production and undersell the Saudi price. Since then, OPEC meetings have centered attention on setting total production and individual country quotas. One difficulty with this approach is that even if the quotas are honored, OPEC's production target may not equal market demand, causing prices to fluctuate sharply, upward or downward. Consequently, Sheik Yamani of Saudi Arabia emphasizes that Saudi Arabia is not constrained by its quota; rather, it is the "swing producer." Presumably this means that Saudi Arabia feels free to increase or decrease its production to equalize OPEC production and market demand at the current market price.

At this time, OPEC prices and production appear to have stabilized. If we can assume that higher oil prices have largely worked their way through the economic system, then rising economic activity will shift the world oil demand schedule in Figure 4.8 outward. It is easy to verify that OPEC will be the prime gainer. Thus the current prognosis seems to be that OPEC has survived its first major test, although it is by no means a certainty. But clearly the OPEC of the mid-1980s does not compare in power to the OPEC of the 1970s. What are the prospects for the future of OPEC? Will OPEC regain its strength and muscle in the late 1980s or 1990s? Or will OPEC continue to exist, but only in a weakened state? Or will OPEC collapse altogether? To attempt to answer these questions, we need an analytical framework within which to analyze the past and predict the future.

ANALYSIS OF OPEC BEHAVIOR

A common complaint of students in economic theory courses is that the material lacks "relevance." Admittedly the absence of applications in such courses may make microeconomic theory appear highly abstract. However, appearance is not necessarily reality. This section illustrates the value of theoretical models in assessing the monopoly power and the stability of OPEC.

While OPEC is a cartel, every cartel has its own unique characteristics. Consequently, shopping for theoretical models that fit OPEC is not a simple matter of reaching into the rack labeled "cartel models" and pulling the right one down. But perhaps the best way to learn this is for you, the reader, to discover it for yourself. Imagine yourself entering an economics department store and proceeding to the basement, where all models of monopoly are located (perfect competition is located on the top floor). After reaching the suit rack labelled "cartel models," you proceed to look at the following three standard cartel models: (1) the multiplant monopoly model, (2) the market-sharing cartel, and (3) the dominant firm/price leadership model. Despite some similarities to OPEC, none of these models offers an appropriate fit to anything as unique and important as OPEC. Our fourth model offers an attempt by your tailors, Professors Griffin and Steele, as they try their hands at developing a customized model for OPEC. While this hybrid model is not a perfect fit, we hope that it provides a useful basis with which to view the past and analyze the future.

Multiplant Monopoly—The Joint Profit-Maximizing Ideal

The simplest theoretical model of a cartel is equivalent to that which describes the behavior of a monopolist operating a number of plants. Rather than permitting each cartel member to own its own plant and make independent price and output decisions, this model assumes the cartel members own shares in the total profits of the cartel and have turned over the initiative for price and output decisions to the main cartel authority. Thus the industry behaves as a multiplant monopoly. Under this form of organization the cartel authority extracts the maximum possible monopoly profits from buyers and avoids the defects usually fatal to real-world cartels.

First, let us show that this type of cartel extracts the full monopoly profit. For simplicity, Figure 4.9 depicts a cartel with three plants. Each plant has a different marginal cost curve (MC_1, MC_2, MC_3). The determination of total cartel output and its division among the various plants is in fact quite simple. The horizontal summation of the marginal cost curves (MC^*) shows the minimum cost of producing any given output level by using the lowest cost facilities first, regardless of the identity of the firm or plant in which production occurs. Given the market demand curve *(D)* for the cartel's product, the cartel authority calculates the marginal revenue schedule (MR) and equates it to the summed marginal cost schedule (MC^*). In Figure 4.9(d), the intersection of marginal cost (MC^*) and marginal revenue (MR) shows the cartel's profit-maximizing output level (Q_m). Corresponding to this output

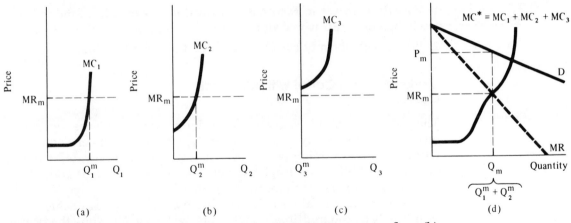

FIGURE 4.9 The multiplant monopoly cartel model. (a) Lowest cost firm. (b) Higher cost firm. (c) Highest cost firm. (d) Total industry.

is the monopoly price P_m. The cartel authority then determines individual firm production by allowing each plant to produce at that output at which the firm's own marginal cost is equal to cartel marginal revenue. In this case, plant 3 is not utilized due to its high marginal cost of production. Plants 1 and 2 produce Q_1^m and Q_2^m, respectively. This solution guarantees the maximum cartel profit, as production takes place only in the lowest-cost plants and marginal cost is equal to marginal revenue in each plant.

An important attribute of this model is the absence of disputes among the cartel members on the basis of the optimal price and output for each plant. Central determination of price and output by the cartel authority guarantees maximum profits, and each member's profits are a predetermined fraction of total cartel profits. Moreover, since individual cartel members do not own the plants separately, they are unconcerned as to the source of production. It should be noted that such arrangements were the goal that the notorious "trusts" sought to achieve in the nineteenth century in the United States. Under existing antitrust laws such practices are now illegal.

The multiplant monopoly type of cartel is the perfect cartel. The perfect cartel maximizes the joint profits of its members and is completely insulated from internal cheating tendencies. Members may disagree as to the cartel's assignment of profit shares, but there is no conflict as to total output and the plants from which output is produced. The picture of OPEC deviates greatly from this ideal. Each OPEC country maintains control over its own production. Furthermore, even side payments to high-cost producers from low-cost producers to induce the former to reduce their production are impractical because they are so costly to negotiate and enforce.

1. For OPEC to act in accordance with this model, what fundamental change in OPEC would have to occur? What factors prevent it?

2. Why is this form of cartel likely to be the most durable?

Market-Sharing Cartel with Identical-Cost Firms

The previous example suggests that if individual plants are separately owned, cartel stability is jeopardized. Since each member country in OPEC retains sovereign power over its own production rate, it might appear that OPEC is a fragile cartel. The purpose of this model is to show that if sellers (a) share markets on a predetermined basis and (b) have similar marginal cost curves, this type of cartel can achieve the same goals as the multiplant monopoly cartel model. Thus the degree of similarity of cost structures combined with the willingness to share markets may prove quite critical.

Figure 4.10 illustrates the case of a three-member cartel with identical cost structures, which has agreed to share markets on a basis of market shares of 40, 40, and 20 percent, respectively. Given the total market demand schedule in Figure 4.10(d), the demand curve facing the first member in Figure 4.10(a) is calculated by taking 40 percent of OPEC demand at every price level. The demand schedules for the second and third members are determined in the same way. Since each member acts independently to maximize its own profits, it equates marginal cost (MC_i) with marginal revenue (MR_i). As shown graphically in Figure 4.10(d), the members choose prices P_1, P_2, and P_3, which curiously enough are all equal. All members desire the same price! By visual inspection it is clear that the sum of desired outputs ($Q_1{}^m + Q_2{}^m + Q_3{}^m$) equals the monopoly output Q_m in Figure 4.10(d). Thus, each member desires the same price, and production is ade-

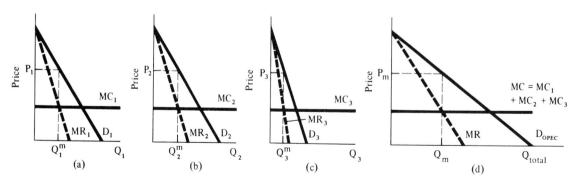

FIGURE 4.10 Market-sharing cartel with identical costs. (a) Member 1 with 40 percent. (b) Member 2 with 40 percent. (c) Member 3 with 20 percent. (d) Total cartel.

quate to clear the market at that price. Moreover this result, based on independent profit maximization by each cartel member, leads to the same profit-maximizing result as if the cartel operated under the multiplant scenario.

Is this merely fortuitous, or must this always be true? Let us first show that the desired price of any cartel member must be the same as for the multiplant cartel authority. Recall that profit maximization occurs when marginal cost equals marginal revenue. Since the long-run marginal costs are the same for all producers, it follows that marginal revenues must be equal:

$$(4.2) \qquad\qquad MR_1 = MR_m$$

Now recall from your principles course in economics the relationship between price, marginal revenue, and the price elasticity of demand ($E_d \geq 0$):

$$(4.3) \qquad\qquad MR = P\left(1 - \frac{1}{E_d}\right)$$

If, for example, the elasticity of demand is 2, the price will be twice marginal revenue. At unitary elasticity, marginal revenue is zero. Substituting equation (4.3) into equation (4.2), we obtain:

$$(4.4) \qquad\qquad P_1\left(1 - \frac{1}{E_{d_1}}\right) = P_m\left(1 - \frac{1}{E_{d_m}}\right)$$

Now in order for each producer to prefer the same price, (i.e., $P_1 = P_m$), it is clear that at the same price the elasticities would have to be identical ($E_{d_1} = E_{d_m}$). Now let us prove that at the same price we do find $E_{d_1} = E_{d_m}$.

$$(4.5) \quad E_{d_1} \equiv -\frac{\Delta Q_1}{\Delta P}\frac{P}{Q_1} = -.4\frac{\Delta Q_m}{\Delta P}\frac{P}{.4Q_m} = -\frac{\Delta Q_m}{\Delta P}\frac{P}{Q_m} \equiv E_{d_m}$$

Notice that if member 1 has 40 percent of OPEC's market, the reciprocal of the slope of its demand curve will be 40 percent of that of the market demand schedule—that is:

$$(4.6) \qquad\qquad \frac{\Delta Q_1}{\Delta P} = 0.4\frac{\Delta Q_m}{\Delta P}$$

Also, from the fact that Q_1 is 40 percent of Q_m it follows that the equality in equation (4.5) holds for all producers. Thus if the price elasticities are the same, so also must the prices in equation (4.4) be identical.

Consequently, the prices independently chosen by the cartel members to maximize individual profits also maximize joint profits because they correspond to the monopolist's profit-maximizing price. It should also be clear that the sum of cartel output must also equal Q_m since by definition $Q_1 = 0.4Q_m$, $Q_2 = 0.4Q_m$, and $Q_3 = 0.2Q_m$.

In summary, if cartel members have identical long-run marginal cost schedules and agree upon predetermined market shares, the monopoly result will be forthcoming. The assumption of substantially identical costs is not too unrealistic for most OPEC cartel members. Marginal production costs in the Middle East range from perhaps 15 cents to 35 cents per barrel. Outside the Persian Gulf area, OPEC members in Venezuela and Indonesia have considerably higher costs—perhaps $1.00 to $2.00 per barrel. Nevertheless, compared to market prices, these differences in costs are not large, especially among the dominant Middle East producers.

In addition, the market shares of OPEC members exhibit appreciable (but by no means complete) stability. As shown in Table 4.3, the output from countries such as Kuwait, United Arab Emirates, Libya, Nigeria, and Indonesia are fairly constant percentages of total OPEC production. After allowance for the Iranian Revolution in 1978–79 and the Iran-Iraq War, the declining market share of Iran and Iraq are understandable. Likewise, the increase in Saudi production in 1980–82 can be directly linked to declining Iranian and Iraqi production. Let us turn to the question of why one might or might not expect stability of market shares.

The market-sharing monopoly model assumes that all members accept their given market shares and make no attempt to increase them. By assumption, no one cheats by attempting to gain a higher market share. This assumption is essential for this particular model. But now let us consider the advantages of being a cheater. What would happen if one cartel member could expand output beyond its assigned market share while all other members refrained from changing their outputs?

Consider the equilibrium at price P_m in Figure 4.10. Suppose the first cartel member is able to sell additional oil in excess of $Q_1{}^m$ while the other members maintain output at $Q_2{}^m$ and $Q_3{}^m$, respectively. What is the elasticity of demand that the first member faces? Assuming the market elasticity of demand (E_d) is 2.0, is it true that the cheater elasticity of demand is also 2.0 as in equation (4.5)? If so, the implication of equation (4.5) is that the first member would not want to expand output beyond $Q_1{}^m$. But the elasticity of demand facing the first member (assuming he cheats) is in fact 5.0, since the demand curve he encounters is the market demand curve for prices below P_m—that is:

$$(4.7) \qquad E_{d_1} = -\frac{\Delta Q_1}{\Delta P}\frac{P_m}{Q_1} = -\frac{\Delta Q}{\Delta P}\frac{P_m}{.4Q_m} = 2.5E_{d_m} = 5.0$$

TABLE 4.3 Percentage Market Shares of OPEC Members, 1973–83

	1973	1974	1975	1976	1977	1978	1979	1980	1981	1982	1983
Saudi Arabia	23.9	26.8	25.1	27.1	28.4	26.9	29.8	36.8	43.6	35.0	28.9
Kuwait	9.5	8.1	7.4	6.8	6.1	6.9	7.8	6.2	5.0	4.5	6.1
United Arab Emirates	4.8	5.3	5.9	6.1	6.2	5.9	5.8	6.4	6.7	6.6	6.5
Iran	18.4	19.1	19.0	18.5	17.5	17.0	9.5	6.2	5.8	10.6	13.8
Iraq	6.4	6.2	8.0	6.8	6.1	8.3	10.8	9.3	4.0	5.0	5.7
Libya	6.9	4.8	5.2	6.1	6.4	6.4	6.5	6.6	5.0	6.6	6.1
Nigeria	6.4	7.2	6.3	6.5	6.5	6.1	7.2	7.6	6.4	7.0	7.1
Venezuela	10.6	9.4	8.3	7.2	6.9	7.0	7.4	8.1	9.3	10.3	10.2
Indonesia	4.2	4.4	4.6	4.7	5.2	5.0	5.0	5.9	7.1	7.3	7.9
Other	8.9	8.7	10.2	10.2	10.7	10.5	10.2	6.9	7.1	7.5	7.7

SOURCE: U.S. Monthly Energy Review.

If indeed the first member could cheat by selling additional oil while the others held their output fixed ($\Delta Q_1 = \Delta Q$), the first member could greatly expand his profits by increasing production, since his marginal revenue would then be greater than his marginal costs. The member with only 20 percent of the market will find that his incentive to cheat is even greater, since he would face a demand curve with an elasticity of 10. The third member's marginal revenue would thus lie far above its marginal cost at the predetermined output of Q_3^m. The smaller the member's market share, the greater will be the profits from successful cheating.

This leads us to the question: Under what conditions will cheating on predetermined market share occur? Game theory, originated by Professors Von Neumann and Morgenstern, does not give a definite answer, but it does provide valuable clues. Consider the familiar example of the prisoner's dilemma. Smith and McAlpin, two criminal conspirators, have both been arrested on a minor charge and there is sufficient evidence to convict both of them for this crime. The prosecutor knows, however, that they are guilty of far more serious crimes for which convictions are impossible unless confessions are obtained. Table 4.4 shows a payoff matrix indicating the number of years in prison Smith and McAlpin will receive, depending upon whether or not a confession is obtained for the more serious crime.

Table 4.4 indicates that if neither confesses to the more serious crime, each will be sentenced to 5 years for the lesser crime. However, should Smith confess and McAlpin fail to confess, Smith could receive clemency and avoid imprisonment by testifying against McAlpin, while McAlpin would then receive 20 years in jail. Conversely, if McAlpin confesses and Smith does not, Smith receives 20 years and McAlpin goes free. If both confess, both would serve 15 years.

What will be the outcome? The answer is not at all obvious, since it depends upon the variety of considerations.[12] These include mutuality of interests, communications, and retaliatory lags. The "mutuality of interests" depends upon the prospects for future association. If the two criminals are long-time confederates and plan to conspire in the future, both may decide not to confess, since they can resume their

TABLE 4.4 Game Theory Payoff Matrix (Years in Prison)

Smith's Strategies	McAlpin's Strategies	
	Don't Confess	Confess
Don't Confess	5, 5	20, 0
Confess	0, 20	15, 15

activities together after 5 years. If they have no such record of past association and future plans, they may decide differently.

A second factor, communications, emphasizes the importance of the two prisoners being able to assure each other than neither will confess. If the two were isolated, Smith, having no assurance of McAlpin's intentions, might decide to confess.

On the other hand, if there is communication and the retaliatory lag is short—that is, if after Smith begins to confess, McAlpin can immediately pursue the same course—there is little incentive for either to confess. Thus retaliatory lags when coupled with the possibility of communications become important factors in determining the outcome.

What is the relevance of this exercise to explain whether a cartel member will cheat to increase its market share? First, the actual values of the payoff matrix are important. If all parties share markets, the payoff is the division of monopoly profits as described in Figure 4.10. The payoff for noncheaters is obviously a reduction in profits relative to a no-cheating situation. If all cheat, the payoff is the loss of all monopoly profits and the reduction of earnings to a merely competitive level. This outcome is analogous to the situation in which both criminals confess. In sum, the set of relative differences in the payoff matrix is an important factor in assessing the costs and benefits of cheating. In addition, mutuality of interests manifests itself in several ways. Feelings of Arab political solidarity no doubt affect behavior among Arab members of OPEC. Members with huge reserves have quite similar interests in the longevity of the cartel, while other members with small reserves may be unconcerned about cartel stability beyond a horizon of perhaps 10 to 15 years, after which their reserves will be substantially depleted. For example, Table 4.5 ranks the OPEC producers by reserves. By taking 1983 production rates as a benchmark, one can divide production into reserves and show the number of years the country could theoretically produce at the 1983 production rate. The years of production at the 1983 rate (or the reserves to production ratio) roughly indicates the period over which the country is likely to remain an important oil producer. Table 4.5 emphasizes the relative importance in terms of reserves of the Persian Gulf members of OPEC vis-à-vis other OPEC producers. Furthermore, the life expectancies of OPEC producers as measured by years of production at 1983 production rates differ greatly, suggesting that those with lower reserves and fewer years of production are more likely to behave independently than are the largest six or seven producers.

Communications and retaliatory lags are also important. Are communications adequate to detect cheating? Is price cutting easily detected? And once cheating is identified, can retaliatory action be taken quickly? Since the retaliation takes place in the form of a price cut to

TABLE 4.5 Characteristics of OPEC Countries Ranked by Importance of Reserves

Country	Reserves (10^9 bbls)	1983 Production (10^9 bbls)	Years of Production at 1983 Rate
Persian Gulf Producers			
Saudi Arabia	166.0	1.88	88
Kuwait	63.9	.33	194
Iran	51.0	.95	54
Iraq	43.0	.33	130
United Arab Emirates	32.2	.41	79
Non-Persian Producers			
Venezuela	24.9	.65	38
Libya	21.3	.37	57
Nigeria	16.6	.45	37
Algeria	9.2	.25	37
Indonesia	9.1	.47	19
Qatar	3.3	.10	33
Ecuador	1.7	.09	19
Gabon	.5	.06	9

SOURCE: "World Oil at a Glance," The Oil and Gas Journal, Vol. 83, No. 52 December 26, 1983.

match the cheater's price, the retaliatory lag is very short. The more serious question is whether communications channels enable the detection of cheating. It would be logical for OPEC to devote considerable resources to providing mechanisms for the detection of cheating and to improvise informal ways of bringing pressure to bear on such cheaters. Furthermore, with most sales to oil companies being public knowledge, the incentive to cheat is substantially reduced.

The market-sharing cartel model takes a step away from the monolithic cartel assumed by the multiplant monopoly model. It recognizes differences in incentives among OPEC countries to abide by predetermined market shares, but how exactly are prices determined? The textbook answer is that since all producers face identical costs and share common perceptions about the elasticity of demand facing each producer, they select price corresponding to the output where marginal costs equal marginal revenue. Upon closer examination, one recognizes that the market elasticity of demand is not known precisely. Different producers may have different estimates. Furthermore, even if the price elasticity were known exactly, some producers with limited reserves would opt for using the short-run price elasticity, while those with huge resource bases would want to utilize the long-run price elasticity. In sum, something more must be added to solve the problem of what will be the OPEC price.

1. Using equation (4.4), show that the third cartel member, with a 20 percent market share, also desires the same monopoly price P_m.

2. Suppose the second cartel member had long-run marginal production costs twice as high as those of other members. What price and output would it prefer? In view of the above discussion of Venezuelan and Indonesian costs, does this help explain why they usually favor high prices?

3. What combinations of OPEC countries are likely to have particularly strong or weak mutuality of interests? Be careful to distinguish between those based on economic and political similarities.

4. Does the rather homogeneous nature of oil compared to, for example, autos, make the cartel more or less stable? Does the fact that competitive responses are limited entirely to price variation facilitate or weaken the tendency to cheat?

The Dominant Firm Price Leadership Model

A shortcoming of the market-sharing models is that the output decisions and corresponding prices come out of the model as if all members choose this outcome with everyone sharing the total OPEC market on a predetermined basis. Such assumptions do not do justice to differences among OPEC members and the critical role of Saudi Arabia in pricing decisions. Evidence from OPEC meetings on oil pricing attests to this fact. At the semiannual sessions at which OPEC has fixed world oil prices since 1974, the Saudi marker crude price is the benchmark crude price around which other producers set their prices. As the earlier discussion emphasizes, the Saudis are clearly the most important producer and play a key role in pricing. The reason is obvious, since with substantial reserve capacity, Saudi Arabia can prevent prices from rising by simply raising its production. Conversely, the Saudis can prevent prices from falling, providing they are willing to substantially reduce their production as they did in 1982.

Let us begin by looking at the dominant firm model as it is usually portrayed in economics textbooks. The typical presumption is that all producers other than the dominant producer behave as competitive fringe producers. Thus other OPEC producers are really no different in behavior than non-OPEC producers. This model assumes that the dominant firm sets a price and all other producers expand their production to the output level where that price equals their marginal cost. The dominant firm then meets the remaining demand by producing enough oil to satisfy market demand. Figure 4.11 depicts the dominant firm model. Assuming that non-OPEC supply has already been subtracted from world demand, we begin with the demand schedule facing OPEC. If OPEC countries other than Saudi Arabia behave as

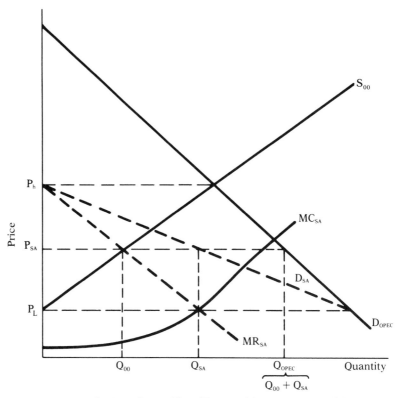

FIGURE 4.11 The Dominant Firm/Competitive Fringe Model.

competitive fringe producers, they will exhibit an upward sloping supply schedule (S_{OO}) that is identical to the sum of their marginal cost
curves.

The problem of deriving the Saudi's demand schedule is simple.
Should the Saudis select a price of P_h, other OPEC countries would
expand production to equal total OPEC demand and the Saudis would
sell nothing. Conversely, at price P_L, the price is so low that even other
OPEC countries cease producing, leaving the whole market to the Saudis. At any price between P_L and P_h, Saudi demand is the horizontal
difference between total OPEC demand (D_{OPEC}) and production by
other OPEC countries (S_{OO}). The dashed line describes the Saudi demand schedule (D_{SA}). It is easy to see that at any price, the Saudis are
the residual seller. Other OPEC countries produce their desired
amounts, leaving the remaining demand to be satisfied by the Saudis.

But how do the Saudis select a price? Obviously, by selecting the
price that corresponds to the output level where the Saudis' marginal
cost (MC_{SA}) equals their marginal revenue (MR_{SA}), so that their profits

are maximized. At Q_{SA}, marginal revenue equals marginal cost and the preferred price must be P_{SA}.

This model seems straightforward enough. The knotty problem of price determination in the market-sharing model is solved, and surely the notion of Saudi Arabia as the dominant producer is appealing. Furthermore, this "cartel" model avoids any problems with intercountry rivalries since, according to this model, Saudi Arabia is the cartel. Other OPEC members may attend meetings in Vienna, Geneva, and Caracas, but they are free riders, behaving no differently than the non-OPEC oil producers. Consequently, this model sweeps away all the intriguing game theoretic aspects as to the conditions under which OPEC members will cheat. But is this simplification legitimate?

At least four pieces of evidence say categorically "no." First, the pattern of considerable stability in market shares among OPEC members suggests that other OPEC producers are exercising output restraint. Second, in 1983 when OPEC production shrank dramatically to 17.6 MMB/D, the output cut was not borne entirely by Saudi Arabia. Virtually all OPEC countries had reduced production. Third, based on years of production at 1983 rates as shown in Table 4.5, the reserve base of most all OPEC countries is sufficient to justify much higher production rates. Finally, regression analysis of each individual OPEC country's production levels on the other OPEC countries' production rates shows a definite positive correlation. That is, OPEC countries tend to raise and lower production jointly. In contrast, non-OPEC countries' production decisions showed no such tendency.[13] Perhaps it is possible to combine the best aspects of the dominant firm model and the market-sharing model.

The Hybrid Model

It should not be surprising that the previous three cartel models (the multiplant monopoly, the market-sharing cartel, and the dominant firm model) do not exactly fit OPEC. After all, every cartel is unique. Why would we expect a standard model to fit anything as extraordinary as OPEC? The first model we selected, the multiplant monopoly, did not fit at all. It just looked atrocious on OPEC. The market-sharing cartel model fit much better, but the price wasn't quite right, nor was Saudi Arabia adequately attired. And then there was the dominant firm model—the price was right but the "competitive fringe" tailoring for countries other than Saudi Arabia was unbecoming. Let us try our own hand at designing a model that better fits OPEC, realizing that a perfect fit is impossible.

As our point of departure, we wish to begin with the dominant firm model in Figure 4.11. Whereas in the dominant firm model OPEC consists of two groups, Saudi Arabia and other OPEC countries, our approach is to distinguish three groups—the cartel core, the price maximizers, and the output maximizers. The cartel core replaces Saudi Arabia as the dominant firm, but its behavior is similar. The cartel core consists of those OPEC members with vast oil reserves, relatively small populations, and more flexible economic development plans such that the relatively low production rates necessary to sustain oil prices at or above monopoly levels are both feasible and desirable. The cartel core is assumed to consist of Saudi Arabia, Kuwait, Qatar, the United Arab Emirates, and Libya. As a group, these countries share markets, behaving as the dominant firm in Figure 4.11. As a group, the cartel core generally prefers to maintain prices during periods of slack demand for OPEC oil by carrying more excess capacity. Their preferences are for relatively lower prices than those preferred by other OPEC members, since, among other reasons, they stand to lose more in the long run due to their large reserves.

For simplicity, we tend to group the remaining OPEC countries as either price maximizers or output maximizers. Like the supply schedule in the dominant firm model, these two OPEC groups form a combined supply schedule which, when subtracted from OPEC demand (D_{OPEC}), gives the demand schedule facing the cartel core. The price maximizers are assumed to consist of Algeria, Iran, and Venezuela. These members have relatively large populations and considerable potential for economic development; but, unlike other OPEC members, their reserves are not high relative to current production rates (as in the cartel core), nor do they appear to be capable of significant expansion in the future (as in the case of the output maximizers). While the price maximizers tend to produce close to full capacity, they are willing to cut production, accepting a smaller market share to achieve higher prices. As shown in Figure 4.12a, the price maximizers' supply schedule, S_{pm}, shows declining production as prices rise above the equilibrium price, P_{OPEC}. An interesting feature of the price maximizers' supply schedule, S_{pm}, is that it is hyperbolic in shape, guaranteeing a constant level of oil revenues at any price/quantity combination. While facing certain pressures to generate oil revenues for domestic economic development, these countries recognize their limited oil reserves and are quite willing to cut production in proportion to any price increase. Thus the market shares of the price maximizers are likely to fall as price increases.

The output maximizers are assumed to behave essentially as competitive producers, selecting that output which equates price to marginal costs. Therefore, the supply schedule for the output maximizers, S_{om}, rises with output, being merely the sum of marginal costs for these token members of the cartel. While they maintain membership in OPEC, the incentives to behave independently are overpowering for these producers. As we shall see later, the identity of these countries matches closely the predicted conditions under which independent be-

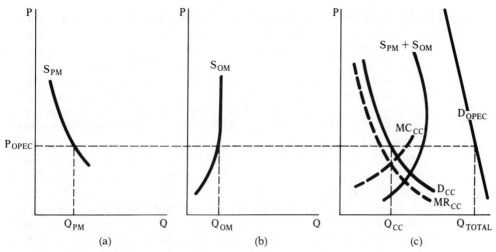

FIGURE 4.12 The hybrid cartel model. (a) Price maximizers. (b) Output maximizers. (c) Combined market.

havior would be expected: (1) the potential to expand production appreciably, (2) relatively small current market shares, and (3) strong internal development pressures.

The sum of the supply responses of the price maximizers (in Figure 4.12a) and the output maximizers (in Figure 4.12b) yields $S_{pm} + S_{om}$ in Figure 4.12c. The difference between OPEC demand and the supply response of the price and output maximizers ($S_{pm} + S_{om}$) yields the cartel core's demand schedule (D_{cc}). The selection of the OPEC price (P_{OPEC}) is then made in an analogous manner to the dominant firm's calculation in Figure 4.11. The cartel core seeks to set a price corresponding to the output level where marginal revenue equals marginal cost. That price corresponds with the cartel core's output of Q_{cc}. Likewise, the price P_{OPEC} brings forth the production of Q_{om} by the price maximizers and Q_{om} by the output maximizers.

The advantage of this model over other earlier contenders is that it recognizes the importance of a cartel core that acts as a dominant firm, setting the market price. At the same time, both the price and output maximizers influence price since their willingness to expand or reduce production affects the remaining market share of the cartel core.

In setting forth three arbitrary groupings to describe the 13 unique OPEC actors, we recognize that these groupings are somewhat artificial. Nevertheless, it is easier to think of three groups rather than 13 countries. There is, however, some justification for placing these countries in these groupings. The rationale for assigning Saudi Arabia, Kuwait, Qatar, the United Arab Emirates, and Libya to the cartel core seems fairly obvious. They are all described by very large oil reserves, small populations, and a physical geography characterized by barren desert regions; and, with the exception of Libya, they are geographically contiguous.

The rationale for assigning Algeria, Iran, and Venezuela to the price maximizers may be less obvious. Ever since the beginning of OPEC, Venezuela has been the primary advocate of higher prices and restraint in production levels, due to its own low ratio of reserves to production and to its relatively low level of reserves per capita. With considerable potential for economic development, Venezuela is interested in high total annual oil export receipts; hence its desire to maximize prices for a relatively low level of exports. Algeria, like Libya, possesses high quality oil close to European markets and has in the past been a vigorous advocate of maximizing the price of its own oil. Algeria, however, has low oil reserves relative to its output rate, low reserves per capita, and promising prospects for internal development. Algeria has probably operated closer to full capacity in oil production than any other member of OPEC, and is a good example of a cartel member that desires to maximize both its price and its output. Iran is much more problematic. Before the 1979 revolution, Iran's policy vacillated between those of the cartel core and the price maximizers in seeking to finance the very ambitious economic and military development programs of its former ruler. Although Iran has absolutely large oil reserves, its population is larger than that of the other price maximizers and its economic development potential is correspondingly greater, due not only to higher population but also to greater resources in other respects. Based on these conditions, it would seem that Iran's production policy may well evolve as that of a price maximizer.

The output maximizers are assumed to consist of Iraq, Nigeria, Indonesia, Ecuador, and Gabon. Logically these OPEC members should prefer relatively greater proportionate output rates, given their relatively large populations, extensive plans for economic development, and relatively low but substantially expansible ratios of reserves per capita. As long as the other members of OPEC, in particular the cartel core, are willing to limit output in order to maintain high prices, the OPEC output maximizers have the incentive to demand a higher market share. It must be conceded that to date, only Iraq has appeared to follow literally the strategy of being an output maximizer by expanding output even during periods of weak market demand, and by making price reductions when necessary. In part, Iraq's program of output expansion stems from its very large potential oil resources base—perhaps 300 billion barrels—relative to which its current output rate is quite low. In a peacetime environment, Iraq tends to expand oil exports in order to finance ambitious internal development programs, and desires to have an expanded role in OPEC as a result of its greater share in the cartel's total output.

Over time, Indonesia is assumed to follow increasingly a policy of output maximization, since its population is the largest of any OPEC member, its development plans depend critically on oil revenues, and its reserves, although not large, are thought to be expansible. Nigeria is the second most populous OPEC member and has larger and probably more expansible reserves than Indonesia. Curiously, Nigeria's behavior has tended to fluctuate between price and output maximization. Gabon is essentially a smaller version of Nigeria with regard to these characteristics. Ecuador, which has perhaps the most problematic future of any OPEC member, should have the motivation to be an output maximizer due to low per capita oil revenues, an expansible resource base, and the capacity for internal economic development

SIX KEYS TO THE LONG-RUN VIABILITY OF OPEC AND THEIR IMPLICATIONS FOR FUTURE OIL PRICES

The hybrid model provides a conceptual lens through which to view past pricing and oil production decisions. When viewed from this perspective, Figure 4.1 describing oil prices and Figue 4.3 describing world oil consumption and non-OPEC production appear quite understandable. Let us recapitulate briefly. In response to the sharply higher oil prices in 1973–74, OPEC was pleasantly surprised to find an extremely price inelastic response in terms of both oil demand and supply from non-OPEC countries. It is not surprising that comforted by stable production despite the four-fold price increase in 1973–74, the Saudis would take advantage of the shortfall in Iranian production in 1979 to double prices again. As market conditions changed in the early 1980s, the cartel core took action to correct the mistake of excessively high prices resulting from the 1979 increase. The price rollback in 1983 from $34 to $29 was led by the cartel core and, as expected, resisted by the price maximizers. As shown in Figure 4.3, by 1983 OPEC production had plummeted to 17.6 MMB/D and production in the cartel core had dropped from 16.5 MMB/D in 1979 to 8.7 MMB/D. There was obvious concern that maintaining the posted price would result in insufficient production in the long run by the cartel. The implications of the hybrid model in Figure 4.12 are clear: decrease the real price of oil, initially, by holding its current price constant. Obviously, in 1983, the cartel core thought this was not strong enough medicine so they chose to reduce the current or nominal price of oil as well.

But what perspective does this give us for the future? If we can forecast the evolution of market conditions as implied in Figure 4.12, we can utilize this model to forecast future oil prices just as we used it to explain past price changes. The market conditions facing the cartel core depend critically on (a) the demand curve facing OPEC and (b) the supply response within OPEC. The following three factors play vital roles in determining the demand schedule facing OPEC: (1) world economic growth, (2) the price elasticity of oil demand, and (3) non-OPEC crude oil supply responses. These three factors are three of the six keys to the long run viability of OPEC to which we subsequently turn. Recall that the demand for OPEC crude is derived by subtracting the non-OPEC supply of crude from the world demand for crude. Over time, the major force shifting world crude demand outward is the rate of world economic growth. Oil is a normal good and the oil demand schedule depends critically on the growth of income. The second factor, the price elasticity of oil demand, is a major determinant of the quantity of oil sold at different prices. The third factor affecting OPEC crude oil demand is the supply response from non-OPEC sources, which may include synthetic oil production. This means that at some price, the synthetic backstop fuel becomes economic to produce, resulting in a price ceiling and large quantities of synthetic oil production.

These three factors are sufficient to describe the demand schedule facing OPEC, but we must also look at the fourth factor—(4) supply responses within OPEC. Even though these four factors completely characterize the hybrid model in Figure 4.12, markets do not perform in a vacuum. We must take a close look at the fifth factor—(5) political, economic, and military developments in the Middle East add a large random element to any attempt to forecast future oil prices and the viability of the cartel. Finally, the sixth factor to be considered is (6) the feasibility of policy actions by crude buyers to attenuate or eliminate OPEC's market power.

1. The Rate of Economic Growth in the Major Consuming Countries

The static graphs illustrating the dominant producer and hybrid models do not capture the effects of economic growth in shifting the world demand for oil outward. For the major consuming countries, the income elasticity for oil products[14] averages about 1.0. This means that with economic growth of 4 percent per year, the demand for oil will rise about 4 percent per year, assuming relative prices are unchanged. Thus even if OPEC is raising the price of oil relative to other energy forms (causing a movement up the demand curve), the quantity response from the shift in the demand schedule owing to economic growth may well offset the reduction in consumption due to higher prices. This means that oil consumption is likely to grow even though its real price is rising over time.

The rate of economic growth affects OPEC pricing in two ways. First, the more rapid the rate of growth in demand and oil consumption, ceteris paribus, the more rapid will be the rate of depletion. By moving the date of exhaustion toward the present, the user cost is increased, leading to a higher marginal cost and a higher monopoly price. In addition to the effects on cost, the rate of economic growth is likely to be critical to OPEC stability. From the hybrid model, we recall that the cartel core acts as a residual supplier. The cartel core is likely to be the prime beneficiary of economic growth and the major loser if world economic growth lags. Slower economic growth means greater excess capacity and greater incentives for the cartel core to seek demand growth via lower prices.

On the face of it, economic growth does not appear to be a particularly important determinant of oil demand. After all, the differences between a 3 percent and a 4 percent growth in economic activity affects oil demand by only 1 percent. Surely, 1 percent is small. But a difference of 1 percent over 10 or 20 years can have a profound effect on oil consumption. Figure 4.13 illustrates the sensitivity of oil consumption over time to differences in the rate of world economic growth. Two important assumptions are invoked. First, the income elasticity is assumed to be unity so that 4 percent economic growth automatically implies 4 percent oil demand growth. Second, the graph presumes that the real price of oil is unchanged over time. In essence,

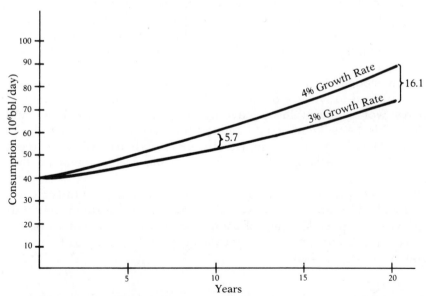

FIGURE 4.13 The effect of economic growth on world oil consumption.

oil prices are assumed to rise only as quickly as does the general inflation rate. As a consequence, only economic growth is affecting consumption in Figure 4.13.

Figure 4.13 assumes an initial noncommunist world oil consumption of 40 MMB/D occurring in year $T = 0$. Two consumption paths are shown; one for 3 percent growth per year and one for 4 percent per year. As shown in Figure 4.13, consumption growth at 4 percent per year implies oil consumption of 59.7 MMB/D after 10 years and 89 MMB/D after 20 years. In contrast, growth at 3 percent per year implies consumption of 54 MMB/D after 10 years and 72.9 MMB/D after 20 years. The differences between the two consumption paths increase over time—5.7 MMB/D after 10 years, 16.1 MMB/D after 20 years, and so forth.

Is a difference of 5.7 MMB/D extra demand important over a 10 year period? Absolutely, yes! Remember that the cartel core is the residual supplier. It meets unfilled demand at the official OPEC price. As the residual supplier, the cartel core would be the sole recipient of the 5.7 MMB/D gain in world oil consumption if economic growth were 4 percent instead of 3 percent. This could be an important addition to the cartel core's production, which in 1984 stood at 8.4 MMB/D.

Is it likely that decade-long averages in economic growth may vary by 1 percent or more? Again an affirmative answer seems likely. Over the decades of the 1960s and 1970s, the average slightly exceeded 4 percent per year, with the 1970s experiencing below average growth. A wide variety of opinion exists regarding the probable value of this variable in the future. Some individuals, whom we might loosely describe as having a "limits to growth" perspective, foresee a sharp diminution in this rate for a variety of reasons including (in their view) a likely reduction in energy availability. Most economists point to long-term trends in the rate of technical progress as evidence for sustained long-run economic growth. Even so, the declining growth in the labor force will lead to lower growth in real GNP even if the growth in output per worker maintains the average growth rate of the 1960s and 1970s. This factor alone could reduce the overall growth rate by .5 percent. Most long-term estimates of GNP growth are in the 3 percent per year range, although there is considerable disagreement on that figure.

We are left with the overall implication: economic growth is clearly the ally of OPEC and if prices remain constant, oil consumption tends to grow over time. The rate of economic growth turns out to be extremely important since the benefits of growth are passed directly through to the cartel core.

 QUESTIONS **1.** In the hybrid model, why is the cartel core the principal beneficiary of economic growth?

2. What factors might tend to restrain the rate of economic growth for the remainder of the century?

3. Give and explain two reasons for the cartel core favoring only modest oil price increases in contrast to most OPEC countries, which favor more rapidly rising prices.

2. The Price Elasticity of Oil Demand

The long-run price elasticity of oil demand will prove to be a critical determinant of both OPEC stability and the rate of future oil price increases. Recall that while the short-run demand schedule is quite inelastic, many long-run possibilities of substitution of nonenergy for energy, and of other fuels for oil are present. The sharp decline in oil consumption for the period 1980–84 can be attributed to the lagged effects of previous price increases as oil consumers adjust from their short-run demand schedules to their long-run demand schedules. OPEC must be concerned with how long it takes for the process of adjustment from the short-run to the long-run demand schedule to occur and just how large the long-run elasticity will be. If the demand response for the period 1980–84 was only the beginning of a process that might last 15 or 20 years, then OPEC should anticipate that lagged price effects may offset the effect of economic growth for many years to come. On the other hand, if the adjustment process occurs within a 5 to 10 year period, then both the effects of the 1973–74 increase and the 1978–79 increase would be more or less completed by the mid-1980s.

To illustrate the importance of the price elasticity of demand for world oil, let us show mathematically the relevance of this coefficient. Recall from simple monopoly theory that profit maximization requires that marginal revenue (MR) be equal to marginal cost (MC). In turn, price is related to marginal revenue through the price elasticity of OPEC's demand (E_{OPEC}).

(4.8)
$$MC = MR = P\left(1 - \frac{1}{E_{OPEC}}\right)$$

From equation (4.8), it is easy to see that the markup over costs, the ratio of price to marginal costs, depends entirely upon OPEC's price elasticity of demand.

(4.9)
$$\frac{P}{MC} = \frac{1}{1 - (1/E_{OPEC})} = \frac{E_{OPEC}}{E_{OPEC} - 1}$$

The reader can verify that if the price elasticity is 2, price will be twice marginal cost. On the other hand, if the elasticity is 1.2, the price is six times cost, representing a markup of 500 percent over cost. The markup varies greatly particularly over the range of elasticities from 1 to 2.

Let us now consider the role of the world oil price elasticity (E_w) and the elasticity of competitive fringe supply (E_{cf}) in determining the price elasticity facing OPEC (E_{OPEC}). Assuming that the OPEC price determines the world price, any given OPEC price change evokes a quantity response in world oil demand and supply from the competitive fringe. It follows that the sum of these two quantity responses gives the effect on OPEC demand:

(4.10)
$$\frac{\Delta Q_{OPEC}}{\Delta P} = \frac{\Delta Q_w}{\Delta P} - \frac{\Delta Q_{cf}}{\Delta P}$$

Multiplying both sides of equation (4.10) by P/Q_{OPEC} and multiplying the right-hand terms by Q_w/Q_w and Q_{cf}/Q_{cf}, we obtain

(4.11)
$$\frac{P}{Q_{OPEC}} \frac{\Delta Q_{OPEC}}{\Delta P} = \frac{P}{Q_{OPEC}} \frac{Q_w}{Q_w} \frac{\Delta Q_w}{\Delta P} - \frac{P}{Q_{OPEC}} \frac{Q_{cf}}{Q_{cf}} \frac{\Delta Q_{cf}}{\Delta P}$$

Rearranging terms and multiplying all terms by -1, we obtain:

(4.12)
$$\frac{P}{Q_{OPEC}} \frac{\Delta Q_{OPEC}}{\Delta P} = - \frac{Q_w}{Q_{OPEC}} \frac{P}{Q_w} \frac{\Delta Q_w}{\Delta P} + \frac{Q_{cf}}{Q_{OPEC}} \frac{P}{Q_{cf}} \frac{\Delta Q_{cf}}{\Delta P}$$

or

(4.13)
$$E_{OPEC} = \frac{Q_w}{Q_{OPEC}} E_w + \frac{Q_{cf}}{Q_{OPEC}} E_{cf}$$

The left-hand side of equation (4.12) is nothing more than OPEC's price elasticity of demand (E_{OPEC}). The first term on the right-hand side is the world oil production (excluding communist areas) relative to OPEC's, times the world oil price elasticity of demand (E_w). The last term in (4.12) is the competitive fringe's share of the market relative to that of OPEC, multiplied by the supply elasticity of the competitive fringe.

To illustrate the importance of the world oil price elasticity, let us examine the effect of varying the world oil price elasticity on OPEC's demand elasticity. Assume that OPEC's production share is approximately one half of noncommunist world production. For pedagogical purposes, also assume that the elasticity of supply from the competitive fringe (E_{cf}) is 0.5. What is OPEC's price elasticity if the world oil price elasticity of demand is also 1?

(4.14) $E_{OPEC} = (2/1)(1) + (1/1)(0.5) = 2.5$

By equation (4.14), OPEC's price elasticity is 2.5, which by equation (4.9) implies a price equal to 1.67 times the marginal cost.

Suppose instead that world oil price elasticity is only 0.5. By equation (4.13), we obtain an elasticity of 1.5:

(4.15) $E_{OPEC} = (2/1)(0.5) + (1/1)(0.5) = 1.5$

This OPEC price elasticity implies a price of 3 times marginal cost.

The relationship between world oil price elasticity and the ratio by which costs are multiplied to obtain prices becomes even more striking for elasticities below 0.5. It is by no means an unimportant question whether the world oil price elasticity is 0.5 or 0.9. Over the likely range of values, small absolute differences in elasticities imply large differences in OPEC's markup and the resulting resource misallocation.

Somehow a long-run price elasticity of 0.7 does not sound very large, but if the oil consumption levels resulting from various prices are compared, we see how sensitive the long-run consumption path really is to price. Let us perform an analysis similar to that performed earlier for alternative economic growth rates. In Figure 4.13, oil prices were held constant and the impact of various economic growth rates on oil consumption was measured. Now, we will hold the economic growth rate constant at 3 percent per year and ask what would be the effect of OPEC shifting to a new real price path at time $T = 0$. For example, in Figure 4.14, it was assumed that OPEC maintained a real price of $30 per barrel based on 1985 dollars for the next 20 years. Now we consider the effects of changing real prices from $30 in 1986 and maintaining the new real price for 20 years thereafter.

In interpreting Figure 4.14, start with the $30 real price path and notice that oil consumption rises exactly like the 3 percent growth path in Figure 4.13. After 10 years consumption reaches 54 MMB/D, and after 20 years it reaches 72.9 MMB/D. The two consumption paths are identical because they utilize identical demand assumptions—3% annual economic growth and a constant real oil price of $30 per barrel. Now assuming the real price is reduced from $30 to $20 per barrel in the first year, oil consumption grows along a much faster path, rising to 64.7 MMB/D after 10 years and to 93 MMB/D after 20 years. These results show the effect of a 0.7 price elasticity of demand (E_w). Notice that initially the effect of the price decrease on consumption is small, but it becomes larger over time. The explanation is that our calculation recognizes that while the long-run elasticities may be 0.7, the short-run demand must be much more inelastic (0.07 in this example). The analysis presumes a long adjustment process whereby

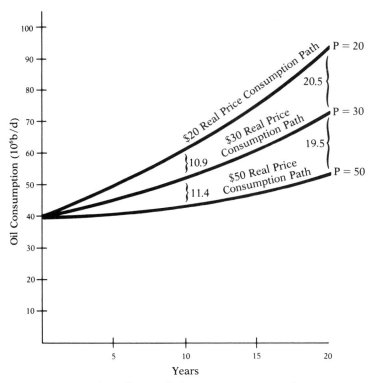

FIGURE 4.14 The effects of alternative price paths on energy consumption with an elasticity of 0.7.

only about 60% of the price effects are felt in the first 10 years. Such an assumption seems plausible though, since the stock of energy-using equipment such as autos, industrial machines, homes, and factories, has a long life and many energy-saving devices must await the basic redesign and replacement of this capital.

Figure 4.14 also illustrates the effect of a real price increase to $50 per barrel (also predicated on a 0.7 long-run price elasticity). Notice the effect of higher prices, particularly after 10 years with demand reaching only 42.6 MMB/D. Thereafter, demand grows at a faster rate, reaching 53.0 MMB/D in the 20th year. Over this latter period, the major impact of the price effects have been felt; although additional lagged conservation effects occur, the effect of economic growth is sufficient to offset them. Particularly for the cartel core, which is interested in its long-run market prospects, the effect after 20 years of a real price increase was to reduce consumption by 19.5 MMB/D. Given that the cartel core's production is only a fraction of OPEC's total, the loss of 19.5 MMB/D in demand for a 66% price increase might actually lower the cartel core's long-run revenues. In effect, even though the world price elasticity of demand may be inelastic at 0.7, the corresponding demand elasticity facing the cartel core may well be quite elastic.

In sum, the magnitude of the price elasticity of world oil demand is very important. Even though demand tends to be very inelastic in the short run, the long-run demand elasticity is much greater, probably falling in the range from 0.5 to 0.9.[15] Particularly in the long run, the effect of high price policies impact directly on the cartel core, so they have a vested interest in selecting prices that are compatible with their long-term horizon. Yet the demand elasticity is not known precisely; because of this, the cartel core must set prices in an uncertain world where miscalculations of a demand elasticity estimate by 0.2 can translate into large losses of cartel core production over time. To compound the pricing dilemma, the cartel core has no easy way of assessing the impact of its current pricing decisions on future demand. The cartel core's problem is akin to planting a forest that takes 20 years to mature, although the growth of the seedlings in the first few years is a poor predictor of the ultimate tree size and only after 10 years is there much basis for estimating ultimate tree size. Unfortunately, if inferior seedlings were planted, there is little that can be done after 10 years.

1. Can you verify the relationships in equation (4.8)?
2. Use equation (4.9) to calculate the markup factors for the following elasticities: 10, 5, 2, 1.5, 1.1. Why will we never observe an elasticity less than 1.0?
3. Suppose the world price elasticity is 0.4. Calculate the markup factor. Do you think the fact that United States imports jumped from 23.3 percent of demand in 1970 to 42.4 percent in 1976 contributed to price movements over this period?
4. Explain why the elasticity of demand facing the cartel core is considerably more elastic than the demand elasticity facing OPEC.

3. The Supply Response from the Competitive Fringe

Equation (4.13) also emphasizes that OPEC's monopoly power depends upon both the quantitative importance and the supply elasticity of the competitive fringe. If, as OPEC increases the price, this indeed leads to new discoveries of oil in the competitive fringe, this will attenuate OPEC's monopoly power. The magnitude of this response, reflected in the competitive fringe's elasticity of supply, can be vital, especially in the current situation facing OPEC. Assuming the above market shares and a world price elasticity of 0.7, let us vary the elasticity of competitive fringe supply to examine its impact on OPEC's price elasticity of demand and markup. First, assuming a competitive fringe supply elasticity of 0.5, we obtain an OPEC price elasticity of 1.9:

(4.16) $\qquad E_{OPEC} = (2/1)(0.7) + (1/1)(0.5) = 1.9$

The implied price from equation (4.16) is approximately 2 times marginal cost.

Now suppose instead that geological opportunities in the North Sea, Mexico, and so on, are not so favorable so that the supply elasticity is only 0.1:

(4.17) $\qquad E_{OPEC} = (2/1)(0.7) + (1/1)(0.1) = 1.5$

Even though the lower supply elasticity lowers OPEC's demand elasticity from 1.9 to only 1.5, the price rises from 2 to 3 times marginal cost. Thus the elasticity of competitive fringe supply is an important determinant of OPEC's monopoly power.

In addition to the elasticity of supply, the quantity of the competitive fringe production is also vital. It matters whether the competitive fringe supplies 1 percent of the market or 30 percent. The increasing relative importance of oil production outside the OPEC countries has no doubt played an important role in OPEC's weakened position in the early 1970s, irrespective of the magnitude of the world demand and competitive fringe's supply elasticities. To illustrate this point, let us contrast the 1973 market shares (two thirds OPEC, one third competitive fringe) with the situation in the mid-1980s (roughly one half OPEC, one half competitive fringe). Utilizing the 1973 market shares together with the 0.7 world price elasticity of demand and 0.5 elasticity of supply from the competitive fringe, we obtain:

(4.18) $\qquad E_{OPEC} = (3/2)(0.7) + (1/2)(0.5) = 1.3$

This elasticity implies an OPEC price of 4.3 times marginal cost. As we saw above, using similar elasticities but mid-1980s market shares, $E_{OPEC} = 1.9$ which translates into a price only approximately two times marginal costs. Thus, even holding the elasticities constant, the greater the quantity of competitive fringe oil production, the more elastic is the demand schedule facing OPEC and the lower is its monopoly power.

Since both the market share and the supply elasticity of non-OPEC producers are important to OPEC's future, it is interesting to speculate about future production from these countries. Whereas econometric research provides reasonably narrow ranges for the price and income elasticities of oil demand, supply elasticities remain elusive numbers. Who would have predicted that Mexican reserves found in the late 1970s may exceed 100 billion barrels? Oil exploration is a

TABLE 4.6 Percentage of Non-OPEC Production by Various Countries (1983)*

U.S.	42.9
Mexico	13.4
U.K.	11.2
Canada	6.9
Egypt	3.4
Norway	3.0
Brunei/Malaysia	2.6
Other Non-OPEC	16.6

*Excluding communist countries.
SOURCE: U.S. Monthly Energy Review.

highly uncertain process. It is clear that the supply elasticity is positive and nontrivial, based on the healthy production increase recorded since 1973 (see Figure 4.3), but it is difficult to say much more.

As shown in Table 4.6, of the 21.1 MMB/D production recorded in 1983 by non-OPEC, noncommunist world producers, the largest single producer was the United States (42.9%), followed by Mexico (13.4%) and the U.K. (11.2%). The North Sea production (consisting of the U.K. and Norway) and Mexico have been the major sources of production growth outside OPEC. Based on Mexican reserves, it is not unreasonable to project still another doubling of production by the early 1990s. But for producers such as the U.S. and Canada, prospects are not as bright. In relatively intensely explored areas, the big fields are found first. Production tends to peak early in a field's life and then decline geometrically. Consequently, higher oil prices stimulate the discovery of new smaller fields, but their addition to production may not be adequate to offset the decline in production from the older, larger fields.

The statistics in Table 4.6 are potentially misleading to the degree that communist countries such as the U.S.S.R. and China develop the capacity to export. After all, the U.S.S.R. is the world's largest oil producer with 1983 production of 11.7 MMB/D. China produces an additional 2.1 MMB/D. Because their internal consumption has roughly matched their production, these countries have not played an appreciable role in the world oil market, but time could change this. Oil is viewed by these countries as a great source of much needed foreign exchange. Heavy exploration programs, particularly in offshore China, might enable these countries to play appreciable roles as non-OPEC producers in the future.

But OPEC's concerns about non-OPEC oil production are not limited to conventional oil. A small but thriving tar sands industry is alive in Canada. Additionally, in the early 1980s when oil prices seemed destined to exceed $50 per barrel, a number of shale oil projects in the U.S. were begun by the major oil companies. While a more detailed discussion of the potential for synthetic oil production is given in Chapter 9, suffice it to say that the reserve bases for tar sands and oil shale are huge, providing an effective backstop fuel price. Thus OPEC must keep a watchful eye on the economics of synthetic oil production as well.

4. Institutional Developments Within OPEC

The classic problem all cartels face is how to restrain overall output to the monopoly level and how to assign the market share given that total output level. To cartelize effectively, OPEC must solve the problem of the 3 C's facing all cartels: concurrence, coordination, and compliance. They must first achieve concurrence on the joint profit-maximizing output for the cartel. Coordination can be achieved by either implicit or explicit agreements to share markets. Finally, some devices must exist to force compliance, since the incentives to cheat will be large. Much to their chagrin, in the early 1970s the international oil companies acted as policing agents for the cartel. The payment of royalties and income taxes based on posted prices, which were fictitious rather than actual transaction prices, in effect meant that every company paid a flat tax per barrel. This flat tax raised the marginal costs of the oil companies, creating a floor below which prices could not fall. By controlling the tax floor and thus the price, OPEC controlled the total quantity of oil sold.

This system also solved the problem of assigning market shares. No member of the cartel could post an appreciably lower tax floor lest others retaliate with matching prices. Thus, with similar tax levies, historical market shares became the natural basis for future market shares. What prevented a country from secretly cutting the tax floor, inducing its concessionaires to sell additional crude? From the game theory results, it is obvious that undetected cheating can be quite lucrative. If all production is sold at cash prices, cheating would easily be detected and price cuts would be matched. Any reduction in the tax floor would be known by all members of the concession. Companies with minor interests in a given concession would quickly demand similar terms from those countries where it happened to hold a majority interest.

Time has altered this system dramatically. Today, most OPEC countries market their crude directly through their state-owned oil companies. This development has added a potentially destabilizing force, since market shares become a variable under the control of the state-owned oil company. In contrast, when the concessionaires handled the marketing function, a country's market share was the outcome of historical supply relations.

Still another problem is that as time passes and conditions change, past historical market shares become less acceptable as a basis for future market shares. For example, following the cessation of the Iran-Iraq War and a resumption of large-scale exports by both countries, will other OPEC countries cut production to enable Iran and Iraq to reestablish production market shares consistent with 1976 or 1977 levels?

For these reasons, it is not surprising that in 1983, OPEC took the historic step of assigning explicit production limits for the various OPEC countries. This could be only the beginning of a whole new set of institutional devices adopted by OPEC to achieve better coordination of output. There is also the related problem of achieving compliance. To date, cheaters such as Iraq have acted with relative impunity. But this only invites others to behave as the non-OPEC, competitive fringe firms do. It remains to be seen how those countries violating the production ceilings will be disciplined by the cartel.

5. Political and Military Developments

Oil markets do not operate in a vacuum, and it would be a mistake to conclude that the hybrid model is capable of predicting future oil prices and OPEC stability independent of the political and military developments in the Middle East. In effect, these political, economic, and military factors set the stage on which energy markets operate. Let us see more precisely what is meant by these factors.

Political Factors. The political divergences between the OPEC members are sufficiently complicated to prevent the development of a comparatively simple two- or three-group discussion. The fundamental division would be between Arab and non-Arab members of OPEC, with each group capable of further subdivision into radical versus more conservative orientations. In the brief discussion that follows, only those aspects of the political climate that have an important bearing on cartel stability will be considered.

The Arab members of OPEC include Saudi Arabia, Kuwait, Libya, Algeria, Iraq, Qatar, and the UAE. These seven members possess about three fourths of the cartel's reserves and productive capacity. These statistics alone are sufficient to establish the dominance of Arab over non-Arab exporters in OPEC. If the Arab group were highly unified, it could control cartel policy to a very considerable degree. Arab political unity was, of course, decisive in mobilizing the cartel's latent monopoly power during and after the 1973 oil embargo. But political unity among the Arab members varies somewhat from issue to issue and from country to country.

There are three important issues that are directly pertinent to Arab political solidarity. The first is Arab ethnic hostility to Israel, which is unanimous but which varies in intensity of manifestation, depending upon the incidence of costs and benefits to particular countries. The second is Arab religious hostility to Soviet communism, which again is widespread, but is strongest in the most orthodox countries; it is qualified in some other countries by the perception of the possible benefit of Soviet alliances. The third is pan-Arab solidarity, both ethnic and religious, which has its strongest appeal in the poorer countries. The oil-rich Arab states are more conscious of the costs to themselves of such broadly based alliances.

The attitude of an Arab member of OPEC toward these issues generally varies with the alignment of its regime in the spectrum of political attitudes, which ranges from radical to reactionary. The radical members of the Arab group include Iraq, Libya, and Algeria. Saudi Arabia is the most conservative of the Arab members. Saudi attitudes and policies are quite influential in Qatar and the UAE. The Kuwait regime is basically conservative but less overtly so because of its proximity to Iraq. But non-OPEC Arab states are very important in conditioning the political climate in the Arab world. This is particularly important regarding Arab attitudes toward Israel, where the views of radical Syria and relatively moderate Egypt are crucial.

Hopes for a lasting peace settlement between Israel and the Arabs, never too high, brightened considerably in 1978 and 1979 with the Camp David Accord. Those who stood to gain from such a settlement included the combatants themselves, the oil importers, the conservative Arab regimes, and perhaps OPEC itself. Those who stood to lose include the more radical Arab regimes and the Soviet Union. The combatants would clearly gain since they would be saved the expense of mobilization and the devastation of warfare. The importers would gain since the danger of periodic supply interruptions and the resulting price increases would be reduced. The conservative Arab states would gain since they would face reduced challenges from the radical regimes, which use the Israeli situation as a basis for intensified agitation. The Soviet Union would lose, since anything that threatens the oil supplies of the major industrialized countries is of advantage to the Soviets. Radical Arab regimes would lose since their prospects for displacing conservative governments would suffer and their Soviet patrons would be reduced in status.

The effect on OPEC itself, however, is uncertain. There are two respects in which cartel stability might be considered to increase in the long run. While embargos increase OPEC power and unity in the short run, the price increases likely to result from future embargos may tend to destabilize OPEC. Additional substantial price hikes could lead to prices well above the profit-maximizing level, as during the Iranian Revolution. Then the lowered production, particularly by the cartel core members, coupled with conservation and the accelerated development of synthetic oil production in non-OPEC countries, would pose serious long-term problems for OPEC. A second factor involves reactions to the reduction in Arab-Israeli tensions. Importers might be led to believe that Arab oil exports were now "secure" and thus become less concerned about developing their own alternative sources of energy.

With regard to Arab anticommunism, one must distinguish between a basic antipathy on religious grounds and the more than occasional willingness of Arab states to cooperate with the Soviets in matters of economics. The religiously orthodox and conservative regimes of the Arabian peninsula are intensely anticommunist, while the radical Arab regimes display varying degrees of enthusiasm or toleration for Soviet alliances. Most radical is Iraq, which has treaties with the Soviet Union and regards itself as being outside the free world. Libya's regime is more religiously orthodox than that of Iraq, but not enough to prevent it from forming Soviet alliances of a military nature. Algeria's radical position within the Arab camp depends less upon its Soviet ties than upon its stance as a champion of pan-Arab unity. On balance, however, the issue of anticommunism tends to form one of the ties between major Arab oil exporters and their customers in the noncommunist world. The producers in the Persian Gulf region justifiably fear Soviet military pressure, against which their own defenses would be unavailing. An important element in future OPEC developments will be the role played by the Soviet Union in the Middle East.

The third issue is that of pan-Arabism. Here the leaders among the OPEC members are Algeria and Libya, although many non-OPEC Arab countries such as Egypt and the Sudan are also prominent in the movement. The popular appeal of the movement is strong, since the Arab countries possess many common elements of historical, cultural, and ethnic kinship. There are, however, strong nationalist loyalties within each state that tend to limit the strength of pan-Arab sentiments. At the most basic economic level, there is the desire of the have-not countries to forge a pan-Arab union with the oil-rich countries and share the wealth of the oil exporters more broadly. Such a prospect compromises the enthusiasm of most Arab oil exporters, particularly those conservative exporters who see pan-Arabism as a thinly veiled maneuver for the replacement of their governments by radical groups. Curiously enough, a lasting peace with Israel might accentuate intra-Arab differences, leading to weakened pan-Arabism and to increased probability of radical coups in conservative Arab regimes.

Even though Iran is not part of the Arab World, events there could greatly influence the leadership and stability of the whole Middle East. Iran, like most countries of the Middle East, is devoutly Moslem.

As in most major religions, there are numerous Moslem sects, but it took the events of 1978 to remind the rest of the world of these differences. The Iranian Revolution resulted in the creation of a fundamentalist Islamic republic under the leadership of Khomeini, a leader of the Shiite Moslem sect. Ironically, a fundamentalist revolution was a direct reaction to the Shah's modernization efforts fueled by the oil revenue influx after 1973–74. While other Moslem sects disassociate themselves from the revolution, Shiite sects are numerically important in Arab and other Middle East countries and are generally supportive of the revolution. The Iranian revolution has opened up a broad range of possibilities; these include internal political upheavals in other Middle East countries with large Shiite sects, and intercountry warfare between countries such as Iran with a fundamentalist government and Iraq, which is openly contemptuous of such a regime.

Military Developments. One cannot engage in a complete survey of political developments and trends without considering the military end of that spectrum. The Iran-Iraq War should serve as a constant reminder of just how tenuous peace is in the Middle East. Fortunately, the war has occurred over a period of falling world demand for OPEC oil, so that its economic impact has been relatively mild. Between the two countries, oil production dropped by nearly 6 MMB/D. Suppose, instead that a production decline of 6 MMB/D had occurred in the mid-1970s, when production in other OPEC countries was at or near capacity! The Iran-Iraq War also illustrates the potential for war to escalate, spreading to other countries. In retaliation for Saudi and Kuwaiti economic aid to Iraq, Iran in 1984 sank tankers carrying oil belonging to the Kuwaitis and Saudis and threatened to block the Straits of Hormuz, the narrow waterway at the entrance of the Persian Gulf. Blocking the flow of all oil out of the Persian Gulf would have reduced world supplies by about 20 percent in 1984.

The possibility of military disruption of the cartel has three aspects of interest to economists. First, there is the possibility that the cartel might be strengthened by conflicts between OPEC countries that reduce the number of countries involved, similar to mergers that reduce the number of rivals in a business cartel. A victory by cartel core countries over the output-maximizing countries might place cartel power more securely in the hands of a few sellers. Alternatively, a victory by output-maximizing countries might alter cartel behavior by increasing production to reflect the revenue needs of the more populous radical Arab countries.

Second, there is the likelihood that the oil fields may be seriously damaged by warfare and sabotage during attempts to occupy the producing areas. This will result, at a minimum, in the interruption of production and/or transportation of oil imports for periods that might easily exceed a year. The danger of sabotage or war damage would be greater if other than Arab forces were involved in occupation attempts. The impact on the cartel might be quite serious if oil supplies were reduced for any significant period of time. OPEC members not suffering damage would certainly increase their exports to practically full capacity levels. Over time they would further expand their capacity and be unlikely to desire to reduce output when the destruction was repaired.

If, however, a significant fraction of total OPEC exports is foreclosed, either through destruction of production facilities or through the continuing sabotage of transport media such as tankers and pipelines, the effect on demand of the unaffected members could be just the opposite. The economies of Japan and Western Europe would literally suffocate if deprived of oil imports for a year, and the resulting collapse of employment, output, world trade, and the structure of national currencies and world financial institutions would leave the remainder of OPEC monopolizing a commodity for which there was no longer an adequate demand—until the passage of a decade or more during which the structure of the world economy might tend to recover its former position. But such a recovery might occur very slowly, and in any event the emerging new world economy would be unlikely to be as dependent upon oil imports as that which it replaces.

Third, there is the reasonable possibility that Soviet occupation of some or all of the Persian Gulf oil fields might be the final outcome of military actions initiated by non-Soviet forces. A Soviet takeover of most of OPEC's reserves would have a decisive impact on the cartel. Since the Soviet Union is perennially starved for export commodities with which it can earn hard currencies to purchase the imported inputs needed to further its own economic development, it could be expected to greatly increase production. It is likely, however, that the Soviet takeover of most of OPEC's reserves would induce importers to make much greater efforts to reduce their dependence on oil imports.

Although such scenarios may seem far-fetched, they cannot be entirely ignored. The attention they merit is the product of (1) the probability of occurrence, and (2) the effect on world oil trade of a given event. The magnitude of the latter factor is so great that the total product is significant even though the probability may be assessed at a low level. The probabilities of such events, while low, are not negligible. That the OPEC price increase of 1973–74 gravely upset a rather delicate balance between the costs and benefits of external military takeover of the major oil exporters has received surprisingly little serious attention. With the qualified exception of Iran, the major Arab oil exporters are militarily weak. As long as oil profits to the exporters were no more than about $1 per barrel, it was questionable whether it would be worth the risk for militarily stronger countries to occupy the oil fields. But with profits per barrel raised to $25 or more, the potential gains are increased relative to the costs.

1. An unidentified observer of the world oil market noted: "The long-range impending shortage of oil is more a political than an economic or geological phenomenon." Discuss. To what extent do economic realities place constraints on political behavior?

2. Who are the beneficiaries of peace in the Middle East and who are the losers? What probability do you attach to (a) future embargos and (b) outright war in the Persian Gulf over the next 20 years? Would you expect these probabilities to increase or decrease compared to the period 1960–80?

6. Policy Actions of Crude Buyers

Until now, the major consuming countries have made no concerted efforts to counter cartel price increases. In the past this inaction stemmed from a feeling that coordinated action is difficult to achieve, and even if it is possible, the range and potential success of such policies are quite restricted.

Without a coordinated international policy in dealings with OPEC, the effect of the response of any one buyer on the cartel price is likely to be small. Table 4.7 shows the shares of OPEC oil sales to various countries. While some countries are major importers, no one country is dominant. In 1983, Japan and the U.S. were OPEC's best customers, each accounting for about 22 percent of OPEC's oil sales. Besides these countries, the percentages for other industrialized countries tend to be 10 percent or less. OPEC's demand elasticity in equation (4.13) is in fact a weighted average of the elasticity responses of the various importers. The weights are determined by the shares in Table 4.7. Con-

TABLE 4.7 Share of Total OPEC Oil Exports Consumed by the Major Importing Countries (1983)

Country	Market Share
United States	22.7
Japan	21.5
France	10.7
Italy	9.5
Benelux Countries	7.5
West Germany	7.3
Spain	5.0
United Kingdom	3.9
Sweden	1.4
Other European Importers	6.8
Other Industrial Importers	3.5
All Other Countries	0.2

SOURCE: International Energy Agency.

sequently, the effect of any one country on OPEC's overall demand elasticity is relatively small. This implies that independent action by any one importer is unlikely to substantially affect OPEC's optimal price. Therefore, some form of combined action involving the largest eight to ten importers appears necessary to place maximum pressure on OPEC.

Although all of the major importers would benefit from any attenuation in OPEC's monopoly power, the range and potential success of likely policy responses seem quite limited. After the 1973 Embargo, some called for a countercartel on goods exported to OPEC by the major importers. Unfortunately, there are several reasons why this is infeasible. First, unless the countercartel charged the higher cartel price to all countries, those non-OPEC countries importing the goods at the low price would simply reexport the goods to OPEC, rendering the cartel ineffective. Perhaps the most serious fault of the policy is that OPEC countries are for the most part not particularly dependent upon imported goods. Western imports are typically luxury items that can be dispensed with.

Another joint program would use coordinated tariff policies to minimize OPEC price increases. Unless demand were perfectly inelastic, the imposition of a tariff would tend to reduce the price received by OPEC even though the price inclusive of the tariff rises. Importing countries also enjoy the tax receipts of the oil tariff. Tariff policies can take several forms including a flat import tax per barrel, an ad valorem tariff, or even a matching tariff geared to OPEC price increases.

The simplest tariff is a flat tariff of, say, $10 per barrel levied on all oil imports. The initial effect of such a tariff would be to raise internal prices of petroleum products by $10 per barrel, suggesting that the tariff is fully shifted onto the consumer. But from principles of economics, we recall that in the long run, the incidence of a tax is borne by both producers and consumers depending on the elasticities of supply and demand. In effect, the tariff will ultimately lower the OPEC price, shifting a portion of the tax to OPEC. For example, if the major consuming countries all imposed the tariff, OPEC might be forced to reduce crude prices by $5 per barrel. Interesting idea! Instead of OPEC imposing taxes on the consuming countries, the consuming countries could levy a tax on OPEC.

Still a more sophisticated tariff is an ad valorem tariff, set as a percentage (say 30%) of the OPEC price. The advantage of an ad valorem tariff is that it provides additional pressure on OPEC to lower prices. Assuming OPEC raised oil prices from $30 to $40 per barrel, the tariff would increase from $9 to $12 per barrel. But for a price decrease from $30 to $20, the tariff would drop from $9 to $6 per barrel.

Still a more ambitious tariff is a matching tariff system, which focuses even more pressure on OPEC to mitigate future OPEC price increases. Normally, when OPEC raises its price by $1 per barrel, the price to the consumer increases by $1, leading to a reduction in the quantity demanded. The decision to raise price is obviously based on the proposition that the net elasticity of demand facing OPEC in equation (4.13) is inelastic. Clearly, if OPEC's oil export demand can be made more elastic by changing domestic economic policies, price increases can be slowed or perhaps halted. Suppose all of the major consuming countries put OPEC on notice that any price increase will be met with a matching tariff increase. For example, the $1-per-barrel OPEC price increase would be matched by a $1-per-barrel tariff imposed by all the consuming countries, meaning that the price of oil domestically would rise by $2 per barrel. The quantity reduction in world demand would be double that obtained for a $1-per-barrel increase, yet OPEC's price would have gone up by only $1 per barrel. In effect, this policy would double the world price elasticity of demand in equation (4.13). Similarly, to the extent that competitive fringe supply emanates from these countries, the supply elasticity would be doubled, since domestic oil prices would increase by $2 per barrel for every $1 per barrel increase by OPEC. In view of the extreme sensitivity of the markup over costs to the world price elasticity for oil shown above, such a policy could be quite effective in holding down future price increases.

Despite the appeal of tariffs, there are two problems. First, to be most effective, tariffs require concerted implementation by the major consuming countries. Because of international trade considerations, no one country would be eager to impose higher energy costs on its own producing industries unilaterally. Second, even if other countries were in agreement, the local opposition to higher energy prices might well be sufficient to defeat such a tariff. Even though the long-run effect would be lower prices, the short-run effect is higher prices, and political resistance is certain to be so strong that many countries would not cooperate in such a program.

As an alternative to a tariff policy, importing countries might use a variant of an import control program to obtain lower oil prices. Professor Adelman has advocated issuing import tickets equal in quantity to the difference between demand and domestic production.[16] These import tickets would be sold to foreign suppliers at public auction. Presumably, if they command a nonzero price, the winning bidder is discounting his imported oil by the amount of the bid. For example, even though the sale price of the oil would be at the official OPEC price, the true price received by the importer would be the official price less the amount paid for the import ticket. Since the importing government auctions the tickets, government tax revenues increase from the ticket sales proceeds. These revenues can in turn be returned to consumers through tax cuts and other devices. An advantage of this approach is that joint country action is not necessary for the implementation of this program. It does not work through the elasticity of world oil demand as in equation (4.13), where each country bears a given weight. Rather the forces tending to lower prices work through the game theory results and the incentive to cheat.

There are two critical unresolved issues facing such a proposal. First, can the winning bidders be identified and their bid prices ascertained? This brings us back to the game theory results, which emphasized that the incentives for undetected cheating were very great. A second point is that even if cheating were undetected and prices fell for a time, responses by OPEC could be anticipated. For example, OPEC might mandate that all OPEC members submit their ticket bids through the OPEC office, thereby eliminating any incentive to cheat. (This step might at least increase intermember tensions within OPEC.) Thus the likelihood of undetected cheating and/or OPEC's response are critical to the success of such a policy. While this approach has appealing attributes, its success seems problematic.

Still another potential response is the development of economically attractive substitutes for OPEC oil. From the discussion of the non-OPEC supply response, we saw the importance of non-OPEC oil production. If through technological advances the costs of synthetic oil can be brought down over time, this could be a very effective constraint on OPEC's monopoly power. Even successful R&D leading to lower costs for other energy forms will no doubt have an impact by making the demand schedule for oil more price elastic, which in turn lowers the markup factor of prices over costs.

Are there organizations capable of organizing a cooperative response by consuming nations? In principle, the International Energy Agency (consisting of 21 OECD countries excluding France) could play a role in promoting international cooperation on tariffs and R&D policy. To date, the agency has succeeded only in devising a highly inadequate oil sharing agreement in the event of a worldwide emergency. Additional details on this agreement are presented in Chapter 6. The failure of the IEA suggests that buyer reactions are likely to be individual rather than collective, thus reducing the effectiveness of the response.

<u>QUESTIONS</u>

1. Outline what you consider to be the most effective buyer responses to OPEC. Now rate them according to political feasibility.

2. Explain the relevance of the free rider phenomenon in undermining the possibility of cooperative arrangements among consuming countries.

<u>Notes</u>

1. See A.D. Johany, "OPEC is not a cartel: a property rights explanation of the rise in crude oil prices," unpublished doctoral dissertation, University of California, Santa Barbara. Also see Walter J.

Mead, "The Performance of Government Energy Regulations," *American Economic Review*, May 1979.

2. See Johany, *op. cit.*

3. See David J. Teece, "OPEC Behavior: An Alternative View," in Griffin and Teece (editors), *OPEC Behavior and World Oil Prices* (London, Allen and Unwin, 1982). Also see J. Cremer and D. Salehi-Isfahani, "Competitive Pricing in the Oil Market: How important is OPEC?", Working Paper, University of Pennsylvania, Philadelphia, 1980.

4. See J.M. Griffin, "OPEC Behavior: A Test of Alternative Hypotheses," *American Economics Review*, forthcoming.

5. Ibid.

6. For a succinct history of the major oil concessions in the Middle East, see Sam Schurr and Paul Homan, *Middle Eastern Oil and the Western World* (New York: Elsevier Press, 1971), Chapters 9 and 10. See also Neil H. Jacoby, *Multinational Oil* (New York: Macmillan, 1974), Chapters 3–7.

7. See M.A. Adelman, *The World Petroleum Market* (Baltimore: Johns Hopkins Press, 1972), Chapter 3.

8. See *New York Times*, September 24, 1980.

9. For a useful discussion of OPEC pricing under uncertainty, see Dermot Gately, John Kyle, and D. Fischer, "Strategies for OPEC's decisions," *European Economic Review*, December 1977.

10. For a more detailed account of events, see Theodore Moran, "Modeling OPEC Behavior: Economic and Political Alternatives," in Griffin and Teece, *op. cit.*

11. For a more extended discussion of OPEC as a cartel, see M.A. Adelman, "OPEC as a Cartel," in Griffin and Teece, *op. cit.*

12. For an acute analysis of the complications of this class of game theory situations, see Daniel Ellsberg, "Theory of the Reluctant Duelist," *American Economic Review*, December 1956.

13. Griffin, *op. cit.*

14. For a survey of world oil models, see Energy Modelling Forum, *World Oil* (Stanford: Energy Modelling Forum, February 1982).

15. Ibid.

16. M.A. Adelman, "Oil Import Quota Auctions," *Challenge*, January–February 1976.

ENVIRONMENTAL ISSUES IN ENERGY DEVELOPMENT 5

INTRODUCTION

Critics of the modern affluent industrial society regard it as keeping bad company. Among its evil companions are the members of the pollution gang: air, water, thermal, nuclear, and solid waste. These critics wish that industrial economies could shun such confederates and go their separate ways. As Falstaff warned Prince Hal, "There is a thing, Harry, which thou hast often heard of, and it is known to many in our land by the name of pitch: this pitch, as ancient writers do report, doth defile; so doth the company thou keepest . . ." Some of the most obvious instances of pollution are associated with energy: most air pollution, some solid waste contamination, a few of the most highly publicized water pollution incidents, much of what is called thermal pollution, and the bulk of the nonmilitary instances of nuclear pollution. The typical observer is tempted to recommend the peremptory banishment of the members of this undesirable gang, and the more extreme environmentalists have urged the execution of them all, through moratoria on nuclear energy, economic growth, and population growth. But before passing sentence, we should first look at the criminal records of the defendants. In some instances there may be extenuating circumstances. It is possible that in a few cases extinction may be imperative. Fines and the payment of damages may suffice in other circumstances. But life sentences at hard labor might typically be more socially just.

It must be recognized that production and pollution are generally joint products of most purposeful activity. In ecological systems all organisms select the inputs to which they are adapted, process them, and eliminate wastes. Within the human body muscular exertion gives rise to fatigue toxins in the cells that must be removed by, and then from, the bloodstream. Through respiration, animals convert an oxygen intake into carbon dioxide, which is also a bloodstream "pollutant" that must be eliminated. For plants, on the other hand, carbon dioxide is an input and oxygen has the status of a pollutant that must be excreted. Human beings must obviously define pollution in human terms, setting appropriate priorities. Two types of pollutants receive attention: the presence of something unwanted, such as sulfur compounds in the air, and the absence of something desired, such as dissolved oxygen in water.

Much pollution is a byproduct of activities involving the production, conversion, and consumption of energy. Such pollution should clearly be controlled by the most economic means. But it is incorrect to conceive of energy per se as inimical to the environment. Energy has been a part of the environment ever since the domestication of fire. It is fortunate that our cave-dwelling ancestors did not see fit to call a halt to the use of fire on air pollution grounds at that early date. Before descending into the particulars of environmental issues, it is useful to sketch in some historical background, showing how the preservation of the environment became a national goal in the 1960s, and how this new goal conflicts with other goals. After that it is appropriate to consider the major types of pollution and assess the contribution of energy sources to such categories. A concluding section then deals with the economics of pollution control, discussing the pros and cons of direct regulation, taxation, and other control methods.

GOALS AND GOAL CONFLICTS

Economists tend to identify a society with its economy, overestimating the predominance of economic motives and activities in the total fabric of a nation's life. On the other hand, political leaders tend to identify the society with its political arrangements and underestimate the constraints that economic factors place upon political strivings. It is not unusual for a nation to set extra-economic goals for itself that can greatly complicate the achievement of ordinary economic objectives. The industrialized nations have consistently given economic goals a prominent position, but by no means an exclusive one. Let us very briefly review the history of national goals in the United States.

American political leaders have generally tried to pursue at least three national goals simultaneously. Two of these are constant—national security and economic prosperity—and they constitute the minimum conditions for a stable society. The third goal is variable in nature, and while it may be complementary to the other two, it can often hamper the accomplishment of either or both of them. In the nineteenth century, the nature of the third goal underwent a slow evolution; while it influenced the means used to achieve the other goals, it generally did not particularly limit the degree to which they could be accomplished. Since the First World War, however, the third goal has changed more frequently in both nature and emphasis, and has posed real problems in the accommodation of mutually inconsistent objectives, as is shown in the following paragraphs.

Although national goals were not readily articulated and propagated before the advent of mass communications media, the goal between about 1790 and 1850 appears to have been economic growth along Jeffersonian lines, stressing agriculture, decentralized control of industry and politics, and a limited government. Between about 1850 and 1920 economic growth continued to be a major goal, but it was pursued more along Hamiltonian lines, stressing industrial expansion, a more centralized government, more participation in world trade, and more spending on defense. As a consequence of industrialization, a forerunner of the modern environmental movement was spawned in the 1880s under the Conservation Movement. The Conservation Movement produced a greater awareness of the richness of America's natural beauty and a desire to protect it for the future.

National consciousness of goals and purposes increased after the First World War. During the 1920s the goal was well expressed by the slogan "Back to Normalcy," which reflected a reactionary desire to return to the simpler, stabler, and more isolated world of the nineteenth century. The national goal in the 1930s was the restoration of full employment, primarily by stimulating the demand for goods and services. Since the Depression was severe and prolonged—a "crisis" that persisted and threatened to become permanent—the national goal of reviving the economy was explicitly articulated by Congress and the President, and national legislative enactments and executive proclamations were increasingly employed to effect this goal. Popular consciousness of a national goal was not only made increasingly widespread and intense, but was actually institutionalized in federal laws and in the later establishment of the Council of Economic Advisers. Following the Second World War, during which national security had preempted all other goals, economic growth once again emerged as an important goal, in part as a means of countering growth in the collectivist camp.

Beginning around 1968, environment preservation and enhancement became a major national goal in its own right. In part this was a reaction to the cost and success of the lunar landing project. Since we can afford to put a man on the moon, why can't we now do many more useful things that seem to be easier to accomplish: clean up the air and water, dispose of trash more effectively, develop biodegradable plastics, and the like?

Three major factors were responsible for the increase in pollutants: population growth, higher per capita incomes, and technological changes. Greater affluence made it possible for more consumers to buy growing amounts of quickly discarded artifacts. Both products and wrappings, particularly the plastic variety, were harder to dispose of by traditional means. Attempts to get rid of wastes in the usual air and water channels caused increasing pollution since the volumes of air and water had not increased. There was a growing awareness that two problems existed. First, air and water have considerable waste disposal capacities, but they were being exceeded in some congested localities. Second, air and water also have other uses than waste disposal, and overly intensive disposal use reduces their capacity to perform other essential functions. A further source of environmental discontent stems from chemical technology. Modern chemistry has devised pesticides, drugs, cosmetics, fertilizers, plastics, and food and fuel additives that ecologists, biochemists, and others have shown to be harmful to the human organism and to ecological systems. Finally, criticism of the automobile was greatly intensified as air pollution from that source increased.

Concern with the environment as a national goal developed rapidly. Intensive exposure of the issues on television and other mass media created a widespread and at times almost morbid concern. Mechanisms to aid in achieving environmental goals were rapidly institutionalized. The executive and legislative branches held hearings, wrote reports, prepared bills, passed laws, and instituted advisory and control agencies and groups. The resulting legislation was uneven in quality and coverage, a natural consequence of the piecemeal approach to a set of problems that required a highly integrated treatment. The general goal of environmental protection was sought by a variety of programs dealing separately with pollution, preservation of the wilderness, waste disposal, urban problems, and many other facets of the total problem area. Even within more narrowly defined subareas, a comprehensive approach was not taken. Separate programs govern not only various types of pollution—land, air, and water—but may cover only a single source of a given type of pollution. The general tendency was to set requirements at too high a level, imposing unnecessary costs and complicating the enforcement process.

With the Arab oil embargo of 1973, the energy crisis replaced the environment as the center of public policy debates. Combatting the energy crisis became a new national goal, with the remedies proposed ranging from crash programs to achieve national self-sufficiency to proposals for nationalization of all energy industries. Solving the energy problem clashed with preserving the environment, and many people were slow to realize that limited domestic energy supplies posed a real problem that would not yield to quick and easy solutions. The passage of special legislation to build the Alaskan pipeline and the decision to accelerate leasing of federally controlled offshore areas provide evidence that the public gave priority to energy over environmental preservation in some important instances. But environmentalists by no means deserted their positions; development of new energy sources continued to be delayed or thwarted in many ways by such opposition.

Of the two, the environmental goal may prove the more perennial. Although it is unlikely, it is at least possible that a series of technological breakthroughs could eventually provide us with adequate supplies of reasonably cheap domestic energy. But the public perception that the environment is adequately protected is, like all ultimately subjective matters, simply a state of mind that may never be attained. Unlike the space race goal, environmental protection has no dramatic solution that occurs at one point in time. The basic causes of pollution—growth in population, income, and productivity—will not subside. If the nation relaxes its efforts in fighting pollution, pollution will become worse and the issue will again become paramount. Concern with the environment thus promises to be as durable a goal as national security.

The major conflicts between environmental and other goals are rather obvious. Reducing pollution may require reductions in the rate of economic growth, particularly if the goal is to reduce pollution by large amounts in a short period of time. Those of the "Limits to Growth" persuasion are willing to limit or even halt economic growth if that is the price that must be paid to abate pollution. Most businessmen and labor organizations feel that the cessation of growth would be disastrous for stability in output and employment, and are less than happy with any brake on economic growth.

The contrast between the policies of the 1970s and the 1980s is instructive. During the late 1970s, environmental controls increased and their implementation was more vigorously prosecuted, but recession predominated in the economic sphere, and periods of economic recovery were brief and incomplete. In the early 1980s, the Reagan administration deemphasized environmental restrictions and reduced the resources devoted to implementation of existing controls. OPEC began experiencing difficulties in price-fixing, and oil prices weakened, facilitating a robust and prolonged economic recovery in the industrial countries. The results were predictable: there was a tendency for people once again to become more concerned with pollution and somewhat less anxious about impeding economic growth. Thus despite its deemphasis in the 1980s, the environment continues to be an important national priority.

MAJOR TYPES OF POLLUTION

The pollution problems associated with energy production and consumption are serious and require efficient solutions. Although economists become impatient with those who demand that all types of pollution be completely eliminated, regardless of the costs, this does not excuse them from looking seriously at the scope of energy-related pollution problems and correctly assessing their social costs. Were humans an amphibious species, we would presumably give air and water pollution equal attention; if we were aquatic, we would give priority to water pollution issues. Since humans are in fact air-breathing creatures, we should rationally be somewhat more concerned about air pollution, and it is here that energy industries cause greatest offense. Physicians have consistently held that the upper respiratory tract is the path of least resistance to infections. Foreign substances in the air, whether solid, liquid, or gaseous, not only are likely to act as primary sources of irritation but are also prone to hamper the body's defense mechanisms against infection and disabling organic alterations.

Although it would be no more appropriate to try to cover all the public health aspects of air pollution in this chapter than it would be to attempt to teach a medical course on a medicine bottle label, some of the more serious problems may be listed and briefly characterized. The respiratory system must absorb those air pollutants which it cannot expel, but it has mechanisms for expelling many of them. Nasal hairs filter out the largest of the solid particles in the air. Smaller particles may adhere to the mucus-coated nasal passageways and be ejected with the expectoration of the mucus. Still smaller particles may be deposited upon the mucus-lined walls of the bronchial tubes for later aspiration and expectoration. Very small particles may be exhaled before they are impacted upon the lining of the respiratory tract. But the smallest particles of all are driven into these linings by the forces of colliding air molecules. Even these absorbed particles may be escorted out of the lungs through engulfment by cells from the affected tissues, which then convey them into the blood or lymph streams or out of the body through eventual expectoration.

But these defense mechanisms can be overwhelmed by having to cope with large volumes of pollutants and with mixtures of different pollutants in different forms. A good example of the latter is the combination of particulate matter and sulfur dioxide. Ordinarily, sulfur dioxide gas is absorbed in the upper respiratory tract without injury. But if particulate matter is also present in the air, the sulfur dioxide may combine with water and coat the particles with sulfuric acid. If the coated particles are small enough to reach the lungs, serious injury may result.

Air pollution has been shown to be an aggravating factor in the following disease conditions: lung cancer, asthma, influenza, pneumonia, emphysema, bronchitis, tuberculosis of the respiratory system, arteriosclerotic heart disease, hypertensive heart disease, rheumatic fever and chronic rheumatic heart disease, certain other diseases of the heart and circulatory system, and certain types of nephritis and nephrosis of the kidneys. Classical smog, discussed later in this chapter, is chiefly harmful because of sulfur compounds. The burning of high-sulfur coal is the chief cause, although discharges from metal smelters may also play a role in some localities. The sulfuric acid in the atmosphere, when taken into the lungs, causes serious lung irritation and increases the resistance of the respiratory tract passageways to the inspiration of air, complicating breathing for the elderly and ill, especially for those suffering from bronchitis and emphysema.

The particles around which sulfuric acid forms are often removed from the air by rainfall. This causes the phenomenon of acid rain, which damages croplands and forests and may distress aquatic life in bodies of water receiving the runoff. The sulfuric acid also damages building surfaces with which it comes into contact. Photochemical smog (also discussed below) is produced primarily by emissions from hydrocarbon-fueled internal combustion machines and contains such irritants as ozone, hydrocarbons, and nitrogen compounds rather than sulfuric substances. Ozone has an unpleasant odor, increases respiratory passageway resistance to breathing, and damages plants and artifacts. Nitrogen compounds are responsible for the opacity of photochemical smog and have toxic effects. Hydrocarbons can combine with nitrogen compounds to produce eye irritation and can also cause serious injury to plant life. But while classical smog is statistically associated with the human mortality rate from respiratory and cardiac disorders, no such statistical relationship has been established between photochemical smog and mortality rates.

Let us now briefly consider the major types of pollution. The usual classification is by the nature of the medium affected by the pollutants: the atmosphere, bodies of water, and the soil. To these may be added thermal pollution, which affects both air and water, and radiation pollution, which affects air, water, and soils. These types of pollutants are to some extent substitutes for each other. Some air pollutants can be removed from fuels prior to combustion or from the combustion gases before their dispersal, but this implies the substitution of more solid or liquid wastes for a reduction in gaseous wastes. A prohibition of both air and water pollution would tend to build up large volumes of solid wastes. Thermal pollution occurs primarily as a byproduct of inefficient energy conversion processes, such as those associated with electric power generation. Here the alternatives are chiefly cooling ponds or cooling towers, but in either case there is the substitution of greater or lesser air pollution for lesser or greater water pollution. Radiation can have adverse impacts on land, water, or air, but its problems are most serious in regard to the solid and liquid wastes produced by nuclear power plants.

AIR POLLUTION

Air is a mixture of elements and compounds, each in its gaseous form. Its crucial constituent is oxygen (21 percent of the atmosphere by volume), which is the only gas that can support the respiration of living matter. The chief component, nitrogen (78 percent), is chemically virtually inert at ordinary temperatures and pressures; the only other gas present in appreciable concentration (0.9 percent) is argon, which is absolutely inert. Air pollution problems of a chemical nature tend to arise when carbon, hydrogen, and sulfur atoms and molecules combine with the oxygen and nitrogen already present in the air to form compounds that injure living tissues and damage property. Air pollution problems that are initially physical in nature arise when particulate matter (ash, soot, dust, etc.) is released into the atmosphere, but the presence of such particles may facilitate subsequent chemical reactions that further increase the adverse effects of chemically polluted air on the environment.

It is instructive to proceed by taking the simplest form of a combustion reaction and showing how various types of air pollutants may be released in case of incomplete or inefficient combustion, or in the presence of "impurities" in the fuel. In a combustion reaction the fuel (which may for example be a compound) combines with oxygen, and as a result of this "burning" energy is released, along with one or more different compounds that result from the rearrangement of the atoms and molecules originally present in the fuel and the oxygen. Widespread interest and concern with nuclear power has acquainted many people with the fact that mass can be transformed into energy in accordance with Einstein's equation, $E = mc^2$ (where E is expressed in energy units, m is measured in mass units, and c is the speed of light). As discussed in Chapter 9, the nuclei of certain heavy atoms can be split apart, resulting usually in the production of two lighter atoms and an energy yield that arises because the combined mass of the two lighter atoms is less than that of the original atom. The loss of mass is not very great, but the ratio between mass and energy is so large that nuclear fission produces enormous energy levels. In every energy reaction, however, there is this necessary relationship of equivalence between energy flows and mass changes. In such a simple example as the winding of a clock spring, the mass of the spring is very minutely increased when fully wound, and subsequently decreases as the energy of the unwinding spring is used to operate the clockworks. Similarly, energy is produced by the "molecular fission" of fuel substances utilized in the form of elements and compounds. But while the binding energy of subatomic particles within the nucleus of the atom is governed by the extremely intense force field of the atomic nucleus, the forces binding the atoms within the molecules of a compound are governed by electromagnetic interactions that are much less intense—only about one millionth as great.

Nevertheless, the forces binding molecules together are appreciable, and since there are so very many molecules involved in fuel combustion reactions, the total energy liberated can be quite large. The energy that is liberated is measured by the so-called heat of combustion of the fuel compound, with fuels having higher heats of combustion being greater sources of energy, other things being equal.

If one is interested only in the energy output of a combustion process, the unattainable ideal goal would be the complete conversion of the mass of the fuel to energy, but this is impossible even in nuclear reactions. Energy and mass are joint products in any combustion process, and it is simply unfortunate from pollution and other standpoints that much of the resulting mass is an unwanted byproduct.

Let us begin by surveying the air pollution potential of the major fuels. Petroleum, which includes both crude oil and natural gas, is primarily a mixture of hydrocarbons, which are compounds in which each molecule contains n atoms of carbon and $2n + 2$ atoms of hydrogen. The simplest hydrocarbon is methane (CH_4), which is the chief constituent of natural gas. The complete combustion of methane would result in the following reaction:

$$CH_4 + 2\,O_2 \rightarrow CO_2 + 2\,H_2O + \text{energy}$$

This states that the reaction of one molecule of methane (CH_4) with two molecules of oxygen (O_2) yields one molecule of carbon dioxide (CO_2), two molecules of water (H_2O), and a quantity of energy, ordinarily released in the form of process heat. From one standpoint this would be a pollution-free combustion reaction, since water is not a pollutant and carbon dioxide would seem to be environmentally benign, having no adverse impact on organisms or artifacts, and indeed being an indispensible input into the metabolism of plants. (As we shall see in a later section, however, in the long run the continued build-up of atmospheric carbon dioxide may cause significant climatic changes, which may result in great economic costs and dislocations.)

The above reaction is oversimplified to the extent that energy inputs are also required to heat the methane to its ignition temperature in order to allow the reaction to proceed, that pure oxygen rather than air is assumed to be used as an input, and that the combustion reaction is assumed to be completely efficient. Accordingly, we should interpret the hypothetical reaction as producing a net energy yield as shown on the right-hand side of the above expression, rather than the actual gross energy yield. The net yield would vary with the efficiency of the process used to bring the methane fuel to its ignition temperature. Also, for complete combustion some excess of oxygen would have to be supplied, rather than the theoretical minimum of two molecules of oxygen for each molecule of methane. In and of itself, an excess input of oxygen (perhaps 5%) would increase the expense of the process but would not contribute to air pollution, since the extra oxygen would simply be released harmlessly into the air. But if incomplete combustion takes place due to the absence of an excess of oxygen, then some carbon dioxide molecules are replaced by carbon monoxide molecules, which may interfere with the respiratory processes of human and animal organisms by replacing oxygen in the hemoglobin of red blood cells and causing partial or total suffocation. Incomplete combustion of methane would therefore imply the following sort of reaction:

$$a \text{ CH}_4 + b \text{ O}_2 \rightarrow c \text{ CO} + d \text{ CO}_2 + e \text{ H}_2\text{O} + \text{energy}$$

where a, b, c, d, and e are the numbers of molecules of the various elements and compounds involved.

Let us now consider the possibility of various impurities in the methane fuel. Of these, the most serious is sulfur, often present in its elemental form in "sour" natural gas. Sulfur combines readily with oxygen to yield sulfur oxides of varying degrees of pollution potential. Let us consider the simplest sour natural gas combustion reaction and its likely consequences:

$$a \text{ CH}_4 + b \text{ S} + c \text{ O}_2 \rightarrow d \text{ CO}_2 + e \text{ H}_2\text{O} + f \text{ SO}_2 + \text{energy}$$

where a through f are again the numbers of molecules present in the reaction. The chief problem is with the resulting sulfur dioxide (SO_2), which can in turn combine with water to yield toxic sulfurous acid (H_2SO_3) as follows:

$$SO_2 + H_2O \rightarrow H_2SO_3$$

Alternatively, sulfur and oxygen can combine to produce sulfur trioxide (SO_3), which then unites with water to produce highly toxic sulfuric acid (H_2SO_4) that is very costly in terms of health impairment and property damages:

$$2 \text{ S} + 3 \text{ O}_2 \rightarrow 2 \text{ SO}_3; \qquad SO_3 + H_2O \rightarrow H_2SO_4$$

Before leaving methane, let us consider the possibility of nitrogen oxide pollutants. We have been assuming pure oxygen as the oxidizing input, but let us now concede that most combustion reactions take place in the presence of air, with its predominant content of usually inert nitrogen. The ideal methane combustion reaction in air would yield the following results:

$$CH_4 + 2 \text{ O}_2 + 7.52 \text{ N}_2 \rightarrow CO_2 + 2 \text{ H}_2\text{O} + 7.52 \text{ N}_2$$

where 7.52 molecules of nitrogen (each consisting of two atoms of nitrogen) per molecule of methane input are both an input to and an output from the reaction. If the reaction takes place at a temperature above approximately 1000°C (1832°F), then atmospheric nitrogen ceases to be chemically inert and combines with oxygen to produce nitrogen oxides. In the first stage nitric oxide (NO) is formed:

$$N_2 + O_2 \rightarrow 2\,NO$$

If an excess of oxygen is present, nitrogen dioxide (NO_2) is formed consequently:

$$2\,NO + O_2 \rightarrow 2\,NO_2$$

In the presence of water, the nitrogen dioxide dissolves, forming a solution of nitrous acid (HNO_2) and nitric acid (HNO_3):

$$2\,NO_2 + H_2O \rightarrow HNO_2 + HNO_3$$

Nitrous acid is unstable and decomposes, forming further nitric oxides; under laboratory conditions all of the oxides of nitrogen are converted into dilute nitric acid, a substance obviously not conducive to health or the preservation of exposed artifacts. The role of nitric oxides in actual air pollution is discussed in the next sections.

If we leave methane and proceed to heavier hydrocarbons, which are liquid rather than gaseous, incomplete or inefficient combustion now gives rise not just to carbon monoxide but to the release of unburned fluid hydrocarbons into the atmosphere. These unburned hydrocarbons can range from methane itself through heavier gaseous hydrocarbons (ethane, propane, butane, pentane) to the lighter liquid hydrocarbons (hexane, heptane, octane) and upward to still heavier molecules. Such hydrocarbons constitute impurities in the atmosphere, regardless of their chemical conversions, and many of them contribute greatly to photochemical smog. Such smog occurs when air containing hydrocarbons and nitrogen compounds is exposed to sunlight and yields pollutants that discolor the sky and irritate plant and animal tissues, as in the Los Angeles Basin. Hydrocarbon emissions have many sources, including evaporation from fuel tanks, release from inefficient carburetors, and from incomplete combustion of overly rich fuel mixtures or improperly adjusted engine operations.

Let us finally turn to coal, which consists primarily of carbon but also contains significant amounts of hydrogen, oxygen, nitrogen, and sulfur in varying concentrations. Coal differs from petroleum, however, in its ash content. Ash results from the presence of mineral residues of the organic materials from which the coal was formed. If we assume coal to be in the form of pure carbon (anthracite coal typically has a carbon content of over 90 percent), then the ideal coal combustion reaction would be $C + O_2 \rightarrow CO_2$ + energy, and no pollution problems would be present except for the long-run risks associated with an increase in the concentration of carbon dioxide in the atmosphere. Unfortunately this is only a gross caricature of the air pollution potential of coal combustion. In addition to the previously discussed problems of sulfur oxides formed by burning high-sulfur coal, and nitrogen oxides that are released when coal is burned at a high temperature, the ash and other solid matter in coal gives rise to particulates, or small solid particles, which give air pollution a physical dimension and complicate its chemical reactions. The chief particulate emissions from coal combustion include soot (unburned carbon), fly ash (consisting of mineral residues in the coal such as silicon and aluminum), and tar, which represents unburned heavy hydrocarbons present in the coal. On the other hand, coal combustion results in relatively low levels of carbon monoxide and hydrocarbon pollution.

While air pollution also results from some nonenergy activities, it can be said that most of it is a byproduct of combustion processes. These combustion processes release chemical and physical pollutants into the atmosphere in the form of gaseous compounds or solid particles. These pollutants reside in the air for limited periods of time before being deposited on land or sea. They may then be absorbed wherever deposited, or may in some cases be reintroduced into the air, as in the dispersal of ashy residues by winds. The atmosphere has a high capacity for absorbing wastes, due to its vast volume and the more or less continuous mixing of its constituent parts by thermal convection currents. The air's capacity to handle wastes by dilution and dispersion, however, may be overtaxed in areas where excessive concentrations of pollutants are emitted. There are five major categories of air pollutants: carbon monoxide, hydrocarbon compounds, sulfur oxides, nitrogen oxides, and particulates. Table 5.1 shows the estimated quantities of these pollutants emitted during the period 1940–1980, in millions of tons per year, over the United States. Unfortunately, research on the damage associated with each of these forms of pollutants does not allow us to place a cost on each. Of these five, a number of studies

TABLE 5.1 Emission Levels for Major Air Pollutants, 1940–1980, in Millions of Tons

Year	Sulfur Oxides	Particulates	Carbon Monoxide	Hydrocarbons	Nitrogen Oxides
1940	18.0	18.9	65.5	15.0	6.1
1950	19.9	18.1	79.0	20.1	8.1
1960	19.5	17.7	97.8	24.7	10.9
1970	28.4	17.9	112.8	27.2	17.6
1975	25.6	10.6	100.2	23.2	18.6
1980	23.4	8.7	95.0	23.0	19.8

SOURCE: *For 1940–1960 computed indexes (1970 = 1):* Nationwide Air Pollutant Emission Trends, 1940–70, *U.S. Environmental Protection Agency. For 1970–1980: "National Air Pollutant Emission Estimates, 1970–1981," U.S. Environmental Protection Agency.*

have established substantial health and property damages associated with sulfur oxides, suggesting that at existing concentrations sulfur oxides are probably the most serious pollutant.

It is evident from this table that between 1940 and 1972, particulates were the only pollutant to decline while the others increased at various rates. This reduction was due simply to the replacement of coal, a solid fuel, by fluid fuels without solid residues. Between 1970 and 1975, however, the impact of air pollution control laws began to be felt. Carbon monoxide emissions fell by 11 percent from 112.8 million tons to 100.2 million. Particulates fell by 41 percent, from 17.9 million tons to 10.6 million; hydrocarbons fell by 15 percent, and sulfur oxides fell by about 10 percent, while nitrogen oxides increased by 6 percent. By 1980, however, even greater progress had been achieved, particularly for sulfur oxides, the most serious pollutant. Nitrogen oxides remain a prominent exception, resulting from engine design advances to enable more complete combustion of hydrocarbons at higher temperatures and pressures.

The statistics in Table 5.1 indicate substantial progress since 1970 in the volume of total pollutants. But for inner city dwellers the gains have been much greater. Government policies have aimed not only at reducing the aggregate quantity of air pollution, but also on reducing the concentration of pollutants in the air in densely populated areas.

As stated earlier, carbon monoxide emissions result from the incomplete combustion of fuels when insufficient oxygen is supplied to the fuel in the combustion chamber. The pronounced increase in carbon monoxide emissions between 1940 and 1972 was due largely to the increased use of fuels by a growing stock of automobiles. Engine emission control devices have been largely responsible for the decline in emissions since 1972. Hydrocarbon emissions increased apace with the growth in the use of petroleum fuels, both oil and gas, in both mobile and stationary power units. Reduced emissions since 1972 have resulted from controls on all such power units.

Table 5.2 shows the percentage of each pollutant resulting from the activities of each of five sectors: transportation, stationary fuel combustion, industrial processing, solid waste disposal, and miscellaneous uses, including such items as forest fires and fires in coal refuse dumps. The last line in this table shows the estimated percentage of each pollutant originating in energy-related activities, defining this category broadly to include energy use in fabrication, processing, and elsewhere. It is apparent that energy-related activities account for the majority of all air pollution, ranging from 57.9 percent of particulates to 98.7 percent of sulfur oxides. The transportation sector is responsible for 64.6 percent of all carbon monoxide emissions, and roughly half of all hydrocarbons and nitrogen compounds, but only a few percent of particulates and sulfur compounds. Of all particulates, 50.3 percent are emitted by the industrial sector, and another 24.6 percent comes from stationary power plants, with almost all the remainder

TABLE 5.2 Emission Levels for Major Air Pollutants, Classified by Source, 1980, in Millions of Tons

	Carbon Monoxide	Particulates	Sulfur Oxides	Hydrocarbons	Nitrogen Oxides
Total emission (in millions of tons)	85.4	17.1	28.9	28.3	28.7
Sources (percent)					
Transportation	64.6	2.2	2.8	45.4	49.6
Fuel combustion (stationary)	1.4	24.6	72.6	2.2	40.4
Industrial	9.9	50.3	23.1	15.4	0.8
Solid waste disposal	7.8	5.0	0.7	6.1	2.0
Miscellaneous	16.3	17.9	0.8	30.9	7.2
All energy uses	76.0	57.9	98.7	64.4	88.8

SOURCE: *Environmental protection Agency.*

from the miscellaneous category. Almost 72.6 percent of sulfur oxides originate with stationary power plants, with the remainder coming largely from industry. Hydrocarbon emissions not accounted for in the transportation sector come largely from storage and processing losses in the petroleum industry and from other industrial processes. Stationary power plants rank second to transportation in the emission of nitrogen oxides, with industry generating very little of this pollutant.

Carbon monoxide pollution in transportation is confined largely to gasoline-powered vehicles, with diesel and jet engines producing very little. The catalyst regeneration process in petroleum refining emits the bulk of carbon monoxide in the industrial sector. Stationary power plants emit little of this pollutant, since their fuel combustion is more complete, yielding carbon dioxide rather than carbon monoxide.

Particulates emitted in energy-related industries come largely from the combustion of coal in stationary power plants and from industrial applications such as the smelting of metals. Substantial volumes of particulates are also generated by forest fires and by the incineration of solid wastes.

By contrast, almost all sulfur oxide emissions are energy-related. Sulfur is found in oil, gas, and coal, but is easily and economically removable only from natural gas. In petroleum refining, hydrogen desulfurizers operating in conjunction with the catalytic cracking process can reduce the sulfur content of the lighter refined products such as gasoline and jet fuels to insignificant levels. But the heavier the product, the higher the sulfur content and (in general) the more costly the extraction process. For example, residual fuel oil, a thick viscous oil used by power plants and for marine bunker fuel, can contain more than 30 times as much sulfur as gasoline. But the major source of sulfur compound emissions is the use of coal and high-sulfur fuel oil in stationary power plants, in both utilities and industry. This coal and high-sulfur fuel oil have a sulfur content of about 2.5 percent, currently being reduced to about 1.0 percent after treatment. Other sulfur emissions come from the petroleum refining industry, both from the hydrogen sulfide stream generated by the desulfurization process itself, and from the regeneration of the catalysts used in catalytic cracking processes.

Hydrocarbon emissions come primarily from gasoline-powered internal-combustion engines and from evaporation at petroleum storage and distribution facilities. Nitrogen oxides come from both mobile and stationary power sources. Hydrocarbon and nitrogen oxide emissions lead to the most highly visible sort of air pollution, photochemical smog. While hydrocarbons are usually emitted due to evaporation from, or incomplete burning of, petroleum fuels, nitrogen oxides result from the burning of fuels at high temperatures and pressures with relatively high efficiency. The high temperatures promote reaction of the fuel substance with atmospheric nitrogen. It is one of the ironies of the automobile air pollution control saga that measures originally designed to reduce carbon monoxide and hydrocarbon emissions caused an increase in nitrogen oxides. Since both carbon monoxide and hydrocarbon emissions in exhaust gases are an indication of incomplete combustion due to oxygen deficiency in the fuel mixture, the remedy appears to lie in increasing the ratio of air to fuel. Unfortunately this leaner fuel mixture burns at a higher temperature, increasing nitrogen oxides by about 40 percent.

Photochemical smog is produced by the action of sunlight on hydrocarbons and nitrogen oxides. The reactions involved are complex and imperfectly understood, but the most important of them cause the production of ozone from nitrogen dioxide and the creation of numerous organic irritants called peroxyacyl nitrates (PAN) from the hydrocarbons. Ozone is toxic in very low concentrations, has a foul odor, complicates respiration, and is very harmful to plant life. Peroxyacyl nitrates act as eye irritants and are also quite harmful to plants.

A final energy-related air pollutant is lead, a highly toxic element released into the atmosphere by the combustion of leaded gasoline. In 1983, about 90,000 tons of lead were thus released, some of which was ingested and stored in the tissues of human beings. But leaded gasoline is in the process of being phased out (the amount of lead released in 1968 was 420,000 tons) because of the requirement that all new cars be equipped with catalytic converters that oxidize the hydrocarbon and carbon monoxide components of the exhaust stream into carbon dioxide and water. Since leaded fuels deactivate these devices, only unleaded gasoline can be used in automobiles produced in recent years. Since the laws began to take effect in the mid-1970s, the consumption of leaded gasoline has fallen sharply and will continue to be phased out, since the average service life of an automobile is limited to about ten years.

Very Long-Run Air Pollution Dilemmas

The Problem of Carbon Dioxide Buildup. In the short and intermediate runs, the solution of the air pollution problem is largely a matter of imposing taxes or standards to improve combustion efficiency, emission quality, and the sulfur content of fuels. Such programs, as we have seen, can within a decade or so reduce the volumes of the major air pollutants that are emitted, without necessarily reducing the level of operation of energy industries themselves. But combustion processes of all sorts release increasing volumes of carbon dioxide each year. There is growing concern over the very long-run effects of an increase in the carbon dioxide content of the atmosphere. This concern stems from (1) the rapid buildup of atmospheric CO_2 since the late 1950s, and (2) the probable consequences of the higher average world temperatures resulting from the increasing CO_2 concentrations. The problem is unusually serious because it is very long term in nature—elevated levels of carbon dioxide will not be reduced for centuries even if current fuel combustion were to be greatly curtailed. In addition, agreements to achieve such curtailment should prove virtually impossible to obtain since elements of market failure are predominant. If one country cuts its rate of fuel combustion, it bears the full cost in terms of reduction in its economic activity level, while the benefits of its action are shared with the entire world, due to the homogeneous dispersion of atmospheric CO_2 worldwide. Third, it appears that the world is already experiencing a long-run warming trend, which is likely to change optimal world crop growth and population density patterns significantly; an additional warming trend from increasing fossil fuel combustion could make matters a great deal worse.[1]

The fundamental problem arises because of the so-called "greenhouse effect." Carbon dioxide is transparent to incoming solar radiation, but largely opaque to the reflection of solar energy back out into space. Thus the higher the atmospheric content of CO_2, the greater the tendency for the air to heat up at lower levels due to the retention of solar heat near the earth's surface. The problem and its possible solutions are complicated by additional difficulties and uncertainties. CO_2 is not the only compound having such an effect; there are a number of so-called "greenhouse gases" such as chlorofluorocarbons, nitrous oxide, methane, and tropospheric ozone; while these gases are produced in smaller volumes than CO_2, they have been rapidly increasing in recent decades, and often have a much more pronounced greenhouse effect per volume unit than carbon dioxide does. In addition, the problem of CO_2 buildup has been accelerated by the worldwide trend toward deforestation, as forests have typically been large consumers of carbon dioxide.

The CO_2 problem is a very long-range problem involving changing ecological equilibrium on a global level. What help can the economist provide? We can only try to identify the known facts, appraise the uncertainties, suggest policies, question their feasibility, and issue warnings. The simplest view is that increasing combustion of fossil fuels increases CO_2 levels, and makes climates warmer worldwide. The resulting increase in heat will on balance increase the length of growing seasons but will significantly reduce rainfall, increasing the size of existing deserts, and will tend to lower total crop production. More ominously, rising ocean temperatures will melt existing ice caps in Greenland and Antarctica, raising ocean levels and inundating coastal areas worldwide. The higher temperatures at the earth's surface will also result in significant purely thermal expansion of the oceans, further raising the level of the sea. It is easy to project astronomical costs from the necessity to protect coasts with lengthy dikes of increasing height, and from the expected decline in world crop harvests.

The evidence for increasing CO_2 concentrations is impressive: between 1958 and 1982 the increase was from 315 to 340 parts per million, or a total of 8 percent over a period of only 24 years—roughly 1/3 of one percent per year. Depending upon one's forecast of the growth in fossil fuel combustion, one can project a doubling of the carbon dioxide concentration in 50 to 250 years. Current studies predict that a doubling of CO_2 concentrations will raise average global temperatures by from 1.5 to 4.5 degrees centigrade. A doubling of the concentration of the other greenhouse gases would jointly raise temperatures by about the same order of magnitude, although the doubling time for the other gases would probably not coincide closely with that for carbon dioxide.

This implies that perhaps by the year 2050 the temperature may be from 3.0 to 9.0 degrees centigrade warmer, which is a rate of heat increase unknown during the period of civilized human life. The impact on agriculture is likely to be significant, and on the whole negative. If we look at the prospects for crops in temperate regions, there are several important effects, which are difficult to assess either individually or in conjunction. First, it appears that higher CO_2 concentrations will promote more rapid crop growth, just as a higher oxygen content in the air would promote animal respiration. For the next few decades an increase in crop yields of about 5 percent might by projected, other things being equal. Unfortunately, however, warmer climates tend to be drier, and a drop in rainfall would cut crop yields by about 5 to 10 percent in areas where rainfall is relied upon for moisture. Where irrigation is relied upon, the outlook is still less favorable, with yield decreases of 25 percent or more foreseeable in areas hard hit by declining precipitation. While there will be some increase in the length of the growing season, this will usually be offset by drier soil conditions.

The problems associated with rising sea levels appear to be somewhat less urgent over the next 50 or more years, but perhaps increasingly troublesome thereafter. It is not widely known that the sea level has been rising by about 3 feet per century over the last 15,000 years, so that a rise of more than 450 feet has occurred since the end of the last ice age. During the last few centuries the rise has been much smaller than the longer-run average—perhaps 8 to 10 inches per century. A warming of the earth's surface would mean rapid heating of land areas but much slower heating of the oceans due to the greater resistance of water, as compared to air, in absorbing heat. Eventually the oceans would warm up, however, and their levels would rise. It is estimated that within the next century a rise of about 16 inches will be due to the melting of alpine and continental glaciers and another 12 inches due to the expansion of warmer waters, for a total of about 28 inches. Really major increases in ocean levels could occur within the next two or three centuries if the west Antarctic ice sheet (large ice masses resting on bedrock below the level of the ocean) were to collapse, with resulting elevations of 15 to 20 feet in mean sea level.

Although a sea rise of 28 inches in 100 years does not sound formidable, it could pose real problems in coastal areas where erosion, storm surges, and encroachment of saline waters upon fresh groundwater aquifers represent hazards that are expensive to combat. For increases of 15 to 20 feet, very expensive dikes and landfills might be the only alternative to abandonment and relocation.

An optimal strategy for coping with all the probable consequences of climate change due to energy-related activities would have to be very comprehensive, global in scale for most purposes, and flexibly adapted to national, regional, and local conditions for many others. Such a strategy would have many elements. First, some CO_2 emissions could be prevented. High taxes on carbon-intensive fuels such as coal could reduce their consumption. This would tend to be a rather costly method for those adopting it, particularly if world adoption of such measures is less than universal. Second, attempts might be made to reduce existing concentrations of carbon dioxide. Again, this strategy would appear to be highly costly. One possible way is to increase the world's standing forests. More trees mean that more carbon is removed from the atmosphere and is fixed (during the life of the tree) in the tree's own structure. More leaves and branches active in the process of photosynthesis "sweep" the air more intensively and remove CO_2 from the air, contributing more oxygen in return.

Third, it might be possible to make countervailing changes in the climate. To this end various agencies might attempt to alter rainfall patterns and the tracks of tropical storms and hurricanes, and to change cloud cover configurations. At present these techniques are not fully developed in their feasibility and reliability, and their use could provoke international confrontations, as when rain, for example, is diverted from one country to another. On a more manageable scale it might be economical to insure greater and more flexible water supplies by building dams, constructing canals and aqueducts, and altering river courses, although here too international and interregional conflicts are very likely.

Fourth, a policy of successive adaptation to changing conditions might be chosen. Through compensatory adaptation, vulnerability could be reduced and impacts could perhaps be gradually absorbed. This would involve considerable migration, changes in agricultural practices, different cultivation patterns, development of new plant varieties, changes in crop mixes and dietary habits, adoption of various regulations in energy-consuming sectors, the improvement of water-use efficiency, and similar measures.

Economists might be expected to prefer the fourth type of program as ways of meeting a gradually developing set of changes in climatic conditions, since it suggests continual incremental adaptation at various margins. This is a reasonable position to hold. Nevertheless, due to difficulties in cooperation over time and space and to lack of foresight, certain problems may arise. Two situations may be pointed out. First, it is possible that more dikes and seawalls will be built than are truly economical. Given the very gradual rate of change in the sea level, seawalls will appear attractive at the outset, and once they have been built, it will always seem preferable to reinforce and extend them rather than to evacuate a given area. Second, as farm lands become more arid, there will be a strong tendency to adopt protective measures limiting imports and to arrange subsidies for continued farming and expanded irrigation facilities. If the region itself has strong political power, it may favor measures that sink increasing sums of money in less and less economical farming methods, increasing the cost of food and the risk of crop failure as long as such uneconomical programs can be maintained.

Before adopting any particular strategy, much more research must be done. Research might first be aimed at clarifying the nature of the carbon cycle. How much of the carbon dioxide emitted from fossil fuels remains in the atmosphere, and for how long? How much is stored in the oceans, on land, and in marine sediments? These questions were asked before, but there may be some urgency in supplying an answer. We know in a general way that carbon in the atmosphere is extracted by growing plants, which use it as an input in their photosynthesis, but which then yield back this carbon when they die and decay. Only part of this carbon is, however, returned to the air; over time much of it is transported to the ocean and buried in marine sediments. How much remains buried is a matter of speculation at present. Due to the limited number of drilling samples taken worldwide to date, the estimates range all the way from one trillion to 500 trillion tons.

The other major economic recommendation is that funds should somehow be provided for the more extensive and accurate worldwide monitoring of atmospheric concentrations of CO_2, other greenhouse gases, volcanic ash, aerosols, ozone, and solar radiation itself. In addition, adequate monitoring should be done to determine changes in surface and atmospheric temperatures, rainfall and cloud cover, snow and sea-ice cover, polar ice-sheet mass balances, sea levels, and radiation fluxes at the top of the atmosphere. The costs of such monitoring, spread over a worldwide base, should not be particularly large; in the present limited state of our knowledge, it would bring more than commensurate benefits.

The Problem of Acid Rain. A final long-term aspect of energy-related air pollution deserving separate consideration is the phenomenon of acid rain—or, more properly speaking, of acid deposition, since the acids in question are conveyed not only by rain but also by fog and snow, and in dry form as chemical precursor gases by direct distribution. Acid deposition incidents may be brief but their consequences, like those of CO_2 build-up, are very long-lasting (although localized rather than global). The problems occur when combustion and other processes release sulfur oxides and nitrogen oxides into the atmosphere, some portions of which are converted to acids that reach the ground in the form of rain, snow, fog, or dry deposits. The acids may be deposited 100 to 1000 miles or more from the source of the emissions, and the environmental damage is most severe for those soils, lakes, trees, fish, and crop species that are particularly susceptible to disruption from increased acidity. While the phenomenon of acid deposition would largely cease in a few months after all surfur and nitrogen oxide emissions ceased, damage to forests and particularly lakes might not be reversed for a number of centuries. Paradoxically, at a time when high-sulfur coal burning has been stabilized, forests in Germany, Sweden, Czechoslavakia, and Poland are suddenly dying. The diagnosis is that previous levels of acid rain slowly weakened the resistance of the forests to drought and disease.

It might appear that control of acid rain would be a simple matter. After all, sulfur oxide emissions have been reduced dramatically. But the problem of acid rain is interwoven with international relations. Much of the acid rain emanating from French, German, Italian, and British industry is ultimately deposited in the Scandinavian countries. On a smaller scale the United States exports acid rain to Canada from utility plants located along the Great Lakes. Under these conditions, the benefits of reducing pollution and the cost of reducing pollution fall quite unevenly, providing little incentive for polluting countries to reduce sulfur emissions. Furthermore, there is genuine disagreement in the academic community about the magnitude of the benefits from reductions in sulfur oxide emissions, because of the apparent long-term effects of acid rain and its interaction with other pollutants. Thus even if one agrees that acid rain must be reduced, the question becomes: "How much?"

One might conclude that not much action will be taken to reduce acid rain. But this overlooks the widespread concern in Europe about continued eradication of the forests. In 1983, virtually all European countries agreed to reduce their sulfur emissions to 70% of their 1983 levels by the year 2000. While this cooperation is an encouraging development, acid rain seems likely to remain a serious long-term pollution problem.

WATER POLLUTION

Energy activities do not loom nearly as large in land and water pollution as they do in air contamination. While most air pollution results from combustion, water pollution has numerous sources: disposal of solid and liquid wastes, surface runoff, thermal pollution, and the like. The physical and economic characteristics of pollution are also somewhat different. If air pollution controls are more strictly enforced than water pollution laws, polluters may try to capture some pollutants in liquid form for disposal in rivers, lakes, and bays. But the capacity of rivers and other inland bodies of water to absorb pollutants is less than that of the air.

Historically, water pollution was the first kind of pollution to be subjected to public control. Fear of epidemics spread by contaminated drinking water led to water treatment by municipalities. This action, however, established the somewhat unfortunate precedent that treatment was applied to the input of the water plant rather than to the output of polluters. This decision is easy to understand in terms of economics. Treatment of water by chlorination was cheap and effective, and costs and benefits were well matched since the expenses incurred by the city benefited only its own water uses. Cleaning up a river as it flowed through the city would be of primary benefit to downstream water users who were beyond the taxing jurisdiction of the city.

Water pollutants can be classified in many ways. Physically they consist of liquids (both mixtures and compounds), suspended solids, larger solids, and energy in the form of heat or radiation. By source, one can distinguish among the pollutants discharged from agriculture (fertilizers, herbicides, pesticides, and erosion sediments), industry (heat, solids, liquids, radiation), mining (sediments, acids, ore wastes), electrical power generation (heat and nuclear wastes), navigation (garbage and fuel wastes), and municipal wastes (sewage, detergents, garbage, trash, and urban drainage, including road salt and suspended sediments). Another important classification is that between biode-gradable and nondegradable wastes, with plastics and many other synthetic organic chemical substances in the latter category.

Rivers have a certain natural capacity to absorb biodegradable pol-lutants. This capacity depends upon several factors, notably upon the amount of dissolved oxygen available to support the microorganisms responsible for waste decomposition. The dissolved oxygen content varies directly with stream turbulence and inversely with temperature of the water. Thus, to preserve the waste-handling capacity of a body of water the temperature must not be increased, and the introduction of substances toxic to the necessary microorganisms must be avoided. Loss of dissolved oxygen results not only in reduction of fish popula-tion but eventually in the creation of an anaerobic environment, within which waste decomposition proceeds to the accompaniment of foul odors and scenic blight.

Energy industries contribute to water pollution primarily through thermal effects and to a much lesser extent through the introduction of fuels into bodies of water. Actual waste discharges by industries in the energy sector into water channels account for only 1 or 2 percent of the biochemical oxygen demand (BOD) of discharged wastes. In contrast, thermally inefficient energy conversion processes are respon-sible for heat pollution; that part of the energy content of the fuel input which is not converted into useful work appears in the form of heat and must somehow be dissipated. Quantitatively the most signif-icant thermal polluters are the relatively fuel-inefficient energy con-verters in the generation of electricity by conventional and nuclear power plants, which are estimated to account for over 70 percent of thermal pollution. The environmental consequences of this thermal pollution consist chiefly of the impairment of the capacity of heated streams to decompose wastes. Thermal pollution of bodies of water can be controlled by further cooling of process waters in cooling tow-ers before they are discharged into streams and lakes.

The environmental impact of crude oil spills at sea has been exag-gerated by the communications media. Crude oil is biodegradable; moreover, there are vast volumes of ocean water available for ade-quate dilution and dispersion unless large spills occur close to shore-lines. It has been estimated that on a worldwide basis, tanker acci-dents account for about 150,000 tons of oil per year, or about 10 percent of the total annual oil release of about 1.5 million tons into the oceans. Offshore drilling accidents worldwide release only about 28,000 tons, while runoff from onshore operations like refining pro-vides about half a million tons per year. Cargo handling in ports is responsible for only a very small amount—some 3000 tons per year—while the majority of all oil introduced into the sea comes from tank-ers that must take on seawater as ballast after delivering their oil car-gos. Of this total of about 850,000 tons, some 80 percent was released by about 12 percent of the world tanker fleet—that portion which does not use the load-on-top method of carriage. Mandatory use of the load-on-top method would thus greatly reduce the presence of oil in the oceans. It is likely, however, that natural sources, such as crude oil seeps from ocean floors, are more than comparable in magnitude with all other sources. Oil spillage on land in the United States is negligible, since losses from pipeline leaks amount to only about 0.006 percent of all oil transported.

SOLID WASTE POLLUTION

The disposal of solid wastes presents a different class of problems. Burial helps, although it can be costly and land-consuming, and there is always the dilemma: How do you bury a pile of dirt? Only Chicago has been imaginative enough to make a virtue of necessity by erecting Mount Trashmore, a garbage-based hill that provides regionally unique recreational opportunities for skiing and tobogganing.

Solid wastes are produced in the United States at an annual rate of about 4.5 billion tons per year, of which about 50 percent is agricultural, 40 percent comes from mining, 7 percent from commercial and residential trash, and only about 3 percent from industry. The classical approach to handling solid wastes has simply been to transport them out of sight to some dumping area, concentrating them without treatment. Sanitary landfills that cover garbage with layers of dirt have been instituted in some areas.

The greatest solid waste disposal problems in energy industries are those associated with coal mining. Solid waste pollution from coal-mining activities and the related health hazards faced by underground miners tend to be concentrated in specific regions and groups. Coal mining is usually regarded as one of the more dangerous industrial occupations. In a competitive labor market, the higher the perceived risk of injury or death, the higher the wage rate that will be required. In any occupation, workers will insist upon a trade-off between higher perceived risks and higher wages. At sufficiently high wage rates, society will obtain equilibrium numbers of deep sea divers, steeplejacks, and drivers of high explosives trucks. While the incidence of fatalities among miners has been slowly declining over the years, the annual number of deaths in underground mines is still significant.

The most expensive of the health hazards of coal mining is the condition known as black lung. The volumes of coal dust produced in certain types of underground mining overwhelm the defenses of the respiratory system and injure the lung cells so as to produce a form of emphysema. Since the passage of the Coal Mine Health and Safety Law of 1969, claims for victim compensation have resulted in payments totaling over half a billion dollars per year. Adding these sums to the price of coal would increase coal costs by about 10 percent.

The surface mining of coal has a much better health and safety record than underground mining, but its environmental impact has been the subject of a variety of criticisms. In strip mining, large power shovels remove the soil above the coal seam and then mine the exposed coal beds. In flat terrain, as soon as the coal is mined, a new trench parallel to the mined area is dug and the overburden soil removed from the new trench is dumped into the mined-out area. As mining progresses the process is repeated again and again. In mountainous terrain, a trench is first cut at the location where the coal seam is exposed at the surface. The overburden is dumped down the slopes of the mountain to settle where it will. As the coal is mined, successively deeper cuts are likely to be made into the mountainside, with the trenches following the contour of the hillsides. If the coal bed is flat while the mountain is steep, at some point the overburden above the coal seam will be too high to remove and other methods of mining must be employed on the exposed seam face.

Overburdens of up to 200 feet have been removed in flat areas, although this exceeds the currently economic limit in mountainous regions. Erosion from unreclaimed strip mine areas is a serious problem, and is naturally more troublesome in regions of pronounced surface relief, where erosion from access roads may be even more intense than the erosion from the spoil banks of piled-up disturbed overburden. Spoil banks may from time to time release boulders on downhill regions, and entire portions of such spoil banks may break away in the form of a landslide. Most coal contains sulfur, and sulfuric acid is formed when water reaches the remains of coal seams, making the spoil banks hostile to plant life. Acids are leached out of the spoil banks by rain, and local streams may become too acidic to support aquatic life.

Most strip-mined land can be readily reclaimed, although at varying costs, with costs for reclaiming contour-mined land being among the highest. Full reclamation, involving restoration of the original surface condition, can be quite expensive, requiring refilling, grading, draining, fertilizing, and seeding operations. It has been estimated that efficient reclamation would add 5 to 15 percent to the cost of strip-mined coal for seams of reasonable thickness.

Other environmental problems associated with coal mining include the seeping of sulfuric acid from abandoned underground mines that have become flooded, the incidence of land subsidence over underground mines, and the prevalence of fires in abandoned coal mines, which cause heat and air pollution, damaging surface vegetation while the fires consume coal reserves. Finally, mine waste heaps, created as a byproduct of the washing of coal to remove impurities, are not only eyesores but are also the source of wind and water pollution, while those that are on fire are also the cause of local air and heat pollution. Still, the amount of land damage from strip mining is often exaggerated. Less than 0.1 percent of the surface area of the country has ever been disturbed by strip mining, although increased reliance on coal and oil shale in the future will increase this fraction.

RADIATION POLLUTION

A radioactive element is one that is structurally unstable at the atomic level, possessing an excess of mass, energy, or electric charge. The radioactive decay of these unstable elements releases three types of radiation, which can be regarded as pollutants since they tend to interfere with vital processes: (1) alpha particles, which consist of expelled helium atom nuclei; (2) beta particles, which consist of fast electrons; and (3) gamma rays, which are pure electromagnetic energy, similar to X-rays but more penetrating.

Radioactive elements achieve eventual stability by radiating excess energy or mass. The more rapid this radiation, the sooner stability is achieved, and the sooner the element ceases to be radioactive. Radioactive elements have half-lives, measured by the amount of time it takes for half of the radioactive nuclei present at any point in time to decay. The shorter the half-life, the more intense and hence dangerous the radiation, but the sooner it ceases. Isotopes with very long half-lives have weaker radiation and are less dangerous. Radiation hazards from materials with short half-lives can be handled by storage for relatively brief periods. Materials with very long half-lives do not have to be handled so carefully since their radiation is weak. It is the class of radioactive materials with intermediate half-lives, roughly from 10 to 100 years, where prolonged storage is necessary, that pose the most difficult problems. (Plutonium is an exception, having a long half-life but also being extremely hazardous.)

Nuclear energy involves the splitting of the nuclei of heavy elements, but does not accomplish their annihilation into pure energy. Only about 0.1 percent of the mass of the heavy nucleus is converted into energy; the remainder of the wreckage of the heavy nucleus usually forms the nuclei of two lighter elements, both structurally unstable and hence radioactive. Since these lighter nuclei usually have an excess of neutrons, the most common form of radiation is beta particles; in this process neutrons are changed to protons by the emission of fast electrons. Alpha particles (such as are emitted by plutonium) carry away excess mass, while gamma rays dispose of excess energy.

Radiation causes damage because these particles and rays have great kinetic energy that can propel them through matter, including living tissues. The collision of these rays and particles with the cells of an organism damages them and may lead to cancer and other disorders, although only after an incubation period of many years. Radiation may also bring about genetic mutations, but time lags of one generation or more may be required. While massive dosages of radiation may be immediately lethal, the effects of small doses absorbed over many years are much milder and can be measured only in a statistical sense, with the interpretation of the statistical record often a matter of some controversy. The situation is further complicated by the presence of natural radiation from the soil, from cosmic rays, and from other sources. Exposure to minimal radiation does not seem to increase the risk of cancer very greatly. Without exposure to other than background levels of natural radiation, for example, the average person has three chances in a thousand of developing leukemia, a variety of blood cancer. Exposure to the minimum recommended additional man-made radiation will increase the risk to only 3.1 chances in a thousand.

Radioactive pollution from nuclear reactors involves solids, liquids, and gases. The water that circulates inside a reactor does not itself become radioactive, but the impurities in the water that result from the corrosion of pipes and valves do become radioactive as the water passes through the reactor core. Much liquid radioactive waste is accumulated during operations, particularly during maintenance and refueling. The circulating water is constantly being filtered to remove radioactive substances, which are then kept for a while in holding tanks to let the materials with short half-lives decay. This water is then slowly released into the cooling water stream, and is thus diluted by mixture with the very large volumes of water returned to the river or lake supplying the reactor.

Gaseous wastes are produced in those reactors where steam is in contact with the core and thus absorbs some of the gaseous fission products. Such gases are stored and then filtered before release to the atmosphere. Solid wastes are primarily concentrated in the uranium fuel rods themselves, although the wastes obtained from filtering the reactor water and gases are concentrated by evaporation, put in barrels, mixed with concrete, and stored in remote locations. The fuel rods are removed from the reactor core after about a year of operation and are stored under water for several months to permit the shorter-lived isotopes to decay. Spent fuel rods were formerly shipped to reprocessing plants where usable fuel materials were salvaged from the fission byproducts, with the short-lived products again being separated and held until they decay. No reprocessing plants are now in operation, and they are prohibited under present federal policy because of the danger of plutonium theft. The remaining "high-level" wastes are then present in liquid form. Since some of the isotopes involved have half-lives of over 100 years, these substances must be stored safely for several centuries. There are already over 100 million gallons of these wastes, mostly generated by military programs, stored at facilities in Hanford, Washington and at the Savannah River plant in South Carolina.

Even under the best of circumstances, controlling radiation pollution from nuclear power operations will be an exacting task. The real hazards lie in the possibility of reactor accidents, or of the diversion of nuclear materials in transit for further processing into the hands of those who wish to put these materials to destructive ends. Strong safeguards are needed against such contingencies.

POLLUTION POTENTIAL OF MAJOR ENERGY SOURCES: A SUMMARY

The pollution potential of the major energy sources can be very briefly summarized. Natural gas is the least polluting due to its comparative freedom from undesirable byproducts of combustion. Petroleum and coal are then considered, followed by hydroelectric and nuclear power. In a brief concluding section the probable environmental drawbacks of new sources of energy are discussed in broad terms.

Natural Gas

Natural gas occasions less air pollution than other conventional fuels for several reasons. First, natural gas has fewer impurities. Second, it is relatively easy and inexpensive to remove these impurities, such as sulfur, from the gas before it is burned. Third, combustion is complete. The hydrocarbons are converted by oxidation to carbon dioxide and water, with the release of energy. No carbon monoxide, unburned hydrocarbons, or particulates are produced.

As do all fossil fuels, natural gas does give rise to carbon dioxide, a potential long-term pollutant. Additionally, natural gas causes nitrogen oxide emissions since its very efficient combustion properties permit high temperatures to be achieved, and whenever the air is heated to 1000°C or above, the oxygen and nitrogen naturally present in the atmosphere are combined into nitric oxide, an ingredient in photochemical smog. Gas has a higher thermal efficiency than coal or oil as a boiler fuel, so its potential for thermal pollution is correspondingly lower.

Crude Oil and Petroleum Products

Crude oil is rarely burned directly as a fuel as is coal or natural gas. Refined products vary in their pollution potential. The two products that have received greatest attention are gasoline and fuel oil. Gasoline used in internal combustion engines emits several pollutants: carbon monoxide, nitrogen oxides, hydrocarbons, and lead. Lead is currently being phased out, and carbon monoxide and hydrocarbon emissions are being combatted by the installation of catalytic converters on new cars. As noted earlier, the more complete combustion has increased nitrogen oxide pollutants. Fuel oils contain sulfur that results in sulfur oxide pollution unless it is removed by various processes. Since the cost of such desulfurization is quite substantial, crude oils that are naturally low in surfur command a considerable price premium.

Coal

Unfortunately, America's most plentiful fuel, coal, is the major source of emissions of particulates and sulfur compounds. At existing concentrations, sulfur oxides are viewed as the most serious form of air pollution. In addition, the problem of acid rain is directly linked to sulfur oxides. But coal has other problems in addition to air pollution. Most of these are related to solid waste from strip mining and the waste piles resulting from the washing of coal at the mine. In addition, there are such adverse environmental effects of underground mining as land subsidence, persistent mine fires, miner lung disease, and fatal accidents. Legislation on mine safety and on strip mining practices has raised coal costs to pay for health and environmental effects. Costs of desulfurization must also be paid by coal buyers if high-sulfur coal is to be used in many localities. The failure to develop low-cost desulfurization processes has reduced the role that coal would otherwise play in the energy market. Despite these environmental problems, coal is still likely to have quite a prominent position. Present trends call for the increased production of more low-sulfur coal, principally strip-mined coal from the western United States.

Hydroelectric Power

Hydroelectric power has a very low pollution impact, although it is not entirely without environmental effects. Its air pollution impact is zero since hydropower is derived from the energy of falling water and no fuels are burned. Water pollution as such can be avoided by proper design of installations. Thermal pollution is, at worst, mild since the conversion of kinetic energy to electricity in large plants takes place at an efficiency of about 85 percent. There is neither solid waste nor radiation.

There are, however, some effects on the ecology and appearance of the river system. Fish migration is at least somewhat impeded. The channel silts up behind the dam. Seasonal flooding is eliminated. Most important from the point of view of many environmentalists is the effect on scenic values. Scenic canyons drowned by lakes are lost to view, and although the lakes behind the dams may be attractive at high water levels, variations in the water level over a period of years usually disfigure the shoreline by causing rock discoloration or changes in vegetation patterns.

Nuclear Power

While nuclear power plants do not give rise to air pollution, they usually cause considerable thermal water pollution because of their low thermal efficiency and consequent need for large amounts of cooling water. Their effect on land surfaces is certainly less than that of coal mining since uranium mining requires much less excavation per unit of energy content of extracted fuels. Radiation pollution is of course the major drawback. While the actual pollution of air and water resources by nuclear plants may be kept to low levels, the long-run hazard of the storage of high-level nuclear wastes underground is hard to appraise. Additional environmental drawbacks concern other aspects of nuclear wastes: Their transportation between reactors and processing plants, with the attendant hazards of accidents, and the fact that in order to enrich uranium much electrical energy is needed, most of which is presently supplied by strip-mined coal with its own pollution complications. Public concern over nuclear reactor accidents increased greatly following the misadventures at the Three Mile Island reactor near Harrisburg, Pennsylvania in March, 1979. In such reactors, the heat developed within the core must be controlled in order to avoid the escape of radioactive materials into the environment. Uncontrolled overheating will ultimately lead to the meltdown of the nuclear fuel mass, the destruction of the core, the probable melt-through of the reactor pressure vessel, and the possible breakthrough of the molten mass of the reactor material through the containment slab. While coolant failure will almost certainly trigger the shutdown of the reactor, catastrophic levels of radiation may escape.

At Three Mile Island, multiple mechanical failures combined with staggering operator errors to produce serious reactor core damage. Fortunately, a meltdown was avoided and radiation emissions were minor. Study groups concluded that inadequate operator training (due in part to the feeling that automatic safety devices have made reactors "people-proof") led personnel to manually override automatic safety devices due to their inadequate understanding of reactor operations. While better training programs will reduce such risks in the future, this incident provides a serious reminder that the probability of a nuclear accident, although absolutely small, is not zero.

New Energy Sources

Although new energy sources are considered at length in Chapter 10, it may be useful to provide the student with some conception of their comparative environmental effects at this point. Some of the new energy sources rely upon combustion and thus have the same air pollution potential as existing fuels, with one or two important exceptions. Other new sources bypass the combustion phase and thus reduce air pollution hazards. Still other sources avoid one type of pollution but aggravate other types.

Synthetic liquid fuels from coal and oil shale can be processed to yield refined products more or less identical to those derived from crude oil. An important advantage of the synthetic approach, however, is that sulfur and other impurities can be removed from coal and shale during the basic conversion process, thus reducing sulfur oxide pollution. But the underground and strip mining operations necessary to extract coal and shale will cause adverse solid waste effects in other parts of the environment. Oil shale has additional waste disposal problems that may give rise to air pollution. For each cubic foot of shale rock processed, more than one cubic foot of light mineral ash is produced; this ash is easily blown aloft by winds and could be dispersed widely unless expensive control methods are employed. Both coal liquefaction and oil shale processing also use large amounts of water, which while physically available are relatively scarce in the western areas of the country where the mining would occur. Coal liquefaction will also result in large volumes of solid wastes, since not all of the coal can be liquefied, leaving solid residues that may not be marketable. Coal gasification poses environmental issues similar to those of coal liquefaction.

The development of geothermal energy will give rise to relatively little air pollution since the heat is produced by steam rather than by fuel combustion, although there are sulfur and other impurities in some geothermal emissions. Geopressurized methane deposits will yield natural gas, but the cost of disposing of large volumes of hot salt water may be prohibitive unless these brines are suitable for disposal offshore in the Gulf of Mexico.

Solar energy appeals to many because of its freedom from the usual pollution problems. Solar home heating units use the sun's energy to heat water directly without any air pollution—not even carbon dioxide. Furthermore, there are no problems with water, solid waste, or radioactive pollution. In addition, energy production is decentralized and thus immune to failures of the distribution system such as occurred in New York City during the 1960s. Besides solar heating, a variety of other solar technologies exist. Even steerably mounted solar reflector panels for electricity production produce steam for electricity generation without the usual byproducts of air pollution. In sum, because of solar's excellent environmental characteristics, many view solar as our most promising fuel source for the future.

Breeder reactors will pose worse radioactive pollution hazards than the present generation of burner reactors, although the mining activities necessary to support them will probably be less extensive. If and when the fusion reactor is commercially available, pollution hazards will decline dramatically, as will the dangers from reactor accidents. The pollution potential is reduced because the only radioactive substance involved is tritium, which is only mildly hazardous. Per unit of possible power output, the radioactivity problems from fusion have been estimated at only 1/10,000 those of fusion. (Hence a fusion reactor would have to "leak" radioactivity about 10,000 times as much as a fission reactor in order to possess a comparable radiation hazard.)

A fusion reactor will not melt down in case of an accident, and the mass of radioactive reactant present is simply insufficient to cause an explosion. Finally, due to very high operating temperatures, fusion reactors might achieve thermal efficiencies of 50 to 60 per cent, about double those of fossil fuel power plants and much higher than nuclear fission reactors. Since higher thermal efficiency means less waste heat to be absorbed by the environment, there will be less thermal pollution of air and water volumes.

If technology advances to the point where solar cells and fuel cells are economical, pollution may also be greatly reduced. Solar cells convert sunlight to electricity directly, while fuel cells combine hydrogen and oxygen to generate electricity, with water as the only byproduct. In general, any energy conversion process that bypasses the combustion step will reduce air pollution, and such processes will also reduce water, thermal, and solid waste pollution.

THE ECONOMICS OF POLLUTION CONTROL
The Fundamental Problem

A common logical error is to identify a source of pollution and automatically conclude the existence of a market failure and thus a welfare loss. Even though pollution examples are often used to illustrate market failures, there is no necessary causal relationship. Recall that externalities exist when private valuations of costs or benefits differ from social valuation of costs and benefits. But the existence of pollution need not automatically imply that the two diverge. First, if the affected parties are relatively few and property rights are well-defined, voluntary agreements between the polluters and affected parties can achieve the socially optimal outcome. These outcomes will rarely result in zero pollution, because the costs would be prohibitive. Second, even when private transactions are not capable of equilibrating private and social valuations, governmental policies may. Even governmental solutions will generally not prohibit pollution, but rather restrict it to socially optimal levels. Thus the critical policy question is not whether pollution exists but rather whether it occurs at socially optimal levels. But how should policy makers go about determining whether optimal levels of pollution are being achieved? The economic approach to pollution control is to view clean air and water as commodities like gasoline and air conditioning, to be provided according to the standard criteria applied to all goods. The last unit of clean air or water should confer a marginal social benefit just equal to the marginal social cost of providing it. Let us consider how externalities can be built into the standard graphical analysis, with its implicit framework for applied welfare analysis.

As an example, consider the case of a large electric power station located in a city in the western United States. This station costs $700 million, generates 5.3 billion kilowatt-hours per year, burns 2.5 million tons of coal, and emits 365 million pounds of sulfur oxides into the atmosphere each year. Let us assume that in this city the coal-powered electric generating station is the only appreciable source of sulfur oxide emissions (SO_x). Furthermore, we shall assume that it is not feasible to move the town or the plant so that the sulfur oxides will not pollute the town. Initially, the plant emits 1 million pounds of SO_x per day, as this is the amount of pollution emitted in the absence of any public action.

Figure 5.1 is a graph relating dollars per pound of SO_x emissions abated to the total quantity of SO_x emissions abated. Starting from a

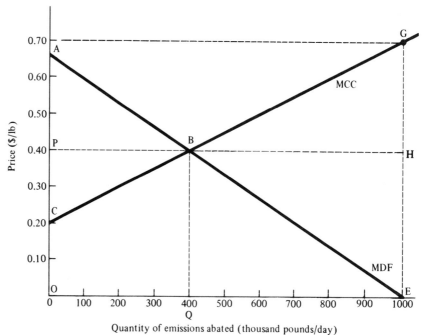

FIGURE 5.1 The simple diagramatics of the pollution problem.

situation with unconstrained emissions of 1 million pounds daily, the question is how much clean air society should optimally purchase. Since every pound of emissions abated amounts to an equivalent unit of clean air, the horizontal axis is measured in terms of pollution abated, or cleaned up. The marginal damage function (MDF) in effect describes the demand for clean air. The MDF is measured by the price the public is willing to pay to have each pound of SO_x reduced. The MDF curve slopes downward to the right as with any demand curve, reflecting the fact that additional units of abated pollution confer marginally smaller benefits. Included in the marginal damage function are the health costs, property losses, and aesthetic costs associated with the SO_x emissions. At initial levels of 1,000,000 pounds of SO_x emissions, the public is willing to pay 67 cents per pound of SO_x to reduce emissions from 1,000,000 to 999,999 pounds. On the other hand, if emissions had already been reduced to 1 pound, the public is willing to pay virtually nothing to have the last pound of SO_x abated. This shape of marginal damage function implies that the marginal health, property, and aesthetic costs rise with increased concentrations of SO_x and fall with decreased concentrations.

The curve labeled MCC is the marginal control cost function, depicting the marginal cost curve of abating SO_x. Also included in these control costs would be the administrative costs associated with policing or enforcing the abatement. The marginal control cost function is entirely analogous to a supply schedule—in this case, the supply schedule for SO_x abatement. The rising marginal control cost schedule reflects the fact that relatively low-cost control technology is available when the first 100,000 pounds of SO_x are removed. However, to eliminate all of the SO_x emissions, the marginal control cost is indeed quite high.

Figure 5.1 shows that the optimal quantity of emissions abated is 400,000 pounds. For the 400,000th pound of SO_x removed, the marginal social benefit of clean air just equals the marginal social cost of providing it. Economic welfare, defined as the difference between social benefits (OABQ) and social costs (OCBQ), is maximized (ABC) when Q = 400,000 pounds. Another way of seeing this is to ask how society can minimize the cost associated with SO_x emissions. These costs associated with SO_x emissions include the damage costs, reflected in the MDF function, and the real resources devoted to pollution control, measured by the MCC function. It is easy to see that when Q = 400,000, the sum of damage plus abatement costs is minimized. The abatement cost for 400,000 pounds is given by area OCBQ, and the damage cost on the remaining 600,000 pounds is QBE. Any other quantity of emissions abated raises the total cost arising from the pollution. For example, with zero emissions abated, the costs associated with SO_x would be measured by the entire area under the marginal damage function (OAE). Conversely, a pollution-free environment would involve the costs under the marginal control cost function (area *OCGE*). This example reinforces the earlier point that even at the optimal level of pollution abatement, a remaining quantity of pollution will exist—in this case 600,000 pounds. On the other hand, there is no reason to believe that the unconstrained level of pollution generated by the market, resulting from no abatement, is socially optimal. Thus informed governmental policies can generate potentially sizeable welfare gains. Let us consider the policy instruments.

The Equivalence of Taxes, Standards, Transferable Pollution Rights, and Subsidies

At a purely abstract level, the choice of pollution control instruments is a moot point. All achieve the same result and have similar implications for energy markets. Consider the above example of the electricity generation plant. Furthermore, assume that (1) the shapes of both the MDF and the MCC function are known, (2) the administrative and policing costs of pollution control instruments are negligible, and (3) neither the plant nor the town can relocate.

Pollution standards have long been the policy maker's most popular approach to pollution control. Pollution standards require explicit quantitative cutbacks in pollution. For example, in Figure 5.1, the optimal pollution standard is one calling for a 400,000-pound reduction in SO_x emissions. Under standards, the plant must pay *OCBQ* to install the pollution abatement equipment. The public bears the cost of the remaining pollution damage (area *QBE*).

A variant of the standards policy is the issuance of transferable pollution rights, which can be bought and sold among polluters. The idea of transferable pollution rights was first set forth by Dales,[4] who visualized the possibility of markets for pollution rights just as we observe markets for offshore drilling rights, water rights, and so forth. Under the above assumptions, the plant could purchase the rights to emit 600,000 pounds of SO_x at a price of $.40 per pound. The firm would thus be required to cut back production by 400,000 pounds of SO_x. Since only 600,000 pounds worth of rights are issued, standards and transferable pollution rights are identical in that they achieve the same quantitative reduction in SO_x. The electric utility is forced to reduce pollution by 400,000 pounds per day and pay the control costs of *OCBQ*.

Pollution taxes, based on equilibrating marginal damage and control costs, also lead to the optimal level of abatement. In the case where the MDF and MCC functions are known exactly, the pollution control agency sets the optimal tax. Firms reduce the pollution up to the point that marginal control costs just equal the tax rate. Beyond that point, it is cheaper to pay the tax than to reduce pollution levels.

In Figure 5.1, the optimal pollution tax is 40 cents per pound of SO_x. The firm consults its marginal control cost function, finding that it is cheaper to abate the SO_x up to 400,000 pounds. For the remaining 600,000 pounds of SO_x it is cheaper to pay the 40 cents per pound tax. The public, via the public agency, receives compensation for the remaining SO_x emissions. Thus the efficiency aspects of taxes and standards are the same in that $Q = 400,000$ is forthcoming in either event. The income distribution consequences do differ in that the public is more than compensated for the unabated emissions under the tax (40 cents × 600,000 minus area BQE) while under the standard the public bears the cost of unabated pollution (area BQE). Overcompensation equals area BHE in Figure 5.1.

Even under a subsidy system designed to bribe the plant to reduce emissions, a subsidy of 40 cents per pound results in abatement of 400,000 pounds. In this case, receiving payment of 40 cents per pound, the plant is now selling two products—electricity and clean air. The plant can improve its profitability by producing clean air up to the point where $P = MC$. Clearly at $Q = 400,000$, marginal control costs just equal 40 cents per pound, the subsidy rate. Again the welfare effects are identical to a tax or a standard. The only difference occurs in the income transfer. In this case, the public not only bears the cost of the unabated pollution (area QBE) but also the payment of the subsidy (40 cents × 400,000 pounds). The plant is a net beneficiary of added producer surplus of PBC.

A Closer Look at Taxes, Standards, Transferable Pollution Rights, and Subsidies

The preceding result, which emphasizes that all four instruments have identical efficiency attributes, is based on some very restrictive assumptions. Now it is time to release these assumptions and reconsider whether we should be indifferent among the choice of pollution control instruments. The preceding analysis implicitly assumes that (1) the price of electricity is unaffected, (2) the utility could not relocate to a less densely populated area, (3) the shapes of the MDF and MCC are known with certainty, and (4) administrative and enforcement costs are zero for all three instruments.

Effects on Related Fuel Markets: The Price and Output of Electricity. Not only should the selection of a pollution control instrument lead to the optimal level of SO_x emissions, but the resulting electricity price should properly reflect the externalities involved in its production. In effect, the price of electricity should internalize these external costs. But do these four policy instruments achieve this?

First, let us put aside the fact that the electricity generation industry is regulated and assume for the moment that it is a typical competitive industry. Associated with the last kilowatt-hour produced is the emission of .069 pounds of SO_x. The .069 pounds of sulfur per kilowatt-hour is obtained by dividing the original sulfur (1,000,000 pounds per day) by the generation of electricity (14.5 million kwh per day or 5.3 billion kwh per year). But with a pollution tax, standard, or transferable pollution rights, the last pound of sulfur has a cost of 40 cents, so the .069 pounds of sulfur associated with the last kilowatt-hour raises the marginal cost of electricity by 2.8 cents per kwh. It is easy to see that in a competitive market, the marginal cost of generating electricity would rise by 2.8 cents and the market price would rise from 10 cents to 12.8 cents per kwh, the marginal social cost of electricity. But is this true in the case of the subsidy? Under a subsidy, exactly what are the marginal private pollution control costs associated with the last kwh of electricity generated? Absolutely zero. At 400,000 pounds abatement, the marginal control cost exactly equals the subsidy rate—imposing no additional cost on the firm. Thus the subsidy prevents the price of electricity from internalizing the externality costs of the SO_x pollution.

How do the results change if we now recognize that the electricity plant is subject to regulation that equates prices with average costs, not marginal costs? If a 2.8 cents per kwh price increase is desirable to equate the marginal social cost of generating electricity with its marginal social benefit, will this occur under regulation?

In this case, taxes (and transferable pollution rights if they must be purchased) come closer to raising the price by 2.8 cents than do the other instruments. First, let us dispose of the subsidy. Under a subsidy, the electric utility earns producers' surplus of area PBC in Figure 5.1, which amounts to $40,000 per day; divided by output of 14.5 million kwh, this yields a *decrease* in average costs of .28 cents per kwh. Thus a subsidy lowers the average cost and, under regulation, the price of electricity will diverge further from the marginal social cost of electricity.

Under standards the electric utility must pay only for the abatement equipment (area OCBQ in Figure 5.1), which amounts to $120,000 per day. The effect of a $120,000 per day increase in total costs is to raise average costs by .8 cents per kwh ($120,000/14,500,000 kwh). Standards or transferable rights would result in a price increase of .8 cents per kwh—far less than the optimal increase of 2.8 cents per kwh but far better than the subsidy.

Under a tax, the electric utility pays the control costs (area OCBQ) plus a tax on the remaining pollution (area QBHE). Together these total $360,000 per day and increase costs by 2.5 cents per kwh. Similarly, costs will be identical for the firm purchasing transferable rights. Thus, under regulation, pollution taxes and possibly transferable pollution rights come closest to equilibrating price and marginal social cost, but even here the increase of 2.5 cents per kwh falls short of the socially optimal increase of 2.8 cents per kwh.

In sum, taxes, standards, transferable pollution rights, and subsidies have ramifications for electricity and other fuel markets in addition to the market for sulfur abatement, and it is important that these markets price electricity and other fuels at socially optimal levels. On all scores, subsidies fail, often sending perverse price signals. In an unregulated competitive setting, taxes, standards, and transferable pollution rights lead to efficient pricing; but under regulation, taxes and possibly transferable pollution rights come closer to internalizing the full marginal social costs into the price.

Effects of Locational Choice. Another long-run consequence of pollution control programs concerns their possible effects on locational choice. In the above example, the power plant and the public were assumed to be unable to relocate. This assumption is valid for most primary energy production because production takes place at the location of the raw energy form. Examples include oil and gas production, coal mining, uranium mining, and geothermal production. It is simply not possible to extract petroleum under the ocean without conducting offshore drilling and production. In these situations, the choice is clear-cut—to produce or not to produce. If the choice is made to produce, the location of the production is already decided.

There are, however, numerous situations where location can be varied, particularly in the production of final energy. The locations of oil refineries and electricity generation plants are open to choice. These facilities can be located either near the primary energy source or near the market that the plant will serve. Similarly, large industrial users of energy with high pollution content have locational choice.

Figure 5.2 depicts the situation in which the power plant in the previous example has a locational choice. If the power plant were located in region B, outside the city, the marginal damage function for region B would be much lower due to the lower population density and the climatic conditions. The criterion of minimizing the costs associated with SO_x emissions leads to relocating the plant in region B where combined damage and control costs are much less (area *OCJK*). Optimal abatement in region B is 100,000 pounds per day. In view of the lower costs associated with region B, economic efficiency calls for relocation of the plant from region A to region B. The sum of costs associated with SO_x would be reduced from area *OCBE* to area *OCJK*.[5]

The question arises as to which instrument will encourage the plant to move to region B. First, consider a subsidy system. Would the plant leave region A with its subsidy of 40 cents per pound of SO_x abated to relocate in region B, where the subsidy is only 25 cents per pound? The loss in producers' surplus would be appreciable. This illustrates an important defect of the subsidy. In order to receive the highest sub-

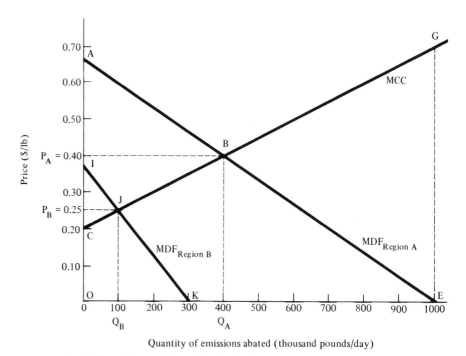

FIGURE 5.2 The effects of locational choice.

sidy, pollution-intensive industries move to the areas where the marginal damage function is the greatest!

In contrast, standards, transferable pollution rights, and taxes provide incentives for relocation to region B. Under a standards program, after relocating to region B, the plant would have to reduce emissions by only 100,000 pounds per day, incurring control costs of $OCJQ_B$. In contrast, the control cost paid by the firm in region A is $OCBQ_A$. Thus there are incentives to relocate. A pollution tax usually provides even stronger incentives to relocate. Not only can the firm reduce its control cost expenditure, but the taxes paid to the public agency can generally be reduced by relocating to region B. In region B, the tax rate is only 25 cents per pound, leading to total taxes of $225,000 per day, which is well below the $240,000 per day paid in region A.[6]

In view of these findings, we dismiss subsidies as a serious candidate, despite their popularity with local chambers of commerce.

Uncertainty About the Shapes of the MDF and MCC Curves. In reality, the public agency does not know the exact shapes of the marginal damage function and the marginal control cost function. There is wide diversity of opinion as to health and ecological effects of various forms of pollution. Similarly, the cost and reliability of current and prospective control equipment are subject to wide disagreement. A particularly germane example is the flue gas desulfurization technology applied in electric power generation plants to control the SO_x emissions from coal-fired plants. In 1972, some reports claimed that the technology was available at low cost while others claimed the feasibility of the technology had not even been established. By the late 1970s, commercial versions of such units were in operation, but the costs far exceeded the initial estimates.

Uncertainty no doubt plays an important role in many externalities associated with energy. These include the health and property damage effects of carbon monoxide, nitrogen oxides, sulfur oxides, and unburned hydrocarbons—all of which are associated with most fuel consumption. In offshore oil production, both the probability of an oil spill and the extent of its damages are very difficult to estimate. In nuclear power production, both the likelihood of an accident coupled with the failure of the emergency core-cooling facility and the extent of the resulting damages are difficult to assess.

Even though the MDF and MCC curves are not known with precision, policy agents must, nevertheless, make decisions. The question is, "What should be the basis for these decisions?" The answer is simply that the MDF and MCC curves must be treated as random variables and that policy agents must attempt to maximize the expected welfare gain. But does this have any implications for the choice of taxes versus standards? Both transferable pollution rights and standards, if enforced, provide a precise quantity of abatement. Taxes, on the other hand, are much more flexible. The resulting abatement depends on where the marginal control cost function equals the tax rate. If the true MCC curve differs from the expected MCC curve, a tax can lead to a different level of abatement than standards (or transferable pollution rights).

The question then becomes, "How serious is the loss of precision with a tax?" To answer this question we must consider the shape of the marginal damage function in the region in which MCC intersects it. Figure 5.3 illustrates two situations in which the imprecision of taxes has very different implications. In the first case, MCC*, the expected marginal control cost function, intersects the expected marginal damage function in a highly inelastic range. For example, such a situation might apply to some poisonous gas that becomes deadly at a given concentration. Since MCC* is not known with certainty, two dashed MCC curves denote a 95 percent confidence interval (MCC* + 2σ, MCC* − 2σ) for the position of MCC*. In this situation, standards would require abatement of Q^*. Similarly, an agency acting on the expected value for MCC* would set a tax at P^*, which would be sufficient to reduce emissions by Q^*, if indeed MCC* turns out to be correct.

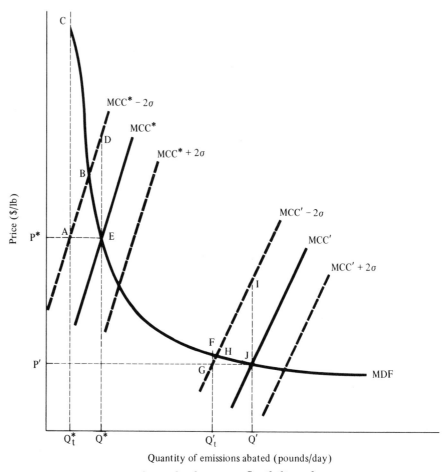

FIGURE 5.3 Precision of standards versus flexibility of taxes.

In situations where the true MCC curve differs from the expected marginal control cost curve (MCC*), taxes give different outcomes from standards and transferable pollution rights. If the true position of the marginal control cost curve is MCC* $- 2\sigma$, then the tax of P^* would result in abatement of only Q_t^*, compared to Q^* resulting from the standard. All instruments result in a welfare loss, but the losses under the tax are greater. Under either standards or transferable pollution rights, the overly rigid standard Q^* (assuming MCC* $- 2\sigma$ is the true cost function) results in a welfare loss of the triangle *BDE* due to excessive control expenditures. However, the welfare loss associated with the tax, area *ABC*, is much greater. In the extreme case in which the MDF is vertical, the welfare losses from a tax approach infinity while those for standards or transferable rights approach zero.

Examples where the MDF function is highly inelastic involve nuclear power production, poisonous gases, and so on. In these situations, the precision of standards or transferable rights is very important because it prevents society from allowing pollution to fall into the very dangerous region where marginal damage costs rise rapidly. A tax lacks this precision and can consequently lead to disastrous results. Suppose that authorities placed too low a tax on radioactive emissions from a nuclear fuel processing plant. The loss could be quite large. On the other hand, with a precise standard or a pollution rights system, the authority might err on the side of being overly cautious. Nevertheless, the welfare loss would be comparatively small. In sum, there are numerous situations where taxes simply are not appropriate and, while one may disagree with the abatement level selected for the standard or transferable rights, they remain conceptually superior policy instruments.

Are there situations where the flexibility of a tax outweighs the benefits of precision with a pollution standard or transferable rights? Consider the case where the expected marginal control cost functions intersect the expected MDF over an elastic section. In Figure 5.3, MCC′ describes the expected value of the marginal control cost function. Based on the expected functions, standards or transferable rights call for abatement of Q' and taxes lead to a tax of P'. Of course, if the actual shape of the marginal control cost function is MCC′, none of the policies would result in a welfare loss. But if the actual marginal control cost function coincides with MCC′ $- 2\sigma$, the outcomes are quite different. Assuming MCC′ $- 2\sigma$ is the true function, overinvestment in pollution equipment would result under either standards or transferable rights. The resulting welfare loss would be *HIJ*. With a tax of P', the tax is slightly lower than the optimal level; consequently the quantity abated is slightly less than the optimal quantity. The welfare loss under the tax, however, is only *FGH*. If the marginal damage function is perfectly elastic, it is easy to show that the tax will result in zero welfare loss while standards or transferable rights would result in a large loss. Thus in the situation where the marginal damage function is believed to be relatively elastic, the precision of standards or transferable rights can lead to large welfare losses and the flexibility of taxes is a desirable attribute.

Indeed, there are numerous situations where the flexibility of a tax is desirable and the precision of either standards or transferable rights is a liability. For example, most empirical research shows that the marginal damage function is horizontal over the observed ranges of SO_x emissions. A tax set equal to the horizontal marginal damage cost would lead to an optimal outcome as firms would purchase abatement equipment up to the point at which the marginal control cost equals the tax rate. The public agency would be relieved of the problem of estimating the expected MCC curve and setting pollution abatement levels, which will surely prove to be wrong. In contrast, a tax allows a flexible response. If low-cost control equipment is not initially available, the quantity abated will be small. With the development of new low-cost technology, firms will automatically adopt these measures, leading to much greater levels of abatement.

Seeming conflicts between energy production and environmental factors can be attenuated through taxes. The existence of pollution taxes assures that firms will reduce pollution to the level economically justified by the tax rate. In contrast to standards or transferable rights, which are typically enforced rigidly or altogether relaxed, taxes maintain a continuing incentive for compliance. Thus, if reductions in emissions are not realistic in the short run, taxes assure they are achieved in the long run. The relaxation of standards, or issuance of additional pollution rights, to deal with short-run exigencies may only invite long-run noncompliance. Alternatively, if the overly ambitious quantity limits are enforced in the short run, this may impose large welfare losses on energy producing and consuming industries.

Administrative Costs with Numerous Polluting Firms. Pollution control instruments need not have similar administrative and enforcement costs, particularly when there are numerous polluters. Public agencies use real resources in acquiring the necessary technical information to adopt responsible policies. Additionally, they must also bear the cost of policing the policy adopted. Since both the information and policing costs are sizeable, we are prompted to ask how taxes, standards, and transferable pollution rights may differ in this regard.

Taxes generally involve less information cost on the part of the public agency. The obvious reason is that information on the aggregate marginal damage function and aggregate marginal control cost function may be adequate to set optimal taxes. Once the tax rate is set, the agency's problem becomes one of collecting the tax, and detecting tax evaders. To reiterate, the agency's information requirements are limited to estimating the intersection of the marginal damage and control cost functions.

Under a standards policy, not only must the aggregate level of abatement be selected, but individual standards for each polluter must be assigned. The information costs of the latter are much greater even though the sum of the individual polluters' marginal control cost functions forms the aggregate marginal control cost function. It is possible to have a good estimate of the aggregate without knowledge of every polluting firm's marginal control cost function. In order for the public agency to set optimal standards, standards for each polluter must be set so that the marginal damage cost of the last unit just equals the marginal control costs of each polluter. In reality, the number of polluters may be large and the public agency does not have a budget adequate to obtain this detailed information. The typical solution is to require all polluters to reduce emissions proportionally. This solution would be fine if all firms had similar marginal control costs. Unfortunately, due to scale economies in abatement technology, large-scale polluters can reduce emissions at lower unit costs than small polluters. The proportional rule forces all polluters to cut back proportionally, even though it would be more efficient if large polluters would cut back a lot, while small polluters would practice only limited abatement. One study has been made using a linear programming model to analyze control cost differences in achieving a given reduction in biochemical oxygen demand (BOD) in the Delaware River estuary. A uniform tax yielded control costs 50 percent less than a standards policy requiring all polluters to achieve proportional reductions.[7] Thus a standards policy is likely to result in either quite high information costs to determine optimal standards for each polluter or unnecessarily high control costs resulting from a proportional rule.

A system of transferable pollution rights overcomes the inefficiencies of standards as they are usually implemented with proportional rules. The beauty of transferable pollution rights is that holders of rights who can sell the right for more than the cost of abatement have an incentive to do so. Likewise, those parties without pollution rights but with very high abatement costs will have an incentive to purchase the pollution rights. The end result is that through the market, those polluters with low abatement costs will find it cheaper to install abatement equipment whereas those polluters with high abatement costs will purchase the pollution rights.

But exactly what are the potential cost savings from allowing the market to sort out high and low cost polluters? Tom Tietenberg surveyed 11 studies comparing the ratio of control costs under various standards policies to the least-cost optimum, and found that costs under standards ranged from 7 percent to 22 times greater than the least-cost solution, with the average being 6.1 times the least-cost optimum.[8] Numbers of this magnitude suggest that transferable pollution rights overcome one of the major objections to standards and yet retain the precision of quantitative limits on total pollution.

Comparisons of policing costs of standards, pollution rights, and taxes do not lead to simple generalizations. All three require policing to be effective. Since all are costly to the firm, there is an incentive to cheat and avoid compliance. In some circumstances, a tax can be the most expensive to administer and enforce. For example, a tax on incinerator emissions from apartment houses may be a good deal more expensive to administer than a standards policy with restrictions on incinerator designs and periods of use. Metering devices are likely to be quite expensive compared to annual inspections and spot checks on the time of legal burnings. On the other hand, there are situations where a tax appears quite easy to collect and enforce. Gasoline taxes are easily collected with virtually no tax evasion. A sulfur tax would also be easy to collect as a metering device is not necessary. At the time of purchase of fuels, the producer of coal or fuel oil could collect the tax based on its sulfur content. The purchaser of the coal or fuel oil could receive tax refunds for the amount of elemental sulfur recovered through flue gas desulfurization, and so on. The difference between the amount of sulfur in the fuel and that recovered is the quantity emitted to the atmosphere and would be the amount taxed.

Institutional and legal practices tend to reduce the effectiveness of standards compared to taxes. Experience suggests that there are several necessary conditions for an effective standards policy. First, agencies must be sufficiently financed to generate their own technical data and to enforce the controls. Second, agencies must represent the public interest rather than the interests of the regulated. Third, procedures for prosecution of violators should motivate quick, decisive compliance under penalty of large fines for violations.

Allen Kneese's discussion of direct controls on water pollution indicates frequent failures in all three aspects.[9] He points out that for lack of manpower, regulators generally depend on firms for estimates of their discharges. It has been estimated that to pursue vigorous enforcement activities in the Missouri basin states, a 25-fold staff expansion would be needed. Unless agencies adopt some ad hoc rules as to pollution reductions for all plants, individual negotiations with each discharger are necessary. Besides requiring significant administrative resources, individual negotiations invite special treatment and delayed action, resulting in a serious conflict of interests.

Developments in the last few years indicate that enforcement is being markedly improved. Major legislation and increased funding for environmental agencies suggest that inadequate resources are becoming a less binding constraint on enforcement. The National Environmental Protection Agency Act gives standing for public suits against agencies for failure to consider environmental impacts. This provides a check on regulatory action and brings into public view regulatory decisions that serve the interests of the regulated. Despite these advances, it is unfortunate that taxes have not been applied more extensively.

Do Environmental Regulations Actually Internalize the Externalities?

There are grounds for doubting that existing environmental regulations actually equate marginal damage and marginal control costs, particularly in the air pollution control area. The preceding theoretical models appear to play little if any role in the minds of policy makers and administrators. This is due chiefly to the legislative preference for legal over economic criteria. Even under the best of circumstances the successful application of economic principles to pollution control will require some trial and error. If the trial is not made, however, errors of various sorts are likely to be universal. This point can be illustrated by taking a brief look at the framework of air pollution regulation.

The Clean Air Act of 1967 provided the basic law governing air pollution control, with primary emphasis on mandated legal standards of air quality. A number of amendments made since that time have reinforced the tendency to employ legal rather than economic means to control pollution. The basic act divided the country into a relatively small number of air quality regions, each of significant geographic extent. Certain individual polluting substances were identified in the basic and later acts, and primary and secondary air quality standards were established with respect to each. In general, these standards provide maximum pollution concentration levels, which are not to be exceeded more than a certain number of times during a certain period, such as once per year. In regions where air quality is initially below the mandated standards, the intent is to employ various legal measures to improve it. In regions where air quality is initially above the standards, the philosophy is to prevent any reduction in air quality. The long-term goal is one of air quality enhancement, to be achieved by improving air quality in areas of deficiency, and by preventing any degradation in areas with relatively clean air. These are certainly laudable goals in themselves, and like all laudable goals should be vigorously pursued if their achievement involves no costs. But since large costs are obviously involved, legislation that either ignores or at least makes no attempt to measure such costs will certainly occasion much inefficiency and inequity.

The current regulatory approach is deficient in two major respects. First, mandated air quality standards are not selected on the basis of the optimal level of abatement (the intersection of marginal damage and control costs), but rather on arbitrary criteria of what is technologically feasible. For example, the idea of disallowing further degradation of the air quality in those areas meeting the national air quality standards eschews costs and benfits and simply sets the status quo as the desirable. The second problem involves the control costs of meeting the mandated standards. No effort has been made to require abatement by those polluters with low-cost control techniques. The end result is a system that deviates greatly from the ideal, but one that nevertheless represents an overall improvement over the previously nonregulated situation.

It is a sad commentary that no adequate studies of the economics of the costs and benefits of the control of each type of pollutant were made before the existing laws were passed. Current knowledge suggests that the required standards are too strict (marginal costs exceed marginal benefits) in many instances and too lenient (marginal costs are less than marginal benefits) in others.

Beyond that, air pollution control has had its political as well as its economic failures, and it is instructive to examine one major instance of each type of policy failure. Economically, it appears that regulation of pollution from mobile sources has been less efficient than that from stationary sources. Specifically, it has not yet been shown that the benefits of reducing carbon monoxide and hydrocarbon emissions from automobiles by requiring catalytic converters have exceeded the costs in terms of higher automobile expenses, higher nitrogen oxide emissions, and greater gasoline consumption. Lave and Seskin, among others, have shown that on the contrary, costs are likely to exceed benefits by a wide margin under existing regulations.[10] Lave reports that control costs of between eight and eleven billion dollars result in benefits of only five billion dollars or less, implying a loss of economic welfare of at least three and perhaps more than six billion dollars. In order to reduce costs to the level of benefits, one could revise the law to require that only those vehicles to be driven in areas of high air pollution, such as Los Angeles and Chicago, be subject to the highest-cost equipment modifications, which would mean that only about 37 percent of all cars would be thus affected. Alternatively, since studies tend to show that nitrogen oxide emissions are harmful only in concentrations above 2.0 grams per composite unit, a relaxation in this standard from the existing 0.4 gram to 2.0 grams would not raise damage costs, but would reduce control costs by several billion dollars. Either measure taken by itself would cut costs by about $5 billion, so that costs would no longer exceed benefits; adopting both would reduce costs below benefits and allow the regulations to increase economic welfare rather than to reduce it.

The greatest policy failure of a political nature occurred in 1977 with the passage of certain amendments to Section 111 of the Clean Air Act, which deals with emission standards for new sources of pollution. Reducing air pollution from sulfur oxides requires among other things a reduction in the sulfur emissions from coal-fired plants. The lowest-cost solution on a national basis requires the substitution of low-sulfur coal for high-sulfur coal, creating more employment in low-sulfur coal mines and reducing employment in high-sulfur coal mines. But if the full social cost of high-sulfur coal is internalized in the prices paid by utilities for coal and coal treatment, and in the prices paid by their customers for the electricity generated by the coal, high-sulfur coal production becomes uneconomical.

Enterprising labor and industry leaders in high-sulfur coal states succeeded in applying pressure to politicians, notably in Ohio and West Virginia, who in turn exerted the leverage necessary to secure the passage of legislation that would force higher costs on all newly constructed electric power plants, whether or not they used low-sulfur coal. By requiring that all such plants use the most expensive means of sulfur removal—stack scrubbing—which is beneficial for high-sulfur coal but unnecessary and uneconomical for low-sulfur coal, the 1977 act artificially reduces the demand for low-sulfur coal and prevents the demand for high-sulfur coal from declining as much as it otherwise would. The result is a resounding policy failure, since the only benefits consist in protecting the incomes of some high-sulfur coal companies and their workers, while the losses in terms of higher costs and continuing air pollution are borne by the rest of the nation. According to the Congressional Budget Office, by the year 2000, national electricity costs will be $3.4 billion higher per year with the scrubbing of high-sulfur coal than with the substitution of low-sulfur coal.[11] The scrubbing technology is said to be so inappropriate for very low-sulfur coal that sulfur actually has to be added to the coal in order to facilitate operations. And it appears that those few states which benefit economically may suffer ecologically. Air pollution and acid rain may very well prove to be higher in Ohio, West Virginia, and neighboring states with the scrubbing of high-sulfur coal than with the use of less intensively controlled low-sulfur coal. Policy makers who yield to the pressure exerted by special interests prove to be very expensive people, since they inflict large and unnecessary costs upon the nation as a whole.

Paradoxically, one of the most encouraging developments, markets for transferable pollution rights, has evolved as a consequence of the current bizarre regulatory framework. The general tendency, particularly in areas with initially adequate air quality, is to begin with a level of air pollution that is provisionally tolerated, but additional pollution is to be avoided under "nondegradation" doctrines. This in effect gives existing polluters property rights in at least that part of their emissions that is tolerated, with economic impact similar to those of "grandfather clauses" that limit new entry into a particular field but sanction the continued operation of existing sellers. Initially, this meant that no new plants could be located in a given air quality region. But new entrants negotiated with existing plants to purchase their pollution rights, and a market for pollution rights has grown steadily despite early governmental opposition.[12]

Furthermore, the fact that transactions have been growing rapidly suggests there are large gains from trade. Millions of dollars in control costs have been saved without worsening air quality, as low-cost emitters have incentives to control more while high-cost emitters have incentives to control less. Society gains because this means that increasingly the low-cost polluters will sell their rights to the high-cost polluters, and total control costs will be minimized for that level of abatement.

1. Do you think a clean environment is a normal good with an income elasticity greater than unity?

2. Discuss how you might go about determining the MDF curve.

3. Can you show graphically that minimizing the damage plus control costs of a pollutant is equivalent to maximizing the welfare gain from cleaner air?

4. Discuss the relative merits of taxes versus standards on the following energy-related pollutants: lead poisoning from gasoline, damage from strip mining, failure of emergency core cooling in nuclear reactors, SO_x emissions, refinery emissions, auto emissions.

5. Suppose that uncertainty exists only in the MDF curve, and show that taxes, standards, and transferable rights yield identical welfare effects. Explain why.

6. Explain why policies that promote relocation may be preferred in dealing with the long-term effects of CO_2.

Notes

1. The most comprehensive summary of recent studies of hazards of CO_2 buildup in the atmosphere is contained in *Changing Climate*, W.A. Nierenberg, editor (National Academy Press, Washington DC, 1983).

2. A recent and highly readable discussion of the problems posed by acid deposition is *Acid Rain*, by Robert H. Boyle (New York: Nick Lyons Books, 1983).

3. G.E. Gordon, "Acid Rain," *Resources*, No. 75, Winter 1984, pp. 6–8.

4. John H. Dales, *Pollution, Property and Prices* (Toronto: University of Toronto Press, 1968).

5. In terms of welfare, the shift to region B leads to a gain of *OAE* (the social benefits from no pollution in region A) less the costs inflicted in region B (area *OCJK*).

6. If the control cost function were extremely price-elastic, tax payments could be greater in region B than in A. In practice, this situation seems unlikely.

7. A.V. Kneese, S. Rolfe, and J. Harned, eds., *Managing the Environment: International Economic Cooperation for Pollution Control* (New York: Ballinger, 1971), Appendix C.

8. See T.H. Tietenberg, *Emissions Trading: An Exercise in Reforming Pollution Policy* (Washington: Resources for the Future, 1985), p. 42.

9. A.V. Kneese, "The Political Economy of Water Quality Management," in *Environmental Decay*, J.S. Bain, editor (Boston: Little, Brown, 1973).

10. Lester Lave and Eugene Seskin, *Air Pollution and Human Health* (Baltimore: Johns Hopkins, 1977).

11. "The Clean Air Act, The Electric Utilities, and the Coal Market," Congressional Budget Office, Washington DC, April 1982.

12. See Tietenberg, *op. cit.*

COPING WITH OIL SUPPLY DISRUPTIONS

It seems obvious that no country desires to depend upon "insecure" (i.e., arbitrarily interruptible) foreign supplies of critically important economic inputs like energy. Nevertheless, such dependence is quite widespread in today's world and can develop in at least three ways. First, as long as the insecurity is merely latent, its potential for disruption may be underestimated or entirely misperceived. Second, if insecure sources are very cheap, risks involved in their use may be rationalized as justifiable. Third, if no secure sources are available, some risks are to be regarded as inevitable. Oil importer awareness of the insecurity of some OPEC oil supplies was dramatically heightened by the Arab oil embargo of 1973. A previously efficiently functioning international oil market showed sudden evidence of severe market failure. Had competition simply been replaced by monopoly? Or were some OPEC members uneconomically tempering monopoly with the pursuit of political goals for their own sake?

At the time of the 1973 embargo, two alternative interpretations of its motivation existed. To some observers, the political considerations involving the Arab-Israeli conflict merely provided the facade for the real concern of the embargo participants—exacting the monopoly price for oil. This view held that economic self-interest dictates the actions of OPEC members. Assuming this view is correct, and further assuming that the exporters are not subject to Soviet takeover, then the oil importers do not really have a national security problem; they face instead a monopoly problem. The oil exporters can be expected to charge the full monopoly price, but they would never want to charge a price in excess of this, nor prohibit oil exports so as to damage the economies of oil importing countries. The oil exporters, in this view, have a vested economic interest in peace and prosperity in the major consuming nations. If the reader regards this view as correct, then national security poses no problem, and he may pass on immediately to the next chapter.

In contrast, most observers take the view that it was politics, not economics, that prompted the embargo of 1973. Strong nationalistic feelings regarding Arab-Israeli differences will in certain circumstances dominate economic self-interest. Arab oil exporters may adopt oil production policies which, even though they inflict some loss upon themselves, inflict even greater losses on importing nations, in order to achieve political goals. The fact that these political motivations sometimes dominate the model of economic self-interest implies that the importers are faced at times with a rational, profit-maximizing cartel and occasionally with an "irrational" adversary desiring to inflict greater losses than it sustains. Additionally, supply interruptions are not always the result of conscious decisions to embargo the importing nations, but are merely a consequence of war or political upheavals in the producing regions. For example, the supply disruptions resulting from the Iranian revolution of 1978–79 and the subsequent Iran-Iraq war were merely unavoidable consequences of the war, rather than the motivation for the war. But whether due to calculated embargo or as a byproduct of war, from the importing nation's perspective the effect is the same.

Oil is the principal energy form in all of the major developed countries, and most of these countries domestically produce only trivial quantities. On the eve of the 1973 embargo, oil products constituted roughly half or more of the energy consumed in the major oil importing countries. For most of the countries, these requirements were met predominantly by imports. For example, imports constituted the following percentages of oil requirements in 1973: Canada (−11%), France (98%), Germany (93%), Italy (99%), Japan (100%), United Kingdom (98%), and the United States (32%). Only the United States and Canada had substantial domestic production. It is noteworthy that the Arab oil embargo sent the world into its greatest economic decline since the Great Depression of the 1930s. Econometric studies of the United States economy by Fried and Schultz showed that it was already headed into a minor recession, but that the embargo significantly deepened the recession and increased its duration. In the United States, unemployment rose from 4.7 percent in the fall of 1973 to over 8.5 percent 16 months later. The inflation rate jumped from 6.1 percent to an 11.4 percent annual rate over the same period. Their study showed that more than 53 percent of the loss in output and 29 percent of the inflation could be attributed to the embargo. Moreover, it is noteworthy that these effects occurred in an economy far less dependent on imported oil than in other consuming countries, where the losses were greater. Despite the economic debacles of the 1973 embargo and the 1979 Iranian revolution and subsequent Iran-Iraq war, the major oil consuming countries remain heavily dependent on imported oil. For these countries, 1984 import levels as a percentage of total oil consumption have not changed appreciably, except for the United Kingdom with its added oil production from the North Sea.

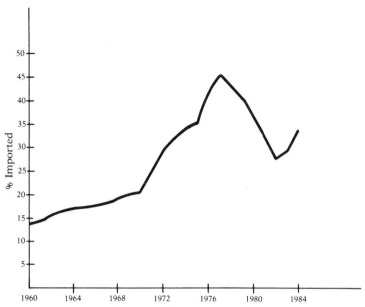

FIGURE 6.1 United States oil imports as a percentage of domestic oil consumption, 1960-1984 (total petroleum liquids basis). (Source: U.S. Bureau of Mines.)

Figure 6.1 shows that percentage imports in the U.S. rose from 32% in 1973 to 46% in 1977. Thereafter declining demand coupled with the completion of the Trans-Alaskan Pipeline helped reduce import dependence to 28% in 1982. Since then imports have resumed their increase, rising to 34% by 1984. A 1985 forecast by Standard Oil of Indiana estimates the percentage imports in the U.S. to be between 52 and 65 percent by the year 2000.

The Rationale for Government Intervention

The fact that the industrialized nations are highly susceptible to future supply disruptions does not automatically prove that a market failure exists and that government intervention is called for. After all, the vagaries inflicted by the weather on many agricultural crops are neither less severe nor more predictable than supply disruptions for oil. There is no public outcry for strategic orange juice or wheat reserves. What is so special about oil? Is it that oil is essential for life while wheat for bread is merely a want? No, obviously not, as we shall soon see.

A close look at a wide variety of commodity markets such as wheat shows active futures markets and numerous speculators who maintain substantial speculative inventories. Speculators acquire buffer inventories, which they hope to sell later at much higher prices. Is there any evidence that the levels of such speculative inventory holdings for these commodities are too small? After all, private investors can assess the probability of a shortage, weighing the probable gain against the inventory holding costs, just as accurately as the government can.

In contrast, a look at U.S. private inventories of crude oil and petroleum products reveals an inventory level just sufficient to enable the smooth day-to-day operations of the oil industry. The absence of large speculative inventories seems at first bizarre given the instability of the world oil market. But is there an explanation? The experience of domestic producers in the 1970s with oil price controls, and before that with natural gas price controls, suggests that price controls would likely be imposed in response to a supply disruption, preventing one from reaping large speculative profits.

Paradoxically, the primary argument favoring government intervention to increase emergency supplies is that private investors underinvest because they assume that price controls would likely be imposed to prevent their earning "obscene" profits. There is another prominent explanation given for the tendency to underinvest in inventories. The social value of emergency supplies during a disruption may well exceed the private value, which is the basis for the private firm's inventory level decision. For example, private demand schedules for oil may not include the external effects brought about by macroeconomic linkages. Put another way, providers of emergency supplies may not be able to appropriate the full social benefits of their inventories. They may receive only a $20 per barrel profit due to the crude price increase, but the full social benefit of that incremental oil in an emergency situation may be $30 or $40 when the macroeconomic effects are factored in. The deviation of social from private benefits remains an intriguing possibility about which little is known.

VARYING CONCEPTIONS OF AND SOLUTIONS TO THE SUPPLY UNCERTAINTY PROBLEM

Today, the problems associated with an oil embargo are viewed primarily in macroeconomic terms—the added inflation and unemployment—and in political terms—restraints on foreign policy in the Middle East. But in the past a disruption of oil supplies has meant quite different problems. Also, the methods chosen to deal with the supply uncertainty problem have changed dramatically from the present methods outlined at the end of this chapter.

At the turn of the century, consuming countries did not regard oil import dependence as a matter for serious concern. Oil products met only a small fraction of energy demand, and many geologists felt promising oil producing areas were restricted to the United States, Russia, and the Dutch East Indies.

The advent of the First World War altered matters considerably, directing the attention of oil importers toward the changes that had occurred both inside their economies and in the world oil industry. All of the major belligerents had become significantly dependent upon petroleum fuels for both military and civilian activities. In particular, the importance of oil to power naval vessels, tanks, trucks, and airplanes was recognized. The security of oil supplies for military purposes became a paramount objective of national policy. As noted in Chapter 4, the major European powers—England, France, and Holland—tried to monopolize oil exploration in the Middle East. Efforts by the U.S. government finally provided the needed leverage for obtaining the participation of U.S. companies in the European-dominated concessions that controlled access to oil lands in the former Turkish empire.

The discovery of oil in politically and economically weak countries provided the major European oil importers with the assurance that they, through their resident oil companies, could receive preferential treatment in times of emergency. Only in the event of war among the major European powers, with attendant disruption of ocean traffic, did an importing country regard its resident companies' foreign oil reserves as less than securely available to it. Years of full availability of cheap oil in increasing volumes had led European oil importers to think that this situation would be permanent. Although supply interruptions during the Arab-Israeli conflicts of 1956 and 1967 did occur, it was probably not until the Libyan negotiations of 1970 that importers began to pause and reflect.

In contrast, the United States attempted to solve its national security problem by limiting import dependence. Of course, only the United States had sufficient domestic oil resources to make import limitation a viable option. Prior to about 1920, the United States was a net exporter of crude oil and refined petroleum products, and naturally had little interest in import control. During the 1920s imports exceeded exports, however, and the excess became very large in the depressed years of the early 1930s. In order to discourage imports, for economic rather than security reasons, a substantial tariff was passed in 1932 on crude oil and heavy product imports, aimed in particular at Venezuelan imports. From 1933 to 1944 export surpluses once again predominated for crude oil.

During the 1950s, imports into the United States began to grow rapidly as the price of Middle East oil fell during this period. As the price of Middle East oil fell below domestic prices, there were strong incentives to import oil. State regulatory agencies, which were set up in the 1930s to promote conservation, controlled the production rate of domestic oil. Initially, they were able to stem the tendency toward lower prices by cutting domestic output by the amount of new imports. This naturally increased tensions between domestic and international companies.

Thus, after the early 1950s, pressure grew to limit imports. In 1957 President Eisenhower requsted all oil importers, large and small, to cooperate in a voluntary program of import limitation. When interests proved to be too divergent for the industry to limit imports on its own initiative, Eisenhower in 1959 made import limitation mandatory.

The implementation of import quotas requires that a total import limit be set, and that the authority to import be distributed among the market participants. There is no point in limiting imports unless the allowed quantity is to be less than that which would prevail in a competitive market; hence any import limitation will reduce total supply in the importing country and raise prices paid by domestic buyers. The recipient of the import quota allotment thus receives a subsidy equal to the difference between the lower foreign price and the higher domestic price. Everyone clamored to be awarded import "tickets." Exporting countries such as Venezuela requested "country quotas" that would in effect raise the price of the imported oil to the domestic level and allow the import subsidy to be captured by the foreign exporters. Domestic refiners insisted that they should be given the tickets, since they were the "natural" buyers of imported oil—a contention that was historically true for some refiners but not others. Domestic producers argued that the benefits of import ticket subsidies should go to producers, who could then use the import subsidy receipts to stimulate domestic exploration and thus reduce the long-run need for oil imports.

As the system evolved, it so happened that imports were reduced below previous levels, that U.S. prices remained above world oil prices, and that the domestic oil industry was for a period of time shielded from the price competition of foreign oil. Although national security was given as the justification for the program, and although the program did contribute to the nation's security, there were a number of inconsistencies and residual beneficiaries.

As of 1959 the price of foreign oil was about $1.25 per barrel less than that of domestic oil. Imports east of the Pacific coast states were limited to 9.0 percent of oil demand in that area, while West Coast refiners were allowed to import as much oil as was needed to equate supply with demand at existing prices. (This division of the country was possible since there were no significant oil movements across the Rocky Mountains, and the West Coast was at that time running out of domestic supplies more rapidly than was the rest of the country.) Import tickets were given to refiners, on a scale that not only provided import allotments to inland refiners (which ordinarily did no importing) but also favored smaller refiners by giving them a higher quota relative to refinery runs than applied to larger refiners. Since refiners now controlled the supply of import "tickets," nonintegrated foreign producers had to make arrangements with refiners in order to market their oil. Refiners holding surplus import tickets "sold" these tickets to refiners who needed them; the value of an import ticket equalled the $1.25 per barrel price gap between foreign and domestic oil. On balance, the system acted as a subsidy to small and inland refiners. Moreover, it protected high-cost domestic oil producers from the competition from lower priced imports. The interesting feature of the oil import program is that foreign price fluctuations had no effect on domestic crude prices. The value of an import ticket would fluctuate in response to foreign prices, but domestic prices were set by domestic supply capabilities and the state regulatory agencies' control over production. After 1972 foreign oil prices rose above domestic levels and import tickets thus became worthless.

Professors Douglas Bohi and Milton Russell have attempted to estimate the protective effect of the import control program during the 1960s. They compared the actual situation with what they estimated would have occurred if free trade in oil had been achieved in 1960 and the U.S. price of $3.06 per barrel had fallen to the world price of around $2.00. Since the lower price would have stimulated domestic consumption and reduced domestic production, imports would certainly have increased significantly. Bohi and Russell concluded that by 1970, imports would have risen to 3.5 billion barrels per year, compared with an actual level of only 700 million barrels. Imports as a percentage of domestic consumption would have risen to 61.4 percent, compared with an actual level of 14.6 percent. Furthermore, imports from the most insecure sources—Arab members of OPEC—would have amounted to 40 percent of all oil consumption in 1970, as compared with an actual rate of less than 5 percent under the control program.[1]

Bohi and Russell estimated the resource cost of the mandatory oil import control program to be about $2.3 billion for the year 1969, the only year for which comprehensive cost data were available. Of this total, $1.4 billion was the estimated cost of carrying excess production capacity under conservation regulation, and $900 million represented the extra production costs of oil produced at costs above the world price level of $2.10 per barrel.[2]

The mandatory oil import program is now history and the United States is grappling with new solutions to the security problem. But what lessons does it offer? There is no doubt that the mandatory oil import program increased national security during that period, in that domestic productive capacity was greater at the higher controlled domestic price than it would have been at world prices. If world oil prices had prevailed in the United States during the 1960s, U.S. production in 1973 on the eve of the Arab Oil Embargo would have been far less. Nevertheless, it does not follow that the program was either optimal or even cost-effective. The program did not differentiate effectively among exporters as to their security prospects. All overseas imports were viewed as insecure regardless of country of origin. No one paused to ask if increased domestic production is the most cost-effective method of achieving security. There is still the more fundamental question: What price premium is justified for secure oil supplies? Under the import control program, domestic prices could theoretically be allowed to rise far above the price of imported oil. Instead of $1.25 per barrel, the security premium might be $5 or $10 per barrel. In order to answer these questions, we will now consider the determination of an optimal import dependence reduction program.

OPTIMAL METHODS OF
REDUCING DEPENDENCE
A Theoretical Basis

The previous discussion of macroeconomic effects as well as military and political considerations suggests that oil supplies subject to possible embargo should receive a lower social valuation than secure oil sources. If market prices were to reflect such a premium, there would be no policy concern. The problem is that due to a variety of governmental powers to ration oil during emergency situations, contracts to deliver "secure" oil could not be honored. Consequently, the structure of world oil prices cannot reflect any security premium.

The supply uncertainty problem represents a market failure of the externality type where the true social cost of nonsecure oil is not reflected in its price. An obvious solution from Chapter 5 is to impose a tax on those oil supplies subject to embargo. But in order to select the optimal tax, we must have information about the marginal damage function, the marginal control or security cost function, and administrative costs. Thus we are forced to look at each of these and in effect to determine the optimal level of security. Our criterion in determining the optimal level of security is the set of policies that minimize the sum of expected damage costs, control or security costs, and administrative costs. After all, if we minimize the sum of these costs, welfare must be maximized.

Let us pose the question of how to purchase the optimal degree of security, so as to minimize the damage to the economies of oil importers during an embargo. Since many countries import oil, their security problem in the face of a common embargo is a group security problem rather than a collection of individual national security issues. Since it is obviously easier to analyze the problems of an isolated importer, let us approach the solution in a series of steps. We first assume a two-country world, with one exporter and one importer, so that no imports are available during an embargo. We next assume two exporters and one importer, where only one exporter indulges in embargo tactics. Third, we add a second importing country and investigate possible relationships between them during an embargo.

The One Importer, One Exporter Case. Before proceding further, we must consider the basis for calculating the marginal damage function. Let us assume that the importing country consumes 10 million barrels per day. The marginal damage function in Figure 6.2 declines with an increasing quantity of secure oil available, and reaches zero when all oil consumption comes from secure sources. In this initial example we abstract from the extra-economic (military and political) costs of an embargo and assume that if all oil imports are cut off, and no domestic oil is available, the economy ceases to operate; then the total social cost of the embargo can be measured in economic terms equal to GNP. If the daily GNP is 10 billion dollars when daily imports are 10 million barrels per day, then the total social cost of an embargo is $10 billion per day. Thus *during* an embargo the area under the marginal damage function in Figure 6.2 from 0 to 10 million barrels per day must equal $10 billion. Clearly, the marginal damage function is likely to slope downward since the marginal effect of the loss of the first barrel of imports is much less than the loss of the 10 millionth barrel. A linear marginal damage function starting at $2000 per barrel for the loss of all crude oil and declining to zero for the first barrel of imports gives an area under the curve equal to $10 billion during the embargo.

Figure 6.2 is not yet complete, even though the MDF schedule does show the economic losses in the event of a supply disruption. If there is no disruption, there is no damage, so the marginal damage function applies only during the probable fraction of time when disruptions occur. In Figure 6.2, the expected marginal damage function is calculated by attaching probabilities to the damages corresponding to various lengths of supply disruptions. The measurement of the expected marginal damage function is by no means a simple matter. Assessing even the macroeconomic effects of an embargo poses substantial difficulties because of the lack of supply-side detail in most macroeconomic models. Another problem is that the probability and duration of an embargo are simply not amenable to close estimation. For example, provision of emergency supplies for 120 days substantially reduces the probability of a short embargo and raises the probability of one lasting more than 120 days. Admittedly, any effort to measure an expected marginal damage function is subject to great error; nevertheless, some informed estimates are better than the alternative—disregarding these damage costs altogether.

In our present simple example, let us assume that the exporter is expected to embargo the importer for a six-month period every five years. Hence the expected marginal damages from an embargo at any time are equal to one-tenth of the actual damages that develop during

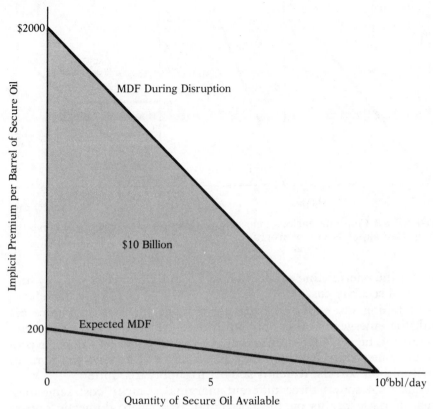

FIGURE 6.2 The marginal damage function at various levels of supply disruption.

the embargo. The expected MDF schedule in Figure 6.2 reflects this assumption.

How can the importing country secure itself against supply interruptions? Let us assume for simplicity that there are only two ways to obtain added domestic supplies during an embargo: either from storage of oil produced (or imported) in excess of consumption in previous periods, or from the production of oil from domestic fields that are kept on a standby basis, to be exploited only during embargos. Figure 6.3 shows how the marginal security cost of relying upon each measure alone, or on both measures together, varies with the rate at which these measures are relied upon for supply security purposes. Let method A be emergency storage, with a rising marginal security cost (MSC_A), such that 1 million barrels per day can be produced at a marginal security cost of $15 per barrel. Let method B be standby production, with more rapidly rising costs, such that only 0.5 million barrels per day can be produced at a marginal security cost (MSC_B) of $15 per barrel. Let method C be the reliance upon both methods A and B

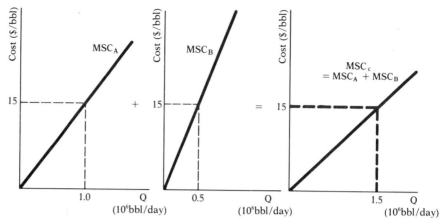

FIGURE 6.3 Combine various emergency oil supply strategies to achieve the lowest-cost supply-security program.

jointly, thus permitting production of 1.5 million barrels per day at a marginal security cost ($MSC_C = MSC_A + MSC_B$) of $15 per barrel.

Combining the expected marginal damage function in Figure 6.2 with the emergency oil supply strategies in Figure 6.3, we construct Figure 6.4. Figure 6.4 assumes that our hypothetical oil importer produces domestically 7 million barrels per day and imports the remaining 3 million barrels, which is subject to supply disruption.

Figure 6.4 shows three different marginal security cost schedules. Each of these begins on the horizontal axis where domestic output ceases at 7 million barrels per day. The marginal security cost of secure domestic oil is by definition zero, as no security premium is granted domestic suppliers. Estimates of marginal security cost are much easier to calculate than expected damage costs, since all that must be estimated is the cost of installing, maintaining, and operating the mix of "embargo insurance" measures to be actually employed. Of the three MSC schedules shown, MSC_C (which utilizes both methods A and B) is obviously preferable since it involves lower marginal cost for additional secure oil than do the other policies or methods. MSC_B, which utilizes only standby production capacity, is inferior to a policy using both standby production and storage. The "method" illustrated by MSC_X is actually no method at all, and is drawn in simply to show what the total expected costs per day of an embargo would be if no defenses against it were undertaken. Under X, an embargo would reduce oil consumption to 7 million barrels per day, and the expected marginal damage would be $60 per barrel. The total costs under policy X arise entirely from damage costs. The total damages would be shown by the area of triangle *ORX*, which is equal to $90 million per day.

Using method B, the intersection of MSC_B with the expected MDF schedule occurs at 8.2 million barrels per day. Thus there would be an additional 1.2 million barrels of oil available through standby production during the embargo. The implicit security premium is $36 per barrel since the marginal security cost of the 1.2 millionth barrel is $36. The total costs under this policy would be the sum of the areas of two triangles: (1) *BVX*, which shows the embargo damages resulting from reducing consumption from 10 to 8.2 million barrels per day ($32.4 million per day), and (2) *OBV*, which shows the total cost of providing the added supplies during the embargo ($21.6 million per day), making the total costs $54 million per day under policy B, which is a savings of $36 million (area *RBO*) over the damages resulting from having no program at all.

Using policy C, however, total supplies during an emergency are increased to 9 million barrels per day, with 2 million added by supply security measures. Remaining damages from reducing oil consumption are area *AWX* ($10 million per day) and total control or security costs are shown by area *OAW* ($20 million per day), so total costs and remaining damages are reduced to $30 million per day. Policy C yields a savings of $24 million (area *OBA*) over those a policy B and $60 million (area *ORA*) over those of policy X.

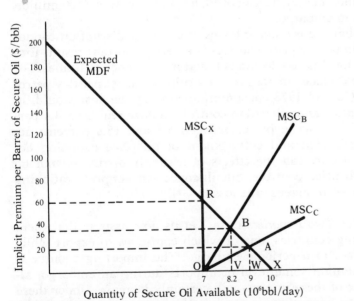

FIGURE 6.4 Determination of the optimal level of provision for secure oil, assuming exports totally embargoed 10 percent of the time, with only a single oil importing country.

It is thus apparent that a single importing country can protect itself to some degree against the damages of an embargo by employing various embargo insurance measures. Figure 6.4 has some interesting implications for the price levels prevailing during supply disruptions. Under a policy utilizing MSC_C, a production shortfall of 1 million barrels per day would force prices up to the society's value of a barrel of oil during an embargo. From Figure 6.4, the security premium is $20 per barrel, but this is the *expected* marginal damage. During an actual supply disruption, Figure 6.2 indicates that a 1 million barrel per day shortfall would push market prices $200 per barrel above the pre-disruption price. A $200 per barrel price hike would indeed ensure the efficient use of oil resources during the embargo. But can the costs of the supply disruption be reduced or avoided by freezing prices? It is argued in Chapter 8 that when an emergency is of short duration, it may be preferable to impose temporary price controls and allocation procedures in the interest of minimizing the macroeconomic effects of a disruption. Let us assume that ideally efficient price controls and quantity rationing are employed, so that the price could stay at the pre-embargo price per barrel. The quantity rationing devices are assumed to distribute the 9 million barrels of oil available to the most productive 90 percent of all consumption. If this were accomplished, the total social cost of the embargo would still consist of the actual damages of $100 million per day (10 times area *AWX*) plus the control costs of $20 million per day (area *OAW*), for a total cost of $120 million per day during an embargo.

The finding that the economic losses of a supply disruption cannot be avoided by imposing price controls is a very important result. Empirical support for this conclusion is found in a number of studies. For example, David Couts estimated that a 4 million barrel per day petroleum shortfall (22% of 1978 consumption) lasting one year would, in the absence of price and allocation controls, reduce real GNP 4.4 percent and, with controls in place, between 5.5 and 15.8 percent (depending on the design and enforcement of nonprice rationing devices).[3] Thus not only can the effects of a supply disruption not be avoided through price controls, but ill-conceived nonprice rationing procedures may even increase the loss in GNP.

The One Importer, Two Exporters Case. Let us now assume that there are two exporting countries, one of which continues to export while the other indulges in a periodic embargo. The importing country is now able to maintain some level of imports during an embargo, although the price of these imports will certainly increase. Under these circumstances the importing country now has another way of mitigating the damages during an embargo; i.e., it simply imports more than usual from the other exporter. While this element of added flexibility tends to further reduce the slope of the MSC schedule, it is still in the interest of the importer to use other measures as well. Assuming an upward sloping supply schedule from the exporter who continues to ship oil, additional supplies will be available, but at higher prices. The incorporation of additional import supply from the nonembargoing country is shown in Figure 6.5. Since imports from the secure country of 1.5 million barrels per day continue along with domestic production of 7 million barrels per day, the marginal social cost schedules emanate from production of 8.5 million barrels per day instead of 7 million barrels daily. Policy C, which is labelled as MSC_C and involves using both standby capacity and oil storage, is no longer likely to be the lowest cost method. The optimal policy set is MSC_D, which involves the use of standby capacity, oil storage, and additional imports from the nonembargoing oil exporter. Figure 6.5 illustrates several important points. First, the presence of a number of importers who are unlikely to participate in embargos and are relatively immune to po-

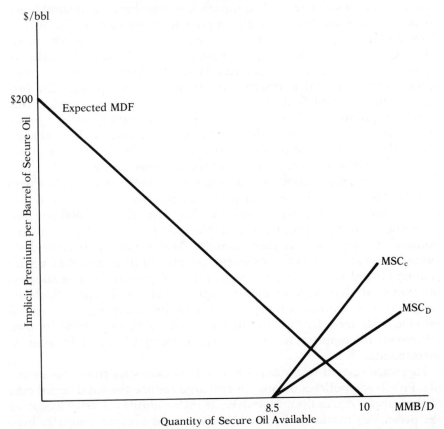

FIGURE 6.5 Security premium in case of embargo from only one of two exporters.

litical disruptions lowers the security premium. Furthermore, additional imports from such countries during disruptions should be a vital component of an optimal security portfolio.

The Two Importers, One Exporter Case. Let us consider the case of two oil importers, each capable of producing 7 MMB/D, and one oil exporter that supplies the other 3 million barrels daily to each importer. Importing country W, the wise country, has adopted policy set C in Figure 6.4 consisting of standby productive capacity and oil storage, so as to limit the expected security premium to $20 per barrel, or a $200 premium during an embargo. Country M, the myopic country, elects to do nothing, in effect placing a security premium of $60 per barrel, or a $600 premium during an embargo.

In an isolated world, prices would rise by $600 per barrel during an embargo in country M, but by only $200 in country W. But in a world with free trade, such price differences would not persist; instead, only one price would be established roughly at $400 per barrel above the pre-embargo price. The critical question is whether it is desirable for country W to share part of its oil supplies with country M. The answer depends on the price. At a market clearing level of $400 per barrel above the pre-embargo level, the answer is clearly yes. The value of imports from country W to country M would clearly be greater than when country W's oil is reserved for its own exclusive use. The producers' surplus at $400 premium per barrel is clearly greater than that at a $200 premium. Not only would the sale to country M be profitable, it would help to lower the combined social cost of the embargo. To the degree that both countries were tied together in trade, country W would benefit indirectly from country M's improvement.

Suppose instead that country W shared its emergency supplies with country M at the pre-embargo price. Despite the transfer at a zero security premium, the market price would soon reflect a $400 per barrel premium in both countries. Thus the only apparent effect is distributional. Country W has given country M one million barrels daily valued at $400 per barrel. Obviously, country W (if it is indeed a wise country) is unlikely to engage in such acts of generosity. But suppose international sharing agreements required such a transfer. Such arrangements would be counterproductive in the long run as they would provide little incentive for the myopic country M to provide its own emergency oil supplies, nor for the wise country W to benefit from its investments.

There are several important implications following from this example. Free trade policies during an embargo reduce the total social cost of the supply disruption. Moreover, if intercountry oil flows occur at the prevailing market price, both the wise and myopic countries benefit, so that there is no reason for the wise country to hoard oil for its own use. Finally, transfers of emergency supplies at the prevailing embargo price premiums provide a strong future inducement for country W to continue investing in emergency supplies and for country M to alter its behavior.

Selection of the Optimal Set of National Security Policies

Figure 6.4 indicates the fundamental problems facing an embargoed economy. With domestic production of 70 percent of requirements, how should one deal with a denial of 30 percent of a country's normal consumption? In Figure 6.4 the optimal policy set consisted of additional emergency supplies of 20 percent and conservation for the remaining 10 percent. Policy makers must assign the relative roles of conservation and emergency supplies. Within the set of policies labeled emergency supplies, there is the decision as to what roles are to be played by increased domestic oil production, oil storage, reserve standby capacity, and so on.

Conservation. An integral part of all national security programs for dealing with embargos is oil conservation. Fortunately, conservation does not necessarily require an elaborate bureaucracy because conservation naturally occurs as a consequence of higher prices. An implication of Figure 6.4 is that as the price rises above the predisruption level, the marginal damage function reflects the value to society of that particular oil. Lower-valued uses of oil will necessarily be curtailed when the market price exceeds the value of such uses.

A conservation program need not be limited to those actions which occur voluntarily in response to higher prices. Particularly when prices are controlled during a disruption, nonprice rationing devices must be used. Other conservation devices include quantity rationing, speed limit reductions, and mandatory thermostat reductions. Policies such as these were employed during the 1973 Arab oil embargo and probably will be utilized again in an impending disruption situation. In this discussion we do not attempt to rank the various methods of achieving conservation, as these are discussed extensively in Chapter 7.

The important point in a conservation policy is recognizing that it has limits. At current consumption rates, a small reduction in consumption can be achieved with minimal changes in life styles. In fact, the loss in social benefits is approximated by the market price, since at the margin the consumer is indifferent between purchasing an oil product and other goods worth the same money. As one moves up the demand curve, achieving greater and greater conservation, the foregone marginal social benefit of each additional percentage of oil saved becomes greater. At some point the foregone marginal social benefits exceed the costs of providing for emergency oil supplies. This defines the limits to a conservation policy.

Figure 6.4 shows that conservation should be used to achieve a reduction of 10 percent. Over this range of oil use, the sacrifice in marginal social benefits in oil consumption, as approximated by the marginal damage function, is less than the cost of providing emergency supplies. In sum, conservation policies should be utilized up to the point that the marginal damage function equals the marginal control cost function consisting of the optimal set of emergency supplies.

Self-Sufficiency in Domestic Oil Production: Drain the United States First. For Japan and the European countries, excepting the United Kingdom and Norway, domestic self-sufficiency in oil production is virtually an impossibility. Nature did not endow these countries with sizeable deposits of even higher cost oil. Consequently, to be self-sufficient in energy production, these countries would have to convert almost completely to other energy forms. At current price differentials among fuels and current technology, such a conversion would inflict impractical costs upon these economies.

For the United States, the choice is a different one. Physical limitations on the petroleum resource base are not as serious. Significant conventional oil reserves and shale oil reserves can be developed providing one is willing to pay the higher cost. Thus the United States probably has the physical reserves to raise domestic production enough to achieve self-sufficiency. Self-sufficiency would likely entail the rapid exploitation of existing conventional oil reserves, extensive exploration in offshore areas, and development of a large scale shale oil industry. The real question is not the physical capability, but the cost of this additional oil production. United States oil production is already high-cost compared to worldwide costs, and the additional oil production to reach self-sufficiency is likely to result in oil costs well above world prices. The domestic price of oil might have to be raised $15 to $30 per barrel above current world prices to achieve complete self-sufficiency. Thus while domestic self-sufficiency may be feasible, it is analogous to an MSC curve that is everywhere above other policies. There exist other, lower-cost alternative methods of providing security.

Another difficulty with pushing domestic oil production up to self-sufficiency is that, because it would exhaust the reserves of lower-cost oil, future generations would have to produce still higher cost reserves to achieve security. The policy of draining America first would significantly increase the cost of national security for future generations.

Drain OPEC First. If it is unwise to embark on self-sufficiency programs that would drain America first, what are the merits of a security program that would drain OPEC first, leaving domestic reserves in the ground? While intuitively quite appealing, such a policy would shift the MSC curve in Figure 6.4 back to the left, so that it begins at 0 percent self-sufficiency rather than 70 percent, since U.S. reserves would be left undeveloped in the ground in order to drain OPEC. After incorporating this change, this would significantly increase the current cost of national security. Even though undeveloped U.S. oil reserves would be formidable, the necessary oil wells, drilling equipment, and pipeline construction could not be developed instantaneously in the event of an embargo. To awaken such a dormant industry might take many years. Thus in the event of an embargo, the United States would have to rely on other methods of achieving national security.

Even though this policy might make it possible for the United States to achieve self-sufficiency at a lower relative cost at some future date, the increased costs of complete vulnerability in the interim would seem to far outweigh any future benefits. Furthermore, this increased vulnerability would increase the probability of an embargo, raising the expected marginal damage function. Thus, just as "drain America first" makes no sense as a long-run strategy, "drain OPEC first" makes no sense as a short-run strategy.

Fiscal and Monetary Policies. A student of macroeconomics is taught that GNP, employment, and inflation can be affected through fiscal and monetary policies. This suggests the possibility that fiscal and monetary policies can be used to offset the deleterious effects of an embargo. For example, to prevent GNP from falling, the government can adopt expansionary policies by lowering taxes, increasing government spending, and increasing the growth in the money supply.[4] In situations where the economy is faced with insufficient aggregate demand, these policy prescriptions are quite effective. However, when the economy is supply-constrained due to a lack of oil, creating additional aggregate demand is not likely to significantly improve the situation. This does not imply that fiscal and monetary policy is completely ineffectual. In the face of rising prices due to shortages during the embargo, there is a tendency to adopt restrictive policies to hold down inflation. Such policies can contribute to the loss in employment, as both the supply and demand sides of the markets are driving output downward. But while fiscal and monetary policies cannot be expected to alleviate the effects of an embargo, if used properly they can prevent a worsening of the economic situation.

Long-Term Contracts. From any one country's view, a seemingly complete solution to a supply disruption problem is to arrange long-term contracts with secure oil exporters. As in the case of Figure 6.5, long-term supply contracts with reliable countries can effectively shift the MSC schedule to the right. In principle, for small importers, such long-term contracts would provide complete insulation from a worldwide supply disruption. Since the long-term contract price would be set previously at pre-embargo levels, it would seem that a country with such contracts could be completely insulated from the apocalypse surrounding it.

But such a narrow view of the world overlooks two basic realities. First, the world's existing oil production can be seen as coming from the same bathtub. Even though one country can establish the right to purchase some portion of the secure oil present in the bathtub, the total amount of secure oil is not increased. Consequently, from a world perspective, security is not enhanced.

Second, it is unrealistic for a country to assume that it can remain unaffected by a worldwide supply disruption. As illustrated in the two importer, one exporter case, high worldwide oil prices during a disruption will create arbitrage incentives that will result in equilibration with world oil prices. Even if a country chose to hoard its oil, the severe macroeconomic dislocations affecting its trading partners would ultimately spread to it.

There are situations where long-term contracts with secure producers can actually enhance world security. Continuing the analogy of the bathtub, if the long-term contract puts more water (oil) in the tub, security is enhanced. Suppose the long-term contract leads to the development of additional productive capacity in secure areas. The existence of such contracts could provide funds necessary for the development of additional productive capacity earmarked for purposes of fulfilling a long-term contract.

International Sharing Agreements. The International Energy Agency was formed as the consuming nations' response to the 1973 Arab oil embargo. All of the major consuming nations except France have agreed that in the event of an embargo against any one member country, all other members will share oil, so as to spread the effect of the embargo evenly over the various members. Additionally, each IEA member agrees to maintain oil storage equal to 90 days of imports, thereby significantly increasing the world's emergency oil supplies. In principle, such an agreement substantially reduces the cost of emergency supplies to any one country and reduces the probability of an embargo against any single country. Some might even argue that it completely resolves the national security problem because participants would realize that an embargo against any one nation would not be able to cripple it, so the embargo tool would never be employed.

Doubts about the effectiveness of the IEA center on the political realities of an embargo and the problems with the pricing of shared oil.[5] While the IEA is no doubt some deterrent to an embargo, agreements among sovereign nations are frequently violated with complete impunity. Suppose country A, a nonembargoed member of IEA, were threatened by embargoing nations that it too would be embargoed if it shared oil with country B, the object of the embargo. It is entirely possible that country A would withdraw from the IEA.

The other objection raised about the IEA is the pricing of shared petroleum. Under the IEA formula, an embargoed country receives rights to purchase a predetermined quantity of the other members' crude oil. Apparently the price of the crude could be set by the IEA secretariat at levels well below world spot prices, giving incentives to purchase more crude than would be the case if world spot prices guided the decision. In effect, mechanical sharing formulas with prices set below world spot levels would only add distortions. An alternative to mechanical sharing formulas, which would fulfill the intended purpose of sharing, would be an agreement among IEA members that no country would impose limitations on its oil companies that would prohibit the reexportation of crude. In effect, the IEA could simply agree to a free market in crude trade among its member countries—a novel idea!

Reserve Standby Capacity. A frequently advocated policy offered by casual observers of the oil industry is to develop large quantities of reserve standby capacity. Owners of existing oil wells could be paid not to produce, saving this production for an emergency. Just as the agricultural soil bank took domestic farm land out of production, oil fields could be shut down until needed. Obviously, government payments would have to be large enough to compensate producers to defer production and to maintain the pumping equipment and the pipeline facilities to transport the oil to the refinery.

The supply schedule based on these costs rises quite sharply and yields very high costs for stripper wells, which produce at a rate of only a few barrels per day. The maintenance cost of the stripper wells implies very high costs per barrel of daily production. The reason is quite simple—the maintenance costs for a well capable of producing 500 barrels per day may be the same as those of the stripper well, yet the 500-barrel-per-day well delivers a much greater flow of oil. Thus only fields having the following characteristics are likely to have acceptably low maintenance costs per barrel: high daily production rates, reasonably low drilling costs per well (to enable infill drilling to increase production), and a location near a major refining center. Clearly, even though Alaskan North Slope wells have high daily production rates, they are very costly to drill, and the expenses of maintaining the pipeline to Valdez on standby would be exorbitant.

There are, however, some fields that meet these conditions, yielding reasonably low costs. Professors Mead and Sorensen show that the Elk

Hills field, a part of the Naval Petroleum Reserve located in southern California, could be economically attractive as a reserve standby facility.[6] By drilling wells in a much closer spacing pattern than is usually followed, this field could produce at a very high output rate during a temporary emergency period. The interesting economic feature to be noted about reserve standby capacity is that the cost per barrel of emergency supplies falls with the length of the embargo. Suppose for example that the annual cost of maintaining a well on standby capacity is $1000 and the rate of production is 100 barrels per day. If the embargo lasts for only one day, the reserve capacity cost is $10 per barrel. However, if the embargo lasts 100 days, the cost of the reserve capacity is only 10 cents per barrel. Particularly to the extent long embargos are expected, the economics of standby reserve capacity become more attractive.

At present, production from the Naval Petroleum Reserve would add perhaps only 200,000 to 300,000 barrels per day to domestic production; in general, few fields would be suited for a standby-reserve basis. The huge Yates field in West Texas may be a promising candidate. Geologically, Yates has all the desirable characteristics—low drilling costs due to a relatively shallow field, extremely prolific wells capable of producing 2,000 to 3,000 barrels per day, and a location near refining centers. Even though in 1984 Yates produced at a rate of 144,000 barrels per day, reservoir tests indicated the field could produce at 352,000 B/D with existing wells. With extensive infill drilling, it is not inconceivable that Yates could produce at a 600,000 B/D rate for 6 to 12 months. But probably the biggest argument is an economic one. Oil reserves in existing fields frequently sell for one-fifth to one-fourth as much as oil that has actually been produced. In contrast the Strategic Petroleum Reserve (SPR) purchases oil at current market prices and then stores them in reservoirs akin to Yates. Imagine the U.S. government buying out U.S. Steel, the owner of Marathon Oil Company (which in turn is the virtually sole owner of Yates), keeping Yates, and selling U.S. Steel's steel plants to a Japanese steel company! Since recent oil industry mergers have transferred oil reserves in the ground at effective prices of $5 to $6 per barrel, the U.S. government might obtain a ready-made SPR at a 75% discount off market price!

Oil Storage. The single most important aspect of U.S. emergency supply policy was the creation of a strategic petroleum reserve, using salt domes located along the Gulf Coast as huge storage facilities. After the mining of salt, great sealed caverns are left deep in the earth's crust that make excellent natural storage facilities with costs only a fraction of those of above-ground steel storage tanks. The major cost of these facilities is simply the interest cost of the stored oil. Standby pipeline facilities are generally near refineries, so that transportation costs are not large.

Oil storage has long been a favorite strategy of European countries, where it is not uncommon to see storage equal to more than 90 days' consumption. In Europe, oil refiners are required by law to maintain 90 or more days' supply. Until explicit government action was taken, U.S. refiners held perhaps 20 to 25 days' consumption or less, which is the amount needed for standard operations. The National Emergency Petroleum Storage Act of 1976 provided for the creation of the Strategic Petroleum Reserve equal to one billion barrels, to have been achieved by 1980. But by 1983, the total stockpile was only about 325 million barrels, and the total goal had been revised downward to 750 million barrels to be achieved by 1989. By 1985, with reserves standing at 500 million barrels, additional purchases were suspended in order to reduce the government deficit. At the 1985 oil import level of about 5 million barrels per day, the actual stockpile would replace fully embargoed imports for a period of 100 days.

Since the supply of available salt domes is very large and imported oil can be purchased at a given price for storage, the long-run supply schedule of emergency supplies from this source tends to be flat over a considerable range. Recent estimates place the annual cost per barrel of this method of storage (including interest costs) at between $3.25 to $4.00 per barrel. In effect, oil storage places a ceiling price on emergency supplies. Other methods, such as reserve standby capacity, should be utilized up to the point that their costs equal the ceiling implied by storage.

Two major questions arise regarding the strategic petroleum reserve (SPR) as the primary element in the U.S. oil security plan. First, what is the optimal size of the SPR? Second, what is or should be the trigger mechanism to initiate withdrawals from the SPR? The answer to the question of the optimal SPR size requires a complicated analytical framework employing dynamic programming techniques together with a host of assumptions regarding the frequency, intensity, and duration of likely future embargos.[7] Almost all studies recommend a reserve greater than 750 million barrels and most recommend a reserve greater than 1 billion barrels.[8]

The trigger mechanism to initiate withdrawals from the SPR currently rests with the President. On the face of it, it would appear to be a simple matter to know when to begin selling oil from the SPR and at what rate, but imagine yourself as President of the U.S. facing the following situation: The Iran-Iraq war spreads as routed Iraqi troops pour into Kuwait and Iranian forces pursue, cutting off all oil shipments from Iran, Iraq, and Kuwait. The loss of 3 million barrels per day of oil supply from world markets sends spot prices up by $10 per barrel. Your economic advisors argue that since in the very short run supply and demand are most inelastic, SPR shipments should begin immediately in volumes of at least 1.5 million barrels per day, offsetting at least half of the shortfall. They argue that such a move would stabilize spot prices and bring about orderly supply and demand adjustments. But your National Security Advisor and Secretary of Defense argue that the SPR should be saved for potentially worse days to come. They fear the conflict will spread into Saudi Arabia, resulting in the loss of another 5 million barrels per day of production. In such event, they argue, war damage and sabotage of these fields will prevent any flow of oil from the Persian Gulf for at least two years. They argue that SPR reserves should be saved until the war picture is more certain. As President you opted for the "wait and see" strategy. The war is then confined to Kuwait and, by the time this becomes apparent, spot prices have risen by $30 above predisruption levels. By the time you begin production from the SPR four months later at a rate of .5 million barrels per day, the economic damage has been done.

Due to the inherent tendency to underutilize the SPR, observers have attempted to formulate a simple set of rules regarding when and how much to withdraw from the SPR. It is extremely difficult to specify the full set of rules that would apply for a large number of situations. The most appealing plan uses the options market as a signalling device for the intensity and duration of supply disruption. Horwich and Weimer go on to offer the following numerical example:[9]

> Operation of the options system can be illustrated with the simple example presented in Table 6.1. Imagine that the world price of oil is stable at thirty dollars per barrel in weeks 1 to 12. Each week during this period the SPR office offers options for purchase at a forward price of thirty-three dollars per barrel nine to twelve weeks in the future. Because most firms expect prices to remain stable, options for only about 1 million of the 12 million barrels offered each week are sold at the minimum acceptable bid of one cent per barrel. Also, because the world price of oil is lower than the forward price on options sold nine to twelve weeks earlier, no options are exercised. Now assume that in week 13 a major crisis with potential for disrupting regional oil supplies begins to develop in the Middle East. Spot prices rise to thirty-one dollars as firms seek to expand their stocks. At the same time, firms also seek to purchase options as an alternative to stocks, bidding the price up by ten cents per barrel in week 13 and twenty cents per barrel in week 14. In week 15 a war breaks out, reducing oil supplies from the Middle East. Spot prices rise to thirty-five dollars per barrel, making it profitable for those who purchased options in weeks 3, 4, 5, and 6 to exercise them. The result is a drawdown of 4 million barrels. From week 16 through week 21, options of 1 million barrels per week are exercised. In week 22 the number of options exercised jumps to 12 million barrels as options sold at the first threat of disruption in week 13 mature. Beginning in week 23, oil prices stabilize at forty dollars per barrel, and option prices once again fall to the minimum acceptable bid. In week 25 the spot price falls below the forward price for options sold nine weeks be-

TABLE 6.1 Illustration of the Options System Drawdown

Week	Market Condition	Spot Price ($/bbl)	Options Sold (millions of bbl)	Option Price ($/bbl)	Current Forward Price ($/bbl)	Options Exercised (millions of bbl)	Week of Purchase of Exercised Option
1	N	30	1	0.01	33.00	0	—
2	N	30	1	0.01	33.00	0	—
3	N	30	1	0.01	33.00	0	—
4	N	30	1	0.01	33.00	0	—
5	N	30	1	0.01	33.00	0	—
6	N	30	1	0.01	33.00	0	—
7	N	30	1	0.01	33.00	0	—
8	N	30	1	0.01	33.00	0	—
9	N	30	1	0.01	33.00	0	—
10	N	30	1	0.01	33.00	0	—
11	N	30	1	0.01	33.00	0	—
12	N	30	1	0.01	33.00	0	—
13	TD	31	12	0.10	34.10	0	—
14	TD	32	12	0.20	35.20	0	—
15	D	35	12	1.00	38.50	4	3, 4, 5, 6
16	D	37	12	2.00	40.70	1	7
17	D	39	12	2.50	42.90	1	8
18	D	42	12	2.00	46.20	1	9
19	D	45	12	1.50	49.50	1	10
20	D	43	12	0.90	47.30	1	11
21	D	42	12	0.50	46.20	1	12
22	D	41	12	0.10	45.10	12	13
23	D	40	6	0.01	44.00	12	14
24	D	40	2	0.01	44.00	12	15
25	D	40	1	0.01	44.00	0	—
26	D	40	1	0.01	44.00	0	—

Note: N = normal; TD = threat of disruption; D = disruption. The average drawdown rate during weeks 15–24 is 657,000 bbl/day. At week 25 the President can continue the drawdown by ordering direct auction of SPR oil.

SOURCE: G. Horwich and D. Weimer, Oil Price Shocks, Market Response, and Contingency Planning (Washington: American Enterprise Institute, 1984), p. 130.

fore, so those options are not exercised, ending the options system drawdown, which had continued into weeks 23 and 24. For the first ten weeks of the disruption, an average drawdown of 657,000 barrels per day has taken place. The President could order direct auctions of SPR oil to continue the drawdown in week 25 or to supplement the drawdown at any earlier time.

The option system has several advantages. First, it substitutes the aggregate of private sector expectations for those of the government as to future market conditions. A second advantage is that it would allow the private sector to anticipate SPR drawdowns and automatically ameliorate sharp upward swings in crude prices. But probably the major advantage of the options idea is that the oil is sold to the highest bidder, assuring that it would be used in its highest socially valued uses.

IMPORT CONTROLS VERSUS TARIFFS

Recall that formulating an optimal national security policy means minimizing the sum of emergency supply costs plus remaining damage costs. This means following the cost-minimizing set of emergency supply and conservation policies to minimize the area OAX in Figure 6.4. The result of this calculation yields P^*, the security premium per barrel of oil.

Does the determination of the security premium have any implications for the pricing of oil?[10] The price axis in Figure 6.4 shows the opportunity cost of another barrel of nonsecure oil versus one less barrel of secure oil. In Figure 6.6 we add this security premium t_0 to the supply schedule from nonsecure sources ($S_{ns} + t_0$), thereby reflecting the true social cost of this oil. At the price $P_{ns} + t_0$, the production from the secure areas equals S and that from nonsecure areas is NS. In principle, this outcome could be achieved by simply imposing a tariff on oil originating from countries likely to participate in an embargo. Imports from secure areas plus domestic production would not be taxed. In practice, the major difficulty in implementing this approach is that the General Agreement on Tariffs and Trade prohibits discriminatory tariffs among GATT members, which include both major oil consumers and producers.[11] As an alternative to a discriminatory tariff, import quotas equal to NS might be assigned to restrict imports from nonsecure countries.

For national security purposes, does it really matter whether we use tariffs or import controls? If import controls are set at NS, the market price of oil is $P_{ns} + t_0$ and domestic supply is S. Similarly, with a tariff of t_0 the market price is $P_{ns} + t_0$, domestic production is S, and imported oil is NS. Even if OPEC changed its price, one might argue that authorities could again solve Figures 6.4 and 6.6 for a new optimal

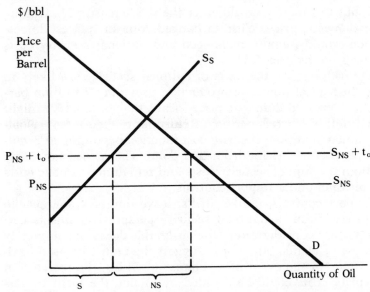

FIGURE 6.6 Determination of the optimal consumption of nonsecure oil: S_s, secure source; S_{ns}, nonsecure source; P_{ns}, nonsecure price; $P_{ns} + t_0$, secure price.

tariff. Corresponding to the new optimal tariff is an optimal level of imports. Thus even with changing prices, it might be argued that the two are equivalent.

But what if one assumes that the government is slow to recalculate the optimal tariff or import control level following an OPEC price change? Suppose instead that the tariff is left at t_0 or import controls are left at NS. In this situation, tariffs and import controls have quite different implications.

Consider the impact of a complete collapse of OPEC, with world prices falling back into the $2 to $3 per barrel range. Looking at Figure 6.6, the reader could pencil in a new price inclusive of tariff that is far below the price $P_{ns} + t_0$. Under a tariff system, domestic prices would fall to the new OPEC price plus the tariff. Domestic production at the low price level would shrink to a very low level and imports would capture the bulk of the market.

In contrast, under an import control system allowing imports of NS with the rights to import being auctioned off by the federal government, the domestic market price would remain at $P_{ns} + t_0$ because, under import controls, domestic supply conditions determine prices irrespective of OPEC actions. Even though the OPEC price fell, there would be no impact on domestic prices. The prices importers were willing to pay would suddenly rise from t_0 to $P_{ns} + t_0$ less the new

OPEC price, but this money would enter the U.S. Treasury, having no effect on the domestic price. With unchanged domestic prices, domestic production would remain unchanged and national security costs would still be given by area OAX.

Under the tariff system, the costs of national security are likely to rise sharply. Instead of domestic production providing 7 million barrels daily, the depressed domestic price means that production might fall back to 3 million barrels per day. Returning to Figure 6.4, visualize drawing a new marginal security cost function beginning at 3 million barrels per day and rising from that point. The reader can easily verify that both the sum of security costs and remaining damage costs are far greater than under import controls.

In sum, import controls, unlike tariffs, leave domestic markets to determine prices. From a national security perspective, this is certainly an important consideration. Obviously, this does not completely rule out the use of tariffs, but it does suggest they must be used flexibly. For example, in the event of a collapse of OPEC, the increase in national security costs could be avoided by raising the tariff to partially offset the price decrease. Given past experience with bureaucratic lags, such actions cannot be taken for granted. On the other hand, there are welfare considerations other than national security that favor tariffs. Let us consider the effect of tariffs versus import controls on the OPEC cartel.

An alternative diagrammatical exposition may serve to illuminate the contrast between tariffs and quotas as leverage devices to affect the price charged by the OPEC cartel. Figure 6.7 shows the comparative effects of tariffs and quotas on oil import demand from OPEC's point of view. Figure 6.7a shows supply and demand for oil in the importing country, with D representing importer demand and S_d domestic supply. It can be seen that if imports were completely prohibited, the equilibrium domestic price would be P_c, with domestic output supplying total domestic demand at the quantity Q_c. But if the world price is P_w and if imports are uncontrolled, total consumption is Q_w, with Q_a produced domestically, and an amount equal to $Q_w - Q_a$ is imported. This amount is shown as Q_m in Figure 6.7b.

Let us assume that, in order to limit imports, a tariff in the amount of t_0 per barrel is imposed, raising the price of imports to $P_w + t_0$. At this price level, total consumption is Q_r while total domestic production is Q_b, with an amount equal to $Q_r - Q_b$ being imported. This volume of imports is shown as Q_e in Figure 6.7b. It thus appears that the imposition of the tariff has reduced total oil demand at the world price P_w from Q_w down to Q_r. This effect can be generalized by simply observing that the impact of a specific tax of a fixed number of dollars per unit on the demand curve for any commodity is determined merely by reducing its demand schedule by the amount of the tax per unit at every price level charged. Thus, domestic demand for oil after

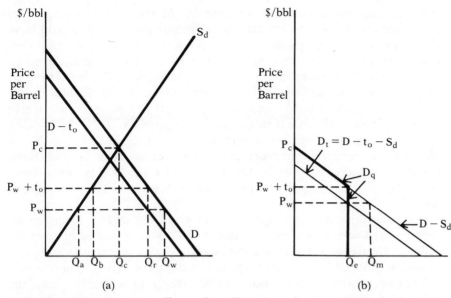

FIGURE 6.7 Comparative effects of tariffs and quotas on oil import demand. (a) Supply and demand for oil in the importing country with oil demand shown before and after the imposition of a tariff on oil imports. (b) Import demand for oil in the importing country, where $D - S_d$ is import demand without quotas or tariffs, D_t is import demand with a tariff, and D_q is import demand with a quota.

the imposition of the tariff (which of course is just a per-unit import tax) falls from D to $D - t_0$.

Figure 6.7b shows the import demand for oil in this particular importing country as seen by the OPEC cartel. In the absence of a tariff, import demand would be determined by merely subtracting total domestic supply S_d from domestic demand D, as shown by the schedule labeled $D - S_d$. Since $D = S_d$ at P_c, import demand is zero at the price P_c, but increases steadily as price falls below P_c and domestic production falls while demand increases. (Some students will recognize $D - S_d$ as constituting the excess demand schedule for oil.) The imposition of a tariff of t_0 dollars per barrel then reduces import demand for oil to the schedule D_t shown in Figure 6.7b. This schedule is derived by subtracting domestic supply from domestic demand minus the tariff, as shown in Figure 6.7a. Therefore, D_t is simply $D - t_0 - S_d$, and represents the net excess demand for oil imports after the imposition of the tariff.

Returning now to Figure 6.7a, we see that total imports under the tariff amount to $Q_r - Q_b$, or the amount Q_e shown in Figure 6.7b. This reduction in imports could have been obtained either by imposing the tariff t_0 per barrel of oil imported or by imposing an absolute quota limit on imports of the same amount Q_e. At the current world price P_w, either a tariff of t_0 per barrel or an import quota of Q_e would have the same effect on prices, imports, domestic production, and consumption. But the demand curve for imports under the quota limit Q_e is shown by the two-segment schedule D_q in Figure 6.7b. We derive D_q by the following reasoning: Imports cannot exceed Q_e in any event; therefore, imports would be equal to Q_e at all prices below the world price plus the tariff. But if prices were to rise above $P_w + t_0$, imports would be reduced, since the import demand schedule $D - S_d$ calls for less than Q_e imports at prices that high. Hence we have very different import demand schedules for OPEC oil under the two systems, since $D_q = D_t$ only at the point where world price remains at its current level P_w.

It can be seen that the quota system gives the OPEC cartel the incentive to raise prices at least to the level $P_w + t_0$, since demand is the same at P_w and at $P_w + t_0$. If OPEC were to raise prices still higher, it would be limited by the elasticity of the demand curve D_q above that price, since $D_q = D - S_D$ above a price of $P_w + t_0$. In any event, the imposition of the import quota Q_e should by itself motivate OPEC to raise the price to the importer by the amount of the tariff t_0. The difference here is that OPEC could get the tariff revenue rather than the importing country.

But if the importer first imposes the tariff t_0, then the demand for OPEC oil is reduced to the schedule D_t in Figure 6.7b. OPEC's profit-maximizing oil price will be lower with a tariff than with a quota because of the downward shift on the entire import demand schedule that results from the imposition of the tariff.

The Magnitude of the Optimal Tariff

If a tariff is preferred because of the effects on OPEC, exactly what should be its magnitude? As the previous section shows, it depends on the OPEC price. The lower the world oil price, the higher the appropriate tariff and vice versa. At current price levels, most studies place the optimal tariff in a range from $2 to $10 per barrel. Professors Horwich and Weimer favor a tariff of $2 per barrel as sufficient to internalize the marginal social cost of the strategic petroleum reserve. Others advocate higher tariffs on the grounds that it would drive down world oil prices and offer an effective vehicle for consuming countries to recapture part of the producer surplus gained by OPEC in the 1970s.

QUESTIONS **1.** Explain why, in minimizing the total costs of providing security, we should use expected damage costs rather than the actual damage costs occurring during a supply disruption.

2. Draw a graph similar to Figure 6.7 assuming a new OPEC price of $5 per barrel, and solve for imports and domestic production under a tariff. Then redraw Figure 6.6, showing the increase in security costs.

3. Suppose that OPEC raised the price instead of lowering it. Assume that the tariff is $2 per barrel and OPEC raises the price by $2. How much will prices go up under a tariff and under an import control system where the rights to NS imports are auctioned? Show that in this situation, a tariff will actually reduce national security costs compared to import controls.

4. If OPEC collapsed, would this signal the end to any possibilities of supply disruptions?

5. For the two importer, one exporter case, draw graphs similar to Figure 6.5 for countries W and M and show how an implicit premium of $40 per barrel would be established under free trade.

6. Besides Horwich's and Weimer's option method for drawing down the SPR, what other mechanisms might you design? Evaluate the strengths and weaknesses of each.

7. In what sense do high world prices reduce security costs?

Notes

1. Douglas Bohi and Milton Russell, *Limiting Oil Imports—An Economic History and Analysis* (Baltimore: Johns Hopkins Press, 1978), pp. 277, 281.

2. Ibid., pp. 285–91.

3. For example, D. Couts, Y. Mansoor, E. Novicky, and T. Schneider, "Economic Analysis of Petroleum Supply Interruption Contingency Actions," D.O.E. Contract CR–1360885 (Washington DC, September 1978). Also see R. G. Hubbard and R. C. Fry, Jr., The Macroeconomic Impacts of Oil Supply Disruptions," Discussion Paper Series E-81-07, Energy and Environmental Policy Center, John F. Kennedy School of Government, Harvard University, June 1982.

4. See Richard J. Gilbert and Knut A. Mork, "Coping with Oil Supply Disruptions," in J. Plummer, editor, *Energy Vulnerability* (Cambridge, MA: Ballinger, 1982), pp. 169–178.

5. See William W. Hogan, "Import Management and Oil Emergencies," in David A. Deese and Joseph S. Nye, editors, *Energy and Security* (Cambridge, MA: Ballinger, 1981), p. 261–301. Also see William W. Hogan, "Policies for Oil Importers," in J. M. Griffin and David J. Teece, editors, *OPEC Behavior and World Oil Prices* (London: Allen and Unwin, 1982), pp. 186–203.

6. Walter Mead and R. Sorenson, "The Economic Value of Standby Crude Oil Production Capacity," *American Economic Review*, May 1979.

7. Thomas J. Teisberg, "A Dynamic Programming Model of the U.S. Strategic Petroleum Reserves," *Bell Journal*, Autumn 1981, pp. 526–546.

8. George Horwich and David Weimer, *Oil Price Shocks, Market Response, and Contingency Planning* (Washington DC: American Enterprise Institute, 1984).

9. See Horwich and Weimer, op. cit., pp. 128–130.

10. See Douglas R. Bohi and W. David Montgomery, *Oil Prices, Energy Security and Import Policy* (Washington DC: Resources for the Future, 1982).

11. This problem can be avoided by having differential treatment among particular countries handled under national security clauses, as was the case with the mandatory oil import control program. Signatories to the General Agreement on Tariffs and Trade recognize such clauses as constituting a legitimate source of authority for decreeing differential trade treatment in instances where security is the point at issue.

CONSERVATION 7

INTRODUCTION

On the face of it, energy conservation is a very simple, noncontroversial concept. Furthermore, unlike increased energy production, which for environmental reasons may be unpopular, energy conservation would appear to be a completely benign policy. A class poll will quickly demonstrate the acceptability of energy conservation, since by inference anyone opposed to conservation must be in favor of waste. But is it really such a simple matter of favoring conservation over waste?

Let us begin by setting forth three definitions of energy conservation, which we will label the layman's definition, the engineering definition, and the economic definition:

(1) The Layman's Definition. Energy conservation is the amount by which energy consumption is reduced from the level that would have occurred otherwise. For example, conservation would be the energy saved from switching off a light or buying a more fuel-efficient car.

(2) The Engineering Definition. Engineers tend to establish a technical benchmark as a standard against which to measure how well energy is being conserved. For example, if it is technically feasible to produce air conditioners with an energy efficiency rating (EER) of 12, energy conservation would be measured in terms of how close the EER rating of air conditioners actually produced approached the feasible technical limit of 12.

(3) The Economic Definition. Like engineers, economists prefer a well-defined benchmark against which to measure conservation. To the economist, conservation occurs at the consumption level where the marginal social benefit equals the marginal social cost of energy. By this definition, the actual level of energy consumption can be too large or too small depending on marginal social costs and benefits. Thus, in

contrast to the layman's, and engineer's definitions, conservation to the economist could actually involve consuming more energy, not less.

If there is a common thread running through all three definitions of energy conservation, it is that all three measures compare existing energy consumption against some benchmark. To the layman, the benchmark is the energy consumption level that would otherwise have occurred. To the engineer, the benchmark is the most technically advanced equipment with the highest EER rating. To the economist, the benchmark is the consumption level at which marginal social benefits and costs are equated. Any of the three definitions would be quite acceptable except for the fact that instinctively we think of conservation as the opposite of waste and, therefore, inherently desirable. For the time being, let us just adopt the layman's definition of conservation to gain some idea of the potential for reducing energy consumption.

THE MATHEMATICS OF ENERGY CONSERVATION

For the period from 1965 to 1973, worldwide consumption of primary energy grew along a 5 percent per year trend line. Consequently, many forecasters preparing their forecasts in 1973 applied that same 5 percent trend line for the period 1973 to 1983. Ten years later they found to their surprise that the annual energy growth rate over this period dropped to 1.6 percent. Figure 7.1 shows that over the period from 1965 to 1973, energy consumption grew from 79.2 million barrels per day of oil equivalent energy (MMB/DOE) to 118.7 MMB/DOE in 1973 and then for the next 10 years (labelled − 10 to 0) grew only to 139.1 MMB/DOE. Now imagine yourself the perplexed energy forecaster required in 1984 to look ahead not 10 years, but 50 years. Does it really matter whether you adopt a 5 percent annual growth rate or a 1.6 percent annual growth rate? Figure 7.1 forcefully illustrates the concept of compound growth. At 5 percent per year, energy consumption doubles every 14 years, quadruples in 28 years and so on. But at 1.6 percent per year, energy consumption doubles only every 44 years and quadruples every 88 years. At a 5 percent per year growth, world energy consumption reaches almost 1,700 MMB/DOE in 50 years, but at the 1.6 percent growth rate, consumption in 50 years reaches about 310 MMB/DOE—a level one fifth as much as the 5 percent path.[1]

Clearly, if the long term growth rate can be lowered from 5 percent to 1.6 percent annually, the potential for energy savings is phenomenal. The shaded area showing potential energy savings in Figure 7.1 amounts to 7.5 trillion barrels of oil equivalent energy—a sum almost twice the 3.9 trillion barrels of oil equivalent energy actually consumed over this period if consumption is held to the 1.6 percent

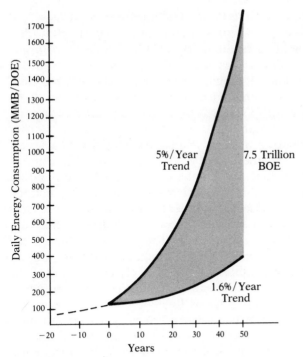

FIGURE 7.1 World energy consumption at various growth rates.

growth path. In effect, for every barrel actually consumed along the 1.6 percent growth path, two barrels were saved.[2]

EVIDENCE ON THE POTENTIAL FOR CONSERVATION

The above mathematical example is quite impressive in demonstrating that *in principle* energy conservation could vastly stretch the world's energy supplies. But the previous example may be a bit deceiving in that it assumes that the trend growth rate can realistically be lowered from 5 percent annually to 1.6 percent annually. Even though an annual growth rate of 1.6 percent was recorded for the 10 year period from 1973 to 1983, it may not be sustainable over 50, 100, or 1000 years, especially when one considers that this period was described as an "energy crisis." This section addresses the question: "Can the long-run trend growth in energy be materially reduced and at the same time allow for a growing full employment economy?"

In the early 1970s, this question was largely unanswered. Many felt that energy and economic activity were tied together by a fixed energy–GNP ratio. To these researchers, the elephant/rabbit stew discussed in Chapter 1 would taste distinctly rabbit. A variety of arguments were offered to support this view. The popular input-output analysis predicated on a Leontief technology would claim a zero elasticity of substitution, as shown in isoquant I_1 in Figure 1.1a. This meant that to produce a dollar's worth of output all material inputs, including energy, must be combined in fixed proportions. Consequently, a 1 percent reduction in energy input translated into a 1 percent reduction in output. Furthermore, work at Resources for the Future by Schurr and others focussed on the energy–GNP ratio.[3] While Schurr and his colleagues demonstrated this ratio appeared to change modestly over time in response to technical changes and structural shifts in the macroeconomy, the implicit presumption was that the energy–GNP ratio was not particularly substitutable against other inputs. Thus increases in the price of energy relative to other inputs would not induce any appreciable substitution of labor, capital, or materials for energy. Finally, when one compares per capita energy consumption in 1973 across countries as in Figure 7.2, we see that a strong positive correlation between per capita energy consumption and the standard of living, measured by per capita real gross domestic product (GDP). (GDP differs from GNP only in that the former excludes net factor payments from abroad.) While correlations do not prove causation, Figure 7.2 suggests that energy consumption and the standard of living are closely and perhaps inextricably intertwined. Therefore, it may not be possible to achieve the U.S. standard of living with the per capita energy consumption of Greece, Turkey, or Spain. Many felt that a permanent lowering of the energy consumption growth rate would only result in a similar lowering of the growth in GNP—an unacceptable price to pay when minimal levels of food, housing, medical attention, and consumer goods are yet to be attained by most of the world's inhabitants. If correct, the implications of such a view are ominous. Energy conservation could not be expected to occur as a natural result of increasing scarcity, reflected in rising prices. Rather, any reduction in energy consumption, to the degree it is achievable at all, must come from mandated changes in energy consuming behavior and an alteration of the mix of products produced to favor a less energy-intensive mix.

Even though the above arguments might seem conclusive, there are some disquieting reasons why we might expect the energy–GNP ratio to respond to economic stimuli. First, our training from principles of economics offers the warning that "needs" are on closer inspection only "wants." In turn, if energy is only a want rather than a necessity, it must respond to the same price mechanism that helps us order our purchases of other goods and services. A price increase in energy, taking everything else as given, will lead to a decrease in its consumption.

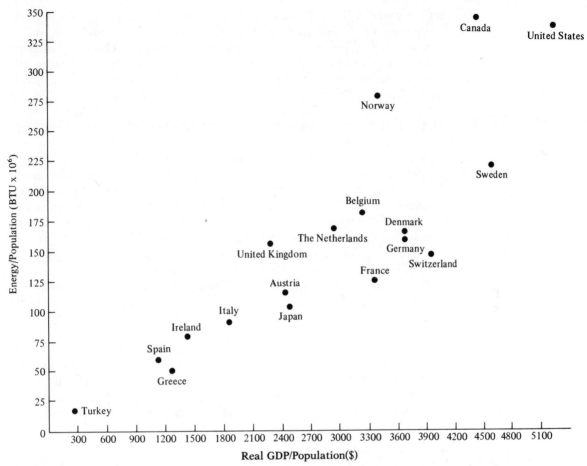

FIGURE 7.2 The relationship between per capita GDP and per capita energy consumption (based on 1973 data).

In effect, the law of demand should apply to energy just as it does to all other goods.

A second troublesome observation is that if the energy–GDP ratio is fixed by technical factors, why does it vary so markedly across countries? Table 7.1 reports the energy–GDP ratio for eight major industrialized countries. In 1982, the energy–GDP ratio varied from a low of 28,400 Btu per dollar of GDP in Japan to 70,900 Btu per dollar in Canada. Now, a variety of factors could explain the differences in energy–GDP ratio other than the price of energy relative to other inputs such as labor, capital, or raw materials. First, in order to calculate GDP in a common currency, exchange rates must typically be used, but exchange rates are not representative of the prices of nontraded goods. Hence, energy–GDP ratios can vary simply due to differences between the exchange rates and the true purchasing power of a country's currency. Second, sectoral differences, reflecting the differing relative sizes of the industrial, agricultural, commercial, and residential sectors, are quite pronounced between countries. Those economies with a large fraction of industrial products are likely to be more energy-intensive per dollar of GDP than a more service-oriented economy. Third, a Btu of one fuel may have the same calorific value for heating water as a Btu of another fuel, but energy is used for much more than heating water. In effect, the thermal efficiency of converting energy to useful work varies considerably depending on the energy-consuming equipment and its specific fuel requirements. For example, it takes 5 Btu of coal to power a steam locomotive whereas 1 Btu of diesel fuel in a diesel locomotive accomplishes the same work.

Another intriguing explanation for at least part of the differences in energy–GDP ratios in Table 7.1 is price. Is it merely an accident that Canada, the economy with the highest energy–GDP ratio, also tended to have relatively cheap energy? Conversely, Japan has the lowest energy–GDP ratio and appears to have high-priced energy.

The Arab Oil Embargo of 1973 and the subsequent oil price increases raised all energy prices, providing a grand but costly experiment. Would the energy–GDP ratios fall owing to price-induced substitution responses, or would they remain fixed in the absence of mandatory restrictions on energy use? Figure 7.3 shows the result of the experiment for the period 1973 to 1983 for the same eight key industrialized economies. Note that all eight economies significantly reduced their energy–GDP ratio. The U.S. recorded the largest absolute drop in energy–GDP, falling from 64,600 Btu per dollar of GDP in 1973

TABLE 7.1 Energy–GDP Ratios in 1982 and Selected Fuel Prices[a]

	1982 Primary Energy/GDP (10^3 Btu/$)	Selected Fuel Prices ($/$10^4$ Btu)			
		Gasoline	Heating Oil	Electricity[b]	Natural Gas
Norway	67.4	19.50	9.52	10.07	—[c]
Canada	70.9	10.14	6.15	9.03	.034
United Kingdom	59.1	16.76	8.56	22.51	.053
United States	48.9	10.40	8.62	20.11	.049
Germany	38.1	17.43	9.16	27.18	.089
Italy	40.0	22.32	9.57	19.97	.084
Sweden	36.1	16.16	8.12	10.65	—[c]
Japan	28.4	21.87	12.42	36.71	.161

[a]Using 1984 exchange rates.
[b]Residential electricity rates.
[c]No consumption.

SOURCE: OECD, *Energy Statistics* and International Energy Agency, *Energy Prices and Taxes*.

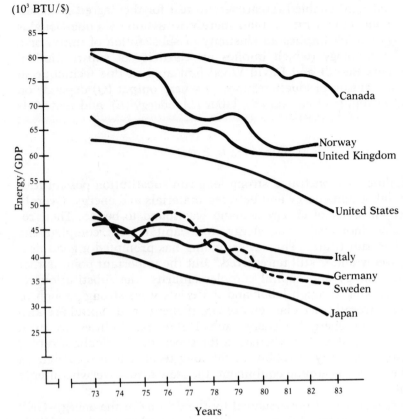

(10³ BTU/$)

Energy/GDP

Canada
Norway
United Kingdom
United States
Italy
Germany
Sweden
Japan

73 74 75 76 77 78 79 80 81 82 83

Years

FIGURE 7.3 Energy–GDP trends over time for eight major energy consuming countries.

SOURCE: See text.

to 48,900 Btu per dollar of GDP in 1983. These results provide compelling evidence that price-induced substitution effects are capable of significantly reducing a country's energy–GDP ratio and play a large role in explaining the differences in energy–GDP ratios between countries. Thus, as the U.S. and Canada face rising energy costs they will adapt their energy using habits to be like those of other countries such as Japan, where energy has long been used quite sparingly. In turn, even Japan has found additional energy substitution possibilities and recorded a 31.6 percent reduction in its energy–GDP ratio over the decade.

While policy makers may have been surprised by the sharp reduction in the energy–GDP ratios, economists were not. Advances in econometrics by the mid-1970s had demonstrated that strong long-run substitution possibilities existed between energy and other inputs. The development of the translog production function by Christensen, Jorgenson, and Lau[4] enabled researchers to test for the degree of substitution among inputs rather than merely to assume a Cobb-Douglas technology (which implies an elasticity of substitution of unity) or a Leontief technology (which implies an elasticity of substitution of zero). Ernest Berndt and David Wood first applied this technique in 1975 to a translog production function where output (Q) depends on the level of inputs of capital (K), labor (L), energy (E), and materials (M):[5]

$$(7.1) \qquad Q = f(K, L, E, M)$$

Their findings demonstrated strong long-run substitution possibilities between labor and energy and between materials and energy. Overall, the price elasticity of energy demand was found to be .45. Their research also indicated that energy and capital were complements rather than substitutes. This latter finding has prompted a good deal of controversy and is still unresolved.[6] But the important point is that even with energy and capital complementarity, the substitution responses working through labor and materials were strong enough to provide an overall price elasticity of .45. If energy and capital are also substitutes, the energy/nonenergy substitution possibilities are even greater. This implies that whereas in the short run the elephant/rabbit stew tasted distinctly of rabbit, in the long term with a reconfigured stock of energy-consuming equipment, the stew tastes overwhelmingly elephant.

If the reader is still unpersuaded by the decline in the energy–GNP ratio and the findings of Berndt and Wood and others, perhaps a little introspection into the decision to insulate one's home would be convincing. As the anecdote "What Goes Into a Conservation-Investment Decision" indicates, there is a tradeoff between buying energy and buying insulation. Figure 7.4 shows the menu of energy-saving investments possible and their corresponding dollar savings in home heating costs. Clearly, it pays to do the cheapest things first—turn down the thermostat, then insulate the ceiling, then the walls, and so forth. The point is that at 1976 prices, it may have paid to stop with insulating the ceiling, but at 1981 fuel prices, it becomes economic to take additional steps such as insulating walls and perhaps installing storm windows.

EVIDENCE ON THE POTENTIAL FOR INTERFUEL COMPETITION

If the long-run possibilities for substitution of nonenergy inputs for energy are appreciable, what are the possibilities for the substitution of one fuel for another? In the short run, the choice of fuel is dictated

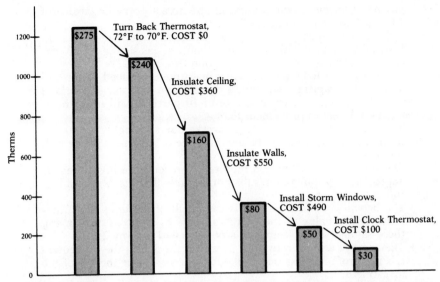

FIGURE 7.4 Annual space heating costs of a representative San Francisco Bay Area family versus energy saving investment costs. (Source: Lee Schipper and Jack Darmstadter, "The Logic of Energy Conservation," in *Technology Review*, January, 1978, p. 42.) Costs are typical figures for the mid-1970s.

almost entirely by the configuration of the energy-consuming equipment. It is as impossible to burn diesel fuel in a gasoline engine as it is to use coal in the breakfast toaster, although burned toast can taste like coal. But over the longer time as fuel-consuming equipment can be modified, the interfuel substitution possibilities can in some cases become much greater.

To some, the question of long-run interfuel substitution is obvious—the long-run elasticity of substitution among fuels is infinite. In effect, the presumption is that energy is fungible. A Btu is a Btu is a Btu. But if this is true, why is it that we observe a wide variety of fuels being consumed even though electricity costs three times more than heating oil? If all fuels are perfect substitutes, we should expect to observe only the lowest cost fuel being consumed.

What Goes Into a Conservation-Investment Decision?

Some conservation decisions—say, repairing a dripping hot-water faucet—require little deliberation. Others require a lot. Suppose a household wanted to reduce heating costs and determined that:
• The house consumes, on the average, 125 million Btu of natural

gas per heating season which, at the area's prevailing price of $4.50 per million Btu, costs $562.50.

- A $400 investment in improved insulation (assumed to last at least fifteen years) will yield annual natural gas savings of 20 percent—which translates into 25 million Btu or $112.50.

This turns out to be a worthwhile investment. (Indeed, if one had access to the capital, one should consider an even larger outlay.) For with an assumed interest rate of 10 percent paid on a three-year, $400 home-improvement loan—

- The unit cost of saving energy works out to roughly $2.10 per million Btu, significantly below the price of gas at $4.50 per million Btu.

- The simple payback period required to recoup the investment is approximately four years, substantially less than its expected lifetime.

- The benefit-cost ratio, which is the result of dividing the cumulative dollar value of the energy savings by the cost of bringing those savings about, comes to a positive and healthy 2 to 1.

- The average annual return on investing the $400—the homeowner's net profit—works out to about 14 percent over the life of the investment.

An investment producing these benefits and recouped in four years is very respectable. True, there are people who—in economic jargon—"discount the future" heavily, placing much greater value on having money now rather than later. They are frequently impatient with the prospect of even that attractive a payback.

Still other factors figure in the conservation decision. Those who expect future energy prices to rise will, if they turn out to be right, benefit from still greater savings. Depending on one's tax bracket, availability of certain federal or state conservation tax credits and the fact that energy savings obviously cannot be taxed (being a reduction in money that would have had to be spent rather than income received) are further pluses. (Hence the 14 percent return on investment is likely to be understated.)

But some aspects of the decision can be problematical. Will the house, if put on the market, command a price reflecting the value of the conservation investment? What about the quality of the insulation or even possible health effects—for example, indoor air pollution from "overtight" insulation?

Big conservation investments—for example, solar hot-water systems—demand still more careful analysis. Consumers are now able to obtain professional advice and information on these matters, but the whole conservation field has not entirely emerged from its shakedown stage.

SOURCE: J. Darmstadter, H.H. Landsberg, H.C. Morton, M.J. Coda, Energy Today and Tomorrow *(Englewood Cliffs, N.J.: Prentice-Hall, 1983), p. 42.*

Figure 7.5 shows the fuel mix in final consumption for eight OECD countries in 1983. The wide differences in mix indicate the considerable flexibility that exists in fuel choice. Obviously if all fuels were perfect substitutes, relative fuel prices would completely dictate fuel choice. It is true that relative fuel prices are the primary determinants of the mix of fuels, but they are not the sole determinants. Per capita

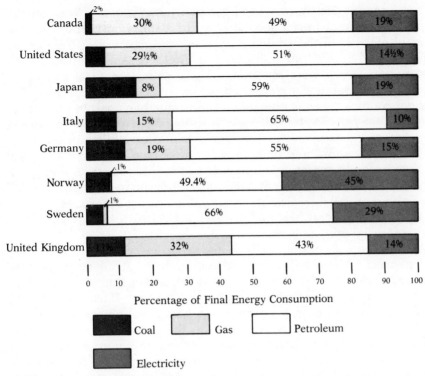

FIGURE 7.5 Intercountry differences in the mix of fuels delivered to final demand in 1983.

income plays a role because of the superior convenience and cleanliness of some fuels. As income rises, there is a transition to these "luxury" fuels. Also, some differences in the fuel mix between countries can be attributed to differing output mixes which require specific fuels. In addition, climate and cultural and institutional differences play lesser roles. These factors can be seen by a brief discussion of the fuel shares in Figure 7.5.

Coal, the dominant fuel throughout the nineteenth century, suffered a marked decline in use during the twentieth century, particularly after the Second World War. As a final energy form for use in industry, transportation, residential, and commercial purposes, it is now of minor importance. Even in traditional coal mining areas such as the United Kingdom and West Germany, coal has only about 11 percent of the market. For the other countries without appreciable indigenous coal production such as Canada, Norway, and Sweden, the percentages range from 2 to 6 percent.

In 1925, when coal provided 96 percent of all primary energy in Western Europe[8] and 74 percent of primary energy in the United States, few scholars would have predicted the importance today of natural gas. At the time, natural gas was nonexistent in Western Europe, with manufactured gas relegated to a small portion of the residential market. In the United States, natural gas was utilized by industries and residential users only in areas of Appalachia and the Southwest, which were fortuitously located near natural gas fields. These data stand in sharp contrast to the situation today. In most European countries, gas is now more important than coal. In the United States, Canada, and the U.K., gas is a major energy form because of significant domestic production. The extreme variability in the share of gas (both natural and manufactured gas), from less than 1 percent in Sweden and Norway to 32 percent in the U.K., suggests that gas is a highly substitutable energy form depending primarily on price and the volumes available. Gas is substitutable against other energy forms as a source of process heat and is also a very clean and convenient fuel for residential and commercial use.

Although not as dramatically as the growth of gas, the share of liquid petroleum fuels has expended markedly in all of the developed economies over the 50 years prior to the Arab Oil Embargo. As a percentage of primary fuels input in Western Europe, Darmstadter et al. report that liquid petroleum fuels grew from 3.2 percent in 1925 to 54.3 percent in 1968. In North America, the growth has been less impressive but still significant, expanding from 18.9 percent in 1925 to 43.6 percent in 1968. In Japan, the share of oil expanded from 4.4 percent in 1925 to 67.1 percent in 1968.[9]

Figure 7.5 reveals that crude oil and its derivatives are still the dominant fuels in virtually all of the OECD countries despite the price increases of the 1970s. The oil percentage is the lowest in the U.K. (43%) and Canada (49%), where natural gas is relatively cheap, but even in these cases it constitutes a major piece of final energy consumption. A partial explanation for the large share of oil products is that gasoline and diesel fuel are used extensively in the transportion sector where interfuel competition is not important. In the United States, gasoline accounts for almost half the liquid share. On the other hand, gasoline provides only about 10 percent of final energy consumption in most European countries. Even allowing for diesel fuels consumed by railroads and trucks, it is clear that a significant portion of oil products are used for process heat. As a source of process heat in the industrial sector, heavy fuel oil competes with coal and gas.

As a share of final energy demand, electricity is roughly equivalent to coal. Figure 7.5 reveals that the share of electricity in final energy consumption ranges between 14 and 19 percent with the exception of Sweden and Norway (29 and 45 percent), where abundant hydroelectric power makes electricity extremely cheap (see Table 7.1). Again it is no coincidence that in countries such as Sweden and Norway, where electricity is cheap relative to other fuels, electricity is used extensively for home heating and even rail transportation.

TABLE 7.2 Comparison of Percentage Petroleum Useage to Total Primary Energy Input in 1973 and 1983

	1973 Percentage Share	1983 Percentage Share	Change in Percentage Share
Denmark	90.9	67.8	− 23.1
Japan	78.2	63.7	− 14.5
Italy	74.8	65.5	− 9.3
Ireland	74.3	52.7	− 21.6
France	69.2	51.7	− 17.5
Turkey	68.9	59.0	− 9.9
Spain	68.2	63.2	− 5.0
Sweden	63.0	51.0	− 12.0
Switzerland	62.3	47.7	− 14.6
Belgium	62.2	49.4	− 12.8
W. Germany	57.7	46.2	− 11.5
U.K.	50.9	39.4	− 11.5
U.S.	46.3	42.9	− 3.4
Canada	45.7	33.8	− 11.9
Netherlands	32.0	45.6	− 13.6
Norway	36.0	23.0	− 8.0

SOURCE: *BP Statistical Review of World Energy, June 1984.*

To gain some idea of the potential magnitude of interfuel substitution, we contrast the share of petroleum as a percentage of total primary energy on the eve of the Arab Oil Embargo and 10 years later. (Note that primary energy input is not equivalent to final energy consumption.) Table 7.2 shows that for 16 developed countries the share of petroleum has been reduced appreciably. For example, Denmark reduced its petroleum share from 90.9 percent to 67.8 percent over the decade. The U.S. recorded the smallest percentage reduction, but even the relative drop from 46.3 percent to 42.9 percent is noteworthy.

In sum, while energy is not fungible, the long-run substitution possibilities are appreciable so that the fuel mix depends critically on fuel prices. These results are particularly encouraging since, when interfuel substitution effects are added to the energy/nonenergy substitution effects, the long-run potential for reducing the consumption of petroleum is indeed great.

THOUGHTS ON THE POLICY IMPORTANCE OF DEFINING CONSERVATION

For policy purposes, does it really matter whether we adopt the layman's, the engineer's, or the economist's definition of conservation?

After all, wouldn't a policy that would be desirable by one definition of conservation also be desirable by some other?

By both the layman's and the engineer's definitions, reductions in the energy–GDP ratio are desirable. In fact, reducing the energy input to the technological minimum energy–GDP ratio would seem to be a worthwhile goal.

But economically, is minimizing the energy intensity of output socially desirable? Consider Figure 7.6, depicting the isoquant for the production of some good produced from labor and energy. The curved isoquant shows the various combinations of labor and energy that can be used to produce 100 units of output. The standard economic solution is that society should minimize the cost ($C = P_L L + P_E E$) of producing 100 units by finding the isocost line, $L = (C/P_L) - (P_E/P_L)E$, that lies closest in to the origin. Since the labor intercept is C/P_L with P_L given, the isocost line lying closest to the origin minimizes costs (C). Figure 7.6 depicts the standard economic solution leading to the choice of L^* labor and E^* energy. Furthermore, if we assume that the prices of energy (P_E) and labor (P_L) reflect their marginal social cost, then any deviation from E^* and L^* would lead to a welfare loss.

Now consider the implications of selecting the least energy intensive output mix, given by E^0 energy and L^0 labor. Unfortunately, using less energy implies using more labor, resulting in a greater total cost of purchasing input combination $E^0 L^0$ than at combination $E^* L^*$.

Only if we make the assumption that only energy has value can the factor combination E^0 energy and L^0 labor be socially justified. Is

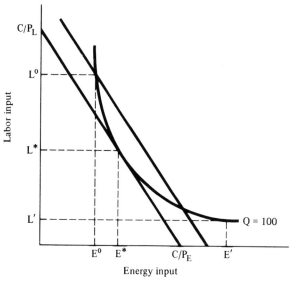

FIGURE 7.6 Society's choice of optimal inputs.

there any evidence to suggest that energy is the only scarce input factor? Clearly, a visit to the supermarket will remind one that many items are scarce. The fact that a good commands a positive price proves that it is scarce.

It is interesting that the assumption necessary to justify minimizing the energy/output ratio (i.e., only energy has value) is entirely analogous to Marx's labor theory of value, except that "Btu" has replaced "labor." Marx argued that the value of a good depended on the amount of labor embodied in its production, since according to Marx, labor is the only scarce factor of production. Because energy embodies only minor labor input in its production, it would command a very low value while labor would have a high price. The labor theory of value would seek to minimize labor input and maximize energy input by choosing factor combination E' energy and L' labor. Thus the proposition that the energy/output ratio should be minimized rests on a new version of the labor theory of value where energy replaces labor as the scarce input factor.

The advantage of the economist's definition of conservation is that it defines the optimal level of energy conservation with respect to an economic benchmark. This benchmark recognizes the scarcity of all inputs and not just energy. E^* is the optimal level of energy consumption because at that level the marginal social benefit of the last unit equals its marginal social cost. For a variety of reasons, observed energy consumption need not equal E^*. Perhaps it is now time to consider causes for these failures. As we shall see, the failures arise as much from governmental actions as from market failures.

QUESTIONS

1. In selecting input combination E^0L^0, what is one assuming about the price of energy relative to labor? Conversely, at $E'L'$, what are the implicit relative prices?

2. In the face of externalities, will the market prices properly reflect marginal social costs? If not, should the energy/output ratio be reduced?

3. List examples of market failures that might justify policies to reduce energy consumption. While price controls on fuel in the United States were not examples of market failures, do they violate the conditions for conservation?

EXAMPLES OF MARKET FAILURES AND GOVERNMENT REGULATORY FAILURES

Do observed market outcomes generally result in the conservationist's ideal—in the pricing of energy such that for the last unit, the marginal social cost equals the marginal social benefit? While the detailed answer to this question goes beyond our purposes here, the following examples should be adequate to show that both government regulatory and market failures often prevent the ideal of conservation from being obtained.

Government Regulatory Failures

Price Controls on Oil and Natural Gas. A distinguishing feature of U.S. and Canadian energy policy of the 1970s was price controls on oil and gas, which resulted in much lower domestic fuel prices than would have occurred in a free market. The subsequent chapter provides a detailed history and analysis of these policies, but for now we simply note their effects on conservation. The effects of price controls are obvious. By setting the market price at a level below the true marginal social benefit of that fuel, domestic oil and gas production was artificially constrained. At the control price, producers were willing to produce only that output where the price equalled the marginal social cost. But at that production rate, the amount demanded exceeded the amount available. In effect, the marginal social benefit of the last unit substantially exceeded the marginal social cost of the last unit, and our conservationist ideal was violated.

Failures in Nonprice Rationing Rules. The failures of price controls were compounded by arbitrary rationing rules, which prevented oil and natural gas from being allocated to their highest valued uses. In markets where prices are free to rise, only those uses with marginal benefits in excess of or equal to the market price are observed. But in a shortage situation with price controls, authorities must make the decision as to who gets what and how much. The shortage of natural gas became increasingly severe in the winter of 1978. Authorities did the obvious things first. Electric power plants that could switch from natural gas to other fuels were ordered to do so. But with the advent of cold weather, the shortage worsened. The decision seemed simple enough—force industrial gas customers to curtail operations, freeing up gas for residential customers. After all, gas customers vote but factories do not. In late December 1978, the factory workers in the huge north Georgia carpet industry received a surprise Christmas gift from the Department of Energy. The D.O.E. curtailed gas sales to the carpet mills, forcing the companies to lay off their workers. The mills were shut down and workers went to homes where they could consume all the natural gas they wanted. There was just one problem—the workers had no paychecks. Had the workers been given the choice of paying higher gas prices and reducing their residential consumption to enable the factories to continue in operation, they would surely have done so. But they were never given the choice. Some fourth or fifth line bureaucrat at the D.O.E. made it for them.

Fuel Tax Policies in Europe. Americans and Canadians visiting Europe are astonished to observe very high prices on gasoline. This seems strange, because petroleum products are traded worldwide and one might expect more-or-less similar prices worldwide. But European governments have historically placed high consumption taxes on gasoline. The intrinsic logic has little to do with equating marginal social costs and benefits. Rather, gasoline taxes are an important source of tax revenues. The taxes are easily collected without appreciable evasion. Furthermore, it is a progressive tax to the degree that upper income individuals tend to drive larger cars and commute over greater distances. In sum, gasoline taxes are a convenient taxing mechanism.

European citizens do pay a price for this taxing system. When taxes are set far above any level justified by externalities or national security considerations, the marginal social benefit of gasoline appreciably exceeds its social cost. Consumers are being forced to restrict consumption below the economically efficient rate of consumption.

Market Failures

Externalities. While not all fuels are subject to appreciable environmental problems, certain fuels pose serious environmental problems. As noted in Chapter 5, policies to internalize these externalities (so that the price of those fuels includes the full marginal social cost) have met with mixed success. In particular, the prices of those fuels giving rise to high sulfur oxide emissions may not internalize their full environmental costs. To the degree the prices of such fuels tend to understate the true marginal social cost, consumption of these fuels occurs at too high a rate.

Consumer Inertia and Ignorance. Perhaps one of the most perplexing market failures rises not because of a false market (price) signal, but rather because of the apparent lack of response to that signal by home owners. In the case of an externality, the price signal set by the market failed to reflect the true marginal social cost of the fuel; here, however, the concern is that consumers somehow fail to respond fully to the price signal sent.

According to Lee Schipper, the typical homeowner has adapted slowly and incompletely to higher fuel prices.[10] His studies show that the American homeowner significantly underinvests in energy-saving devices that could be economically justified. In effect, homeowners could invest in additional energy saving devices that could yield a return of perhaps 15 percent, but instead, they choose not to. This raises the interesting question: "Why?" Is the consumer incapable of computing the costs and benefits? This seems paradoxical since, in the case of automobiles, consumers adjusted rather quickly to rising gasoline prices in the 1970s. Even though federal standards set minimum levels of miles per gallon for new cars, the public demanded a mix of vehicles with even higher miles per gallon. Still another explanation is that most homes are built by contractors and then sold to the public. But if these additional energy-saving devices are worthwhile, why didn't the contractor offer such cost-saving devices to astute home buyers? Perhaps even the astute home buyer is reluctant to demand such construction, since at some time in the future when he sells the house to some nondiscriminating buyer, he will be unable to recoup the money paid for the energy saving devices. It should be apparent that information is a commodity itself and, particularly with respect to some energy-saving devices, it can be quite costly to acquire. The exerpt from "What Goes Into a Conservation-Investment Decision" illustrates the various factors involved.

METHODS OF ACHIEVING ENERGY CONSERVATION

Let us proceed on the assumption that governmental authorities have identified a situation in which conservation is not being achieved. For example, assume that the marginal social cost of energy exceeds the marginal social benefits. Energy consumption must be cut back to the economically optimal level. But what policy instruments are to be used? The subsequent sections illustrate that there are a variety of possible conservation policy instruments, each with quite different efficiency implications. We shall separate these policy instruments into two categories: those relying on price methods and those relying on nonprice methods. Within each group, there are alternative policies with various efficiency attributes.

Nonprice Methods of Conservation

Direct Quantity Rationing. In a planned economy, energy conservation would probably be achieved by explicit quantity rationing of fuels among various users. Planners would simply reduce fuel deliveries to those sectors where the fuel is viewed as a "low-priority" use. If our planners were "democratic," the cutbacks might be proportional across all industries and homes. Even in relatively market-oriented economies, direct quantity rationing of energy is usually considered a viable alternative. Even in noncrisis times, the United States has employed direct quantity rationing to ban all consumption of natural gas in electric utilities beginning in 1985.

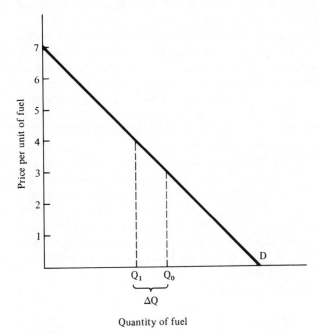

FIGURE 7.7 Alternative conservation methods.

What are the advantages and limitations of direct quantity rationing? Figure 7.7 depicts a standard demand schedule for a given fuel. Quantity Q_0 depicts current consumption and Q_1 depicts the economically efficient consumption level. The difference $Q_0 - Q_1$ shows the desired reduction in consumption. At the quantity Q_0, the prevailing market price is \$3 ($P_0 = 3$). If prices, instead of direct quantity rationing, were used to promote conservation of ΔQ, authorities would simply add a tax sufficient to raise the price from \$3 to \$4. As a consequence of the price rising from \$3 to \$4, those fuel uses which had social benefits in excess of \$4 would continue to be bought, while those fuel uses with social benefits between \$3 and \$4 would drop out, and some other fuel or good would be consumed in its place.

Did the price mechanism assure that the lowest-valued uses of the fuel were curtailed? Obviously this is the case, as the loss in social benefits from conservation of ΔQ is smallest for this area. From the graph, the loss in social benefits from the conservation policy is \$3.50 times ΔQ. Suppose instead that nonprice rationing selected the first ΔQ units lying between \$6 and \$7 rationed; the loss in social benefits would be \$6.50 times ΔQ. Clearly, the price system identifies and excludes the ΔQ units lying at the margin (between \$3 and \$4) and thereby minimizes the loss in social benefits. Now if the goal of conservation is to maximize the welfare gain or minimize the welfare loss, any loss in social benefits must be minimized, which is exactly what the price rationing system does.

But how would a direct quantity rationing scheme work? Can it also minimize the loss in social benefits? The answer is no, unless government planners are omniscient. To assure that only uses with marginal social benefits of less than $4 are rationed, planners must know each firm's and individual's demand schedule. Knowledge of the aggregate market elasticity of demand is not enough, since quantity rationing is performed at the micro level. Not having this information, planners typically try to approximate the market result by labeling certain fuel uses to be rationed as "low-priority," such as the consumption of natural gas by electric utilities. What this approach amounts to is the assumption that the price elasticity of demand facing the "low-priority" users is extremely high while the elasticities for the "high-priority" users are very low. One need only consider the case of a southern California utility subject to sulfur oxide problems from coal and heavy fuel oil coupled with nuclear plant location difficulties to realize that natural gas is not a low-priority fuel.

Despite these efficiency problems, direct quantity rationing remains popular because it avoids the income distribution effects of higher energy prices. Consumers of the remaining quantity Q_1 of fuel avoid paying the additional $1 per unit tax under a quantity rationing scheme. Particularly in the short run when demand is highly price-inelastic, price rationing can involve substantial income transfers. Let us suppose that at the time of the 1973 Arab oil embargo, it had been deemed necessary to cut gasoline consumption by 10 percent. Assuming a very inelastic short-run price elasticity of 0.1, prices would have to double to achieve a reduction in gasoline consumption of 10 percent in the short run. Based on the 1973 average price of 36 cents per gallon, the price would have risen to 72 cents per gallon. If 1973 consumption had been reduced by 10 percent, consumption would have fallen to 92.8 billion gallons. In this example, consumers would be paying $33 billion more than previously. Based on the 1973 labor force, the income transfer per worker would amount to $360 per year. Even though this money would have resulted in increased government tax revenues and could have been used to reduce personal income taxes, consumers were understandably skeptical.

Public Exhortation. Economists, reasoning from the model of the utility-maximizing individual, generally tend to smile when one advocates the use of public exhortation. Without some method to force compliance through either higher prices or direct quantity controls, the standard model of microeconomic theory would predict zero compliance. On the other hand, politicians have viewed public exhortation as a sometimes quite effective policy tool. One need only look back to the Second World War for a variety of examples where public exhortation proved quite effective. Well, then, who is right?

During the 1973 Arab oil embargo, President Nixon together with the press and TV urged the public to voluntarily conserve electricity by turning down the lights. General Electric (GE) undertook a study of this episode[11] to see if these public exhortations had any effects on consumption and, if so, whether their effects were transitory or permanent. The GE study showed that voluntary conservation achieved fairly significant gains during the embargo, reducing the demand for electricity by about 5 percent. Another interesting finding of the GE report is that when the embargo ended, consumption rates quickly returned to normal levels, despite continued but less intensive public exhortation to conserve energy. It appears that public exhortation can achieve significant effects, particularly if the public views the crisis as genuine and of a fairly short-run nature.

As a short-term solution where the crisis aspects are obvious, voluntary conservation has a role to play in achieving at least modest fuel reductions. Since the short-run price elasticity of fuels tends to be quite low, voluntary methods avoid the large income transfers associated with the use of market prices and the unnecessary welfare losses from arbitrary quantity rationing schemes.

Fuel Efficiency Standards. An increasingly popular nonprice method of conserving energy is mandating that energy-consuming equipment have certain efficiency characteristics. For example, in the United States, auto manufacturers were required by law to market a mix of cars averaging 20 miles per gallon in 1980 and 27.5 miles per gallon by 1985. Fitting under a similar rubric is home insulation standards to meet FHA requirements. Federal legislation has already required producers of home appliances to report the unit's energy efficiency ratio (EER). Subsequent legislation could require that selected appliances meet certain minimum standards for fuel efficiency. This would mean that cheap, inefficient window air conditioners, refrigerators, and so on would be banned from the market. Germany has already instituted standards for industrial boilers, and Canada has a mandatory minimum furnace efficiency program.[12]

The rationale for fuel efficiency standards is twofold. First, as with all nonprice methods of conserving energy, the income distributional effects of higher fuel prices are avoided. Second, it corrects market failures due to imperfect information that could lead people to choose more fuel-inefficient equipment than they otherwise would. Presumably, when low-fuel-efficiency appliances and autos are banned, the consumer is forced to buy the fuel-efficient model. Similarly, local housing standards as in Sweden requiring triple-glazed windows (three glass panes with air spaces between them) overcomes problems of consumer and contractor ignorance.

But efficiency standards may prove much less desirable than they first appear to be. Fuel inefficiency does not necessarily imply economic inefficiency. For example, consider the choice between buying a high-efficiency air conditioner for $275 or a low-efficiency model for $200. Is it irrational to buy the low-efficiency unit? Assuming similar repair costs and appliance life, the answer clearly depends on the present value of electricity cost savings over the life of the unit. If these cost savings exceed $75, the high-efficiency unit should be purchased; the reverse is true if the savings are less than $75. A critical element in the calculation is the anticipated utilization rate of the air conditioner. If the consumer lives in Connecticut and needs air conditioning only 5 to 10 days in the summer, the low-efficiency unit is probably preferred, while a resident of the Southwest would choose the high-efficiency unit, which would be in operation for 3 to 4 months.

There remains the problem that while the high-fuel-efficiency appliance may be optimal, it may not be purchased. The Southwestern consumer may irrationally choose the low-fuel-efficiency model unless prevented by law. Even with energy efficiency ratings displayed on the appliances, the fuel savings from such an appliance are by no means apparent. The average consumer is ill equipped to measure kilowatt-hour savings and then to convert these to dollar savings. Opponents of efficiency standards would argue that this problem could be corrected by providing more readily accessible government information showing annual dollar savings for various localities. To them, the remedy is more information, not less consumer choice.

Price Methods of Achieving Conservation

Fuel Taxes. A prominent aspect of European energy policy is the primary reliance on fuel taxes, as indicated by the gasoline and heating oil prices shown in Table 7.1. Taxes on gasoline exceed $2.00 per gallon in many countries. Smaller but nontrivial taxes have been levied on other petroleum products. The popularity of fuel taxes is due primarily to their ease of collection and their large revenue potential. In addition, taxes on petroleum products afford some protection to the domestic coal industries. The United States stands in sharp contrast, with Federal taxes of only 13 cents per gallon on gasoline and smaller state gasoline taxes.

As has been shown above, a fuel tax is the most economically efficient method of achieving a given reduction in energy consumption. Opposition to fuel taxes is typically centered on two interrelated propositions. The first is that fuel taxes will result in large income distributional effects. The second is that because the demand for the fuel is so price-inelastic, taxes are not effective in achieving conservation.

The two propositions are interrelated in that the more price-inelastic the demand schedule, the larger the income transfer, and the smaller the reduction in quantity demand.

A little introspection will amply convince us that in the short run, the demand for energy is highly inelastic with respect to price. In the short run, the stock of energy-consuming equipment is fixed. In addition, its efficiency characteristics are given, leaving only the utilization rate to be varied. In the winter of 1973, we were struck with the old gas guzzlers; the only choice was to drive less. Therefore, it should come as no surprise that most econometric studies place the short-run price elasticity of gasoline and other fuels quite low. Therefore, the taxes required to reach a given conservation target are likely to be indeed high, resulting in appreciable income transfers.

Econometric evidence suggests that the long-run price elasticities are indeed much greater than the short-run elasticities.[13] In the long run the magnitude of the taxes required to achieve a given quantity reduction is not nearly so large, implying much lower income transfers. Before turning to actual elasticity results, consider why the long-run elasticities could be much larger than the short-run elasticities. In the short run, the only channel of response is through varying the utilization rate. With time, both the size of the stock of energy-consuming equipment and its fuel efficiency characteristics are variable. For example, approximately every ten years the stock of cars is turned over, allowing the substitution of fewer cars or more fuel-efficient cars or both. For many other users of energy, such as industrial boilers, the long run is an even longer period, as these facilities tend to be longer-lived than autos.

Table 7.3 reports long-run price elasticities for four major fuel cate-

TABLE 7.3 Long-Run Price Elasticities for Energy and Fuels[a]

Sector	Energy	Petroleum Products	Gas (Natural and Manufactured)	Coal	Electricity
Industrial	0.4	0.71	1.14	1.17	0.46
Transportation	1.1	.96[b]	0.71	0.71	0.71
Residential and commercial	0.93	1.24	2.26	NA[c]	0.88
Electricity generation	0	4.27	0.98	0.86	NA

[a]Based on U.S. data, average elasticities, 1960–1972.
[b]Motor gasoline only. See Baltagi and Griffin, "Gasoline Demand in the OECD," *European Economic Review*, 1983.
[c]NA = not applicable, as there was very little consumption of the fuel in this sector.
SOURCE: *J. M. Griffin*, Energy Conservation in the OECD, 1980 to 2000 (Cambridge: Ballinger, 1979).

gories: coal, gas, petroleum products, and electricity. Since the price elasticity may vary depending on the sector in which the fuel is consumed, separate elasticities are reported for the industrial sector, the transportation sector, the residential and commercial sectors, and the electricity generation sector. These results show the elasticities for the United States, which was one of the 18 OECD countries included in the study. Notice that many of the elasticities exceed unity, and even the most inelastic response (electricity in the industrial sector) has a price elasticity of 0.46. Perhaps the most surprising result is that the long-run elasticity of gasoline (transportation sector) is 0.9 as contrasted with the short-run elasticities ranging around 0.1. The reader should be cautioned that these long-run responses may take ten to twenty years to achieve.

Let us return to the example of gasoline consumption and examine the income transfers associated with the use of gasoline taxes to promote conservation. We choose a more conservative estimate of the long-run price elasticity for gasoline from a study by Professor James Sweeney of Stanford University. Professor Sweeney's study is of methodological interest because his model separately explains the choice of auto stock, fuel efficiency, and vehicle miles (utilization). Sweeney found a long-run price elasticity of 0.78.[14] His long-run elasticity is based on replacing the current stock of automobiles with a more fuel-efficient auto fleet.

Recall that in 1973, with a short-run price elasticity of 0.1, a 100 percent price increase is needed to achieve a 10 percent change in gasoline consumption, resulting in a $33 billion income transfer. Now suppose society is concerned only with reducing consumption by 10 percent over a time horizon of, say, 10 years. Assuming a price elasticity of 0.78, gasoline prices would have to rise by only 13 percent rather than 100 percent. In this case, the long-run income transfer is $4.2 billion, or about $45 per worker. The problem of the large income transfer aspect is reduced by a factor of 8, suggesting that fuel taxes can play effective and politically palatable roles in long-run conservation policies.

Taxes on Energy-Consuming Equipment. There are a variety of methods of taxing energy-consuming equipment, including taxes on the stock of equipment and taxes on equipment with low fuel efficiency. In Europe, it is common practice to pay a substantial excise tax at the time of purchase of a new car. In addition, some countries such as France encourage the use of more fuel-efficient autos through a horsepower tax. In many states in the United States, annual automobile registration fees are based on the weight of cars.

General taxes on energy equipment, unlike fuel taxes, do not necessarily minimize the loss in social benefits for a given degree of fuel conservation. Whereas a fuel tax works through all three channels of substitution—stock, fuel efficiency, and utilization—a tax on fuel-consuming equipment works through at most two of the channels. For example, a tax on autos raises the price of autos, causing a reduction in the stock of cars. There is no reason to expect the auto tax to improve either the efficiency of the stock or the utilization rate. Auto utilization may even increase with fewer cars on the road.

Nevertheless, a tax on the efficiency of autos is not always inferior to a fuel tax. One proposal considered by the U.S. Congress was to reduce gasoline consumption through an efficiency tax on new car sales. For example, for each mile per gallon below some threshold level, say 25 miles per gallon, a $100 tax would be applied. A car getting 20 miles to the gallon would pay a tax of $500 at the time of its purchase. It is also possible to subsidize purchasers of small cars with this tax revenue. For example, a subsidy of $100 could be paid for each mile per gallon that exceeded the threshold level of 25 miles per gallon. Thus the purchase price of a 35-mile-per-gallon Toyota would be reduced by $1000.

Viewed in a long-run context, Professor Sweeney's analysis found that gasoline taxes work almost entirely through the efficiency of the auto fleet—the same mechanism as the efficiency tax. Assuming these findings to be valid, the fuel efficiency tax would yield welfare characteristics similar to the gasoline tax—both would minimize the loss in social benefits from the reduction in consumption. Furthermore, it would avoid the large income transfers associated with a gasoline tax. In sum, there appear to be situations where taxes on the energy-consuming equipment or its fuel efficiency are economically efficient and stand a better chance of obtaining congressional approval than a simple fuel tax.

QUESTIONS

1. Explain in words why price rationing is more economically efficient than quantity rationing.

2. What are the necessary conditions for a successful program of public exhortation? What are its relative strengths and weaknesses compared to a direct quantity rationing and a fuels tax?

3. Use a numerical example to show that the income transfer is inversely proportional to the price elasticity of demand.

4. Discuss how a gasoline tax could be phased in over time to achieve the desired long-run adjustment in auto efficiency and yet avoid the large income transfer in the short run.

5. Suppose gasoline prices affected only the miles driven. Can you suggest a tax that would have the same effect as a gasoline tax? Would it involve smaller income transfers?

ENERGY CONSERVATION ON THE SUPPLY SIDE: CONSERVATION IN PRODUCTION

Conservation is no easier to define for production than for consumption. Laws requiring adherence to conservation practices generally define conservation as the "avoidance of waste" in the production of energy resources. Ultimately, however, waste must be defined in economic rather than physical terms. Let us first consider the implications of defining conservation in a physical or engineering sense as the maximization of recovery of an energy resource from a given deposit. For example, a program for maximizing physical recovery of oil and gas would include four elements. First, one or more development wells would have to be drilled in most cases to supplement the discovery well and drain those portions of the reservoir which will yield spontaneous fluid flows, referred to as "primary production." Second, at various subsequent times it would be necessary to install additional equipment to stimulate further production by augmenting or replacing natural reservoir drive mechanisms. Pumps would be placed in wells that had ceased to flow naturally. Reservoir pressure could be maintained by "secondary recovery" techniques such as injecting water or gas into the productive formation. Third, at later times, chemicals or heat could be introduced into the reservoir in "tertiary recovery" programs. Finally, the complete recovery of all hydrocarbons would require mining oil-bearing rock and extracting the oil from the rock by physical and chemical means. This is clearly an extreme notion of conservation, since such procedures could easily use more energy than they produce. A more sensible definition of waste must be sought.

Consider our economic definition—produce oil until the marginal social benefit equals the marginal social cost of the last barrel. Stated differently, we wish to recover all the oil and gas that costs no more to produce than it is worth to society. Assuming perfect competition and no externalities, the use of such a definition would maximize the present discounted value of a reservoir. Furthermore, in seeking to maximize the present value of the resource, private producers will also maximize its social value.[15]

Note that the use of the economic definition does not imply (1) the absolute minimization of total costs, (2) the maximization of production, or (3) the minimization of the reservoir's productive life. One could minimize costs by drilling only a single well, but this would either reduce total output or increase the total time required to drain the reservoir, or both. Similarly, it will never be economical to maximize total output by wringing the last drop of oil from the reservoir sponge. Given present technology, the actual mining of reservoir sediments is not economical, and tertiary recovery technology has not been widely applied until quite recently. Finally, while a barrel produced today is worth more than a barrel produced tomorrow, it is not economical to minimize the time required to produce the contents of the reservoir. Rapid production not only requires a larger investment in well drilling but also greatly reduces the effectiveness of the reservoir's natural drive mechanisms, reducing ultimate recovery from the reservoir.

Still, the physical and economic definitions of conservation are not totally opposed. While they imply different concepts of "waste," there is agreement that easily avoidable physical waste implies economic inefficiency. The advantage of the economic definition is its recognition that increased recovery is costly in that society's other resources must be diverted to increase recovery, and this should not be done unless the resources you get are more valuable than the ones you give up.

Although the wastes of oil and gas production practices in the early decades of the industry's history can readily be exaggerated by dwelling only upon the very worst instances, purely physical waste was, by current conservation standards, remarkably high during that period. In the early decades of the oil industry in the United States, many oil and gas fields were found in settled areas where the land was held by numerous small owners. In most countries, accepted legal doctrine gives the rights to subsurface minerals to the state; hence the temptation for private investors to explore for minerals is minimized. But in the United States the owner of the surface also owns the subsurface with whatever minerals it may contain. Hence a discovery well in an area of numerous small farms could, and often did, provide the occasion for a drilling spree, as adjoining landowners drilled as rapidly as possible to prevent the discoverer from exclusively draining the common oil reservoir that might underlie the surface properties of many farmers. Such overdrilling and rapid production led to wasteful dissipation of the natural reservoir energy that normally will propel oil to the surface for a period in a new flush field. This sharply raised costs and lowered ultimate recovery. As long as each landowner felt that his neighbors were draining the oil that was rightfully his, however, he felt compelled to drill as many wells as he could, and produce as rapidly as possible, in order to prevent the possibility of adverse drainage.

The legal system might have stepped in at this point and exerted its influence to prevent landowners from draining their neighbors. After all, if each landholder owned only the oil and gas beneath his acreage, it would be illegal for him to drain petroleum from beneath the property line of others. But the relevant question—How much oil is located under each surface tract?—could not be answered at that time with any confidence by reservoir engineers, to say nothing of judges. If no one knows where the oil came from, who owns it? An ingenious judge soon identified an applicable simple principle: the rule of capture.

This legal notion was developed centuries earlier in England to handle disputes over the decoying of wild game. Such animals in their free state constitute a scarce but unowned resource, since they freely migrate across property lines. It was understood that one might legally capture game animals if they "trespass" on one's own property, but one might not shoot them over the fence while they were on another's land. The issue in this dispute was different: Is it permissible for a landowner to entice wild game from the property of a neighbor onto his own land, using decoys or lures? Once across the fence, the game could legally be captured. The rule of capture holds such decoying to be legal. From this precedent it was an easy leap to construe oil and gas in the reservoir as scarce, unappropriated natural resources, which could be lured from beneath one's neighbor's land by locating well bores as hydrocarbon decoys. Judges thus gave landowners the signal to drill as rapidly and intensively as possible if they were to prevent their wild hydrocarbons from being lured away by their neighbors' wells! In fairness to judges, this was the only practical solution because it was, and is, impossible to determine the original location of oil produced from a reservoir. Under this solution, though, it was logical for adjoining landowners to drill a row of "offset" wells all along their fence lines, their wells being directly opposite those of their neighbors. When oil was discovered within city limits, in certain small east Texas towns, the multiplication of derricks on tiny town lot plots provided a ridiculous spectacle. Although the rule of capture may have been a godsend to judges burdened with heavy case loads, it was anathema to the goal of economic efficiency.

What should have been done? Had all the judges been trained and dedicated economists, how might they have ruled? The fundamental unit of petroleum production is the reservoir, not the well. If it were possible to ascertain all the economically relevant characteristics of a reservoir shortly after discovery, a judge could engage as consultants a staff of engineers and economists who could formulate a unified plan for reservoir development, alloting each landowner the proper share of the reservoir. While the field must be developed as a unit, several operators could act as cooperating managers. The operators would cooperate in production within a particular field but would be free to compete with each other as regards production from other fields, and would of course compete directly in downstream operations. As long as there were a large number of individual reservoirs with different firms acting as operators, no abridgment of competition need arise from the unitization of individual reservoirs.

Unitization Versus Rule of Capture: A Hypothetical Example

Perhaps it is useful to construct a hypothetical example contrasting unitization with the rule of capture. Let us begin by assuming 25 adjoining square tracts of land, each 100 acres in extent, covering a total area of slightly under four square miles. Each tract is owned by a different individual. Let us further assume that an initial discovery well is drilled in the very center of the central tract, and as soon as oil is discovered, the characteristics of the reservoir are correctly inferred (even though such knowledge is usually obtainable only after enough time has passed to permit a substantial amount of development drilling to be done, and production experience to be analyzed).

Assuming that the state has a compulsory unitization law, the field can be developed efficiently with a minimum number of wells. The spacing, depth, and recovery from each well will depend on many factors, including the nature of the reservoir drive mechanism. Let us consider a simple gas-cap drive formation, as shown in Figures 7.8a and 7.8b. The oil sands are trapped in a gap between two masses of non-oil bearing rock, occupying the space between a lower cone of rock and the underside of another cone of non-oil rock. Since gas is lighter than oil, there is a cap of gas on top of the oil sands. When the oil reservoir is penetrated by well bores, the difference between the reservoir pressure and the pressure at the wellhead causes the hydrocarbons to flow naturally out the well bores. As oil is produced, the gas cap expands very slightly in response to the reduction in reservoir pressure. Thus the reservoir mechanism is driven by the pressure of the gas cap expanding from above, and over time as more oil is produced the gas-oil interface falls. The optimal number and placement of wells calls for 13 wells in two concentric circles about the discovery well A. The discovery well A is assumed to be on a tract containing 4 percent of total reserves (see 4 in lower right corner of the tract). But it would be a mistake to produce well A, since the loss of the gas cap would severely reduce reservoir pressure and reduce recovery of the other 12 wells. Therefore, under unitization, well A is plugged until all the oil in the reservoir is produced; then it can be re-opened to produce the gas, since the gas can no longer serve the purpose of expelling the oil. Even though the eight tracts adjacent to the central tract contain 48 percent of reserves, the four wells B_1 through B_4 will produce only 20 percent of total production (5% for each well, as shown in upper left corner of tract), being plugged when the gas-oil interface reaches that depth. The outer tracts, containing 48% of reserves, ultimately produce 80 percent of reserves (10 percent for each well) through the eight wells denoted as C_1 through C_8. The reason for the large recovery by the structurally low wells is that as the gas cap expands with production, oil from interior tracts will migrate to the outer wells, C_1 to C_8.

The optimal production strategy from the gas-cap reservoir implies that the production resulting from wells located in a given landowner's tract does not closely match what the landowner receives. The allocation of shares in the unit is based on the original determination

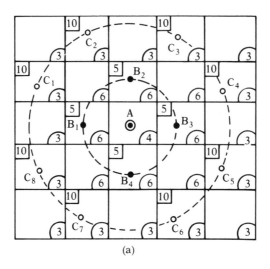

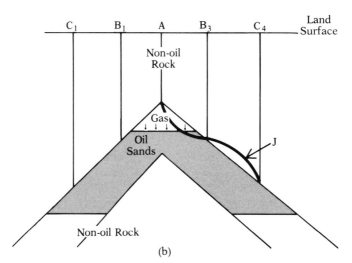

FIGURE 7.8(a) and (b) Optimum well configuration for achieving maximum economic recovery of oil and gas from a simple gas-cap drive formation.

of oil underlying each tract. For example, the central tract receives payment for 4 percent of oil production even though well A is plugged for later gas production. Of the eight inner tracts, the four with wells located on them produce 5 percent each of total reserves and yet receive payment for 6 percent shares, while the four tracts without wells receive payment for 6 percent shares even though there is no production on the tract. Similarly, for the other tracts, those without wells receive 3 percent shares for producing nothing while those tracts with wells produce 10 percent of reserves yet receive only a 3 percent share.

Consequently, the unitization agreement requires substantial redistributive transfers among the 25 tract owners, but this transfer will occur since, by assumption, the oil reservoir has been subject to *compulsory* unitization.

Let us now ask what would happen if there were no compulsory unitization law, and drilling took place under the rule of capture. Would we expect rationality to prevail so that the 25 tract owners agree to unitize the reservoir voluntarily, with each party receiving the shares outlined under the compulsory unitization agreement? Experience clearly shows the answer to be no. The rule of capture would instead result in large overdrilling and the recovery of only a fraction of the oil recovered under unitization. First of all, numerous additional wells would be drilled, with an average of perhaps as many as 10 wells on each of the 25 tracts. The strategy is to locate wells along property lines to prevent drainage of one's reserves by adjoining landowners. In turn, the adjoining landowner is likely to drill offset wells across the fence to prevent the neighbor's wells from draining his tract. Thus instead of 13 wells draining the 250 acres, we might easily observe 250 wells or more. To place this excess drilling problem in perspective, Morris Adelman estimated in 1964 that excessive drilling costs were running about $4 billion per year.[16] For just one field, the Slaughter field in West Texas, excessive well costs were estimated at over $150 million. The severity of this problem is also revealed in international well and output data. In 1980, the U.S. had 88 percent of the world's active oil wells but only 14 percent of world oil production.

Coordinated field development through unitization not only can reduce such costs, but will also lead to substantial increases in ultimate oil recovery. Under competitive development, production rates are very high. Firms try to drain oil from the neighboring area by producing too rapidly, which lowers pressure in the vicinity of the well-bore, attracting oil from surrounding higher pressure areas. With rapid production, however, natural gas (which can move more rapidly than oil through the reservoir rock) pushes past the oil, and the ratio of gas to oil production rises. Less gas in the reservoir means that the remaining hydrocarbons are more viscous and it will take more pressure to move them through the rock. Lowered gas also means less pressure. Since gas is much less valuable than oil, the gas that is produced will ideally be reinjected back into field, reducing hydrocarbon viscosity and raising pressure. Such recycling activities, however, are quite costly and in practice are seldom found in reservoirs that are not unitized. As a result, early unitization sharply increases oil recovery, from two to ten times in solution gas fields. Despite these large gains, in practice unitization is difficult to achieve, particularly early in a field's productive life when the potential gains from reduced drilling costs and increased recovery are greatest.

But if the increased recovery and savings in drilling costs are so large, why doesn't voluntary unitization occur? If the relevant parties couldn't reach a unitization agreement, why wouldn't it pay someone to buy up all of the leases in a field and then unitize it? Curiously, private contracting breaks down severely for one principal reason—uncertainty.[17] The central problem with voluntary unitization lies in the inability of firms to reach agreement on relative lease values so that unit shares can be assigned. A lease's value is determined by the amount of hydrocarbons originally in place and the net migration the lease could achieve under open production. It is quite difficult to assess this value early, and sometimes even late, in field life. An oil field varies like ordinary surface terrain, and the only information about the structure of the pool comes from the well bores. It is extremely difficult to construct a composite map of the reservoir from the 13 well bores in Figure 7.8b. In Figure 7.8b, line J, measuring thickness of the oil sand, is just as plausible based on the available data as are the straight lines shown. If line J is the true reservoir boundary, however, the outer leases have much more oil than the inner leases. The choice between J as the boundary and the original straight line could reallocate millions of dollars across firms. Voluntary unitization is not a very effective solution to the common pool problem because of these types of difficulties. The only time it works very well is when almost nothing is known about the reservoir. In that case firms do not get into disputes about the reservoir's exact shape and can reach agreement. This occurs frequently on federal lands in Wyoming and other Western states, but is uncommon elsewhere. The result of the failure to unitize voluntarily is prorationing regulation. Prorationing is a much less efficient way than unitization to develop an oil field but is, nevertheless, much more efficient than open production.

Prorationing: A Second Best Policy

With the legal doctrine of the rule of capture in the ascendancy, the only way out seemed to be the adoption of specific laws that would supersede that doctrine. The first state conservation laws were passed before 1900, and covered such matters as avoidance of ground water pollution and excessive flaring of natural gas. Not until after the First World War, however, were the major producing states motivated to pass laws attacking both the physical and economic problems of wasteful production practices. Texas in 1919 first passed laws preventing extremely close spacing of wells. This law, however, was generally ineffective because it did not provide a way to stop dense drilling on small tracts. Landowners on these tracts gained exemptions from spacing rules because they had a legal right to the hydrocarbons under their land even if it were no larger than a single lot in a town. The only solution was to force these small landowners together to form a drilling unit—a grouping of land large enough to merit its own well. Texas law did not permit this and so was ineffective at stopping dense small-tract drilling. Oklahoma solved this problem in 1935 by passing compulsory "pooling" laws that permitted small tracts to be forced together, making spacing laws effective.

Besides spacing rules, the largest factor in limiting common pool abuses was prorationing—limitation of output rates in a reservoir generally, but still permitting individual lease owners to operate their own leases. Prorationing first developed voluntarily on the huge Yates field in West Texas.[18] Yates initially had only nine operators and one, Mid-Kansas (later Marathon), had over 60 percent of the field. Initially, there was also only one pipeline into the field, owned by Humble. Given the very concentrated nature of holdings, and pressure from Humble, the firms were able to reach an agreement that restricted drilling and production. This led to a sharp reduction of drilling costs, and the field's output was maintained because natural pressure was not dissipated from overly rapid production. The lesson was not lost on the industry—soon there were similar efforts to control production in a large number of fields. Few fields, however, were blessed with Yates' highly concentrated ownership. In these less concentrated fields agreements were negotiated, but they broke down repeatedly as individual lease owners cheated to increase their output shares. In the face of repeated failure of private contracting for prorationing controls, firms petitioned state authorities to impose controls.

Oklahoma first promulgated a statewide prorationing law, permitting the state regulatory commission to determine total state output and allocate the total well by well. Texas followed suit in 1930, ordering that state production be limited to market demand.

In 1932 the United States Supreme Court upheld the Oklahoma law on grounds that limiting production to market demand prevented physical waste, with any price effects being merely incidental. During the next few years the basis for market demand prorationing was established by both state and federal action. The major producing states adopted conservation statutes that included the market demand provision, and the federal government passed the Connally "Hot Oil" Act, making illegal the interstate shipment of oil produced in excess of state quotas. By 1935 the system of conservation laws was working in such a way as to stabilize prices and production and to eliminate some of the extremes of physical waste experienced in earlier years. But the emphasis was obviously more on price stability than on waste prevention. Gas continued to be flared in significant volumes until after the Second World War.

The early prorationing approach was to look at the status quo, count the number of wells in the field, and divide the total output quota for the field more or less equally among all wells. If a particular well did not have the productive capacity to make its quota, the tendency on the part of regulators was to serve the interests of "equity" by reducing the output from the entire field to the point at which the least productive well could obtain its "fair share" of total field output! Such inefficiency-promoting inclinations came naturally to state regulators who, being elected officials, were understandably sensitive to the preferences of the numerous groups of small operators and royalty owners. But practical considerations usually prevented egalitarian programs from being carried to ridiculous extremes. Wells with very low potential could be granted blanket exemptions on grounds that these exceptions would not compromise the total program. Furthermore, wells with greater productive capacities could be given higher production "allowables" if some factual basis existed for legally rationalizing decisions that might increase economic efficiency. There were three major ways in which a well could qualify for a higher-than-average production quota: (1) deeper production; (2) wider spacing; or (3) a higher maximum efficient rate (MER) of production due to reservoir characteristics.[19]

The rationale for granting larger allowables to deeper wells was simply that such wells had higher costs and therefore should be rewarded with higher output quotas. But this is not necessarily economically efficient; relative subsidies to deeper drilling are desirable only if deeper drilling is fundamentally more promising. Allowables based on acreage might have a firmer basis. The general rule in the early days of prorationing was to give every existing producer at least some guaranteed market access through the awarding of an output quota. But if allowables were to be awarded strictly on a per-well basis, more wells would be drilled than were necessary to develop a field. To reduce rewards for overdrilling, regulators increased the production rates for more widely spaced wells. Such acreage allowables were economically defensible as long as all the acreage in question was oil-bearing. Shrewd operators, however, might drill at the edges of a field and include substantial amounts of "scenery" acreage in their leases, thus obtaining acreage allotments for nonproductive land.

Both economists and reservoir engineers would be likely to select MER as the single most valid basis for conservation regulation, although they might disagree as to its precise definition. Engineers might take the absolute conservationist (or preservationist) view that ultimate physical recovery should be maximized. The MER would thus be defined as the production rate just below that which causes a decline in total recovery. The chief reservation of the economist to this approach is that too slow a production rate may be required; it is better to produce 20 million barrels over 20 years than to produce 22 million over a century. The economist would prefer that MER be defined as that rate of output which maximizes the present discounted value of the stream of net future receipts from oil production in the reservoir. The chief difference is the role of the price of oil. Under the engineering approach the price level does not enter explicitly into the calculations, while it is of crucial importance in the economic definition. A regulatory commission employing an economic definition of MER would not only be compelled to consider prices very closely, but would also tend to affect prices by its decision.

In practice, not enough is known about the characteristics of most reservoirs to permit more than a general estimate of even an engineering-based MER. Adequate studies may be performed on the largest and most important reservoirs and fields, but rule-of-thumb estimates may have to suffice for most smaller reservoirs. Under market demand prorationing, the MER merely serves as an upper limit on production levels; during the years when output was curtailed to stabilize domestic prices, allowables in major fields might be only a small fraction of engineering-based MERs.

What can be concluded regarding the impact of conservation regulation on prices and recovery rates? Before 1930 (particularly in the early years) there was much physical waste in the field production of oil and gas. After 1935 such wastes were considerably reduced. What factors were responsible for this improvement? Technological advances probably played the largest role, with conservation regulation having a complex impact on production practices, on the nature of the market, and on the direction of technological innovation. Technological developments were particularly important in the conservation of natural gas. Until methods were developed to transport large volumes of gas economically through long-distance pipelines, the gas that could not be sold locally was generally flared. "Sour" natural gas with its high sulfur content could not be transported or burned in conventional equipment because of its corrosive effects. Hence vast quantities of sour natural gas were burned in very-low-productivity uses like the production of carbon black until technological innovations allowed the economical desulfurization of sour gas. Furthermore, innovations in secondary recovery operations permitted the recycling of natural gas to maintain field pressures and thus cut down on the volumes of gas vented and flared.

At some point, however—perhaps between 1910 and 1925—advancing technology could have laid the foundation for better conceived conservation laws. Compulsory unitization could have been imposed upon large reservoirs at the earliest possible date. Compulsory unitization would have enabled the earlier introduction of secondary recovery techniques, which would have significantly increased ultimate recovery from these reservoirs. As for conservation of natural gas, early emphasis could have been on recycling. In recent years, most of the producing states have passed mandatory unitization laws that apply to newly discovered reservoirs. Nevertheless, considerable production still originates from many of the older fields, which have not undergone unitization.

1. Under a rule of capture, what type of market failure do we observe?

2. Discuss the following: "Efforts by state conservation agencies to limit well drilling, increase the spacing of wells, and reduce production represented treatment of the symptoms of the disease and not the cause of the disease."

3. Even though unitization was not mandatory, why wouldn't the economic self-interest of the leaseholders in a reservoir lead to voluntary unitization?

SUMMARY

Conservation in the consumption and production of energy is best thought of in economic terms. We define conservation as that output or consumption rate at which the marginal social cost just equals the marginal social benefit. This condition is generally satisfied in a competitive market, free of externalities. On the production side, this implies that producers should follow production strategies that maximize the present value of the resource.

The potential for altering energy consumption in the long run is enormous. Historical experience reveals that energy and economic growth are causally related, but prices and technology can significantly alter the energy–GDP ratio over time. International evidence on interfuel substitution likewise suggests that within fairly broad limits one fuel can be substituted for another, confirming the feasibility of fuel-specific energy conservation programs.

Using less energy is not always better, particularly if the marginal social benefits of added production exceed their marginal social costs. As an example, the Btu theory of value is an outgrowth of the mistaken view that only energy is scarce. Nevertheless, there are legitimate instances where markets fail to equate marginal social costs and benefits. Policies of price controls, noninternalized externalities, and consumer inertia are but a few examples on the consumption side.

The discussion of policy instruments emphasizes the importance of using price methods of allocating energy. Arbitrary rationing rules may reduce the redistributive consequences of higher prices, but suffer from being highly inefficient. Other policies such as fuel efficiency standards and public exhortation have more limited roles, being applicable in a much narrower set of circumstances.

In the production of oil and gas in the United States, the "rule of capture" coupled with private ownership of subsurface minerals has resulted in a serious market failure. Unitization, the first best ideal, fails to occur voluntarily despite the huge gains. The large redistribution that must occur under unitization, and the uncertainty in ascertaining reasonable estimates of oil underlying each tract, prevent voluntary unitization from occurring despite the huge possible gains.

Given the failure of voluntary unitization and the belated application of compulsory unitization to new fields, a second best policy described as prorationing regulation has evolved. Prorationing seeks to remedy the symptoms of the inefficiency—excessive drilling, overproduction, and flaring of natural gas—rather than the underlying illness—the failure to achieve unitization through efficient contracting.

1. For example, to solve for production after 50 years with a 5 percent annual growth rate, we solve the equation:

$$Q_t = Q_0 e^{0.05t}$$

Setting $t = 50$ and setting base year consumption Q_0 at 139, we get:

$$Q_{50} = 139e^{0.05(50)}$$
$$\ln Q_{50} = \ln 139 + .05(50)$$
$$\ln Q_{50} = 7.43$$
$$Q_{50} = 1693$$

By a similar technique one can solve for Q_{50} when the growth rate is 1.6 percent per year.

2. To compute cumulative production over the 50 year horizon, we integrate the equation defining consumption at every year over the period:

$$\text{Cumulative} = Q_0 \int_0^{50} e^{0.05t} dt$$
$$= \frac{Q_0}{0.05} \int_0^{50} e^{0.05t} d(0.05t)$$
$$= \frac{Q_0}{0.05} [e^{0.05t}]_0^{50}$$
$$= \frac{139}{0.05} [e^{0.05(50)} - e^0]$$
$$= \frac{139}{0.05} [12.18 - 1]$$
$$= 31,087 \text{ MMB/DOE.}$$

The multiplication of this daily rate by 365 days per year yields a total of 11.4 trillion barrels of oil equivalent energy over 50 years. Similarly, one can show that cumulative production along the 1.6 percent trend is 3.9 trillion BOE, yielding a difference between the two paths of 7.5 trillion BOE.

3. See Sam Schurr and B. Netschert, *Energy in the American Economy: 1850–1975* (Baltimore: Johns Hopkins Press, 1960).

4. L. Christensen, D. Jorgenson, and L. Lau, "Transcendental Logarithmic Production Frontiers," *Review of Economics and Statistics*, February 1973, pp. 28–45.

5. Ernest Berndt and David Wood, "Technology, Prices, and the Derived Demand for Energy," *Review of Economics and Statistics*, August 1975, pp. 259–268.

6. For a review, see J.M. Griffin, "The Energy-Capital Complementarity Controversy: A Progress Report on Reconciliation Attempts," in Berndt and Field, eds., *Modelling and Measuring Natural Resource Substitution* (Cambridge, Mass.: M.I.T. Press, 1981).

7. See R.L. Gordon, *The Evolution of Energy Policy in Western Europe: The Reluctant Retreat from Coal* (New York: Praeger, 1970).

8. J. Darmstadter, P. Teitelbaum, and J. Polach, *Energy in the World Economy* (Baltimore: Johns Hopkins Press, 1971), p. 14.

9. Ibid.

10. See Lee Schipper, "Raising the Productivity of Energy Utilization," *Annual Review of Energy*, Vol. 1, 1976. Also see Lee Schipper, Stephen Meyers, and Henry Kelly, *Coming in From the Cold: Energy-Wise Housing in Sweden* (Washington: Seven Locks Press, 1985).

11. H. Asher and R. Haberman, Jr., *Analysis of Recent Fluctuations in Electricity Consumption* (Washington, D.C.: General Electric Center for Energy Systems, 1978).

12. See O.E.C.D., *Energy Conservation in the International Energy Agency: 1976 Review* (Paris, 1976), p. 14.

13. For an extensive revision, see Douglas R. Bohi, *Analyzing Demand Behavior: A Study of Energy Elasticities* (Washington, D.C.: Johns Hopkins Press, 1981).

14. James L. Sweeney, "The Demand for Gasoline in the United States: A Vintage Capital Model" in *Workshops on Energy Supply and Demand* (Paris: International Energy Agency, 1978).

15. See Stephen L. MacDonald, *Petroleum Conservation in the United States* (Baltimore: Johns Hopkins Press, 1970), Ch. 5.

16. M.A. Adelman, "Efficiency of Resource Use in Crude Petroleum," *Southern Economic Journal*, October 1965, pp. 101–122.

17. See Gary D. Libecap and Steven N. Wiggins, "Contractual Responses to the Common Pool: Prorationing of Crude Oil Production," *American Economic Review*, March 1984.

18. See Libecap and Wiggins for an elaboration.

19. For an extensive review, see Wallace J. Lovejoy and Paul T. Homan, *Economic Aspects of Oil Conservation Regulation* (Baltimore: Johns Hopkins Press, 1967).

FEDERAL TAXATION AND PRICE REGULATION OF ENERGY PRODUCTION 8

INTRODUCTION

Students of the price histories of commodities have long observed that the prices of raw materials tend to fluctuate more sharply and more frequently than those of consumer goods in their final manufactured forms. Such fluctuations are not welcomed by either producers or consumers, and attempts at price stabilization or regulation have been a recurring feature in a number of raw materials markets. The initiative may come from producers, with or without the support of their national governments, as in the case of cartels. The initiative may also come from consumers, who have price controls as their goal. At its most ambitious reach, international commodity agreements may be undertaken to stabilize prices or limit price movements, with the participants including producers, consumers, and national governments of both importing and exporting countries.

Crude oil and natural gas are characterized by very inelastic short-run demand and supply schedules, which when coupled with substantial fluctuations in both supply and demand, lead to considerable fluctuations in market-clearing prices. This chapter undertakes to discuss the measures that the federal government in the United States has taken to control prices and producer income in the crude oil and natural gas markets in the last fifty years, with emphasis on the post-embargo period. The chief methods used have been price controls to place relatively low ceilings on producer receipts, or, when prices are decontrolled, taxes to recapture part of the producer surplus resulting from higher prices. In the more distant past, prices were stabilized indirectly through state production control. While this chapter recounts the U.S. experience with price controls and windfall profits taxes, U.S. policy is not unique. Canadian price and tax policies appear closely related to U.S. practices, and methods of taxing producer surplus in numerous other producing countries are similar in many respects to U.S. tax policy.

A prominent aspect of U.S. energy policy has been government regulation of the prices charged for crude oil and natural gas. During the 1970s price regulation held the prices of oil and gas well below the levels that would have prevailed in a free market. By the late 1970s, however, the costs of underpricing domestic energy resources—overconsumption, underproduction, and higher OPEC oil imports—began to be more apparent to policy makers in the federal government, and phased-in price decontrol for oil and for some categories of natural gas was contemplated. In 1977, for example, the average price paid for domestically produced oil was $9.55 per barrel compared to the world price of $14.53 per barrel. The price received for natural gas at the wellhead committed to the regulated interstate market (gas sold to buyers in other states) was $1.42 per thousand cubic feet (mcf) in 1977. In the unregulated intrastate market in Texas, the average price was $1.93 per mcf in 1977. Price discrepancies were even larger in earlier years. During this period, activities in Congress provided the basis for various degrees of price decontrol. The Natural Gas Policy Act of 1978 provided for the gradual decontrol of most natural gas, and the Windfall Profit Tax Act of 1980 facilitated the price decontrol of crude oil.

From newspaper reports of congressional deliberations during the 1970s it might appear that price regulations were new policies inaugurated in the 1970s. During the 1960s, there was little congressional concern with price regulation. Furthermore, given congressional action in the late 1970s to decontrol oil prices and to gradually deregulate most natural gas prices by the mid-1980s, it might even appear that price controls were a short-lived aspect of energy policy, inconsequential in the future. But this would be an incorrect conclusion. Government price regulation had its roots in the 1930s and has had a pervasive effect on U.S. energy supply and demand during much of the period since. Today, even though oil and most gas prices have been freed from controls, the Windfall Profit Tax remains and the advocates of price controls are both influential and politically strong. Thus, price regulation as a policy alternative is likely to remain a distinct possibility.

This chapter is best thought of as a five-course dinner with the following courses: (1) as a cocktail, a taste of post-embargo developments in oil price regulation; (2) as an appetizer, a similar account of recent gas price regulation; (3) as the main entree, a discussion of the conditions under which price controls may or may not increase economic welfare; (4) as dessert, an evaluation of the difficulties faced by price regulators, and (5) a final sobering cup of coffee to remind the dinner guests that distortions of the market arise not only from market failures but also from regulatory failures.

OIL PRICE REGULATIONS

A Brief Overview

The history of governmental price regulation can be divided into three distinct eras roughly spanning the periods 1935 to 1970, 1971 to 1980, and 1980 to present. During the period 1935 to 1970, government policies led to prices above what they otherwise would have been. Over this period, the role of government in determining price was subtle, but nevertheless quite effective. The discovery of huge oil fields in Texas and Oklahoma in the 1920s and early 1930s coupled with flush production under the rule of capture sent oil prices plummeting to $.67 per barrel in 1933. As noted in Chapter 7, statewide prorationing regulations were instituted to control production. Even though such regulation was ostensibly designed to promote conservation, controlling quantity is equivalent to controlling price. In this scheme, the federal government played a less apparent but quite supportive role by outlawing the sale of oil produced in excess of state production allowables and staunching the flow of cheap imported oil in 1959 through the Mandatory Oil Import Program.

Just as the first era resulted in oil prices above competitive levels, the era 1971 to 1980 led to prices well below an unregulated market outcome. In an unregulated setting, competitive fringe producers would have received sharply higher prices for their oil in accord with OPEC price increases, but this was not the case in the U.S. Price controls on domestic crude oil coupled with an "Entitlements Program" equalized the price of foreign and domestic crude to refiners, so that consumers ultimately paid a weighted average price based on the prices of foreign crude oil and domestic price-controlled crude oil. By the late 1970s, the effects of price controls were obvious—price controls artificially stimulated consumption and discouraged domestic production, increasing U.S. dependency on oil imports. Because of these perverse incentives, it has even been suggested that the legislation creating and extending price controls might better be renamed the "OPEC Assistance Act."

Finally, the third era was born in 1980 with the arrival of the Windfall Profit Tax. With the Windfall Profit Tax came decontrol of crude prices and an excise tax placed on domestic crude to capture part of the "windfall profits" that would occur as a consequence of decontrol. Compared to the previous era, the welfare loss from overconsumption was corrected and the distortions from domestic underproduction were attenuated. Nevertheless, the question remains: "Why should an oil producer be penalized for finding oil domestically by facing an excise tax on domestic oil production through the Windfall Profit Tax?"

Historical Origins

Regulation of the price of crude oil initially came about indirectly due to an interaction of state and federal regulations. As noted in Chapter 7, in the 1930s, in order to conserve crude oil, the oil-producing states created state regulatory agencies to limit the rate of crude oil production. A byproduct of this conservation policy, termed prorationing, was to restrain total production and thereby to set price indirectly. This control over price was unchallenged until the mid-1950s, when the cost of imported oil fell appreciably below domestic prices. Suddenly, imports restrained the power of the regulatory agencies to set prices. Following an unsuccessful attempt to restrict imports on a voluntary basis, President Eisenhower in 1959 imposed mandatory import controls, using national security considerations as a justification. Oil imports east of the Rocky Mountains were limited to 12.2 percent of domestic requirements. With imported oil no longer the marginal source, the large producing states, Texas and Louisiana, once again found themselves in a position not unlike that of Saudi Arabia in the dominant firm model of Chapter 4. With Texas and Louisiana supplying the marginal crude oil and their state regulatory agencies able to restrict production, the domestic price of oil was artificially maintained $1.00 to $1.50 per barrel above the price of imports delivered to the United States.[2] Thus federal regulations limiting imports coupled with the state regulatory commissions' control over domestic production meant that crude oil prices were effectively set by state regulatory commissions.

Beginning in 1971, control over oil prices was gradually transferred from the state to the federal level. Oil prices periodically fell under President Nixon's wage and price control policies. Under Phase IV of wage and price controls, a system was devised that attempted both to encourage increased exploration and development of additional oil production, and also to protect consumers from rising prices of petroleum products. Production from a given property up to 1972 production rates was categorized as "old" oil, receiving a price of 35 cents per barrel above the May 15, 1973 price. "New" oil consisted of production in excess of 1972 levels or from new properties, and its price was not controlled. A third category of oil called "released" oil was created to encourage increased production. For each barrel of new oil, a company would be allowed to release one barrel of old oil from price controls.

Post-Embargo Price Controls

As the price of imported oil skyrocketed during the embargo of the winter of 1973–74, the price controls on domestic oil kept U.S. prices well below world prices. The average price of domestic oil in early

1974 stood at $7.18 per barrel compared to $12.52 for imported oil. Demand in early 1974 was at elevated levels, due to panic buying as motorists continually kept gasoline tanks full, fearing that shortages might materialize at any time. As long as demand was very high, refiners who used higher-priced imported oil could pass on their high crude oil costs in the prices of their refined products, and still find adequate numbers of customers. Price controls on refined petroleum products such as gasoline were also improvised during the embargo period, such that prices were limited to costs plus a certain pre-embargo profit margin per gallon sold. This meant that gasoline refined from domestic oil could be sold at ceiling prices that were much lower than those allotted to gasoline refined from higher-cost imported oil. It is obviously inefficient to charge different prices for the same good, but as long as demand was at elevated levels, customers not able to buy gasoline from lower-priced sellers would purchase from higher-cost outlets, and the sellers of higher-priced gasoline were able to sell at the ceiling prices allowed under regulation.

With the cessation of the embargo and the restoration of greater confidence in future gasoline supplies, the demand for gasoline declined appreciably during 1974. Now the sellers of gasoline refined from imported oil could no longer market their product at the regulated ceiling price. After buyers purchased available supplies from sellers of gasoline refined from lower-cost "old" domestic crude oil, there was not enough demand to support higher prices by the sellers of gasoline derived from "new" domestic oil and oil imports. The refiners and sellers of products derived from high-cost oil faced a crisis. The crude oil price control scheme had broken down at the level of refined products demand.

To regulators, the "solution" was easy: equalize the cost of crude across all refiners. The "entitlements" scheme was thus born. This scheme in effect transferred the title to a large percentage of old domestic oil from its actual producers to those who imported oil. Let us assume for the purposes of a simple example that half of the oil processed by U.S. refineries is domestically produced old oil, which is price controlled at $5 per barrel, and other half is imported oil costing $10. (We disregard new domestic oil because of its relative unimportance.) Under the breathtaking doctrine of entitlements, every refinery in the country was "entitled" to process a mix of oil that is 50% low-cost domestic and 50% imported oil. Since we are assuming that half the U.S. refineries in fact processed their own domestic oil, and half of them exclusively processed imported oil, entitlements generated huge income transfers. An entitlement was issued with each barrel of imported oil, allowing the purchase of one barrel of low-cost domestic oil. Refiners processing essentially domestic oil had to purchase entitlements in order to buy domestic oil. In this example domestic oil producers refining their own oil in their own refineries were incensed at being compelled to buy entitlements from oil importers for the "privilege" of refining their own oil.

Despite the obvious equity problems, the entitlements scheme did equalize the per-barrel crude oil costs of all refiners and thus allowed all sellers to charge the same legal maximum price for petroleum products. In the present example it works this way: For every 100 barrels of crude oil refined, suppose 50 barrels are imported at $10 per barrel and 50 barrels are purchased domestically at the controlled price of $5. Hence the 100 barrels costs $750, so the average cost of crude oil is $7.50 per barrel. Now suppose refiner A processes only the 50 barrels of domestic crude, while refiner B processes the 50 barrels of foreign crude. In the absence of entitlements refiner A's crude costs are $250 and refiner B's crude costs are $500. To equalize crude costs across refiners, with each barrel of imported oil went the entitlement to purchase a certain amount of low cost domestic oil. In this case, with imports equalling domestic production, for each barrel of imported crude an entitlement was issued to purchase one barrel of low cost domestic crude. In principle, each refiner could process a 50–50 mix of foreign and domestic crude with an average cost of $7.50 per barrel. But in reality, refiner A would simply purchase refiner B's 50 entitlements to domestic oil at a price of $2.50 per entitlement and continue operating as before. In either case, the average cost to both refiners would be $7.50 per barrel.

Welfare Analysis of Price Controls Per Se

A reasonably simple diagram will suffice to show the welfare losses resulting from price controls on crude oil in early 1974, and from the price controls plus the entitlements scheme in late 1974. Figure 8.1 shows U.S. demand in early 1974 as the schedule D'_{US}, while demand in late 1974 is shown by the demand curve D_{US}. The curve D_{US} lies to left of D'_{US} due to the decline in demand in late 1974 as shortage fears subsided. The horizontal line labelled P_{OPEC} indicates that at $12.52 per barrel the U.S. can purchase whatever quantity of imported oil it desires. The domestic supply schedule S reflects the long-run supply curve of a competitive industry free from price control, and producing outputs limited only by marginal production cost relative to demand. In the absence of price controls, domestic oil would be bid up to price parity with OPEC oil, domestic suppliers would produce a quantity Q_s, and imports of $Q_d - Q_s$ would meet that part of demand which could not be domestically supplied at the OPEC price. In this case domestic oil producers would earn producer surplus equal to the area OAB, the difference between total revenues and the total production cost, represented by the area under the domestic supply curve.

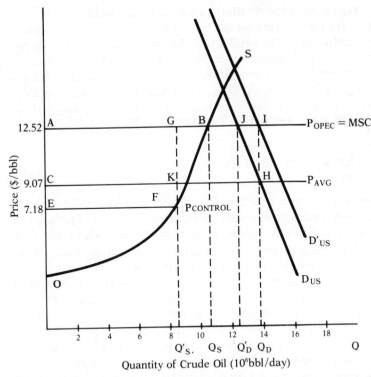

FIGURE 8.1 The effects of price controls and entitlements on the U.S. crude oil market. (D'_{US} = U.S. demand in early 1974; D_{US} = U.S. demand in late 1974.)

If we assume that all price-controlled oil sold for an average value of $7.18 per barrel in early 1974, and all imported oil for $12.52 per barrel, it can easily be shown what impact price controls had on economic welfare in the crude oil market. Consumers purchased oil produced domestically under price control in the amount of Q'_s barrels per day, receiving additional consumer surplus equal to the area *AEFG*, or about $45.4 million per day. The consumers realized this saving because they were able to buy about 8.5 million barrels of oil per day at $7.18 instead of the world price of $12.52. Producer surplus, on the other hand, was more greatly reduced under price controls, from area *OAB* down to area *OEF*. The loss in producer surplus (area *AEFB*) was about $53.1 million per day. Hence economic welfare in the crude oil market declined by area *FGB* or about $7.7 million per day ($2.8 billion per year). Of the $53.1 million daily decline in producer surplus, $45.4 million per day represented a direct transfer to consumer surplus through underpricing the actual level of production realized with regulation; the deadweight area of net reduction in economic welfare, area *FGB*, represented domestic producer surplus lost due to the reduction of U.S. production below its competitive level, and amounts to the $7.7 million per day mentioned above. Note that under price controls per se, the welfare loss, area *FGB*, arises entirely from domestic underproduction. There is no loss from underconsumption, since for the marginal barrel of imported crude the marginal social benefit equals the marginal social cost.

Welfare Analysis of Price Controls Plus Entitlements

Now let us see what happens when demand falls in late 1974 and entitlements are imposed. Let demand fall from D'_{US} to D_{US}. The market equilibrium without controls would now be at point *J*, where the new lower demand curve intersects the world supply-price schedule at P_{OPEC} = $12.52. This would reduce total demand to Q_d, eliminating oil imports in the amount of $Q'_d - Q_d$. It was this loss in their business volume at the world price that the oil importers successfully prevented by securing the adoption of the entitlements scheme. With entitlements the marginal price to the consumer was reduced to P_{AVG}, which was a weighted average of imported oil costing $12.52 per barrel and domestic oil selling at $7.18. The lower price approximately restores consumption to the original early 1974 quantity of Q'_d. With total domestic production at Q'_s and total imports at $Q'_d - Q'_s$, the ratio of domestic production to total demand was about 64.4 percent. The weighted average of domestic and total demand costs was $9.07 per barrel, so under the entitlements program the costs of refinery input to refiners producing low-cost domestic oil had to be increased by $1.89 per barrel ($9.07 minus $7.18) and the costs to refiners purchasing imported oil had to be reduced by $3.45 per barrel ($12.52 minus $9.07). This was easily accomplished by issuing 1.81 entitlements (the right to purchase 1.81 domestic barrels) for every barrel of imported oil. [The 1.81 ratio is arrived at by taking the ratio of the percentage domestic oil to imported oil (1.81 = 0.644/0.356)]. With the market value of one entitlement at $1.89 per barrel [the difference between the average price ($9.07) and the domestic control price ($7.18)], every barrel of imported crude received a subsidy of 1.81 entitlements worth $3.45 per barrel of imported oil. The entitlements program resulted in a substantial income transfer of $16.1 million per day as refiners of domestic crude were forced to pay $1.89 per barrel times 8.5 million barrels per day for the right to refine their own domestic crude. The $16.1 million dollars paid out to "buy entitlements" is of course used to subsidize the importation of foreign oil. In Figure 8.1, area *CEFK* is the cost of entitlements to domestic refiners, and the exactly equivalent area *GKHI* is the subsidy received by refiners of imported oil. The per-barrel subsidy to importation is higher than the per-barrel tribute paid by domestic refiners, since the volume of imports is smaller than the volume of domestic production under price control: the $16.1 million in question is now divided by only 4.7 million barrels, so the per-barrel subsidy to importers is $3.45, bringing the net cost of imported oil down to equality with the net cost of domestic production, at $9.07 per barrel. Curiously, the entitlements scheme had the perverse effect of underpricing domestic oil and then subsidizing imports by lowering the net price of imported oil to U.S. refiners. The regulation cut the effective import price by $3.45 per barrel on the amount of oil actually imported into the U.S.

In the previous section, we saw that price controls prior to entitlements resulted in a welfare loss of FGB or $7.7 million per day. Referring back to Figure 8.1, it is clear that in the absence of price controls, U.S. oil consumption would decline from Q'_D to Q_D as demand shifts from D'_S to D_S, with a constant OPEC price of $12.52. One of the main purposes of equalizing crude oil costs among refiners, however, was to prevent the decline in consumption. Unfortunately this could only be done by pricing imported oil at a marginal private cost that is below the true marginal social cost by the amount of the subsidy. Thus, in addition to the existing welfare loss of $7.7 million dollars per day that prevailed under simple domestic price control with U.S. demand at D', there is an additional deadweight loss due to the overconsumption resulting from pricing imports at less than their true marginal social cost. This loss is shown by the area JIH (or $2.6 million per day), which is obtained by subtracting the incremental social benefits of quantity $Q'_D - Q_D$ from the incremental social costs. This brings the total deadweight loss of price controls plus entitlements to $10.3 million per day, or $3.8 billion per year.

The "equilibrium" achieved under entitlements is short-run in nature, since the basis for paying entitlements depends upon the total supply of price-regulated domestic oil, as well as upon domestic demand and the OPEC price. Even if domestic demand and the OPEC price were to remain constant over time, the supply of "old" domestic oil will steadily decline through natural depletion and through disincentive effects of price control on optimal maintenance programs. As the captive supply of underpriced oil declines, the weighted average price (P_{AVG}) will rise, and total consumption will fall. The average entitlement per barrel paid on old oil will rise (as the weighted average price rises with the controlled price constant) while the average entitlement received per barrel imported will decline. In the long run, when domestic production is extinguished, entitlements would disappear and the domestic price would rise to the world price. Had the program been allowed to run its fatal course, it would have succeeded in transferring consumer surplus from producers to both consumers and oil exporters in the intermediate run, but in the long run would have hastened depletion of domestic reserves and left consumers at the mercy of the oil exporters.

Events Leading to the End of Price Controls and Entitlements

The program was not allowed to persist indefinitely, however, for several reasons. First, regulatory loopholes led to widespread abuses of the program. The increase in OPEC prices after the Iranian revolution of 1978–79 created huge incentives to transform old, low-priced oil into high-cost new oil. The "daisy chain" scam was invented by crude traders who amassed fortunes overnight. Under entitlement regulations, crude oil "reselling" was allowed to enable crude to move from the field to refineries. An allowed maximum resale profit of approximately 50 cents per barrel was stipulated for each transaction. But regulations did not limit the number of transactions! Thus the same barrel of oil could usually be legally "resold" many times, with the price rising about 50 cents on each resale. Most such resales were simply paper transactions. A crude trader could set up three or four wholly owned corporations and create paper crude transactions between them, taking a barrel of old oil originally purchased at a price of $6 or $7 and making about 50 cents per barrel on each transaction in the daisy chain until finally the crude was sold to a refiner at the *highest price* allowed on new oil. At least one reseller legally earned more than one billion dollars—the first "regulatory billionaire" in economic history.

The Department of Energy was even more embarrassed by the courts. Many cases brought against affluent resellers were lost, since the law invited and even encouraged such actions. Legislation under President Carter had called for crude oil price decontrol and an end to entitlements by October 1981, but President Reagan terminated the program still earlier, shortly after his inauguration in January 1981.

Other factors also contributed to the political battle to end oil price control and the entitlements regime. Economists generally were against it, as were those who were concerned with national security. European critics were also very numerous. But powerful oil importers resisted forcefully. Since inefficient regulation creates vested interests in resource misallocation, those oil companies that on balance gained by the program tended to oppose its elimination. Nevertheless, it seems likely that the single most important force behind the ultimate demise of oil price controls was the desire of various governmental groups, both federal and state, to transfer consumer surplus into government tax revenues. Thus in 1980, Congress replaced price controls with the Windfall Profit Tax.

Consumers had been more or less passive beneficiaries of the price control program. The political unpopularity of oil companies, particularly in the period of the Arab oil embargo and the first big OPEC price hike, helped consumers to obtain a large transfer of consumers' surplus in their favor with little organized effort on their own. But since consumers are too large and heterogeneous a group to organize effectively, their ability to preserve their sizeable short-run gains proved inadequate over time. Economists argued that domestic prices should be raised to the OPEC level in order to achieve price-induced conservation, increase domestic production, and reduce oil imports. Politicians heard part of the message. Higher prices to consumers would reduce consumption, and conservation was good—but why reward producers with higher prices, when the difference between the OPEC price and the short-run domestic production cost could be heavily taxed without obvious immediate effects on domestic supply? A windfall profit tax would yield enormous revenues over a long period of time that could be used to fund the Synthetic Fuel Corporation, a fund to enable poor people to receive assistance from energy bills, and large sums of uncommitted revenues for a variety of federal projects.

The Windfall Profit Tax of 1980

The "windfall profit tax" as finally passed by Congress should perhaps have been called more accurately the "windfall revenue act" since the tax was not placed upon profits as such, but is more akin to a per-barrel excise tax, where the tax rate varies depending on the sale price of the oil. The act itself is tedious beyond belief, impossible to comprehend in economic terms because of logical inconsistencies, and represents perhaps the single most complicated tax law category in the entire Internal Revenue code—which is saying a very great deal. The windfall profit tax liability of production from any particular well depends upon more than fifty variables relating to real and imaginary characteristics of a historical, geological, technological, geographic, and purely regulatory nature. Thus it is impossible to discuss the tax without radical simplification of its endless complexities. The most pertinent data are summarized in Table 8.1.

It is apparent that a major distinction is made between old and new oil, and a further distinction exists between old oil from marginal "stripper" wells and old oil from supramarginal flowing wells. Old oil generally is taxed at a 70 percent rate applied to the difference between the price received by the seller and the base price given in Table 8.1. Furthermore, the base prices in Table 8.1 will vary from crude to crude and escalate with price inflation over time. In 1980, at the time of the passage of the Windfall Profit Tax Act, the average base price of all nonmarginal old oil (Tier 1 oil) was about $12.85. Thus if it were anticipated that prices after decontrol would rise to the OPEC level of perhaps $40 per barrel, the federal government anticipated a bonanza. From a price of $40, the base price of $12.85 would be de-

TABLE 8.1 Federal Windfall Profit Tax: 1980 Rates and Base Prices

Tier Number	Type of Oil Production	Tax Rate	1980 Average Base Price
1	Old oil (discovered before 1979)	70%*	$12.85
2	Stripper well oil	60%*	15.15
3	New oil (discovered after 1978)	30%*	16.60
	(Also applies to heavy oil and to oil produced from tertiary recovery processes)		

*The tax rate is only 50% for old oil and 30% for stripper oil for the first 1,000 barrels per day of output by nonintegrated producers.

ducted, leaving taxable income of $27.15 per barrel. A 70 percent windfall revenue tax would thus yield $19.00 per barrel to the federal government. For Tier 2 oil (old oil from stripper wells), the tax rate is 60 percent and the average base price is $15.15, so at $40 per barrel the government tax take would be $14.91 [0.6 × ($40.00 − 15.15)]. For Tier 3 oil (new oil) the tax rate is only 30 percent and the average base price in 1980 was about $16.60, so at $40 per barrel the government tax take would be only $7.02. Thus the windfall profits tax acted to increase government tax revenues and to reduce consumer surplus.

Exemptions from the windfall profit tax were accorded to oil owned by state and local governments, Indian tribes, and certain charities, as well as new oil in most of Alaska. The original legislation also provided that once cumulative revenues reached $227.3 billion, the tax would be phased out over a period of 33 months, but complete phase-out could not arrive before January 1, 1988 or after January 1, 1991.

Hopes in Washington were high that a tremendous revenue bonanza would flow from the windfall profit tax, but actual experience has not satisfied such sanguine expectations. Over $16 billion was collected in 1981 from major integrated oil companies, but OPEC prices weakened in 1982 and the price cut to $29 in March 1983 disappointed the expectations of fiscal authorities that OPEC prices would continue to rise year by year. Instead of prices in the $50 range during the early 1980s, the prospect was for prices below $30 per barrel. In addition, the relatively low tax rates on heavy and tertiary oil stimulated considerable production increases in the Tier 3 categories, which reduced the average per barrel windfall profits tax revenues.

Economic criticism of the windfall profit tax centers on several points. In the first place, the tax is an excise tax, not a true profits tax, and thus tends to discourage domestic exploration and encourages the premature abandonment of marginal oil wells. For example, there are drilling prospects that are economic at $30 per barrel, but which become unattractive after subtracting $10 per barrel for windfall profits.

Additionally, on stripper wells, production declines slowly and producers must balance marginal costs with marginal revenues to compute the economic limit—the level of oil production below which operating costs exceed revenues. The windfall profits tax raises the minimum production rate necessary to continue production and forces earlier abandonment of existing oil reservoirs. In the second place, the bulk of the tax revenues should probably be devoted to the development of new domestic sources of energy. Original plans at one time called for the financing of the Synthetic Fuels Corporation to the extent of over $80 billion from windfall profit tax revenues—an entirely appropriate idea, provided that financing could be limited to sufficiently promising projects. But, as subsequently noted in Chapter 9, the Synthetic Fuels Corporation had done very little by the mid-1980s, partly due to a negative attitude on the part of the Reagan administration toward public financing of research and development of new fuels.

It would be instructive to devise a diagram similar to that of Figure 8.1 to show the impact of the windfall profits tax on economic welfare, as contrasted with a competitive market and with price controls and entitlements. Unfortunately, the impact of the tax on different categories of oil is too complex to permit simple diagrammatical representation. To a first approximation it would be feasible to show the impact of the tax on each type of regulated oil, but the information required to construct the relevant supply schedules is lacking. The best compromise might be to compare the impact of price controls in early 1974 with a hypothetical windfall profit tax imposed in 1974 at 1974 OPEC prices and at the tax rates adopted in 1980, but with a cost basis appropriate to 1974 costs. Figure 8.2 shows the results of such an exercise.

Welfare Effects of the Windfall Profit Tax

It is assumed that all oil supplied in 1974 is initially classified as Tier 1, old oil, so the domestic supply function is the supply function for old oil. It is assumed that the base price allowed in 1974 would have been the actual average price of old oil under price controls in 1974, or $7.18 per barrel. Since the OPEC price is $12.52, a tax of 70 percent of the difference between $12.52 and $7.18 is a tax of $3.74 per barrel, which it is assumed will be paid by all domestic oil producers. Hence the demand curve for oil, as seen by domestic producers, is reduced by the amount of the unit windfall tax of $3.74, and thus declines to $8.78. At this price, domestic output amounts to Q_s'', producer surplus is increased by area $MEFN$, and government tax revenues by area $AMNL$. This outcome represents a considerable welfare gain over price controls set at $7.18 with an output of Q_s'. Economic welfare is in-

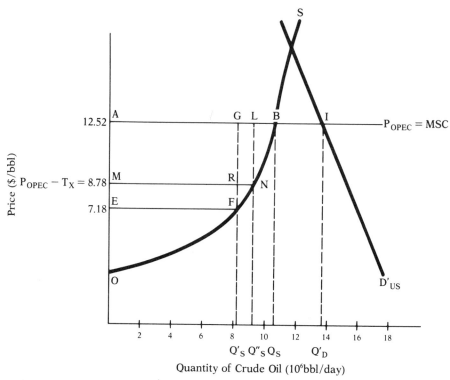

FIGURE 8.2 The estimated impact of a windfall profit tax on the U.S. crude oil market in early 1974.

creased by the value of area *GFNL*, or by about $5.7 million per day. Area *GFNL* shows, for an increase in domestic production of $Q''_s - Q'_s$, that incremental social benefits exceed total social costs. Relative to the price control situation, consumers lose while producers and the federal government gain. Consumer surplus is reduced by area *AEFG*, a total of $45.4 million per day. At the same time, producer surplus is increased by area *MEFN* for $14.8 million per day and tax revenues increase by area *AMNL* for another $36.3 million per day. Thus the gain in economic welfare is the previously identified area *GFNL*, for $5.7 million per day.

Still, the windfall profit tax is inferior in welfare terms to a situation in which there are no taxes or price controls. Moving to a competitive equilibrium for domestic production at point B, tax receipts would fall by area *AMNL* ($36.3 million per day) while producer surplus would rise by area *AMNB*, or $38.3 million per day. Thus the loss in economic welfare is given by area *LNB* ($2 million per day) which represents reduction in producer surplus not compensated for by an increase in federal tax receipts. Hence, given the situation in early 1974, the welfare loss under price regulation was $7.7 million while that under a comparable windfall profit tax would be only $2.0 million. In later 1974, with a decline in demand and the adoption of entitlements, the welfare loss rose to $10.3 million, while with a windfall profit tax domestic and imported oil would sell at the same price, avoiding any opportunity of subsidizing oil imports. Thus the welfare loss would remain at $2.0 million per day.

Even so, it must be repeated that the windfall profit tax is still inferior to a no-tax situation, or to a perfectly designed tax on true producer profits, each of which would increase domestic output to point *B* in Figure 8.2, and eliminate welfare losses entirely. Although the windfall profit tax statute calls for it to phase out by 1993, most students of the political process doubt this. In the meantime, we are left with a tax that discourages domestic exploration and production, implicitly sending the signal that domestic oil production is inferior to imported oil.

1. Given the shares of domestic and imported oil, show that every $1 increase in OPEC's crude price increases the average price of crude to the consumer by roughly $.35 per barrel under entitlements. Can you show that this reduces the U.S. demand elasticity for imported crude by roughly .35?
2. Explain why area *CEFK* in Figure 8.1, the amount paid for entitlements by refiners of domestic crude, will just equal area *GKHI*, the receipts of refiners processing imported oil.

PRICE CONTROLS ON NATURAL GAS

A Brief Overview

Regulation of oil and natural gas prices evolved through quite different channels. The Natural Gas Act of 1938 established the Federal Power Commission (FPC) and empowered it to regulate the transportation fee a gas pipeline could charge for interstate deliveries. Initially, it was presumed that the Natural Gas Act regulated only the interstate pipelines. Since long-run average costs decline as pipeline diameters increase, the pipeline industry was obviously characterized by natural monopoly, and was therefore an appropriate target for traditional public utility regulation. In 1954, the Supreme Court *(Phillips vs. Wisconsin)* interpreted some ambiguous language in the 1938 statute to mean that the FPC's responsibility to regulate price extended back to the wellhead and thus the price charged by gas producers (Phillips). Following a subsequent Supreme Court decision, in 1959 the

FPC instituted an area-wide pricing scheme. The area-wide pricing scheme at first created two vintages of gas. "New" gas supplies could be sold at the level of the highest price at which a sale in the area has been previously certified. "Old" gas supplies received the average price for all sales in the areas.[1] Subsequently, the commission found it necessary to create additional vintages of new gas supplies, each selling at a still higher price.

The umbrella of FPC price regulation did not extend to intrastate gas sales, where separate markets flourished free of regulation. During the 1960s, intrastate gas buyers, which were not subject to interstate price regulation, were able to purchase all their requirements by offering a slight premium over the FPC price for the latest vintage of interstate gas. With intrastate buyers getting first choice, interstate markets absorbed the residual or left-over gas. Over the 1960s, interstate buyers purchased the marginal supplies; therefore, intrastate prices were only slightly above the price set by the FPC in the interstate market. But, beginning in the early 1970s, the rapidly growing intrastate demand for gas in the southwestern states had become more than sufficient to absorb the available supply of newly discovered gas at a price considerably higher than that set by the FPC. With the FPC's interstate price well below the intrastate price, consumers outside the Southwest were effectively cut off from new gas supplies and had to face increasing shortages as demand increased. In 1978, compromise legislation both extended price controls to intrastate gas, and at the same time set up a timetable for a phased decontrol of most gas prices.

The Early Period: 1938–1960

In view of the discussion of oil price regulation, one might think it difficult to find a market that has been more thoroughly distorted by regulation than the crude oil market, but such is not the case. The natural gas market has been even more systematically deformed, disfigured, and wrenched out of shape as a result of a longer period of even more perverse price controls than ever existed for crude oil.

Until the 1930s, natural gas was in excess supply relative to market demand, since the technology necessary for building long-distance gas pipelines had not yet been developed. Most of the large quantities of associated gas produced with crude oil was simply flared at the wellhead. With gas as a joint product produced in fixed proportions with oil production, its marginal production cost could be regarded as zero, and gas was marketed on a byproduct basis for whatever price it would bring. Relatively little gas was reinjected to maintain reservoir pressures in the early days, and the small volumes that were sold were generally marketed to nearby industrial plants. Prices were typically in the neighborhood of one cent per thousand cubic feet—the Btu equivalent of 5 cents per barrel of oil!

Following World War II, gas pipeline technology advanced, opening up the huge Northeastern market for natural gas produced in the Southwest. But excess supply still prevailed, and the first pipelines were in a position to dictate their own terms: low prices, long-term contracts (20 years was standard), and usually no provisions for price escalation even over as long a time period as two decades.

Demand continued to grow phenomenally as new pipelines were completed and producers began reinjecting gas back into producing formations in order to increase total oil recovery. The market price of gas increased briskly as demand rose and the supply surplus disappeared. Petroleum exploration activities became more gas oriented. During the middle and later 1950s the old gas supply contracts came up for renewal after 20 years, and something like a ten-fold price increase was registered, from an original 1.5 cents to about 15 cents. Pipelines and consumers were unduly upset, and they naturally preferred arrangements that would continue indefinitely the low prices established in past years. Lawyers for the State of Wisconsin successfully argued that some ambiguous wording in the Natural Gas Act of 1938 required that the Federal Power Commission (FPC) regulate the wellhead price of natural gas. Until this time, the FPC had assumed that the intent of the language was to regulate only the gas pipelines, which, like other utilities with aspects of natural monopoly, had become subject to public utility regulation. But in 1954 in *Phillips vs. Wisconsin*, the court ruled that the FPC must regulate and approve the prices charged by natural gas producers in the fields.

Once the FPC began to implement the court's mandate, the natural gas industry was transformed from a growing and dynamic market into a cemetary plot consisting of three graves, in which, side by side, the remains of three separate sub-markets were to be mummified: the gas production business, gas pipelines, and gas utilities. It is understandable that gas pipelines and gas utilities would be subject to public utility regulations. Gas pipelines were originally regulated by the Natural Gas Act of 1938 as natural monopolies, due to their decreasing cost characteristics. Between any two points, one large pipeline would have much lower costs than ten smaller pipelines. Gas utilities were a "natural monopoly" of a somewhat different type than pipelines. Although gas distribution costs do not necessarily decline steadily as gas consumption increases, it is quite true that gas distribution costs will be higher and increase more rapidly as the number of gas utility companies increases, due to the duplication of fixed investment and its relative underutilization. Gas utility price regulation aimed at preventing the exploitation of consumers through the setting of monopoly rates.

But the occupant of the third grave had no natural monopoly characteristics, and such regulation would not work for field production of gas. Cost-based price regulation was infeasible since gas producers had very different cost structures depending on their past fortunes in oil and gas exploration. Paradoxically, rewarding a high-cost seller with higher prices would simply price him out of the market relative to lower-cost competitors. Conflicts were endless, and during the period 1954–1960 over 2000 unresolved rate case proceedings piled up at the FPC.

Area Rate Regulation: 1960–1978

With the case-by-case approach rendered hopeless by economic facts in the market, the FPC after 1960 began a series of attempts to regulate gas prices on an "Area Rate" basis, whereby the U.S. was divided into a small number of gas producing areas, and the goal was to set a separate rate for each area at a level that would provide the average producer with a reasonable rate of return on his formula-based average costs. In practice, this process took several years, during which time costs were steadily increasing. A proceeding begun in 1961 might be completed by 1964, but would only cover a certain "vintage" of gas production. New proceedings then might begin in 1964, covering a later vintage of gas discovered and developed at higher costs. The prices that were eventually allowed tended to be below the true long-run marginal cost, so over time gas exploration efforts declined and new supplies fell at the same time that demand for the underpriced commodity was increasing.

There was, however, one safety valve: the intrastate market. Until 1978, only interstate prices were controlled because the Natural Gas Act of 1938 regulated only interstate gas sales. Before 1978, new gas reserves were increasingly committed to the intrastate market, where competitive prices still prevailed. But as mentioned earlier, these competitive intrastate prices were not necessarily higher than those prevailing under regulation, particularly in the early years. In the 1960s, most of the demand was in the interstate market, while supplies made available to the interstate market steadily increased. For a number of years intrastate prices were only marginally higher than interstate prices, but intrastate markets were still the preferred outlets for new gas since price escalation clauses were permissible in the intrastate market, and sources of additional flexibility existed.

Intrastate prices rose significantly above interstate prices after 1971, and new supplies to the interstate market dried up. Energy-intensive industries increasingly relocated in the states where gas was available, even at a higher price. To regulators, the "solution" was obvious: regulate the intrastate market, seeing that gas is shared equitably between the two groups of consumers.

This conflict was one of the major strands leading up to the passage of the Natural Gas Policy Act of 1978. Political pressures for gas decontrol had been mounting. Interstate consumers were now willing to pay higher prices just to get some new gas. Many in the government wanted more gas production to bolster the domestic energy sector and reduce oil imports. Producers were bitter over the extent of gas underpricing, particularly for some old gas which received less than 30 cents per mcf while new gas was selling for seven times as much. Economists were eager for the long-overdue decontrol, and differed chiefly in their preferences either for immediate decontrol or for a phased-in deregulation to lessen the shock, which might otherwise have to be absorbed by a sluggish economy.

The act that emerged from lengthy deliberations did provide for a phased-in price decontrol of many categories of gas, but in general compounded pre-existing confusion by multiplying the number of pricing categories. No less than 27 separate primary price categories were now provided for a homogeneous commodity. While certain categories of new gas were to be decontrolled by January 1, 1985, old gas would never be released from regulation. Prices were to be allowed to rise by an inflation factor, and for some categories of new high-cost gas, found at depths below 12,000 feet, complete decontrol occurred immediately. To gain the support of eastern legislators, the intrastate gas market came under the price controls umbrella, assuring immediate supplies of gas to the Northeast.

The general expectation of the 1978 act seems to have been that new gas prices would rise to their true competitive wellhead values, while old gas would continue to be underpriced for the benefit of the consumer as long as it lasted. These expectations were not to be realized. Gas prices increased more rapidly than had been anticipated, largely because pipelines with large quantities of cheap old gas could bid above-market prices for new gas and pass the higher average cost of supplies along to utility companies. The utilities in turn could cover these charges by averaging in the cost of this new gas with other old gas supplies they might have from other pipeline contracts and presenting a higher gas bill to their consumers. Gas pipelines could do this because their profits depended upon maintaining a high percentage of pipeline capacity utilization, and not upon the margin between purchase cost and resale price, which was closely regulated. Natural gas prices also increased for other reasons. The Federal Energy Regulatory Commission (successor to the FPC in gas price control matters) favored gas price increases for reasons of economic efficiency, and took a number of steps to facilitate price hikes, especially for new gas. The most important categories of new gas were completely decontrolled by FERC action in 1979, and prices of old gas began to rise in ways that, although economically beneficial, have yet to be explained by the FERC. By mid-1982, for example, over 10 percent of all old gas was selling at prices above legal ceilings. Deep gas had skyrocketed to over $9.00 per mcf by 1980, contrasted with certain vintages of old gas that were selling for $.50 per mcf. Thus a combination of higher prices for both new and old gas increased natural gas prices quite significantly during the period 1978–84, and it is very interesting to investigate the reasons for these increases.

Much of the blame for the rapid increase in the price of new gas has been directed at gas pipeline companies, particularly those with large supplies of underpriced old gas, but in a broader context these pipelines acted as agents rather than principals. The more fundamental causes of pipeline imprudence are (1) the whole scheme of gas price regulation, which over a period of years systematically underpriced new as well as old gas and hence created continual excess demand for any gas available at regulated prices; (2) inefficient price regulation of utility companies, which should have been required to charge prices based on the marginal cost of gas supplies rather than the weighted average cost; (3) less than optimal regulation of pipeline companies, such that their incentives to operate efficiently were impaired; and (4) a legal tradition of very inflexible long-term contracts for the sale of gas to pipelines.

Let us return to our graveyard analogy. Regulation had by 1978 been extended to all phases of the natural gas market. Regulators were responsible for setting rates that provided a "reasonable" return to each of the three phases of the industry. Since gas was persistently underpriced in the market, whatever could be produced could readily be sold. Regulated companies often lead a rather sheltered life. They focus their skills on the manipulation of the regulators, and not on keeping abreast of the whole market at all times. Why bother to pinpoint total potential gas demand when you can sell all you can produce, or resell all you can buy? Since the early 1960s, many forces had combined to produce an increasing excess demand for gas, including environmental regulations that placed a premium on gas as a fuel because of its freedom from major air pollution problems. Pipelines in particular were convinced as of 1978–80 that the gas shortage would be perpetual, since they felt oil prices would continue to rise over time, and under the new regulations, gas prices would never quite catch up. Thus it followed that they should control as many gas reserves as they could: get the gas reserves under contract, regardless of price or contract terms.

After deregulation of high-cost new gas, supplies increased sharply in response to the very high prices offered by pipelines. A gas pipeline company with large reserves under contract at less than 50 cents per mcf could afford to contract for new reserves at $5.00 or more per mcf and still keep its weighted average of acquisition costs at or below the price that a utility company could pass on to its customers—at least, to its residential customers.

Not only did the price of new and deep gas increase sharply, but the gas producers insisted upon contract terms, other than price, that were very favorable to them: high deliverability rates, favorable "take-or-pay" provisions (under the terms of which pipelines were obligated to pay for specified volumes of gas each month, even though they did not take them), "most favored nation" clauses, which guaranteed that higher prices paid to anyone else in a field would automatically trigger an increase to all producers in that field, and similar provisions.

The pipeline companies' strategy was based on the assumption that gas consumption would never fall, since OPEC prices would always rise and gas prices would always lag behind oil prices. But gas consumption eventually fell. By the 1980s, high OPEC prices had induced energy conservation efforts everywhere. Initially oil consumption suffered before gas consumption declined. By late 1981 oil prices were slowly falling and gas prices were still rapidly increasing under the provisions of the 1978 gas act. It is apparent that some time in 1982 oil and gas prices converged and the gas market finally cleared. For the first time in roughly 20 years, excess demand for gas no longer existed. Furthermore, gas demand then declined somewhat as oil prices continued to fall. But FERC regulation prevented gas price decreases, and in fact guaranteed ceiling prices that included a monthly inflation escalation adjustment for all gas. Oil began to recapture some of the industrial market from gas. The domestic petrochemical industry's demand for gas fell as foreign competition, using low-cost Middle East natural gas, displaced much U.S. petrochemical output.

Within a surprisingly short period of time, gas prices came to be determined by competition and not by regulation. Under these circumstances, guaranteed price escalation under inflation adjustment clauses became a disadvantage, and the "take-or-pay" contracts signed in earlier years by pipeline companies became the casket in which pipelines were to be buried.

Analytics of "Rolled In" Pricing

Perhaps the following simplified example in Figure 8.3, describing the demand for natural gas by gas utilities, will illustrate the dilemma facing pipeline companies. Our hypothetical pipeline had long-term contracts to purchase 10 units of old natural gas at a price of $1 per mcf with a perfectly inelastic supply of old gas (S_{OG}). The obvious strategy is to sell only the 10 units to the gas utility for $3.40/mcf, collecting monopoly profits of $24. But rate of return regulation prevents the pipeline from such behavior. Regulation requires that gas be resold to gas utilities at cost. The pipeline's only source of profit is the

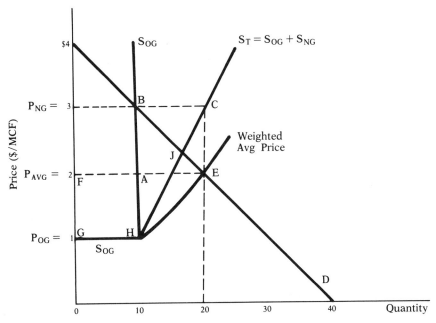

FIGURE 8.3 Hypothetical determination of natural gas market equilibrium, when a gas pipeline has contracts for 10 units of old gas at a price of $1.00 per mcf.

transportation charge based on the volume of gas transported to the gas utility.

Another obvious outcome is for the gas utility to purchase only the 10 units and resell the gas to residential and industrial customers for a huge profit. But again, this is impossible. Gas utilities must resell the gas to the public at its average cost. Since the gas utility's profits are tied to the total volume of gas provided to the public, there is again an incentive to acquire more than the 10 units of old gas.

The total supply (S_T) of gas to the market is made up of old gas supply (S_{OG}) plus new gas (S_{NG}), which is assumed to be deregulated and competitively supplied. According to Figure 8.3, the solution is to purchase 10 units of new gas at $3/mcf, which together with the 10 units of old gas at $1/mcf gives an average gas price (P_{AVG}) of $2/mcf. The combination of a $2/mcf average price and 20 units of gas is just sufficient to clear the market demand. Equilibrium is achieved at point E, since this is the intersection between the demand curve and the weighted average price of old and new gas. Note that at the equilibrium solution, the below-average price paid to old gas is used as a subsidy for new gas production. Area $AFGH$, the amount by which old gas is underpaid, just equals the area $ABCE$, the subsidy to new gas production. The regulatory framework utilizing average cost pricing for gas requires that these two areas must always be equal. This pricing system is called "rolled in" pricing, as the price of new supplies is simply rolled into the cost base together with old gas prices.

From an economic perspective, "rolled in" pricing is obviously wasteful. The welfare loss is *JEC* since the socially optimal production level is where S_T intersects D, but that is not the point of the story. As long as demand was shifting to the right, implying excess demand at the average price P_{AVG}, the pipelines were justified in paying higher and higher prices for new gas. Furthermore, with growing demand, granting "take or pay" provisions to new gas producers on the new high-cost gas was seemingly costless, since there would be no reason not to purchase this gas.

In 1982, suddenly the world changed: there was no excess demand, and the demand for gas shifted inward as oil prices fell, presenting pipelines with an impossible dilemma. It was not possible to renegotiate the price of new gas and at the same time reduce purchases. Both price and delivery quantities of new gas had been set in concrete with fixed prices and the "take or pay" provision.

What did the pipelines do? Seemingly, the only option was to fight. If pipelines had to pay for gas they could not sell, it was clearly less expensive to them to pay for unpurchased cheap gas than for unpurchased expensive gas. So in the early 1980s, the natural gas market witnessed the paradox of low-cost reserves being shut-in or underproduced, while high-cost new gas was being produced as close to capacity as demand would permit. Such a policy maximizes total supply cost rather than minimizes it! Nevertheless, it was perfectly logical for pipelines to behave this way under existing legal, regulatory, and market constraints.

This was no solution, however, because as old gas was shut-in, the average price of gas to the consumer rose, causing additional reductions in natural gas consumption. As gas consumption fell further, pipelines were finally forced to cut purchases of high-cost new gas, in violation of contract terms, and lawsuits rapidly multiplied. If contracts on new gas were enforced, many pipelines faced bankruptcy. Bills were introduced in Congress to abrogate the terms of gas contracts already in existence, a rather novel proposal in the context of orthodox contract law. As the January 1, 1985 deadline for gas price deregulation approached, demand was falling, prices to consumers were rising, gas producers were suffering from a burden of shut-in production, many pipelines were grasping at the straws of legal doctrines such as *force majeure* to save them from ruin, and the FERC was having difficulties explaining how old gas prices could have risen so rapidly under continued price regulation.

The fundamental cause of all these market dislocations was the tradition of underpricing gas through regulation. As long as gas was underpriced, excess demand existed and it was obviously more important for the gas industry to forecast FERC policy than to forecast gas demand. Once the all-embracing nature of the regulatory context is understood, the self-confessed "imprudence" and "stupidity" of the pipelines becomes more comprehensible. Through 1980, gas producers, pipelines, and utility companies were guaranteed fixed rates of return on all the business volumes they could generate, and if the FERC could be induced to raise prices somewhat, the market demand was there because of the continuing fact of excess demand at an artificially low price. Producer profits could be increased without cutting rates earned by pipelines and utilities, and so on. But once the gas market cleared, no such price slack existed, and higher earnings in one phase of the gas market could only be achieved at the expense of lower earnings elsewhere.

Gas industry policy has been in need of complete redirection for decades, and the crisis of the mid-1980s presents opportunities for basic changes. It is to be hoped that these changes will embody major reforms rather than a new set of blunders. What are the alternatives? Paradoxically, the partial gas price decontrol of 1985 may help to lower prices, not to raise them, through the ending of continuous inflationary adjustments and certain other upward movements in some categories of price-regulated gas.

It is straightforward to prescribe where policy should ultimately take us. It is less obvious how to get there. From Figure 8.3, it should be clear that "rolled in" pricing coupled with differential pricing of new and old gas creates gross market distortions. Given "rolled in" pricing, policy should aim for a single price of gas, irrespective of when it was found or how difficult it was to find. Does this mean immediate decontrol of all gas vintages still held under controls? In the event of complete decontrol, gas producers individually would be motivated to exploit all the terms in existing contracts to maximize price hikes, particularly those relating to receiving prices equal to the highest price received by any producer in a given field. If high-cost new gas production exists with contract prices well above competitive levels—and such production is rather widespread, as shown in previous examples—then gas producers will simply price themselves out of the market. Not only would utility companies be unlikely to recognize such high prices, when passed on to them by the pipelines, as eligible for inclusion in the rate base, but utility demand itself would dwindle away as final user demand proved inadequate to sustain consumption levels at much higher prices. Industrial users would switch first, leaving residential users with a higher fixed cost allocation (for both pipeline and utility investment) to be covered in their rates. This in turn would provoke revolt by residential users, with the probable passage of laws in some states that would regulate gas utilities more harshly. There would be demands everywhere for fresh legislation to "solve" the new gas price problems.

Thus a worst-case scenario can readily be devised that would result in disaster. On the other hand, gas producers as a group may see reasons to act more temperately. Since the gas pipelines are their only customers, it would not seem optimal to take steps that would destroy them. Voluntary renegotiations, contract by contract, might lead to more efficient resource allocation than the passage of extremely detailed national laws changing the terms of individual gas contracts. A major problem with voluntary renegotiations is that producers may be less willing to negotiate than pipelines. Existing contracts seem to give them an advantage in the event of decontrol; the market realities of excess supply at existing prices mean that they are likely to lose revenues at the present time, to the extent that prices are exposed to short-run competitive forces. Most producers believe that currently depressed prices will disappear in the long run as the present gas surplus is worked through, so they feel that delay will work in their interest. Under such circumstances negotiations may not begin readily or proceed rapidly.

The foregoing discussion of the disastrous results of oil and gas price regulation should not necessarily be construed as implying that price regulation is necessarily a mistake in any and every market context. We turn now to an examination of the arguments for and against price regulation, beginning with an assessment of the arguments that favor regulation.

1. Can you explain how price controls on natural gas increased the demand for crude oil, and imported crude in particular?

2. Show that the welfare loss in Figure 8.3 of area *JEC* could be avoided by allowing all natural gas to sell at a similar price, thus equating the "rolled in" price and the price for marginal supplies.

3. Another alternative is to retain differential pricing for gas but abandon "rolled in" pricing. One possible approach would be to set prices at marginal costs for new gas supplies and allow savings on inframarginal gas to be passed along to customers via a reduction in the fixed overhead charge. Can you sketch out some of the details of such a plan? Do you think it should be administratively practical?

THE AFFIRMATIVE RATIONALE
FOR PRICE CONTROLS

Preventing Macroeconomic
Dislocations

In 1973, U.S. price controls on domestic oil were motivated by the awareness that domestic crude oil prices would rise sharply as these were bid up in competition with imported sources. In turn, the rising price of domestic oil would raise the price of energy generally, since the short-run supply schedules for other fuels tended to be quite inelastic. During 1973, inflation fires had been damped as the U.S. consumer price index increased by only 2.5 percent. By 1974 the inflation rate had jumped to 7.1 percent, and in 1975 reached 11.4 percent per year. During 1974 and 1975, the price of energy rose sharply despite the effects of price controls. By 1975, the average price of oil (including imports) had reached $10.38 per barrel. This was a substantial increase over the 1973 average of $3.94 per barrel. The average price of electricity paid by residential users increased from 2.38 cents per kilowatt-hour in 1973 to 3.2 cents per kwh in 1975. The average cost of coal increased from 41.9 cents per million Btu in 1973 to 86.4 per million Btu in 1975.

The subsequent story is quite predictable: The rising costs of living in turn led workers to escalate wage demands in order to maintain the same real standard of living. The rising wages force all prices upward, prompting government policies to slow the economy in an attempt to control inflation. By 1975 unemployment averaged 8.5 percent, giving the United States the worst of both worlds—high inflation and high unemployment. Since many other factors were also at work during this period, it would be incorrect to assign all of the blame to the OPEC oil price increase. Econometric studies of the U.S. economy have shown that about 28 percent of the increase in inflation over this period can be ascribed to rising energy prices.[4] Thus a case for price controls can be made to avoid the macroeconomic dislocations coming from rapidly rising energy prices.

Protecting Consumers

While energy does not constitute as high a fraction of consumer expenditure as housing or food, it is nevertheless significant, and energy price increases can be expected to lower society's real standard of living. In 1972, U.S. consumers, either directly through the energy purchased or indirectly through the energy contained in products purchased, spent $446 per capita.[5] Based on a per capita personal disposable income of $3836, energy expenditures accounted for 11.6 percent of the consumer budget. Certainly with the price increases since 1972, this fraction is considerably higher today. To the extent that energy price increases can be avoided, consumers maintain the consumer surplus they would otherwise lose with the price increase. As noted earlier, the system of crude oil price controls in effect during 1971–80 permitted a large-scale transfer of income from producers to consumers. Recall that Figure 8.1 illustrates the situation for price controls on crude oil in the United States using 1974 data. The horizontal line labeled P_{OPEC} indicates that at $12.52 per barrel, the United States could purchase whatever quantity of imports it desires. In the absence of price controls and entitlements, domestic oil would be bid up to parity with OPEC oil, domestic suppliers would supply that quantity Q_s, and imports of $Q_d - Q_s$ would meet unfilled demand. Domestic oil producers would earn producers' surplus of area OAB.

The effect of price controls with entitlements is to transfer a large portion of that producer surplus to consumers in the form of consumer surplus. By placing price controls of $P_{control}$ on domestic oil at $7.18 per barrel, regulators can average down the price of oil to $9.07 per barrel by mixing the imported oil at P_{OPEC} ($12.52) with domestic oil at $P_{control}$ ($7.18) through the entitlements program.

The gain in consumer surplus resulting from price controls with entitlements is area $ACHJ$, which amounted to $45.4 million per day or $16.6 billion annually, which is about $76 for every American.

As indicated previously, price controls on natural gas did not result in such simple redistributions from producers to consumers. Unlike oil, there were no appreciable quantities of imported gas. Furthermore, regulators did not allow the market to clear. Consumers could not buy all the natural gas they desired at some market price. The demand curve for natural gas was in fact artificially shifted back to distinguish two classes of consumers: Those rationed customers excluded from the market and those unrationed customers permitted to continue purchasing gas. Figure 8.4 describes these two demand

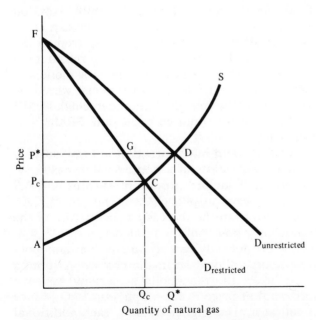

FIGURE 8.4 Price controls in the natural gas market.

schedules. $D_{unrestricted}$ shows what demand would materialize in the absence of any rationing. $D_{restricted}$ shows the demand schedule for that group of consumers able to purchase gas at the controlled price. In effect, regulators set the price that results in a forthcoming supply of Q_c. Next, they define the group of consumers eligible to purchase the gas such that the restricted demand schedule just intersects at that quantity.

As anticipated, price controls lead to a loss in producers' surplus of P^*P_cCD. Those consumers lucky enough not to be excluded are able to buy gas at P_c instead of P^*. They enjoy a gain in consumer surplus of P^*P_cCG. Thus, as in the case of crude oil, producers are subsidizing consumers. However, this is not the complete story. Those consumers excluded from purchasing gas at P_c who would have been willing to pay P^* suffer a loss in consumer surplus of area FGD. In practice, the excluded consumers consist of new homeowners wishing to use natural gas and industrial users. Since the former is a reasonably small group and the latter are nonvoting consumers, there is a tendency to overlook this effect, yet these consumers suffer real welfare losses.

Avoiding Monopoly Profits and Improving Resource Allocation

For the sake of argument let us assume, as many citizens do, that the domestic oil and gas industry is a monopoly. Even though there are numerous firms in the industry, we saw in Chapter 4 that if firms shared markets equally and faced similar costs, a monopoly solution could occur. Beginning with the monopoly assumption, we can show that price controls enable monopoly profits to be transferred to the consumer and output to be expanded, thereby improving resource allocation. Figure 8.5 assumes the natural gas industry is a monopoly and investigates the effect of price controls. The monopolist would select that output level Q_m where the marginal revenue schedule MR intersects the industry's long-run marginal cost schedule LRMC. The resulting monopoly price is P_m.

Even a competitive industry would have earned producers' surplus owing to the user costs and rising costs of a nonrenewable resource, but the monopolist foregoes the standard producers' surplus of OP_cB to gain the higher level of producers' surplus OP_mAC. The area P_cP_mAE of producers' surplus arises not from the increasing cost nature of the industry, but from the monopoly power of the producers.

Parodoxically, price controls not only can eliminate this monopoly profit, but can improve resource allocation in the process. Assuming the regulated price is set at P_c, the monopolist's marginal revenue curve now becomes horizontal at price P_c for outputs up to Q_c. Since the monopolist cannot sell at a price higher than P_c, each additional unit commands the same price and marginal revenue for outputs up

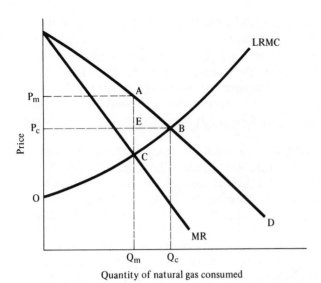

FIGURE 8.5 Effect of price controls on a monopoly.

to Q_c. The profit-maximizing monopolist facing price controls sets marginal revenue (P_c) equal to marginal costs, leading to output Q_c. Under price controls, the monopolist actually increases output, leading to greater supply and elimination of the distortion caused by monopoly! Furthermore, the monopoly profit P_cP_mAE is put into the hands of consumers in the form of a gain in consumer surplus of P_cP_mAB.

THE EVIDENCE TO SUPPORT OR REJECT THESE RATIONALES

The Macroeconomic Effects of Higher Energy Prices

It is obvious that a sudden large increase in energy prices can have deleterious macroeconomic effects. In situations such as the Arab oil embargo of 1973, policy makers assumed they were facing a temporary price increase and felt justified in attempting to minimize the macroeconomic dislocations through the use of price controls. In effect, the short-term macroeconomic gains of avoiding an inflationary push may well offset the microeconomic welfare losses from nonprice rationing mechanisms, particularly if the duration of the price controls is only a few weeks or months.

The problem is that policy makers can seldom distinguish between temporary price changes and permanent price changes, but permanent price controls can inflict serious distortions as we have seen earlier. Furthermore, price controls actually impede the forces that would otherwise cause the price increase to be temporary. For example, price controls with entitlements actually increased the demand for OPEC crude oil, making it less likely that price would fall compared to the nonprice control policy.

The experience of the 1970s suggests that policy makers are unlikely to be able to make such distinctions. Remember that temporary oil price controls imposed in 1971 lasted until 1981, and even then required the implementation of a Windfall Profit Tax that may expire in 1993.

Protecting the Consumer

There is little doubt that price controls generally lead to a subsidization of consumers by producers. The relevant question though is whether this subsidization is socially desirable. Let us return to Figure 8.1 and recompute the efficiency effects of this subsidization. The price controls in effect in 1974 definitely distorted resource allocation by lowering the price of oil in the United States below its marginal social cost. Note that while the social costs to OPEC of a barrel of oil may be only a few dollars, for U.S. welfare calculations, the relevant social cost is P_{OPEC}, as this measures OPEC's command over real U.S. resources. Note that since P_{AVG} is less than P_{OPEC}, one effect of U.S. price controls in 1974 was to artificially stimulate consumption from Q_d to Q_d'. The resulting welfare loss is the triangle *JIH*.

There is an additional welfare loss on the supply side of the market. Figure 8.1 shows that even with price controls, producers' surplus or profits have risen sharply over 1973 price levels. If firms are already earning some windfall profits, why should one believe that still greater profits through price decontrol would increase production from Q_s to Q_s'? The answer lies in the fact that profits are high on low-cost oil found many years ago. However, to create the investment in new high-cost exploration or tertiary recovery on oil fields, a price increase to P_{OPEC} is necessary to elicit the additional production $Q_s - Q_s'$. Since the United States is importing this additional oil at a real cost of P_{OPEC} and domestic suppliers could produce the additional amount $Q_s - Q_s'$ at a lower marginal social cost, a second source of welfare loss is evident. Focusing on the output interval $Q_s - Q_s'$, we see that the difference in marginal social costs between imported and domestic oil is the triangle *GBF*. Thus the welfare loss from price control is the sum of the two triangles *JIH* and *FGB*. From the previous welfare calculations, area *FGB* was estimated to be $7.7 million per day and area *JIH* was estimated at $2.5 million per day. Together the two areas imply a welfare loss of $3.8 billion annually.

In sum, the consumer protection argument in support of price controls results in a misallocation of resources and significant welfare losses. The logic in support of artificially low petroleum prices could equally apply to food, housing, or automobiles. For example, suppose government authorities decided to subsidize interest rates to homeowners by borrowing money at 10 percent and loaning it to homeowners for 2 percent. Homeowners would benefit from the reduced mortgage payments, but taxes would have to increase to pay for the mortgage subsidy, reflecting the truism that "there ain't no such thing as a free lunch."

The only difference between the mortgage example and petroleum price controls situations is that in the latter it is the oil companies, rather than the government, that bear the cost of the subsidy. But do the oil companies ultimately bear the cost of the subsidy? The foregone producers' surplus would be taxed by the U.S. Treasury at a rate of 46 percent. In addition, the producers' surplus from new federal offshore leasing would tend to be captured by the government in the form of higher lease bonuses or royalties paid by the oil companies. The remainder would accrue to the stockholders either in the form of retained earnings to support new exploration or as dividends paid to stockholders. Increased dividend payments would be subject to personal income taxes, and the increased value of stock shares owing to successful exploration would be subject to personal income taxes at the time the stock is sold. Thus the seeming free lunch provided by the oil companies no longer seems so free!

Nevertheless, stockholders in oil companies and the U.S. Treasury are not identical with the average consumer, and crude oil price decontrol after 1980 did involve substantial income transfers. Prior to decontrol, reluctance to accept the impact of such income transfers occasioned substantial and continuous welfare losses through distortions of resource allocation in the U.S. oil market. But at no time was the issue simply one *either* of distorting resource allocation *or* of permitting substantial income redistribution. Rather, turning to the equity versus efficiency discussion in Chapter 2, these two issues can clearly be separated by selecting price policies to promote economic efficiency and at the same time using tax policies to modify income redistribution effects. A cut in personal income taxes, made possible through higher tax revenues from increased oil company profits, would have been one plausible solution. The actual solution — price decontrol with a substantial windfall profit tax—was merely one of many possible alternatives, and inferior to most of them.

1. Suppose that a tax equal to the difference between foreign and domestically controlled crude prices had been imposed in 1974. Can you show that the welfare loss would be limited to area *FGB*? Were efforts to distinguish old and new oil helpful in reducing the welfare loss?

2. Recall the assertion that price controls on perfectly inelastically supplied products have no effects. Many would argue that since the supply of previously discovered reserves is inelastic with respect to current prices, there are no welfare losses from price controls. Is this true? Consider how producer expectations regarding the conditions under which today's newly discovered reserves may be developed and produced in the future have been influenced (and perhaps undermined) by experience during the period of price controls.

3. Utilizing the welfare loss formulas, can you show that implicit in the calculation of a welfare loss for area *FGB* of $7.7 million per day was an elasticity of supply estimate of 0.44? Also, can you show that if area *JIH* equals $2.6 million per day, the implied price elasticity of demand is 0.3?

The Monopoly Profits Argument

The earlier discussion showed that if the oil industry acts as a monopoly, then price controls can redistribute the monopoly profits back to consumers and at the same time improve resource allocation by increasing output. In Figure 8.5, the welfare gain resulting from price controls is triangle *ABC*. If the monopoly assumption is correct, there is a legitimate case to be made for price controls or some other policy to reduce prices and increase output.[6]

The fact that the monopoly assumption is critical to the whole justification for price controls is seen by comparing the consumer protection argument with the monopoly profits argument. The consumer protection argument was not based on monopoly power. Rather, in Figures 8.1 and 8.4 the industry was assumed to be competitive. Under competitive assumptions, price controls lead to lower domestic outputs and significant welfare losses. On the other hand, when one assumes a monopolistic rather than competitive market structure, we saw in Figure 8.5 that price controls led to a welfare gain and increased output.

In sum, the only economic justification for long-run price controls rests on the assumption that the industry is characterized by monopoly behavior. Stated differently, the critical policy question is whether the oil industry approximates the competitive behavior posited in Figures 8.1 through 8.4 or the monopoly behavior in Figure 8.5. Let us now investigate the validity of this assumption.

THE DOMESTIC PETROLEUM INDUSTRY: BASICALLY COMPETITIVE?

The Industrial Organization Framework of Analysis

In order to assess the competitive nature of the petroleum industry, we shall adopt the framework of analysis employed extensively in the industrial organization literature to examine such questions.[7] This approach calls for a detailed look at the structure, conduct, and economic performance of the firms in the market. Under market structure we consider such variables as entry conditions and the number of producers, because monopoly and competition are quite different in these respects. After having defined the basic structural conditions within which firms operate, one must examine the conduct of firms vis-à-vis one another. Are there certain industry practices or institutional arrangements that tend to be exclusionary and anticompetitive? Finally, one must also look at the industry's economic performance. Economic theory would suggest that monopoly will manifest itself through excess profits. Therefore, one test of economic performance is whether the industry earns monopoly rents. A second test involves the industry's research and development (R&D) performance, and how it might change if industry structure were altered. It is well established that the diffusion of new technology occurs at a faster rate in a competitive market structure. Even though large firms are typically necessary to incur the costs of innovation, there is generally little support for the proposition that the largest firm is the most technologically progressive. Therefore, R&D performance is likely to be the highest in a market characterized by numerous firms of a size large enough to carry on vigorous R&D programs.[8]

Before embarking on an analysis of structure, conduct, and performance, we must pause to ask: "In what market?" There is a tendency to be imprecise in this definition, with the end result being a faulty analysis. The relevant market must be defined in terms of both the product and the geographic market. For purposes of examining the price controls issue, we shall define the relevant products as crude oil and natural gas, which are frequently jointly produced. Excluded, then, are finished petroleum products such as gasoline, heating oil, and so on. Since crude oil is sold in market transactions to refiners, it is not necessary to examine market conditions in the refining and retailing of petroleum products, even though most large oil companies perform these activities. Natural gas is sold directly to the pipeline companies. Critics of the industry, such as Allvine, have noted that competition in gasoline marketing among major oil companies is typically restricted to nonprice methods such as advertising, service station location, service, and so on, resulting in considerable economic waste.[9] The analysis here focuses only on crude oil and natural gas production, since it is at this level that the standard competitive supply response is relevant for the price controls question. In the following chapter, we consider whether an oil company should be allowed to perform these various activities, but this question is not critical to the analysis here.

There remains the geographic definition of the market. The critical question posed by Figures 8.1 and 8.4 versus Figure 8.5 involves the existence of competition in domestic markets. Since there are no appreciable imports of natural gas because of its high transportation costs, domestic conditions clearly set price and output. In contrast, in the market for crude oil, OPEC effectively sets the price, but the question is whether domestic oil companies are coconspirators or independently minded competitive fringe producers. In the monopoly case, domestic price controls will raise production, as in Figure 8.5, while under competition, price controls will lower production, as in Figure 8.1.

The domestic oil and gas market will be analyzed at a national level. The rationale is that crude oil produced in the Southwest is sold to refiners in the Midwest and Northeast. Similarly, there is an extensive grid of natural gas pipelines throughout most of the United States, allowing natural gas to be sold in a virtual national market. Thus both crude oil and natural gas produced in different regions are likely to compete with similar fuels produced in other regions, so that appreciable price differentials, reflecting more than transportation costs, cannot persist for extended periods.

Structural Evidence

To many experts in the field of industrial organization, market structure is more important than conduct or economic performance because if structural conditions preclude a competitive market situation, the results on conduct and economic performance are foregone conclusions. Tests of market structure frequently center on the entry conditions and the number and relative importance of existing producers.

Entry conditions are of vital importance because monopoly profits cannot persist over the long run if there are no significant barriers to entry. Entry barriers can occur in the form of scale economies, large capital outlays, specialized technology, and institutional restraints on access to promising lands or a market.

In the onshore exploration for oil and natural gas, there have been virtually no entry barriers, as evidenced by the fact that in 1982 there were 3478 producers of crude oil and natural gas. The existence of a competitive group of service industries makes the necessary technology, manpower, and equipment readily available to independent oil operators. Seismographic and geologic evaluations along with the drilling, logging, and equipping of wells can all be contracted. In fact, even the major oil companies generally contract for these services.

Exploration firms generally have equal access to promising properties. Promising oil formations can be leased from the numerous private land owners or, in the case of government-owned mineral rights, tracts can be leased from the government in competitive lease sales. Another potential constraint, the capital to conduct a given exploration activity, seldom exceeds $5 million. Such funds could be raised through banks and the sale of working interests to private investors. Finally, state laws typically assure all producers of a market for their oil. So-called "rateable take" laws require that if a refiner purchases oil in a given oil field, it cannot discriminate against any producer in the field by refusing to purchase its oil. For example, any crude oil purchaser buying in a given field must be willing to purchase the same percentage of production, irrespective of who produced the oil. Thus if Texaco elects to purchase all of its own crude oil in a given field, it must also be willing to take crude oil at the same rate from other producers in the field.

Even though the bulk of production still comes from onshore, offshore and Alaskan oil production is becoming increasingly important. Offshore exploration and production is subject to more stringent entry conditions, as players in this game may have to expend $10 or $20 million just to obtain a government lease on an offshore tract. In 1982, an offshore well in Louisiana at a depth of 8700 feet cost an average $1,976,000, contrasted with a cost of $568,000 for the same well onshore. Since a field could easily involve 15 or 20 wells, the table stakes for the offshore game are many times the cost of the onshore game. The major difference, however, appears limited to the cash outlays. The service industries available for onshore drilling have expanded into the offshore market, so that offshore technology, equipment, and manpower do not appear to offer a significant entry barrier. Similarly, access to government leases is through competitive auctions.

Some indication of the number of offshore competitors is given by the fact that the number of participants in government offshore lease sales has increased from 33 bidders in the first sale in 1954 to over 100 in lease sales during the 1980s. One explanation for why as many as 100 firms could participate in such a high-stakes poker game is risk sharing. By selling fractional interests in an offshore tract, companies can spread the risk and reduce their maximum loss to some manageable level. It is for this reason that many smaller firms participate in bidding combines, taking a fractional interest in a number of offshore tracts rather than assuming complete ownership of just one tract.

Let us assume that instead of the relatively minor entry barriers suggested by this analysis, we found that entry barriers were such that no new firms could enter. This would raise the question of whether there exists enough competition among existing firms for the industry to be competitive. A simple count showing 3478 gas producers obscures the fact that there could be one firm with 99 percent of the market and 3477 firms sharing only 1 percent of the market. For this reason, economists have frequently calculated concentration ratios, showing the percentage of the market controlled by the largest four firms, the largest eight firms, and so on. The conventional wisdom is that when such ratios are relatively low, the likelihood of tacit collusion to achieve a monopoly outcome is indeed low. Thus even if entry were blocked, low concentration ratios would indicate that the stability and permanence of any collusive agreement among firms to limit output would be fragile indeed. Recall from Chapter 4 that firms with small market shares face an extremely elastic demand schedule, conducive to output expansion. On the other hand, if the largest four firms controlled 95 percent of the market, they would probably recognize the interdependence of their pricing and output actions and thus tacitly collude to raise price and restrict output. Obviously, much research has focused on the relationship between concentration and profitability. Some studies find a positive linear relationship between the two. Others show a dichotomous response—no relationship until some threshold concentration level is reached, beyond which a positive linear relationship between concentration and profitability exists. Those studies showing a threshold effect typically place the threshold measured in terms of the four-firm concentration ratio somewhere between 50 and 70 percent. Still other studies claim there is no relationship![10] In view of these disparate findings, one should be careful in drawing strong inferences. For concentration ratios below the 50 to 70 percent threshold level, the empirical findings do agree that the tendency for collusion is weak, if present at all.

A study by the Federal Trade Commission shows that concentration is relatively low in the production of oil and natural gas. Table 8.2 shows various concentration ratios for crude oil as they have changed over the period from 1955 to 1981. Over the 26-year period, concentration increased from 18.1 to 26.2 percent in 1981. In 1981, the largest producer, Exxon, had less than 10 percent of the market. Nevertheless, the concentration ratios are well below the average for all manufacturing industries, which was 41 percent for four firms and 62 percent for eight firms in 1981. Additionally, the market shares of the 15 major oil companies have changed markedly over time, suggesting firms do not collude to share markets. For example, in 1955 Phillips was the major interstate gas producer, followed by Standard Oil of Indiana, Exxon, Union, and Cities Service. Gulf Oil was a distant ninth. By 1968, Exxon had moved into first, and Gulf was third. Phillips had fallen to fourth, Union to eighth, and Cities Service to fourteenth.[11] Even allowing for future increases in the concentration ratio as offshore and Alaskan production increases, these data are certainly not

TABLE 8.2 U.S. Net Crude Oil, Condensate, and Natural Gas Liquids
Production Concentration Ratios

	1955	1960	1965	1970	1974	1981
4 Firms	18.1	20.8	23.9	26.3	26.0	26.2
8 Firms	30.3	33.5	38.5	41.7	41.7	41.4
15 Firms	41.0	44.2	50.3	57.1	57.9	57.8
20 Firms	46.3	49.1	55.0	60	61	61.6

SOURCE: *U.S. Federal Trade Commission*, Concentration Levels and Trends in the Energy Sector of the U.S. Economy, *1984; and corporate annual reports.*

suggestive of the small-numbers situation in which tacit collusion is likely to occur. Almost 40 percent of the industry's production comes from independent producers, no one of which controls more than 1 percent of the market. These operators offer vigorous competition to the major companies. It is precisely for these reasons that numerous mergers involving major oil companies in the 1980s have not been challenged by the Reagan Administration's Justice Department. Some of these mergers have involved very large producers (Standard Oil of California's acquisition of Gulf and Texaco's purchase of Getty). However, the view was that while such mergers will raise concentration, it remains relatively low and other structural factors point to ease of entry. In sum, structural tests point to a basically competitive market structure, despite the trend toward increasing concentration.

1. Contrast the results of concentration ratios for the international oil market in Chapter 4 with those in Table 8.2. What can you conclude about the likelihood of tacit collusion in each market? | QUESTIONS
2. Are entry barriers similar in the Middle East and in the U.S. domestic market? Contrast technology, lease acquisition, and availability of markets.

Conduct

The battle lines separating the industry's critics from its defenders are typically centered on the subject of conduct. Even though the large number of producers is probably sufficient to prevent tacit collusion, it does not rule out overt collusion or noncompetitive industry practices. In particular, we shall consider conduct as it relates to joint ventures, product exchange agreements, and state prorationing regulation.

Joint Venture Activities. Joint venture activity in the petroleum industry is a widespread phenomenon, manifesting itself in joint lease acquisition, joint ownership of pipelines, joint ownership of and production from oil and gas leases, and international joint ventures. From the discussion in Chapter 4, recall that international joint ventures and the concessionary system created interdependencies among producers that substantially weakened the incentives for independent competitive actions. On the other hand, monopolization is not the only motive for participating in joint ventures. Joint ventures permit the sharing of unusually large risks, enabling smaller firms and investors to jointly enter an industry they would not be able to enter individually. The ability to spread risk by selling fractional interests in leases and production can be an important factor in facilitating entry. A second justification is that in situations involving economies of scale, separate operations would involve inefficient operations. In petroleum exploration and production, the reservoir or even the entire field is the optimal unit of operation. Parties owning wells in a given field can enhance ultimate recovery and reduce operating costs by jointly operating the field as a unit. As noted in Chapter 7, unitization or operation of the field as a single unit has strong support as a conservation device. Also, scale economies in pipeline size make it less costly for 10 firms to own a pipeline jointly than for 10 firms to build separate lines each one-tenth the size.

From a public policy perspective, the most fascinating questions revolve around joint bidding for offshore oil and gas leases. Joint venture bidding has become a prominent characteristic of government offshore lease sales. Even though 100 or more firms may participate in a lease sale, the number of bidding units is much smaller; moreover, not all bidding units submit bids on every tract offered. This raises the question of whether joint bidding serves as a vehicle to reduce the number of potential bidders, thereby lowering the winning bid prices and allowing oil companies to earn the producers' surplus that would otherwise go to the government. John Wilson, a harsh critic of the oil industry, stated in congressional testimony in 1973: "My own view is that the offshore leasing program, as currently administered by the Interior Department, has become one of the most onerous anticompetitive cartelization devices at work in our domestic gas producing industry."[12]

Joint bidding could potentially promote anticompetitive effects through two mechanisms. The first mechanism occurs through intergroup competition for desirable leases. Joint bidding may reduce the number of bidding combines to such a small number that groups will collude, agreeing to share leases on some predetermined basis. All of the evidence rejects this type of intergroup collusion. For example, in the March 1974 offshore Louisiana lease sale, the winning bidders paid $2.09 billion, while the next highest bids totaled $1.33 billion. The winning bidders paid $763 million more than they would have needed to if they had colluded.

The second potentially anticompetitive mechanism associated with joint bidding is that it reduces the number of potential bidders on any given tract, resulting in a winning bid that might not include all of the producers' surplus.

Presumably a major economic justification for joint bidding is increased risk sharing, thereby enabling greater participation. The asset position of a firm is critical to showing whether or not its participation would be much more limited if it were limited to the submission of solo bids. Prior to 1975, joint bidding was a common practice, even among the largest 16 oil companies in offshore operations. If a firm is sufficiently large, it is probably indifferent between owning 100 percent of one lease or a 50 percent interest in two leases. For these firms, the requirement of solo bidding will typically add more bidders and potentially increase the total bids. However, for firms with low asset positions, a requirement to submit solo bids would effectively preclude many firms from bidding. For small firms bidding independently, the cost of obtaining geological information may be prohibitive. As a member of a bidding combine, the risk-averse firm can act in a fairly risk-neutral manner, but if forced to bid solo, its bids would always be less than the expected present value of excess profits from the lease.

Recognition of these two divergent tendencies led the U.S. Department of the Interior to change its bidding policy in 1975 to forbid joint bidding among companies with worldwide oil equivalent (oil and natural gas and natural gas liquids) production in excess of 1.6 million barrels per day. In 1977, these companies included Exxon, Shell, Texaco, Standard of California, Gulf, Mobil, and British Petroleum. Firms in this category are believed to have sufficient production that they can be risk-neutral while solo bidding. For firms below this level of production, joint bidding is encouraged as a means of spreading risk and increasing both the number and magnitude of bids. While one can disagree about the particulars of the production level set by the Department of Interior, the reform appears definitely an improvement over past practices.

Barter Exchange Agreements. An intriguing and perhaps poorly understood industry practice is that of engaging in barter transactions such as crude oil swapping. As in the case of joint ventures, there are legitimate economic justifications for such exchanges. For example, crude oil transactions (either sales or exchanges) can reduce transportation costs by allowing refiners to process nearby oil rather than to purchase its own oil from a distant field and to transport it to the refinery. Similarly, crude swapping enables cost saving in refining because different refineries are designed to process different types of crude oil (sweet or high-sulfur sour crudes with varying degrees of viscosity). By engaging in crude swaps, refiners can balance the mix of crude input to the specifications of their refinery design, enabling lower cost and a greater fraction of the high-valued, lighter petroleum products. In addition, the ability to swap crude oil enables refiners to maintain lower inventories and also to avoid supply disruptions caused by temporary shortage/surplus situations. There seems little doubt that these are legitimate transactional efficiencies, beneficial to the firms and society in terms of lowering social costs of production.

On the other hand, the fact that these transactions generally involve exchanges for like products rather than cash sales raises the possibility of anticompetitive motives. Are barter exchange transactions motivated for efficiency reasons or for exclusionary reasons? The fact that transactions occur in terms of oil, rather than dollars, raises the question of whether these agreements erect a type of entry barrier. One explanation is that barter is a means of precluding small producers and refiners who have nothing to swap, but would like to sell or buy.[13] To the extent that oil is a preferred medium of exchange to dollars, small operators cannot enjoy the savings associated with such exchanges. Future research should be able to ascertain to what degree barter is a preferred medium of exchange and the extent to which these practices preclude smaller operators.

State Prorationing Regulation. State regulatory commissions have played curious roles in both fostering competition and precluding it. State "rateable take" laws assure independent producers of a market for their crude oil. On the other hand, it was noted that since the 1930s state regulatory agencies regulated production, thereby effectively setting the domestic price of crude. In effect, state regulatory agencies were able to accomplish what the oil companies could not achieve on their own initiative.[14] The predictions of the monopoly model are entirely consistent with prorationing over this period. By restraining production, price could be increased. Conversely, lower prices corresponded to greater output.

Complete unitization of all the various oil fields would eliminate the need for state prorationing, as the producers in each field could collectively choose the efficient rate of production. While progress is being made in the unitization area, it is not likely to be complete, leaving the state regulatory commissions with considerable potential power over supply. Whether this power is exercised or not depends in part on the presence or absence of import controls. If import quotas were once again imposed, then domestic prices would be determined by domestic production.[15] Since the state regulatory commissions can set production, there is the distinct likelihood that they might exercise this monopoly power, just as they did in the 1950s and 1960s, when import controls were in place.

If there are no quantitative limitations on imports, the domestic price level will be determined, as in Figure 8.1, by the world oil price plus transportation and tariff costs (if any). In this situation, the regulatory commission has no power to fix prices. Production cutbacks would only increase imports, leaving OPEC's price unchanged. There would be no incentive to cut back production, since state severance taxes increase with output (holding price constant), so that they can be expected to allow all-out production. In fact, market demand prorationing was abandoned by the Texas Railroad Commission in 1973.

QUESTIONS

1. What differences exist between the type of joint ventures in the Middle East and those for United States federal offshore drilling?
2. Show graphically that import controls would place the state regulatory agencies in a position to fix price, while with a tariff system, the domestic price level is set by OPEC plus the relevant tariff and transport costs.

Industry Performance

The standard measures of performance, profitability, and R&D activity are generally supportive of the industry's claim of being workably competitive. In measuring profitability in the petroleum industry, it is important to remember that absolute levels of profitability reflect the size of the industry, not monopoly power. Petroleum companies by any standard of measurement are large. They account for five of the top 10 corporations on *Fortune's* list of the 500 largest industrial companies in the United States. Ten of the top 20 firms and 15 of the top 50 are petroleum companies. Therefore, it is not surprising that in 1983, the five largest oil companies showed profits of $6.6 billion. For policy purposes, it is not the absolute level of profits, but rather the rate of return on capital, that is important. The received wisdom is that industries permanently able to earn rates of return well in excess of the average do so because of monopoly power or their own efficiency. One caveat should be added. Chapter 3 showed that even firms in a competitive industry producing a renewable resource will earn a producers' surplus owing to the user cost of the resource.

For our purposes, the optimal measure of profitability would be the industry's rate of return on capital invested in domestic exploration and production activities. Unfortunately, the profit statements of firms distinguish neither between foreign and domestic earnings nor between the vertical stages of integration at which profits are earned. Thus the profits of the petroleum industry include foreign operations and earnings associated with refining. The effect of including foreign exploration earnings is clearly to bias upward the average rate of return. This may be partially offset by lower earnings in domestic marketing and refining, so that the latter could conceivably cancel the former effect. Another problem arises in that historical data measure

TABLE 8.3 Return on Equity of Petroleum Companies, 1965–1982[a]

Year	Percentage Return on Equity	
	Petroleum Industry	All Manufacturing
1965	11.9	13.8
1966	12.6	14.1
1967	12.9	12.6
1968	12.9	13.2
1969	12.1	12.7
1970	10.9	10.3
1971	11.2	10.9
1972	10.8	12.1
1973	15.6	14.5
1974	19.6	15.2
1975	13.9	12.6
1976	14.8	15.0
1977	14.2	15.0
1978	12.9	14.1
1979	15.4	13.9
1980	16.5	14.8
1981	15.6	14.4
1982	14.1	14.1

[a]Excludes transportation companies, public utilities, and financial corporations.
SOURCE: Citibank (New York).

the rate of return on stockholders' equity, thus excluding the debt component of capital. To the extent that industries with very different ratios of debt to equity are compared, this can also bias the results. In this particular example, the conclusions do not appear to be affected whether one uses return on capital or return on stockholders' equity.[16]

With these qualifications in mind, Table 8.3 shows the average rates of return on stockholders' equity for the period 1965–1982 for both the petroleum industry and all manufacturing industry. For the period before the Arab oil embargo in 1973, the petroleum industry exhibits lower returns than the average for all industry. This is somewhat surprising, since producer surplus owing to user costs should have pushed profits at least above the average.

Industry critics have been quick to point to industry profits since 1973 as proof of monopoly power. These profits would no doubt have been even greater in the absence of price controls and the Windfall Profit Tax. Even purely competitive markets can exhibit excess profits during market disequilibrium, and certainly the events since 1973 indicate such a situation. Even under price controls, the producers' surplus earned on low-cost oil found 20 and 30 years ago suddenly became quite large. As firms explore for high-cost oil, the rate of return on equity (a mixture of equity invested 20 years ago and recent investments) would be expected to fall back toward normal levels. This would appear to be the pattern in 1975–1977 and 1981–1983. The OPEC price hikes of 1979–1980 again caused oil industry profit rates to rise above those of all manufacturing industries in 1979–1981, but by 1982 the earnings rates were again the same.

Another indicator of the competitive performance of the industry is the increase in drilling and exploration activity as prices increased under price controls in the 1970s. Recall that under the monopoly model, rising prices reduce oil demand and thus the need to add to productive capacity via drilling activity. In contrast, under competition, rising prices encourage producers to develop previously uneconomic oil deposits. Conversely, falling prices discourage drilling activity. Figure 8.6 plots the number of wells drilled in the U.S. for the period from 1965 to 1983. The dashed line shows the average price

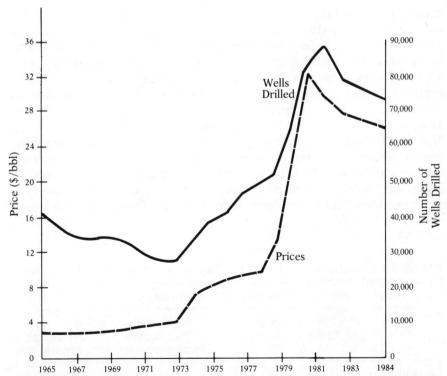

FIGURE 8.6 The relationship between U.S. average crude oil prices and drilling activity, 1965–1983.

SOURCES: American Petroleum Institute and United States Department of Energy.

paid for U.S. crude. Visual inspection is sufficient to convince one that crude prices and drilling activity are strongly positively correlated. The supply response is entirely consistent with the competitive paradigm that the supply curve of a competitive industry slopes upward and higher prices should evoke a substantial increase in oil exploration activity.

Another prominent measure of industry performance is the research and development (R&D) activity of the industry. Generally, the U.S. exploration and production industry is thought to be highly progressive in generating new technology. Prominent examples over the last 25 years have been the advances in offshore exploration technology and enhanced secondary and tertiary recovery techniques. Offshore exploration can now be conducted in water depths greater than 2000 feet. Oil fields that would typically yield only 15 to 20 percent of the oil present in the reservoir now yield 50 percent and more due to advanced recovery techniques. These advances would not have been forthcoming without major commitments to R&D expenditure. In 1982, petroleum companies spent $960 million, of which about 70 percent went for energy R&D.

What is the result of these expenditures? In measuring R&D performance, it is desirable to measure the outputs in terms of successful innovations rather than just the dollar expenditures. Also, it would be desirable to weight successful innovations based on their commercial importance. Teece and Armour have performed half the task by compiling a list of 85 important innovations over the period 1959–1976 in exploration and production and identifying the firm or firms first to commercialize the new innovation.[17] Table 8.4 summarizes the Teece-Armour results. The results for the firms were ranked based on each firm's 1970 rank as a domestic crude oil producer. By comparing the innovative activity of the top four, top eight, and top 20 crude producers, we can assess the relative R&D performance of these firms. In effect, did the top four crude producers account for a greater fraction of innovations than their share of crude production? Table 8.6 shows

TABLE 8.4 Exploration and Production Innovations, Total Innovations, and Domestic Crude Petroleum for Top 4, Top 8, and Top 20 Firms (by Crude Production) for 1959–1976 Percentage of Total Industry

	Percentage of Crude Production in 1970	Total Number of Innovations Participated In	Percentage of Innovations
Top 4 firms	26.3	37	29
Top 8 firms	41.7	70	69
Top 20 firms	60.5	86	79

that the largest four oil producers with 26 percent of the market accounted for 29 percent of the innovations. The top eight were particularly impressive, accounting for 69 percent of the innovations and only 41.7 percent of production. The top 20 producers, with 60.5 percent of the crude production, accounted for 79 percent of the innovations. These results are quite supportive of the R&D role played by the large oil companies. In addition to the R&D performed by oil companies, the oil field service industry has also tended to conduct vigorous R&D programs. In fact, the remaining 21 percent of innovations not accounted for in Table 8.4 are attributed to service companies such as Schlumberger, GSI, and Dresser-Atlas.

A Brief Recapitulation

If the sole economic justification for permanent price controls on crude oil and natural gas is monopoly power, one would expect overwhelming evidence in support of this hypothesis. Particularly given the existence of other industries containing obvious monopoly power and yet continuing to operate in the absence of price controls, one would expect a strong case. The evidence we and most other students of the industry have examined provides little support for the monopoly power hypothesis. The major anticompetitive questions center on the new merger wave, state prorationing regulation (which has benign effects in the absence of import controls), and possible barter exchange agreements. These questions hardly seem serious enough to justify price controls. They could be more effectively dealt with on an individual basis through unitization reform and antitrust relief. While we believe this conclusion would be broadly supported by students of the industry, a majority is not immune to error. Therefore, the interested student is urged to delve deeper, reviewing the original research,[18] and taking a particularly close look at the works of the industry's most ardent critics.[19]

PROBLEMS IN ADMINISTERING PRICES

One difficulty in policy deliberations regarding price administration is that there may be a tendency to compare the pricing performance of an idealized, omniscient government agency with the market result of an industry that only roughly approximates the competitive ideal. The former always wins. Recall that in Figure 8.5, the pricing authority somehow set the optimal price that equated marginal social costs and benefits, leading to a significant welfare gain. The natural gas pricing performance of the Federal Power Commission (FPC) affords an excellent opportunity to discover inherent difficulties in government price administration. The FPC experienced difficulties in (1) taking a long-term perspective, (2) obtaining reliable estimates of supply and demand elasticities, (3) resisting external political pressures, (4) dealing with divergent producer expectations, (5) administering in the presence of external market forces, and (6) devising efficient corrective policies.

Difficulties in Taking a Long-Term Perspective

If government agencies are to administer gas prices effectively, a long-term perspective must be used in setting prices. Even though supplies may be adequate to meet demand at current prices, this does not assure future supply/demand equilibria. In oil and natural gas exploration, there are considerable lags between price increases and the supply response. First, higher prices lead to increased exploration and leasing activity, after which exploration drilling confirms or rejects the existence of reserves. Subsequent development drilling is necessary to delimit field size and increase productive capacity. At this point, the producer is able to make these reserves available to interstate pipelines on long-term supply contracts. This complete process can easily take 7 to 10 years. Unless authorities adopt such a long-term perspective, price regulation can itself cause welfare losses by creating surplus/shortage situations. Figure 8.7 presents data for the period 1964–1983 for interstate production capacity, demand, and the prices allowed for new gas sales. The right-hand axis shows FPC pricing behavior. Beginning in 1961, the FPC adopted a vintage method of pricing. Even though new vintages of gas were created in 1961, 1968, and 1971, the price was virtually frozen over the period 1961–1971. The left-hand axis measures productive capacity and demand in the interstate market. As late as 1964, capacity was almost twice as large as demand. In 1972, just eight years later, demand exceeded productive capacity. Since FPC rationing rules were in force between 1972 and 1981, one cannot know unrestricted demand. The dotted line for demand after 1972 is only a rough projection based on past demand growth.

From the behavior of prices over the period 1964–1972, the commission appears to have been completely myopic. Only in August 1971, six months before physical shortages were reported, were the wellhead prices increased—an increase that proved trivial compared to the increases granted in 1974 and in 1976.

In retrospect, it is difficult to understand why the commission did not anticipate the shortage and act to increase prices in the mid-1960s. Note that over the period 1964–1967 productive capacity increased, but at a much slower rate than demand. This fact alone should have indicated a future shortage. Beginning in 1969, the hand-

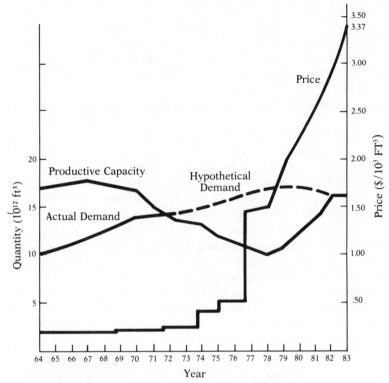

FIGURE 8.7 Natural gas wellhead prices, demand, and productive capacity under FPC regulation. Estimates of productive capacity are based on a reserves-to-production ratio of 11 prior to 1972.

(SOURCE: Federal Power Commission Annual Yearbook, Washington D.C., annually.) 1983 data are preliminary.

writing was on the wall, but the commission was unable to read it. Productive capacity was now declining as reserves declined because production exceeded additions to reserves.

Difficulties in Obtaining Reliable Estimates of Supply and Demand Elasticities

While it may have been apparent that the FPC should have moved far sooner to increase prices, the question then becomes how much. Unlike the idealized situation in Figure 8.5, where the supply and demand schedules are known, regulators do not know the exact magnitude of the price elasticities of supply and demand, which are so critical to setting optimal prices. Also, the effects of economic growth and inflation complicate the analysis. Inflation increases exploration costs, shifting the supply schedule upward over time. At the same time, inflation and economic growth shift the demand schedule outward. To further complicate matters, the price behavior of substitute fuels such as coal and oil products affects gas supply as well as demand. Consumer choices to switch from one fuel to another are influenced by relative prices and may take many years. In addition, the price of crude oil affects the supply of natural gas, since about one-third of the gas found is "associated gas," that is, gas produced in association with oil. Oil prices influence the rate of exploration activity, which in turn affects the amount of gas and oil discovered. Thus, crude oil is a joint product with natural gas on the supply side and yet is a substitute for natural gas in customer markets. For these reasons, econometric model builders face perhaps the most challenging problems in the natural gas market. A number of econometric models have been constructed and applied to estimate the market clearing price where supply equals demand. As an example, an econometric model developed by Professors Edward Erickson and Robert Spann first appeared at the time of the FPC deliberations leading to a price increase from 20.5 cents to 26 cents in August 1971. In 1971, the Erickson/Spann model showed that a price between 24 cents and 30 cents per mcf could be appropriate to eliminate the estimated shortage.[20] As shown in Figure 8.7, subsequent price increases and widening shortages lend an element of comedy to these and other forecasts. In sum, because of the complexities of the crude oil and natural gas markets, it is unrealistic to think that governmental planners can rely extensively on models to set prices in an optimal manner.

Difficulties in Resisting External Political Pressures

Examination of the factors affecting FPC pricing policies over the period shows that politics dominated economics. Federal Power Commission commissioners appointed by President Eisenhower generally felt quite strongly that the FPC had no business regulating gas prices. Over the period 1954–1960, the commission in effect approved market-determined prices. This practice came under severe criticism in a report on regulatory agencies to President-elect Kennedy. James Landis, author of the well-known report, had this to say: "The Federal Power Commission without question represents the outstanding example in the federal government of the breakdown of the administrative process."[21] Other reports, including those by Nader's Raiders, echoed the same trenchant criticism.

In view of these criticisms, it is not surprising that the new commission would feel compelled "to make regulation work." Out of this evolved an "in-line" price formula, which effectively put a lid on price increases. The commission no doubt came to view the pricing issue as an adversary proceeding, with producers on one side wanting higher prices and consumers on the other wanting lower prices.[22] The "in-line" pricing formula set price on the basis of average costs, based on production and exploration outlays. In effect, this approach is analogous to setting price equal to marginal production cost, as in the examples in Chapter 3. Completely absent from the calculation of costs is any allowance for user costs, reflecting the inherent scarcity of this nonrenewable resource. Consumers during the 1960s were, of course, the major beneficiary of regulation, but today's consumers can hardly claim to benefit. Artificially low prices stimulated overconsumption during this period, allowing natural gas to serve extensively as a boiler fuel for electricity generation. These low-cost reserves are now depleted, forcing production out of much-higher-cost reserves today. The regulatory experience over this period suggests an important lesson: unregulated markets cannot overlook the user cost component in arrriving at costs, while regulators can and will.

Difficulties with Divergent Producer Expectations

The fact that natural gas, unlike perishable foods, can be stored for future sales, adds another complicating element. In seeking to maximize the present value of gas reserves, must we necessarily look at the user costs of gas in the current period as well as the future? Recall from Chapter 3 that producers want to maximize the present value of their gas reserves. How does the firm behave under price regulation? Obviously, if the FPC allowed prices to rise so that the present value of user costs was the same at every point in time, gas producers would have no incentive to hold back production. However, FPC price regulation meant that once the gas is committed to contract, its price is likely to remain fixed forever. However, there was the likelihood that the "newest" gas committed to contract in that year would have a higher price than "older" gas committed the previous year. Two extreme situations can occur, depending on producers' expectations about present and future contract prices. If producers believe contract prices in future years will be identical to existing prices, they will rush to sign production contracts in order to produce the gas as quickly as possible. In this case, the user cost in the current period U_0 equals the user cost in all future periods U_i [see equation (3.6)]. But since firms look at the present value of user costs, U_0 is clearly the highest. Thus if producers expect constant contract prices on new gas in the future, accelerated current production will occur.

On the other hand, suppose producers expect that the FPC will offer higher contract prices in the future. Producers may very well decide to wait before signing a production contract. In effect, producers will wait to commit gas in the period when they think the present value of the reserves will be the highest. Because user costs are only a fraction of total marginal costs, expectations that next year's contract price will be 4 or 5 percent higher may be sufficient to defer current production.

What lessons do producers' expectations offer about the current gas shortages? Between 1972 and 1981, contract prices of gas rose from 26 cents per mcf to over $6.00 per mcf. The obvious cause of the persisting shortage is that inexpensive onshore gas is no longer available. But producer expectations have been an important contributing factor. Having witnessed such tremendous price increases over this period, wasn't it likely that producers expected even higher future prices? The greater the expectation of higher future prices, the lower the current production; consequently, the more likely the future price increase becomes!

The market mechanism has an important advantage over a regulatory commission in dealing with price expectations. Unlike the FPC, the market leaves open the possibility of lower prices in the future, so that the producer does face a downside risk from waiting. With the FPC setting prices, producers assumed the FPC would never lower prices. With a perception of trivial downside risk from lower prices, the case for waiting is indeed strong.

Administering in the Presence of External Market Forces

The FPC's power to regulate the wellhead price of gas applied only to gas sold for resale in interstate markets. Until the Natural Gas Policy Act of 1978, natural gas produced and consumed in the intrastate market did not fall under the commission's regulatory umbrella. The existence of an unregulated market capable of competing for the same natural gas desired in the FPC-controlled interstate market created added difficulties for the FPC.[23] Figure 8.8 shows that if the FPC sets too low a control price, the shortage in the interstate market is magnified. In Figure 8.8 the total demand for gas, D_{total}, is the sum of intrastate demand D_{intra} and interstate demand D_{inter}. The supply schedule S depicts the long-run supply schedule for a competitive industry. At equilibrium price P^*, total supply and demand are equilibrated at output Q^*. Of the output Q^*, Q_a^* is sold in intrastate markets and Q_e^* is sold in interstate markets.

In the situation in which the FPC sets a lower than equilibrium price P^r, producers will supply only Q^r since the cost of producing additional units exceeds the market price. Since total output is reduced to Q^r, clearly regulation in the case of a competitive industry leads to lower production. The existence of an unregulated intrastate market exacerbates the shortage. Because of the lower price P^r, intrastate producers actually increase consumption from Q_a^* to Q_a^r, leaving

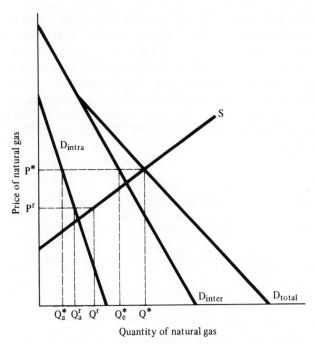

FIGURE 8.8 Regulation in the presence of an unregulated market.

only $Q^r - Q_a^r$ for interstate markets. In sum, FPC price regulation of P^r resulted in $Q^* - Q^r$ less gas being produced. Not only was this shortage absorbed by the interstate market, but additional gas going to intrastate users $Q_a^r - Q_a^*$ came from supplies that would have otherwise gone to interstate consumers. It is surprising that it took until 1978 to recognize the untenable situation interstate consumers found themselves in.

Devising Efficient Corrective Policies

By 1978, it was apparent to everyone that price controls had failed. Regulation had failed to protect consumers and had entombed the gas producers, the pipeline companies, and gas utilities. A sad feature of our legislative system is its inability to wipe the regulatory black-board clean. Instead the Natural Gas Policy Act of 1978 was a political compromise between forces favoring increased regulation and propo-nents of deregulation. The Act offered something for each group—it extended price controls over the intrastate market and at the same time set in motion a formula for partial decontrol in 1985. While com-promises in the political arena are a socially beneficial manner of weighing opposing interest groups, in the economic policy sphere compromise may distort resource allocation even further. The provisions for complete decontrol of deep gas and rapidly rising prices of new gas set in motion incentives to produce and contract for high-cost gas with stringent "take or pay" provisions. The result was even higher prices to consumers and widespread default on gas purchase contracts with the likelihood of numerous bankruptcies. By 1985, the question was what type of corrective legislation, if any, is appropriate to deal with the latest fiasco.

Notes

1. For an economic analysis of this regulation, see Edmund Kitch, "Regulation of the Field Market for Natural Gas," *Journal of Law and Economics* (October 1968), pp. 245–254. For an analysis of more recent events, see Robert Helms, *Natural Gas Regulation* (Washington, D.C.: American Enterprise Institute, 1974).

2. See U.S. Cabinet Task Force on Oil Import Control, *The Oil Import Question* (Washington, D.C.: U.S. Government Printing Office, 1970).

3. For an elaboration of this regulation, see Paul MacAvoy, *Federal Energy Administration Regulation: Report of the President's Task Force* (Washington, D.C.: American Enterprise Institute, 1977).

4. E.R. Fried and Charles L. Schultze, "Overview," in *Higher Oil Prices and the World Economy*, edited by E.R. Fried and C. Schultze (Washington, D.C.: Brookings Institution, 1975).

5. Irving Hoch, *Energy Use in the United States by States and Regions* (Baltimore: Johns Hopkins Press, 1978), p. 90.

6. Students of industrial organization would point out that structural deconcentration or remedies to alter industry conduct through the antitrust laws offer another means to the same ends.

7. See F.M. Scherer, *Industrial Market Structure and Economic Performance* (Chicago: Rand McNally, 1970).

8. See Edwin Mansfield, *Industrial Research and Technological Innovation* (New York: Norton, 1968), pp. 21–43.

9. F. Allvine and R. Patterson, *Highway Robbery* (Lafayette: Indiana University Press, 1974).

10. See Harold Demsetz, "Two Systems of Belief about Monopoly," in *Industrial Concentration: The New Learning*, (Boston: Little, Brown, 1974).

11. See Clark Hawkins, "Structure of the Natural Gas Producing Industry," in *Regulation of the Natural Gas Producing Industry*, edited by Keith Brown (Baltimore: Johns Hopkins Press, 1970).

12. John W. Wilson, testimony before U.S. Senate Subcommittee on

Antitrust and Monopoly, June 27, 1973. See also Paul Davidson, "Divestiture and the Economics and Energy Supplies," in *Research and Development in Energy*, edited by David Teece (Palo Alto, Calif.: Stanford University Institute for Energy Studies, 1977).

13. This issue is more germane to the refining industry than to crude oil or natural gas production, as rateable take laws assure producers of a market.

14. Thomas Duchesneau, *Competition in the U.S. Energy Industry* (Cambridge: Ballinger, 1975), pp. 121–129.

15. This can be seen by subtracting a fixed quantity of imports from the demand schedule in Figure 8.2. The domestic price is determined by the intersection of the new demand schedule and domestic production.

16. *Forbes Magazine* annually reports the median rate of return on capital for essentially domestic petroleum firms and compares this with the median rate of return for all industries. Relatively speaking, these results are quite similar to those given in Table 8.3. In 1976, the petroleum firms earned 10.2 percent compared with 9.8 percent for all industries.

17. D.J. Teece and Henry Armour, "Innovation and Divestiture in the U.S. Oil Industry," in Teece, *Research and Development in Energy*, p. 118 (see Note 12).

18. Major monographs in the field include M.G. DeChazeau and A.E. Kahn, *Integration and Competition in the Petroleum Industry* (New Haven: Yale University Press, 1959); Paul MacAvoy, *Price Formation in Natural Gas Fields: A Study of Competition, Monopsony and Regulation* (New Haven: Yale University Press, 1962); T. Duchesneau, *Competition in the U.S. Energy Industry* (Cambridge: Ballinger, 1975); W.A. Johnson, R.E. Messick, S. VanVactor, and R.F. Wyant, *Competition in the Oil Industry* (Washington, D.C.: Energy Policy Research Project, George Washington University, 1976); Joseph P. Kalt, *The Economics and Politics of Oil Price Regulation* (Cambridge, Mass.: MIT Press, 1981).

19. See Wilson's testimony, Davidson, "Divestiture," Allvine and Patterson, *Highway Robbery*, and also Walter Measday, "Feasibility of Petroleum Industry Divestiture," in Teece, *Research and Development in Energy*, pp. 175–192 (see Note 12).

20. Prices apply to southern Louisiana area rates; see E.W. Erickson and R.M. Spann, "Supply Response in a Regulated Industry: The Case of Natural Gas," *Bell Journal of Economics* (Spring 1971), pp. 94–121.

21. James M. Landis, *Report on Regulatory Agencies to the President Elect* submitted by the chairman of the Subcommittee on Admin-

istrative Practices and Procedures to the Senate Committee on the Judiciary, 86th Congress, Second Session, 1960.

22. For an insightful account by an FPC commissioner, see Charles Ross, "Producer Regulation: A Commissioner's Viewpoint," in Brown, *Regulation of the Natural Gas Producing Industry*, pp. 90–112 (see Note 11).

23. For a review, see Milton Russell, "Producer Regulation for the 1970's," in Brown, *Regulation of the Natural Gas Producing Industry*, pp. 219–237 (see Note 11).

ENERGY SOURCES FOR THE TWENTY-FIRST CENTURY 9

A persuasive case can be made for developing new sources of energy without undue delay. Reduced to its essentials, the reasoning is as follows. Since the industrial revolution, the availability of relatively cheap energy sources has been an important factor in facilitating long-term economic growth. Economic history reveals that the age of firewood was superseded by the age of coal, which was in turn superseded by the age of petroleum beginning in the 1920s. Today, over two-thirds of world energy consumption still comes from oil and natural gas. But since the OPEC price hikes of 1973–80, petroleum is no longer a cheap fuel. Furthermore, even at the higher energy prices, we are not replacing world petroleum reserves as rapidly as they are being consumed. Even though real oil prices may decline for a time with OPEC's diminished market power, over a longer horizon of 20 to 50 years the results of Chapter 3 are inescapable—in the absence of major technological advances, the real price of petroleum will rise. The rate of increase over this period is likely to depend on technological advances in extracting existing energy sources and the price at which backstop fuels become available. Given the long lead times in research and development, our R&D decisions today will affect the economics and availability of these backstop fuels for the twenty-first century.

Not only is the development of new lower cost energy sources important for future generations, it can be important today, even though the new technology may not be implemented for 10 or 20 years. But how can a technology that will not be economic for 20 years be of any benefit to current energy consumers? Recall from Chapter 3 the discussion of the Hotelling price path and the backstop fuel price. Figure 3.5 shows that the price will rise at rate r until it hits the backstop fuel price, and thereafter the availability of the new backstop fuel in infinitely elastic supply constrains price to be constant. In Hotelling's framework, conventional oil production ceases at the instant the price path reaches the backstop price because the user costs no longer rise at rate r, meaning that the present value of production during the pe-

337

riod of backstop fuel production will be less than during the earlier period when prices were rising at rate r. Therefore, a conventional oil producer would never choose to sell his reserves at a lower present value. Combining the results that (a) prices must rise at rate r until reaching the backstop and (b) conventional oil reserves must be just exhausted at the point of reaching the backstop price, we know that there can be only one price satisfying both conditions. If the price path is set too high the backstop will be reached too soon with oil left over; consumption rates at the higher prices will not be sufficient to use up conventional oil reserves. Conversely, if prices are set too low today, it will take a longer period for the rising price path to reach the backstop. Furthermore, along the lower price price path, consumption will proceed at a faster rate, using up conventional oil reserves well before the price path would normally reach the backstop.

Figure 9.1 examines the effect on today's fuel (P_0) of a technological breakthrough reducing the backstop fuel price from P_B to P_B'. Corresponding to the new backstop fuel price will be a new price path lowering today's fuel price from P_0 to P_0'. The new price path will lie below the old price path because along the lower price path consumption rates will be faster, thus assuring that conventional oil reserves will be produced by period t_B', when the price reaches the new lower backstop.

The implication of this result is quite profound: Technological breakthroughs can significantly lower the current price path even though the new backstop may not be reached until many years in the future. The welfare gains from technological breakthroughs are potentially large. To the degree that new technology lowers the marginal social cost of conventional oil, society receives a major welfare gain.

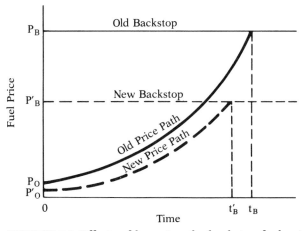

FIGURE 9.1 Effects of lowering the backstop fuel price.

The welfare gain is analogous to the area between two supply curves—the old supply curve, based on the old backstop technology, and the new supply curve, based on the new backstop technology. For these reasons, new energy technologies are exciting subjects about which to speculate.

This much seems clear and reasonable. But what is the most probable candidate for a backstop fuel? What sort of transition from oil and gas to one or more backstop fuels is most likely? The ideal scenario, less popular with economists than with journalists, is a swift transition from dirty, dangerous depletable fuels to clean, benign, nondepletable energy sources, achieved in a single decisive step. There are a number of "magic words" in the energy debate. The two words with the greatest "white magic" power are "conservation" and "solar." Conversely, the "black magic" of the energy rhetorician is most powerfully evoked by the words "pollution" and "nuclear." Five to ten years ago everyone "knew" the solution to the energy problem: conservation in the short run, and solar energy in the long run. The many uncertainties regarding the length of the transition period involved and the economic feasibility of solar power were glossed over, to the point where a skeptical observer might say that the program was largely taken on faith.

There are only two nondepletable sources of energy, solar power in its various forms and nuclear fusion. Based on current cost estimates, neither of these promises to be fully developed as a comprehensive substitute or backstop for petroleum in the next 20 to 50 years. More likely, the evolution of the world energy sector will pass through two or more complementary and sequential backstop fuels before the transition to nondepletable sources is achieved. The following list of candidates for backstop fuels, in their order of economic promise, might serve as a point of departure:

1. Synthetic fluid fuels (liquid and gaseous) from nonpetroleum sources:
   a. Oil shales
   b. Tar sands
   c. Coal
2. Various forms of solar energy, usually suitable more for stationary than for mobile power source applications:
   a. Solar thermal energy conversion: heating and cooling; power generation
   b. Photovoltaic cells
   c. Ocean thermal energy conversion
   d. Biomass, wind power, wave action, and other solar energy applications

3. Fuel cells and related technologies
4. Nuclear power developments
    a. Improved burner reactors
    b. Breeder reactor prospects
    c. Nuclear fusion prospects
5. Other sources, usually classed as "exotic"—a hydrogen-based fuel sector, geothermal, tidal power, etc.

Just as mineral reserves do not disappear all at once, new energy sources will not appear immediately and cause instant abandonment of old sources. Over the life of an energy form, the unit cost of a fuel is likely to follow a U-shaped pattern, declining at first, then rising in the latter years. Initially, the unit costs of the new energy source usually decline from high to moderate levels as technological problems are solved and learning effects accumulate. Over time, however, the resource base becomes increasingly depleted and higher raw materials costs are experienced, raising costs as a function of the cumulative production from the resource itself. Figure 9.2 shows the possible time path of replacement of one backstop fuel by another as production costs slowly rise for each fuel. Thus with several fuels utilized over time, jointly and in sequence, the curve of increasing energy costs does not follow those that would be imposed by exclusive reliance upon a

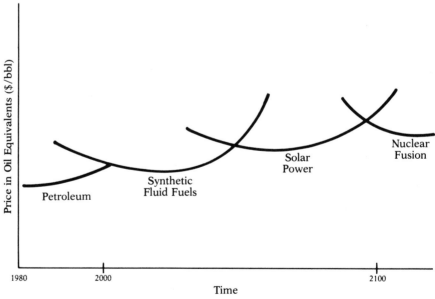

FIGURE 9.2 Unit cost of energy (converted to dollars per barrel of oil equivalent) from various fuel sources as a function of time.

single fuel, but rather rises in a slower fashion, with the suggestion of a scalloped configuration, as in Figure 9.2.

Figure 9.2 embodies one possible forecast of future energy source reliance. As crude oil becomes higher in price, synthetic fuels are phased in, but after an extended period even this source experiences higher costs. Solar energy then becomes more widely economical, but at some point in the future there is a breakthrough in nuclear fusion technology that enables fusion power to be used very widely, and at lower costs than most other energy forms. This is merely one possibility and should not be regarded as a high-probability forecast.

SYNTHETIC FLUID FUELS

Some creatures, such as snakes and locusts, periodically shed their skins. Other creatures such as turtles do not. It is often efficient for a growing or changing organism to shed its skin, but to shed one's skeleton is not conducive to survival—it is just biologically too extravagant. Analogous reasoning would suggest that an industrial nation's energy "skeleton" of pipelines, refineries, and liquid and gaseous fuel distribution systems should not be unnecessarily abandoned as the nature of the energy economy changes. Unless vast investments in such facilities are to be written off as a total loss, synthetic fluid fuels must be developed to replace natural petroleum as input into existing energy systems.

Synthetic fluid fuels can be supplied in either liquid or gaseous forms, and can be derived from a variety of raw materials, such as oil shales, tar sands, and various types of coal. In order to serve as a backstop fuel, the material must be sufficiently plentiful to allow large-scale production for a period of many decades or even centuries. Coal, oil shales, and tar sands all possess enormous volumes of physical resources, enough to last for well over a century at a minimum. Processing costs are more difficult to predict. Several large plants are currently producing synthetic crude oil from tar sands deposits in Canada at production costs low enough to allow substantial profits at current world oil prices. Production is certain to increase in the future, but the volumes involved, although absolutely large, are as yet far from sufficient to permit tar sands oil to supply a substantial fraction of the energy consumption now provided for by crude oil. Shale oil would seem to be the next most promising source of synthetic fuels, but since commercial-scale plants have yet to be constructed, the economics of oil shale processing has not been established. Finally, the least promising of the three types of synthetics is synthetic crude and gas produced from coal. As we shall see, without major technical breakthroughs, oil prices must rise significantly before they will become economic.

Tar Sands

Tar sands are petroleum deposits that are so viscous that primary oil production is impossible. The petroleum material in tar sands may be solid or semisolid. This description typically includes the tar sands of Canada as well as the heavy oil reserves of California and Venezuela. The potential reserve base for tar sands is large compared to existing reserve estimates for oil (26.8 billion barrels in 1983). For example, heavy oil in place is estimated at over 100 billion barrels in California and 700 to 3,000 billion barrels in the Orinoco River Basin in Venezuela. Estimates are that 20 billion barrels may be recovered in California and up to 500 billion barrels in Venezuela. The world's largest tar sand deposits are estimated at 1,000 billion barrels in the Athabasca tar sands of Alberta, Canada. Even the tar sands of Eastern Utah contain resources roughly equal to existing U.S. oil reserves (30 billion barrels).

Tar sands economics has already been proven, at least for surface-mined reserves with the characteristics of those currently being exploited in Canada. Here the nature of the resource permits lower mining and processing costs than are likely to prevail for the typical tar sands project. Sun Oil first began tar sands production in 1967, but it appears that the process was carried on at a loss until the price hikes of the 1970s made tar sands oil definitely profitable. Since that time, additional large new plants have been built, or are under construction, and the chief barrier to entry at present is the restrictive licensing policy of the Provincial government of Alberta. Beginning in 1978, Syncrude of Canada has operated a much larger project on an adjoining lease to Sun's operation with an allowable output limit of 129,000 barrels per day. With a peak mining rate of 300,000 tons of tar sands material per day, the Syncrude plant represents the largest mining operation in the world. In 1979, Alsands, a consortium of nine major oil companies, received provisional approval to construct a similar plant to produce 140,000 barrels per day by 1986. It has been estimated that the Athabasca deposits alone contain more than 60 billion barrels of oil at depths sufficiently shallow to make strip mining economical. Such a resource base would permit a production rate of several million barrels per day. To this could be added the output that would be obtainable from the Cold Lake and Peace River deposits. While deeper mining would increase costs, it is clear that the economic potential of Canadian tar sands oil is quite significant. This fact makes current and prospective future Canadian energy policy failures very expensive to the world at large.

Strip mining of Athabasca tar sands involves extraction of the predominately loose and moist rocky deposits and mixing them with hot water to separate the bitumen material from the mineral in the rock matrix. Vast volumes of water are required—about a ton of water for a ton of tar sands rock—and large ponds must be provided to allow the process water to precipitate finely divided clays before it can be reused. The tar sands themselves are about 85 percent sand and clay, 5 percent water, and only 10 percent bitumen. About 90 percent of the bitumen is recovered by the hot-water process, and the resulting heavy oil is upgraded to a lighter product status by delayed coking. Environmental problems are sizeable but are not unmanageable in the Alberta wilderness. Water is superabundant in this land of lakes and marshes, and there is ample space for large process water treatment reservoirs. Disposal of solid wastes is another large volume problem, since the production of one ton of tar sands oil leaves about 10 tons of solid residue, largely sand and clay. Again, ample waste disposal space exists in the sparsely inhabited regions that are involved, and a land-fill configuration that minimizes water flow through the residue, coupled with revegetation arrangements, is usually required.

It is difficult to generalize about costs, but an order of magnitude estimate would place both capital and operating costs in the range of about $10 per barrel, before allowing for overhead costs and the various contributions to governments. At a wellhead price of roughly $30 there is room for profit, although periodic cost escalations remain likely and the prospect for price reductions cannot be ruled out. The fact of rapidly increasing investment constrained only by the Albertan government testifies to the confidence of producers in the ultimate profitability of tar sands in Canada.

The prospects for heavy oil development likewise appear promising. In California, advances in thermal recovery techniques involve the injection of steam into heavy oil sands to improve the viscosity of the oil sufficiently to recover it by artificial lift wells. By 1990, the National Petroleum Council estimates, heavy oil production will reach 2.1 million barrels per day.

Oil Shales

The historical description of oil shale economics is that it "is always economic at $5 per barrel more than the prevailing price at that time." Even when oil prices were $3 per barrel, oil shale was "right around the corner" as illustrated in Professor Steele's 1957 Ph.D. Dissertation, which projected large-scale production by 1966! Today, oil shale is still "right around the corner." Perhaps oil shale enthusiasts have been so mesmerized by the immense potential of U.S. shale deposits that they have underestimated its costs and environmental limitations. In the Green River Formation in the adjoining corners of Colorado, Utah, and Idaho, all grades of oil shale represent 1,800 billion barrels, enough to supply the U.S. for 339 years at 1984 consumption levels. But as we shall see, potential is not reality and oil shale may remain "right around the corner" without significantly higher prices.

The technology of oil shale is not particularly exotic, which is an advantage. All that is required to separate the kerogen from the marl-stone is enough heat to drive off the volatile compounds and the proper facilities for collecting them in liquid and gaseous form. The chief problems are those of materials handling: how to crush and convey the shale rock; how to secure the optimal exposure of the shale to the heat in the retort so as to maximize kerogen yields, and so on. Heat must be supplied to initiate the thermal distillation process. Hydrogen must be added to the liquid output to obtain a product suitable for petroleum refineries. Water must be obtained to facilitate operations and support resident populations.

But conventional mining of shale oil has two environmental problems reducing its popularity. In the retorting process, the byproduct shale actually expands in volume, exacerbating the land reclamation problems. Every cubic yard of shale extracted is converted into 1.2 cubic yards of spent shale. Additionally, the high water requirements coupled with the limited water supplies of the West and economically suboptimal water use legislation limit the size of such an industry to 1.5 to 2 million barrels per day. To expand the industry above this level would require pipelining water in from the Missouri River Basin. Because of these difficulties, experimentation with in situ processes has long captivated technological interests. The idea is that by lighting underground fires, the oil component can be liquefied and can then be pumped to the surface, avoiding the shale disposal and large water requirements problems. Unfortunately, in situ processes have proved difficult to operate on a commercial scale and must await further technical breakthroughs.

It appeared in the later 1970s that the era of shale oil had finally arrived. Large OPEC price hikes in 1973–79 stimulated considerable research and development in shale oil. As of early 1978 about eight major projects were in various stages of investigation, the most important of which was the Colony project, a joint venture between Exxon and Arco, which had an output goal of 45,000 barrels per day. Then in 1980, the federal government established the Synthetic Fuels Corporation (SFC) with a budget of over $80 billion to support private investment in this area. In the early 1980s, output goals were established: 500,000 barrels per day of synthetics would be produced by 1987 and 2 million barrels per day by 1992. But within a few years it was obvious that those goals would never be met. At the time the SFC was established, hopes were high in some quarters that rising oil prices would provide enough stimulus for private companies to produce synthetics without public subsidy. But falling oil prices and declining oil demand suddenly changed the climate. In the spring of 1982 Exxon withdrew from the Colony project, citing, in addition to the obvious burdens of lower oil price projections, high interest rates and escalating cost projections. The original cost of $3.5 billion had doubled by 1982.

At the same time, during the Reagan administration the philosophy was adverse to such subsidy. Of an original total of $88 billion ultimately authorizable, amounts available dropped to a maximum of $20 billion, and then to less than $15 billion for synthetics. An upper limit of $3 billion for any one project was imposed. As of mid-1984, less than one billion dollars of subsidies had been committed, all in the form of loan or price guarantees. By 1984 SFC had extended price guarantees to only a handful of projects, totalling about $750 million. Under such arrangements the SFC stands ready to provide a certain maximum amount of subsidy payments if market prices for synthetics should drop below the guaranteed price. Such fixed limits would cover a large volume of production at a higher market price, but lesser volumes at lower market prices due to the greater unit subsidy required. In addition to the very small number of projects in operation, another dozen or so proposals were under consideration in 1984. The total output goal of the four approved shale oil projects was only 65,000 barrels per day. The approved projects were of various types. The largest is the Union Oil Company of California's Colorado shale oil project, with 10,000 barrels per day output for phase I and 40,000 more barrels per day for phase II. Phase I production has a price guarantee of $42.50 per barrel. The Cathedral Bluffs project of Tenneco and Occidental, also in Colorado, has an output goal of 15,000 barrels per day.

The prognosis for a shale oil industry seems clear. Until oil prices demonstrate more firmness and an unmistakable upward trend, shale oil projects will continue to receive much study and research, but no new plants will be built. There is a widely held view that oil prices will resume their upward trend in the 1990s. If these predictions are correct, a shale oil industry may await the turn of the century.

Coal Liquefaction and Gasification

If shale oil awaits the turn of the century, synthetic oil and gas from coal seem likely to be in for a still longer wait. The huge reserves of coal in the U.S. and worldwide suggest that synthetics could serve as a backstop fuel for many years. But the question is: "How high is the backstop price?" The answer seems to be higher than for shale oil, although the prospects of coal gasification appear considerably more encouraging than for coal liquefaction. Since coal can be mined and used directly as a boiler fuel for process heat, it would be uneconomic to liquefy it and then burn it as a stationary power source. Coal liquefaction becomes economical only when there is a demand for liquid fuels per se, as in the transportation market. It will always cost more to produce a Btu of energy from liquefied coal than from unprocessed coal, and the cost of processing is high.

Even though shale oil seems more promising economically, coal liquefaction does have some advantages over shale oil. Coal deposits are widespread, and exist closer to markets and water sources than do oil shale reserves. Waste disposal costs should be lower. Desulfurization of high-sulfur coal during liquefaction should make such coal much more attractive in markets where air pollution is a problem. But coal's disadvantages are considerable. The technology of processing presents more difficulties and has not been demonstrated on a large scale. The ratio of hydrogen to carbon in the solid coal input (.5 to .9) is lower than the desired ratio in the synthetic fuel output (1.5), so during processing hydrogen must be added or carbon must be thrown away, and both alternatives are expensive. In contrast, the ratio of hydrogen to carbon in oil shale (1.6) is higher, so the problem will not be as large for shale oil.

Coal liquefaction can be achieved by a variety of methods. One process begins with the gasification of coal into a mixture of hydrogen, carbon monoxide, and methane. This gas is then converted into liquid form by catalytic means. The hydrogenation process requires the mixture of powdered coal with coal-derived oil and hydrogen gas and the exposure of this mixture to a catalyst at high temperatures. This reaction yields oil, liquefied coal, and a residue of ash and nonliquefied coal called char. The chief technical difficulties lie in separating the solid and liquid components of this mixture.

Coal gasification is somewhat more complex, the actual complexity depending upon whether the goal is to obtain a low-Btu-content gas that must be used locally, or a high-Btu gas that can be transported by pipeline. In coal gasification, the carbon and hydrogen content of the coal is separated from its other constituents and converted into gas. Crushed coal is treated in a gasifier under pressure with oxygen and steam. If a low-Btu gas is desired, the output from the gasifier is cleaned by removing tar, dust, and sulfur, and the resulting product, a mixture of carbon monoxide and hydrogen, is used locally for power generation. The waste product is coal ash. If a high-Btu gas similar to natural gas is desired, the output from the gasifier is further processed. Methods differ, but in general the low-Btu gas is combined with fresh steam, which reacts with the carbon monoxide in the gas to yield hydrogen and carbon dioxide. A catalyst is then employed to facilitate the formation of methane, the chief constituent of natural gas, by accelerating the combination of hydrogen with the remaining carbon dioxide.

Under the regulatory framework of price controls, a coal gasification industry was almost born. Under price controls, domestic gas supplies in the United States declined and utilities sought alternative sources of supply such as gas from coal. In the mid-1970s a number of processes were under active investigation, which ranged in cost from $3 to $7 per million Btu. This price was considerably higher than the average cost of natural gas under regulation—but when no new natural gas was available, this price seemed reasonable to utilities. Utilities would be able to pass the higher costs of gasified coal along to the final consumer rather gradually by averaging in this higher-cost gas with their lower-cost natural gas under price controls. A utility could pay $5 per million Btu for synthetic gas to cover 10% of its sales as long as the price on the remaining 90% of gas contracts was $2 per million Btu. The effect on the average price facing gas customers was to raise the price from $2.00 to $2.30 per million Btu.

Conditions began to change after the Natural Gas Act of 1978, which provided for much higher prices for newly discovered gas and even increases for some older gas under contract. As the average price of natural gas rose, the marginal value of synthetic gas declined. Plans for producing gas from coal were accordingly postponed or abandoned. Nevertheless, the SFC has enabled a few projects to escape cancellation.

The Great Plains project, in the start-up phase in 1984, has a planned capacity of 23,000 barrels per day oil equivalent of synthetic natural gas. The Dow Syngas project in Louisiana has an output rate of 5,000 barrels per day of oil equivalent, and the Cool Water project adds another 4,000 barrels per day in the form of synthetic gas. The coal gasification projects are primarily cases involving special circumstances where the coal is partly gasified, the solid residue being burned in boilers and the coal gas being used to run gas turbines. Over the longer term, the prospects for coal gasification are more promising. The fundamental situation is similar to that of shale oil. Future demand for fuel in gaseous form is certain to increase due to the low air pollution potential for such fuels. High-sulfur coal can be desulfurized during gasification and the clean gas can be transported to industrial and utility markets. By the first decade of the twenty-first century coal gasification should be increasingly resorted to. Rising energy prices will hasten the advent of coal gasification as well as shale oil.

Coal liquefaction presents greater technological problems than shale oil production or coal gasification, and its commercialization seems farther in the future than that of the other synthetic fuels derived from resources abundant within the borders of the United States. During the period of rapidly rising crude oil prices, however, several alternative processes were studied intensively: the solvent-refining process of Gulf Oil, a hydrogenation process by Hydrocarbons Research and Ashland Oil, and the Exxon donor-solvent process, involving both solvent refining and catalytic hydrogenation. None of these investigations involved commercial-scale plants; the largest pilot plant was designed to handle only about 500 tons per day of throughput. These projects were also postponed or abandoned when the world oil price declined in the early 1980s. The Exxon process, for example, proved a technical success but an economic failure. Exxon spent a total of $341 million to build and operate a 250-ton-per-day pilot plant in Baytown, Texas. Between 1980 and 1982, 90,000 tons of coal were successfully converted into about 65,000 barrels of synthetic oil and gas equivalent. Only about three-quarters of a barrel of fluid was produced per ton of coal. The actual cost of the fluids produced translates to $5,246 per barrel! But it was estimated that on a commercial plant scale a cost of $50 (in 1980 dollars) per barrel could be achieved. Technological advances of this sort insure that if oil prices rise high enough, coal liquefaction will be economical on a substantial scale. Thus liquefied coal will be another backstop fuel for future energy needs in the twenty-first century as energy prices rise and as advancing technology steadily reduces costs.

OTHER BACKSTOP FUELS: CERTAIN APPLICATIONS OF SOLAR ENERGY

It is safe to assume that synthetic fluid fuels will serve for an extended period of time, probably during the twenty-first century, as a backstop fuel when backstop fuels are essential. But it will not be the only backstop fuel. As mentioned earlier, a chief appeal of synthetic fluid fuels is that they can substitute closely and on a very large scale for petroleum fluid fuels throughout the range of mobile and stationary energy applications. It is, in a sense, a single "one hundred percent" solution. But as energy prices change relative to other prices, the whole structure of the energy sector changes, in consumption as well as in production. In the absence of a single 100 percent solution, ten 10 percent solutions or twenty 5 percent solutions may have to suffice. Solar energy as a backstop fuel offers not so much a blanket substitute for existing fuels as a number of partial substitutes in a wide variety of different applications. Let us now turn to solar energy, and appraise its potential as a backstop fuel in all its various manifestations.

Solar energy certainly has great power to seize the imagination of the general public. Its chief advantage is its inexhaustibility, and freedom from pollution effects. But there are some drawbacks. Sunlight is two-dimensional; it has a natural surface intensity, but achieving power concentrations comparable to those easily obtained from three-dimensional fossil fuels requires elaborate and expensive focusing. Sunlight is also intermittent, and the storage of solar power in concentrated forms (similar to the concentrated chemical potential energy of fossil fuels) requires much ingenuity and expense. Nevertheless, while solar energy is no panacea, the sun is here to stay, and we should look at the economic potential of solar energy in all its forms.

The sun is essentially a huge fusion reactor which supplies the earth with electromagnetic radiation with an energy content of roughly 1 kilowatt per square meter at the earth's surface during daylight hours.

Man has used this radiation for light and heat, and of course has benefitted from the plant and animal products of photosynthesis, but has yet to harness sunlight to provide economical energy in mechanical, chemical, or electrical form. Solar energy can more readily be employed in thermal form, where the major problem is to store excess heat provided during daytime in order to raise temperatures at night. Most solar energy processes currently under investigation contemplate the use of solar heat to operate heat engines of various types and accomplish mechanical work. Other processes aim at the direct conversion of sunlight to electrical energy through photovoltaic cells. Still other processes contemplate even more exotic use of solar energy.

Solar Heating. The distinction between passive and active solar heating is indeed important economically. Whereas active solar heating requires elaborate solar collector plates and the circulation of heated water as a source for home heating, passive solar heating involves a number of simple architectural changes. Passive solar techniques are today widely applied in new home construction. Most of the techniques involve at least placing windows along the southern exposure of the home to catch the winter sunlight. Floor surfaces may be brick or tile to collect this heat for use later in the evening when the sun goes down.

Active solar heating units can range from simple solar hot water heaters to complete home heating units. Solar hot water heaters are becoming increasingly popular and economic in many regions for several reasons. First, many hot water uses such as running the dishwasher or bathing children can be adjusted to match peak water production. Secondly, the cost of adding a backup electric heating element is rather small; this is needed to cover those periods when solar heated water production is inadequate. Paradoxically, it is precisely for these reasons that the economics of solar home heating is much less encouraging. Using flat plate solar energy collectors on rooftops, the average house would require an outlay of perhaps $20,000 to $30,000 to generate enough energy to supply 50 percent of annual heating needs. This in itself is very costly, but an additional full-capacity conventional system would have to be installed for use during shady days. The main difficulty is that solar energy for heating is most abundant in those sunny areas such as Arizona where heating demand is naturally low. Due to high cost, relatively few solar-heated homes exist today, and market prospects are best for high-priced homes where solar heating is a prestige feature.

It is likely that the costs of certain elements, such as the flat plates themselves, can be reduced as a result of development of mass production techniques. But this must await the appearance of a mass market, and major companies are postponing the risk of entry into a market that may not be there until the provision of government subsidy programs to solar energy system buyers. Even with considerably reduced costs there is no assurance that solar heating will prove economical until fossil fuel prices rise considerably above current levels.

Solar Cells. One of the most compelling goals of solar power research is the development of an economical solar cell. Solar cells convert radiant energy directly into electricity, taking advantage of the photovoltaic properties of certain materials such as silicon, cadmium, and gallium. When sunlight is absorbed by these materials, some electrons are separated from their atoms. If these electrons can be induced to move in one direction and the positively charged ions in the other, a small electrical field (about 0.5 volt) is created in each cell. If a large number of solar cells are connected in series, useful power levels result. Capital cost is the big drawback. At present the silicon cells require the use of crystalline silicon, produced at great expense in small batches and assembled by hand in individual cells. By 1984 the cost for flat arrays of cells had fallen to $7.00 to $10.00 per watt, which compares quite unfavorably with levels of $0.45 to $0.60 per watt for fossil fuel and nuclear power plants. Further cost reductions are likely if the use of amorphous silicon in place of expensive crystalline silicon becomes possible—a development that is already under way.

Solar cells enjoy great support from public authorities because of their environmental advantages. Their impact is largely benign, they use an essentially undepletable source of energy, and they can be built in sizes down to those appropriate for use in individual residences. Use of solar cells (if cheap enough) could simplify complex energy systems of generation, transmission, and distribution, and to a considerable extent decentralize the control of energy consumption. This aspect of solar cells is of interest to political and social observers as well as economists.

There is evidence that costs are declining. Competitive bids for 250–350 kilowatt solar cell concentrator systems were $6.00 per watt in 1978 and $4.25 per watt in 1984. Further significant breakthroughs in the use of amorphous silicon appear necessary before solar cells can become economic at today's oil prices.

Solar Thermal Energy Conversion. Solar thermal energy conversion is another way of using solar power. It requires less research and development than solar cells, since the cost gap is less and the methods and materials used are already familiar in other applications. The basic idea is simply to collect heat from the sun by reflection from mirrors and concentrate it by focusing it on vessels containing heat exchange elements, which will heat a fluid capable of operating a steam-electric generating plant. The problems encountered in this application are similar to those of solar heating of residences: solar radiation contains diffuse energy in relatively low concentration, and since sunlight is intermittent there must be either adequate power storage or an alternative source of energy.

Solar thermal energy conversion first became a reality when the experimental 10-million-watt Barstow, California plant began operations in 1982. In this installation 1818 heliostats, each with a reflecting area of about 400 square feet, surround a tower about 300 feet high and reflect solar radiation to a boiler atop the tower. Water is the heat exchange fluid and superheated steam is produced. The output from the plant is connected to the Southern California Edison grid, and enough power is developed to supply the needs of about 7,000 people. The technology is extremely land intensive, as this plant covers 130 acres and produces 1 percent of the output of a standard nuclear plant.

Several factors influence costs. First, there is the relatively large collection area that is needed, roughly 1 square mile for every 100 million watts. Second, there is the need to concentrate solar radiation to achieve the 1000°F temperature needed for the solar boiler. Storage is another important factor. The storage of energy in any form is a relatively costly and inefficient process; storage "bargains" are hard to come by, and even hydropower dams and batteries have high capital costs. Storage is doubly important for solar power plants, since they face fluctuations both in demand and in energy supply. A solar thermal plant might conceivably employ pumped storage, pumping water into an elevated reservoir during periods of slack demand when generation capacity would otherwise go unused, and then recapturing the potential energy of the elevated water by letting it run downhill into turbines during periods of high power demand. But this requires much water, which is typically very scarce in the desert areas best suited for solar power.

The environmental impact of solar thermal conversion would appear to be generally benign. The main barriers are economic. The Energy Research and Development Agency estimated that their 100-million-watt demonstration plant, planned for the 1980s, will cost about $5500 per kilowatt in 1984 dollars, or about ten times the capital cost of more conventional generating plants. Since solar fuel costs are close to zero, higher capital costs would tend to be partially offset by lower operating costs. But even with major capital cost breakthroughs, solar thermal power will be a regional rather than a national industry.

Ocean Thermal Energy Conversion. The solar energy which strikes the earth's surface is largely expended in heating the oceans. But oceans and seas are of unequal depths, and are situated at different latitudes. Temperature differences between tropical and polar waters create slow currents, such as the Gulf Stream, which are thousands of miles in length. Visionaries have suggested placing huge turbines in the Gulf Stream, which through rotation in the 5-mile-per-hour current would generate electrical power—hydroelectric plants without dams. Solar energy also creates sea waves and winds, which might conceivably be harnessed. However, solar energy could more readily be tapped by taking advantage of the temperature gradients between the surfaces of the oceans and their lower depths. Solar radiation heats the oceans from above, and the heat is gradually transferred to greater depths by convection. In tropical and subtropical latitudes there may be a temperature difference of 40°F between the surface waters and those one-half mile or more below the surface. Although this is a relatively small difference in temperature, the volumes of water available are so great that it might be economically feasible to design huge heat engines to generate electrical power by employing heat exchangers to exploit this temperature difference and drive turbines and generators. But the thermal energy efficiency of this system would be quite low owing to the small difference in temperature between the inlet and outlet streams. Maximum efficiency would be about 6 percent, but in practice only 2 or 3 percent efficiency is expected.

Such plants might produce more than electricity. Generating plants could transmit their current through large ocean-bottom power lines. But in other plants all or part of the output could be chemical in nature. The electricity could be used to produce hydrogen electrolytically from seawater, and the hydrogen could be sent to shore by pipeline, where it could be used in fuel cells and for other energy purposes. The plants could also produce oxygen, methanol, ammonia, and other industrial chemicals.

Even though these plants do not involve any novel technology, scale-up risk is present, since these plants will be much larger than any other heat-exchange facilities ever built. The development of economically corrosion-free materials for the exchangers is also a matter of uncertainty. Nevertheless, the promise of ocean thermal energy conversion is sufficiently attractive that the Department of Energy is funding a 100-million-watt demonstration plant with a 1987 operation date. The chief attractions of this method are that it is the only solar energy system which can operate continuously at full power and that the problems of collecting and storing solar energy have already been solved by virtue of the oceans' serving as a giant solar heat sink. But the costs that have been projected have a wide range of uncertainty, and projections may prove to be on the low side. Current costs lie in the range from $2000 to $3000 per kilowatt for capital costs, much above those of conventional and nuclear plants and solar thermal energy projects.

Wind Energy. Solar energy provides the driving force for atmospheric currents, and thus is responsible for wind power. The atmosphere acts as a huge heat engine which is heated from below, in contrast to the surface heating of the oceans. Solar heating warms the air at the earth's surface, and this warmer air rises until increasing distance from the earth cools it. But the atmosphere is heated unevenly because of the variable distribution of clouds, moisture, and surface topography. Uneven heating means that air masses achieve different temperatures and rise, fall, or shift position, thus creating wind currents. Winds seldom move at uniform speeds, but accelerate and decelerate, arise and disappear.

The technology is reasonably simple. Propellers mounted on shafts rotate in response to air currents and the shaft turns a generator. Due to the sporadic nature of winds, no one considers the use of wind power to generate base-load electrical power. Instead, wind generators would be used to supplement other sources of power. In large-scale applications, storage of generated electricity would be an important feature. The velocity and directional constancy of winds increase with altitude above the earth, but so do the costs of windmill construction. Costs per kilowatt-hour depend critically upon the speed of the wind. Small wind generators are currently on the market, which can supply 1 to 10 kilowatts at wind speeds of 10 to 18 miles per hour at costs between $5000 and $15,000. Costs per kilowatt-hour might be in the range of $0.07 to $0.18 with such devices. Some of the smaller machines incorporate storage through batteries or compressed-air facilities.

The U.S. federal wind power program has fostered the development of both large and small wind power machines. Mod 2, for example, built by Boeing, has a tower height of 200 feet and a blade span of 300 feet, and is rated at 2.5 million watts in a moderate wind. Boeing estimated that in quantity production the one hundredth machine would cost about $2.5 million in 1980 dollars, or about $1000 per kilowatt, which is reasonably competitive with other new energy sources. However, due to the variability of winds in some areas, only about one-third of the rated full capacity of a windmill may be achieved on average. But windmill designs have yet to be optimized, for either large or small scale applications. In 1981 a 4-million-watt wind dynamo was built in southern Wyoming, marking the beginning of what may become the widespread supplementation of hydroelectric power with wind power, where wind power is generated when the wind is strong, and the water in the reservoir can be saved to generate power when the wind is weak.

In the early 1980s several utility companies began to install wind power units on wind "farms," particularly in regions of California where strong sea breezes prevail. Southern California Edison began with the construction of a 3-million-watt windmill near Palm Springs. By the mid-1980s, numerous wind power installations were present in the breezy areas of Southern California, with estimated costs of $0.05

per kilowatt hour. Hawaii Light and Power contracted for the installation of 80 million watts in the northeastern part of Oahu.

Biomass Cultivation. The conversion of solar energy into plant materials by photosynthesis and the further conversion of stored plant and animal materials into more concentrated forms such as coal and petroleum resulted over millions of years in the formation of fossil fuels. Total fossil fuel reserves at present (including oil shales and tar sands) represent, however, only about two weeks' supply of solar energy. The reason for this low ratio is that only a very small fraction of the sun's energy is captured through photosynthesis, and only a tiny fraction of this amount is subsequently concentrated in fossil form. It might be useful to try to obtain more fuels from photosynthetic processes by discovering and cultivating improved plant species that would maximize the production of biomass, or organic solids in the form of carbohydrates and hydrocarbons. This biomass could be processed into fuels, or biologically converted by bacteria to yield methane. Hydrogen might even be produced directly by enzyme action on biomass.

Vegetable crops cultivated for food typically convert sunlight into biomass at very low efficiencies, ranging from 0.1 to 0.5 percent. Many plants, such as weeds and trees, have much higher conversion efficiencies, in the range of 3 to 5 percent. Tree farming for biomass harvesting would require drying of the fuel and would result in fuel costs at the power plant of $3.25 or more per million Btu of heat content. While land plants in natural ecosystems show a net productivity of about 5 to 25 tons of dry biomass per acre per year, water plants show greater productivity where nutrients are abundant. Water hyacinths yield up to 85 tons per year. Water plants can be grown in shallow ponds, and with the addition of nutrients such as plant and animal wastes, very high yields result. But even if the entire U.S. corn crop were converted to alcohol fuel, it would replace about one-fourth of current U.S. oil consumption.

Hydroelectric Power. Hydroelectric power is another manifestation of solar energy, since the sun's energy is required to evaporate water and condense it into the rainfall which provides the stream flow harnessed by power plants. Hydroelectric power generated at very large dam or waterfall sites is currently produced at very low costs. There are many environmental advantages: no air pollution, little waste heat, and no need to mine mineral fuels. The chief drawbacks are perhaps esthetic: scenic river canyons are drowned, favoring the activities of sedentary outdoor types (fishing and boating) over those of more energetic inclination (hiking and climbing). Unfortunately, the potential for expanded hydroelectric power in the developed countries is quite limited.

NUCLEAR ENERGY DEVELOPMENTS

In the 1970s, most observers felt that nuclear would be the backstop fuel to replace petroleum, but experience since the Three Mile Island accident suggests otherwise. Both in Europe and in the U.S., the commitment to build new nuclear plants has dwindled. But nuclear's decline in popularity depends critically on the public's perceptions of safety, and public perceptions have been known to be fickle. Thus it is instructive to look at nuclear fuels as potential backstops, depending on public perceptions and so forth. Fission reactors may provide us with nuclear power for decades or for generations, depending upon the long-run supply of uranium. Breeder reactors, if made technically and politically acceptable, could prolong the era of fission reactors from generations to perhaps centuries. But the prospects of literally unlimited nuclear energy—from the human point of view—must await the perfecting of the fusion reactor. We will consider each source of nuclear energy in turn, paying attention to both advantages and drawbacks.

The main thrust of federal energy R&D has been in nuclear energy. This policy has long been criticized on grounds that the comparative promise of nuclear energy has never been proportional to the share of funds allocated, and that a more balanced and comprehensive federal program should have been pursued. Early enthusiasm for atomic energy was based largely on utopian thinking. But even though a kilogram of uranium-235 could release enormous energy, the energy cost of finding and concentrating the raw materials necessary to produce that kilogram exceeded the useful yield of energy in generating electric power in 1945, and continued to do so until the 1970s. Thus atomic energy was for a long time a net consumer of energy rather than a producer.

Despite this fact, there was never any chance that nuclear power would fail to receive continuing public subsidy. The permanent involvement of the military in the production of weapons-grade uranium (93 percent U-235) insured a capability for producing the much less concentrated reactor-grade uranium (3 percent U-235), and there was the sanguine expectation that "peaceful uses" of atomic power would be a salutary byproduct of military necessities.

Burner versus Breeder Reactors. Current reactors "burn" U-235 to produce heat, which is then used to produce steam, turn turbine blades, and generate electricity as in more conventional utility plants. Commercial development of the burner reactor came as a byproduct of military efforts to develop nuclear power plants for submarines. Federal nuclear R&D funds have in contrast long been focused on the development of "breeder" reactors, which not only consume U-235 as a fuel, but also convert other radioactive substances such as uranium-238 and thorium-232 into fissile compounds as the result of neutron absorption. In naturally occurring uranium only seven atoms in every thousand are in the form of the isotope U-235. Their concentration to 30 per thousand is necessary to make current burner reactors operate. The appeal of the breeder reactor is precisely its ability to transmute U-238 atoms, which are plentiful, into U-235, greatly increasing the fraction of elemental uranium metal that can be fissioned. The original promoters of nuclear energy in the 1940s foresaw breeder reactor production of electricity as the goal and regarded burner reactors as a temporary expedient.

While the promise of the breeder reactor from this perspective is impressive, the economic advantages of "breeding" are actually smaller, since the cost of the uranium input itself is very small relative to the total cost of nuclear power generation. The reasons for intense government emphasis on breeders are other than economic, and are not entirely clear. Scientific interest developed out of the enthusiasm of physicists and engineers for developing a complex new technology for its own sake. Justifying the spending of public funds, however, required other reasons. It was possible to assert that the supply of uranium was desperately limited, so that breeders would be needed within a few decades due to resource depletion. Such arguments seem overstated and without substantial merit. Uranium is not naturally abundant, but it is very widely distributed in low concentrations. There are numerous regions in the United States where uranium ores are found. The relatively brief period of active widespread exploration in the 1950s resulted in the discovery of so much uranium ore that further exploration was discouraged for a number of years. Although proven reserves are currently not excessive relative to anticipated demands in the future, the United States is now in about the same position with regard to uranium resources as it was with regard to oil in the 1920s, when little systematic exploration had been done relative to the entire resource base and much more oil remained to be discovered than had been found up to that time.

Although increasing amounts of electricity have been generated by burner reactors since the late 1950s, the operation was economically subsidized and was in fact even a deficit process in energy terms until the late 1960s. While energy was naturally required to mine uranium ore and construct the reactor plant and equipment, the largest energy input was in the concentration or "enrichment" of the uranium ore, a process that required very large quantities of electric power. Economists tend to smile at scientists who look at energy balances, preferring themselves to look at profitability as reflected through supply and demand. Assuming rational energy pricing, it is true that any process which operates at an energy deficit is very likely to operate at an economic deficit. But nuclear energy has been heavily subsidized in four ways: (1) all R&D work is done at public expense; (2) utilities are supplied with enriched uranium at prices that do not cover the total cost of enrichment: (3) radioactive wastes are disposed of at public expense; and (4) utilities are supplied with public liability insurance at rates below those that would be charged by private companies, assuming that the latter ever felt in a position to offer such insurance. The magnitudes of these subsidies are difficult to estimate, but they are very significant. The enrichment subsidy, for example, is particularly resistant to estimation. The government's cost of uranium enrichment is a closely guarded secret, as are all details of the federal nuclear program.

Until the Arab oil embargo of 1973, the economics of nuclear power had always been uncertain. Utility companies did not begin to order nuclear reactors in any volume until the major equipment suppliers undertook a policy of promotionally low pricing in the early 1960s, hoping that economies would materialize as business developed and experience grew. Such hopes were not justified, and utilities and contractors were both disappointed as costs rose above estimations, delays occurred in construction, and reliability proved inadequate. Nevertheless, the plants were eventually built, and after the energy price increases since 1973, nuclear power generation appeared to be economically viable. Federal regulations penalizing the use of high-sulfur coal, the decline in domestic natural gas supplies under federal price control, and the high cost of low-sulfur fuel oil deflected utility plant investment away from fossil fuels and toward nuclear installations. But by the time this trend was well under way, it had become very difficult to obtain the necessary sites and permits for new nuclear plants due to increasing opposition on safety and environmental grounds.

There are a number of paradoxes, technical and otherwise, about nuclear power. While nuclear energy is regarded by the layman as embodying the most sophisticated sort of technology, the burner reactor now in use in the United States is essentially a glorified water heater, extracting less than 1 percent of the total energy in the uranium input and converting that extracted heat energy into electricity at a relatively low thermal efficiency of only about 32 percent. But nuclear enthusiasts insist that even after all this inefficiency it is still wondrous that so much energy is obtained from so little mass. Laymen generally have been misled by the apparent accessibility of the relationship between matter and energy, as given in Einstein's special theory of relativity: $E = mc^2$. Here E is energy, m is mass, and c is the speed of light (i.e., the speed of electromagnetic radiation). From this equation it readily follows that the conversion of 1 pound of mass into energy would yield 38.9 trillion Btu, or enough to raise the temperature of 4 cubic miles of seawater by 1 degree Fahrenheit. But the fallacy is that matter cannot in practice be entirely converted into energy. Protons and neutrons cannot be destroyed. Nuclear energy is released by a rearrangement of the subatomic particles in the nuclear fuel. This rearrangement results in a small loss of mass. In the commercial fission reaction, only 0.1 percent of the mass of the nuclear fuel is actually converted into energy. Thus mass is far from being totally annihilated in the fission reactor—by a factor of 1000 to 1.

Will the advent of the breeder reactor greatly reduce energy costs? This is not very likely, since the cost of uranium today is only a small part of nuclear energy costs, and cutting uranium costs all the way to zero would not exert much downward leverage on total costs. If a true shortage of uranium ultimately develops, then of course uranium costs would eventually increase and the breeder would make a real contribution in retarding the date of arrival of some genuine future uranium shortage. But breeding is an expensive and relatively slow process, which has hazards all its own. The term breeder is itself misleading, since it conveys the impressions that the reactor actually creates new mass, so that the more fuel it uses the more surplus fuel it creates, and that the longer it runs the greater the supply of fissionable isotopes becomes. On the contrary, 140 pounds of uranium, for example, will never under any circumstances provide more than 140 pounds of fissionable fuel. Of this 140 pounds, only 1 pound will be U-235. With burner reactors only this pound (and not even all of it) could be used. With breeder reactors, all of the 139 pounds of U-238 might conceivably be converted into plutonium-239 to be used as fuel in the breeding process. Given present technology, and abstracting from economic limitations, only about 60 percent of the U-238 could be converted into reactor fuel. This still implies that perhaps 84 pounds of fissile material could be obtained from 140 pounds of uranium. A multiplier of 84 to 1 would seem to provide a lot of leverage for the uranium supply. Still, it is not infinite. By the time the 84th pound of fuel is consumed, there is no further fuel produced. Hence the term breeder is fundamentally misleading. The reaction is more like a jailbreak, where stable atoms are liberated by being converted into more usable fissile forms, allowing energy to escape. The term jailbreak reactor would be preferable, since only so many prisoners can be liberated from a given jail.

The breeder reactor provokes widespread opposition on both safety and economic grounds. Not only is there some small danger of catastrophic reactor accident, but the operation of a system of breeder reactors involves the accumulation of surplus plutonium fuel that must be periodically removed from the reactor and shipped to other plants for fuel use. Plutonium is one of the most lethal of all the radioactive byproducts of nuclear power generation, and as such it has a natural appeal to terrorists and to nations unable to make nuclear bombs by concentrating U-235. Furthermore, plutonium bombs are easier for nuclear amateurs to make. It is difficult to assess the magnitude of risk from this hazard, but it seems only prudent to award it a significant value.

As described in Chapter 5, the operator-error mishap involved in the Three Mile Island burner reactor, although resulting in remarkably little apparent damage, was enough to discredit nuclear power safety entirely in the eyes of millions of observers. Thus the ranks of nuclear industry critics, already large, were further swollen. Still, this was the first potentially serious accident in a burner reactor after several hundred reactor-years of operation. But the safety record of the as yet commercially unborn breeder reactor industry in the United States is far worse. In 1961, one of the three experimental liquid metal fast breeder reactors suffered a core meltdown in Idaho, killing three workers, and in 1966 the experimental Enrico Fermi plant near Detroit was shut down after part of its core melted down following a cooling system blockage.

Economic criticisms center around two issues. While breeders promise lower long-run fuel costs, their capital costs are much higher than those of burner reactors, making total costs higher. If there is no real shortage of uranium, the breeder is a white elephant. Second, the gestation period of a breeder reactor may be disappointingly long. The "doubling times" of breeders now under consideration range from 10 to 20 or more years, but the longer the time required for a breeder with a given fuel charge to generate an equal additional fuel charge, the less promising the economics.

Nuclear Fusion. Nuclear energy can be obtained not only by the fission of heavy elements but also by the fusion of lighter elements. Here, however, more work must be done on the system in order to achieve an energy output, and the technical problems are much more formidable. In the economically most promising reaction, two hydrogen isotope atoms are combined to produce a single helium atom, together with the release of energy. The amount of mass converted into energy is about 0.37 percent of the mass of the two original hydrogen isotope atoms—almost four times as much as in the fission reaction. But there are many difficulties. First, the fuel inputs consist of deuterium (hydrogen-2) and tritium (hydrogen-3). Although the abundance of deuterium is only about 1 atom in 6500 atoms of ordinary hydrogen, the supply of hydrogen from sea water is superabundant, and the ease of separation of deuterium from hydrogen is so great that the cost of obtaining deuterium for fuel use is not significant. Tritium, however, is of only microscopic abundance in nature and must be obtained by nuclear bombardment of lithium, itself an element of rather limited occurrence. Thus the fusion reaction must also depend upon the fissioning of lithium to yield tritium. But of still greater importance is the very high temperature required to achieve thermonuclear fusion, roughly 100,000,000°C. While thermonuclear fusion is the source of the sun's energy, the sun's fusion reaction (somewhat different from those employed on earth) takes place at a much lower temperature—perhaps 15,000,000°C—but at pressures higher than have yet been achieved on earth.

Heating the deuterium-tritium fuel mixture to 100,000,000°C converts it into a plasma state (dissociation of electrons from atomic nuclei), which is intensely unstable and difficult to contain. But the plasma must be contained to permit the reaction to proceed; it must be stable in order to be contained, and it has to possess the necessary density in order for the reaction to be sustained. The most promising reactor contains the plasma in a doughnut shape by magnetic forces for a sufficiently long time period at a sufficiently high temperature and at a sufficiently low density to achieve the reaction. So far the three problems of time interval, temperature, and density have not all been solved simultaneously. While it has proved possible to achieve temperatures of over 100,000,000°C, they have not been maintained long enough to permit the fusion reaction to begin. And while the plasma state has been stabilized for a sufficient time interval and at sufficiently low densities, the heat achieved has not been adequate. So far the only significant energy release from fusion has been from hydrogen bombs (using atomic bombs to initiate the reaction), where there is of course no concern for containment or sustaining a controlled reaction.

A perfected fusion reactor would have enormous advantages. Most inspiring is the virtually unlimited supply of seawater for providing hydrogen fuel. The oceans become a fuel resource, with each gallon of seawater having a recoverable energy content equal to that of 300 gallons of gasoline. Pollution and safety problems are also much reduced. There will not be a sufficiently large mass of hydrogen in the reactor at any one time to permit an explosive reaction. There are no radioactive byproducts that require transportation to other sites for processing or fuel use. The only radioactive product is the tritium isotope, which is only mildly harmful, has a short half-life, and is not biologically active as a gas. The only real hazard is that of tritium combining with oxygen to produce radioactive water, but good reactor design should reduce this hazard to an acceptable level. Since fusion reactions take place at high efficiencies, perhaps on the order of 60 percent, there will be less thermal pollution in the form of waste heat.

The commercial success of the fusion reaction probably lies decades away unless an entire series of currently unanticipated major technical breakthroughs occur very soon. While the coordination of any very large-scale joint research and development program presents many organizational problems, those in fusion research appear particularly severe. The general problem is that there can be only so much flexibility in a given project design, and each of the groups involved tends to appropriate for itself all of the design flexibility, leaving other groups with virtually impossible tasks to perform. It is as if every input factor employed in a process yielding a commodity that could be sold at a profit tried to appropriate the entirety of that unit profit for itself alone.

OTHER ENERGY SOURCES

Fuel Cells. Most processes for converting fuels into electric energy are unable to achieve a net efficiency of more than about 40 percent since they convert chemical potential energy into thermal energy and then convert the thermal energy into mechanical and finally into electrical energy. The fuel cell, however, is able to convert chemical potential energy directly into electrical energy and thus avoids the inefficiency of thermal conversions.

The fuel cell principle is the reverse of electrolysis. Hydrogen and oxygen can be electrolytically separated from water by supplying enough energy to break the bonds between those two elements. In the hydrogen fuel cell, hydrogen and oxygen are combined to produce water and the energy released by the reaction is obtained in the form of electricity. The cell is constructed like a battery and contains a porous fuel electrode (anode), through which the hydrogen is fed, and another porous oxidizer electrode (cathode), through which the oxygen is introduced. These electrodes are separated by an intermediate electrolyte. Chemical reactions within the cell create electrical voltages at the electrodes. These can be utilized by connecting an electrical load to these electrodes.

Fuel cells have not been widely used outside the space program for economic reasons. High capital costs and relatively short operating lives mean expensive electricity. In addition, the cost of hydrogen fuel is significant and is likely to increase if hydrogen continues to be produced from natural gas and light petroleum liquids. But there is surely room for cost reduction. Early fuel cells built for the space program cost from $100,000 to $400,000 per kilowatt; those used in military applications cost about $30,000, but firms today are doing research on utility applications with a goal of costs in the $500-per-kilowatt range, which would be competitive. In 1984 costs had been apparently reduced to the range of $1500 to $2000 per kilowatt. By the mid-1980s, several dozen fuel cell projects were being operated on an experimental basis, and it was hoped that production and operating experience would bring about further cost-saving innovations. Current efforts, which do not involve mass production, have already lowered capital costs and have increased operating life significantly. True mass production for larger markets would greatly increase the probability of achieving the cost reductions needed to make fuel cells competitive. Once fuel cell costs are cut to competitive levels, their use should spread very rapidly; they could be used in central generation stations, high-output power plants to supplement central station facilities, low-output power plants for remote locations and unattended operations, and units for on-site conversion of hydrogen to electricity in residences and small commercial installations.

Initial fuel cell installations have been made in applications where there is a premium on reducing air pollution further in an already polluted airshed, or in which users are attracted to a self-contained modular energy system embodying clean and advanced technology, as in schools, gymnasiums, and municipal centers. In the former category, we find new municipal power generating plants in the United States and Japan. The Manhattan plant in New York City has a capacity of 4.5 megawatts, obtains hydrogen by reforming naphtha, and operates at an efficiency of 37 percent, before allowing for thermal energy recovered from process heat and hot water byproducts. The Tokyo plant, of equal wattage, began operations in 1983. In the latter category, the U.S. Department of Energy sponsored 40 smaller wattage demonstration units, such as the two 40-kilowatt units providing light and heat at Racquetball World in Fountain City, California.

The new units embody the best of current technology, but second generation cells with exotic components could operate with efficiencies near 90 percent. Westinghouse plans to install two 7.5 megawatt prototype electricity plants by 1988, and commercial utility plants on larger scales are projected for the United States and Japan in the 1990s. Federal government support for fuel cell development was over $30 million per year in the mid-1980s.

Energy from Recovery of Wastes. A limited but still useful amount of energy could be recovered from the processing of municipal, industrial, and agricultural wastes. The economic return to such activities is very sensitive to the cost of collecting these wastes, however, and a combination of the services of garbage disposal and fuel production might make an otherwise unpromising venture economically viable. In this respect processing municipal garbage may be profitable since many cities have run out of sites for disposal of garbage by conventional landfill operations, and incineration without unacceptable pollution is costly. Power plants could offer to dispose of municipal garbage at a price marginally less than the city's cost of otherwise disposing of these wastes, and thus obtain its fuel input at a negative price. Processing this input, however, would be more or less costly depending upon the method employed. The simplest way is direct incineration in a water-wall burner, a chamber the walls of which contain water-filled pipes. Burning the unprocessed garbage generates steam for a power plant or for other uses, but the ashes that remain must be disposed of at some cost.

Depending upon the price received for accepting city garbage, the cost of generating energy from trash conversion appears to be between $2.70 and $3.60 per million Btu in 1984 dollars. Progress in trash conversion is slow, however, since this activity requires close cooperation among municipal governments, conversion contractors, and utility companies, within a context where there are no precedents or guidelines for cooperating. For these and other reasons, including the fact that many cities still have adequate land for garbage disposal by dumping and filling, it is unlikely that garbage conversion will add greatly to national fuel resources in the next 10 or 20 years. Even if all the municipal solid waste in the nation were converted to fuel, it would provide the energy equivalent of only about 1 million barrels of oil per day, some 3 percent of energy use. Apart from municipal garbage, it appears that perhaps 72 million tons of organic biomass might be reclaimed from other wastes originating in the agricultural, industrial, and municipal sewage sectors. At the rate of about 1.25 barrels of oil per ton of wastes, this would provide a maximum of about 250,000 barrels of oil per day. Again, this is not a very large part of total national energy consumption, and the economics of processing these nonmunicipal wastes is even more uncertain than that of municipal trash conversion.

Geothermal Energy. Inside the earth is an enormous amount of internally generated and stored heat, which cannot be overlooked as an energy source. If molten rock or magma extends in isolated columns to within a few kilometers of the earth's surface, the adjoining rocks are subjected to great heat. If water is trapped above the magma in a permeable stratum between two impermeable strata, the water may be converted into superheated steam, which can escape through fissures in the upper stratum. This steam can escape in the form of a surface geyser, and we have a dry steam field. The magma may also heat other bodies of subsurface water to lesser temperatures such that a mixture of steam and water is produced, creating what is called a wet steam field. At still lower temperatures the water is hot but below the boiling point. Finally, there are dry geothermal reservoirs consisting of large masses of very hot rocks (up to 700°F), which contain no water.

At present only the dry steam fields appear to be economically attractive, but research is proceeding on ways to use other geothermal resources as well. A dry steam field is developed in a manner analogous to that for an oil field. The field must contain steam heated to at least 350°F and should not be more than about 10,000 feet deep. Wells are then drilled into the steam formation and the steam is fed directly to a generation plant. Only a single field is now in operation, the Geysers field in California, but it is increasing its capacity rapidly and may achieve an output of 3 billion watts. (An oil input of about 75,000 barrels per day would be required to generate this much electricity at average fossil fuel plant thermal efficiencies.)

The total energy potential of geothermal sources is impressive, and much of it should be economically feasible at present energy prices. But geothermal steam resources are depletable. Only a finite amount of water is trapped above magma intrusions. How long a given field will last is a matter of speculation. The large Lardarello field in Italy has been producing increasing energy since 1904. For most geothermal sites an estimated life of 50 years is regarded as conservative.

Geopressurized Methane. Geopressurized methane is a potentially very important geothermal resource. Oil- and gas-bearing sedimentary basins line the Texas and Louisiana Gulf coasts. Much evidence indicates that there are sedimentary deposits lying below these oil and gas fields but above intrusive masses of heated magma, which contain trapped hot water, steam, and natural gas. Drilling into these deposits might make available vast amounts of energy in the form not only of steam but also of methane dissolved under pressure in the heated water.

It is believed that the geopressurized methane fields along the Gulf Coast were originally deep oil and gas reservoirs that were later subjected to intense heating by the approach of magma bodies from below. Under great heat and pressure the oil that originally existed in these reservoirs was broken down into methane gas, which saturated the salt water content of the reservoir rocks. When these waters become so saturated with gas that no more could be contained, the excess gas leaked upward, forming the shallower gas fields along the coast. The problem therefore is to drill deeper, below the known coastal gas fields, and penetrate the geopressurized methane fields, producing enough of the hot water to lower the formation pressures sufficiently to bring the gas up out of solution. Once gas production is initiated in this manner it can probably be continued for a long period of time, since the estimated volume of geopressurized methane on the Gulf Coast is enormous—perhaps 50 quadrillion cubic feet, or about 250 times the current proved reserves of gas.

Despite such potential, efforts to date have been disappointing. The water/methane gas ratio has been higher than expected, reducing yields and raising water disposal costs. In the absence of major technical breakthroughs, gas prices of two to three times 1985 levels may be necessary before geopressurized methane becomes economic.

Tidal Energy. Tidal energy is derived from the combined kinetic and potential energy of the sun-moon-earth system and is not a variety of solar energy. Total power capable of generation at a given site varies with the area of the enclosed tidal basin and with the square of the height of the tide, or tidal range. The United States contains only two regions with tides of over 15 feet: Passamaquoddy Bay in Maine and Cook Inlet in Alaska. The Maine bay is bounded by Canada so that its development would involve all the tensions inherent in international cooperation, and the amount of energy obtainable from the U.S. sector is quite small—only about 1.8 billion kwh per year. The potential tidal energy of the Alaskan Cook Inlet is much greater, at 75 billion kwh per year, but water depths of 300 feet at the mouth of the inlet, the presence of drift ice and silt, and the possibility of earthquakes make it very unlikely that this area will be developed in the next 25 years. Abroad, prospects are not much better. There are only two tidal power plants operating in the entire world, one in France and one in the Soviet Union, which is an indication of the difficulty of harnessing such a diffuse and episodic energy source as tides.

Hydrogen as a Fuel. In addition to being an ideal fuel for fuel cells, hydrogen is needed to produce synthetic liquid and gaseous fuels from coal by increasing the ratio of hydrogen to carbon in the input materials. Hydrogen is also needed to refine petroleum and shale oil, and it is possible to make such fuels as methanol or gasoline out of hydrogen and atmospheric carbon dioxide. Hydrogen itself can be used as fuel; with its high heat of combustion it can be burned to produce thermal energy for heating or for steam-electric generation. If a fuel storage system could be devised, hydrogen could even be used to power motor vehicles.

The chief obstacle in the path of movement toward a "hydrogen economy" is the high cost of producing hydrogen from sources other than petroleum. While hydrogen can be generated relatively inexpensively from natural gas and light oils, these fuels are themselves scarce and the opportunity cost of using them for hydrogen production is high. The major reserves of hydrogen are in seawater, but at present its electrolysis takes as much or more energy than can be obtained from the subsequent combustion of the hydrogen output. The perfection of an economical solar cell would provide a good source of energy for water electrolysis—low-voltage direct current—and solar cells might be used to make hydrogen on a large scale. Ocean thermal energy conversion plants could also use the energy they generate to produce hydrogen and oxygen from seawater. Since the capital costs of solar energy plants are high and the fuel costs are practically zero, it is optimal to utilize these plants as continuously as possible. Hence capacity not used to generate power during periods of slack demand could be employed in the production of hydrogen, which could be stored as a gas to be used at a later time, in fuel cells or in other devices, to supplement the output of solar plants during periods of peak demand.

If electricity costs $0.10 per kwh, then hydrogen produced by electrolysis would cost in the range of $3.65 per million Btu. Still, cheaper ways of producing hydrogen must be found before its use as a fuel can become widespread. At present it appears unlikely that the necessary breakthroughs will be made in time for hydrogen to play a major role as an energy source per se before the end of this century. But it is likely that increasing resources will be devoted to hydrogen research, since the use of hydrogen in the production of synthetic fuels and in refining will become increasingly necessary in coming decades.

IMPLICATIONS FOR FEDERAL RESEARCH AND DEVELOPMENT POLICY

The review of the previous list of energy sources provides both the private and public sectors with an extensive R&D menu. The question becomes, "How should the federal government allocate its energy R&D expenditures among the various alternatives, given that there is already much R&D performed in the private sector?" It is important to remember that the justification for government expenditure rests upon a market failure argument. Because an innovating firm cannot typically appropriate all of the social benefit from a new innovation, it will tend to underinvest. Stated differently, the social rate of return exceeds the private rate of return, so that government R&D is needed to increase investment up to the point where the social rate of return equals the market rate of discount.

Does the appropriability argument mean across-the-board expenditures on all technologies? Some energy technologies are so far from becoming economic and the likelihood of new breakthroughs so limited that the social rate of discount falls below the market rate of discount. Such projects are poor R&D bets. It is only those projects where the expected social rate of return exceeds or equals the market rate of discount which are eligible, and then only to the extent that appropriability is a problem. Moreover, the appropriability problem is likely to be more serious for basic research involving the invention of a new technique than for a firm engaged in the commercial development of a new technology. The latter is almost certain to capture a sizeable part of the benefit from the new technology, while the former has yet to prove the viability of the new technology. For this reason the appropriability problem is likely to be more serious in basic and applied research than in development. Federal funds should be allocated accordingly.

Part of the costs and uncertainties facing an innovating firm are the direct result of government policies, but these costs and uncertainties may not represent true social costs. By eliminating or reducing such barriers, government can accelerate the development of new energy technology and enhance economic welfare. Examples of such barriers include a host of bureaucratic licensing requirements and uncertain future environmental regulations. Even if very stringent environmental restrictions were placed on shale oil operations that would apply for the life of the plant, investors would prefer this to a situation where restrictions change every few years. Investors are reluctant to invest $2 billion or more on a project that could be made uneconomic at the whim of some federal agency. Since government imposes these costs, there is no reason the government cannot eliminate them.

We have an interesting asymmetry between the reactions of business and of government to market uncertainties. If the public sector wishes to hasten the development of new energy technologies, it appropriately seeks to provide the private sector with various inducements and guarantees that are aimed at reducing the adverse gap between marginal social benefits and marginal private benefits that usually prevails in matters of innovating new technologies. If both business and government forecasts of future market conditions are consistent, then an incentive package can be arranged that will be sufficient to initiate the desired projects. If conditions later change, as they did in 1982–85 with conditions becoming more adverse, the project is in jeopardy unless the incentives can be adjusted satisfactorily. Often this is administratively impossible, and the private contractor can minimize losses only by postponing or cancelling the project. If the government agency still desires the innovation of the new technology, it may come to feel that there is little alternative to direct public involvement if projects are ever to get off the ground. It may reason that there is a long-term public interest in the establishment of new energy technologies, and that industry should not be in a position to abort operating programs on the basis of what may prove to be short-run signals from changed current market conditions. Consequently the government may desire to be very much the senior partner in joint ventures where private companies essentially supply the hardware packages. This attitude is understandable and is defensible if government goals focus upon "information and insurance" objectives; these can be satisfied by building facilities large enough to throw light on the technology, economics, and possible hazards of new projects, but not large enough to contribute significantly to total energy supply. For commercial-scale plants, obviously future market conditions are crucial and, to the extent that these can be inferred from present conditions, either caution or enthusiasm might properly be displayed by private firms.

The government's task is thus in part to provide steadily funded programs that will yield valuable information regardless of current short-term trends in market conditions. It is a sad commentary that government R&D policy is perhaps even more changeable than oil prices. Rather than reducing governmentally imposed costs and attempting to provide long-term support for projects providing valuable information, policies appear schizophrenic, varying with administrations and swings in oil prices. Under President Carter, the emphasis was on spending vast sums to reach arbitrarily determined levels of synthetic fuels production by 1990. Under President Reagan, support for energy R&D has languished with no clear objectives. While declining oil prices in the mid-1980s may have contributed to a general feeling of malaise about energy R&D, the development of low-cost backstop fuels could produce a welfare gain of enormous proportions.

QUESTIONS

1. The usual justification given for public R&D expenditures is the nonappropriability problem. Simply stated, a successful innovator seldom appropriates the full economic benefits of his innovation. Consequently, the firm's private rate of return is less than the social rate of return, and additional public R&D is justified to offset the underinvestment in the private sector. Think of examples of the nonappropriability problem. Are patent laws designed to mitigate the problem? What types of R&D projects are likely to pose the most serious appropriability problems?

2. Suppose a major technical breakthrough lowered the backstop fuel cost from $70 to $50 per barrel. What effect would this have on today's energy price and economic welfare?

3. Imagine yourself the director of the Synthetic Fuels Corporation with a fixed budget. What criteria should you use in funding various projects? Is it useful to set explicit targets for synthetic fuel production by the year 2000?

Notes

1. The cost estimates that are presented have been drawn from a variety of sources, including interviews with companies pursuing R&D efforts in new energy sources. The most valuable single source is *Energy Futures* by Herman and Cannon (New York: Ballinger, 1976). Another useful source is the two-volume work *Modern Energy Technology* edited by Fogiel (New York: Research and Education Association, 1975).

References for Consultation

S. Herman and J. S. Cannon, *Energy Futures* (New York: Ballinger, 1976).

Max Fogiel, editor, *Modern Energy Technology*, 2 volumes (New York: Research and Education Association, 1975).

A. Hammon, W. Metz, and T. Maugh, *Energy and the Future* (New York: American Association for the Advancement of Science, 1973).

J. Hollomon and M. Grenon, *Energy Research and Development* (New York: Ballinger, 1975).

L. C. Ruedisili and M. W. Firebaugh, *Perspectives on Energy* (New York: Oxford University Press, 1972).

C. Russell, *Elements of Energy Conversion* (New York: Pergamon Press, 1967).

S. Penner and L. Icerman, *Energy: Demands, Resources, Impact, Technology, and Policy* (Reading, Mass.: Addison-Wesley, 1974).

Organization for Economic Cooperation and Development, *Energy R&D* (Paris: OECD, 1975).

J. Fowler, *Energy and the Environment* (New York: McGraw-Hill, 1975).

R. Romer, *Energy: An Introduction to Physics* (San Francisco: Freeman, 1976).

SUGGESTED POLICY DIRECTIONS

By now, the reader should be convinced that the energy problem cannot be distilled to a single well-defined problem such as characterized in the narrow and simplistic viewpoints outlined in Chapter 1. The challenge to any discipline is the ability to analyze a set of complex and interrelated problems and propose workable remedies. We hope that by now you, the reader, share with us the conviction that economics offers a powerful and exciting conceptual lens through which to observe and analyze energy markets. This book suggests that rather than there being only one energy problem, there are at least six energy problems, corresponding to the six previous chapters. In looking at each energy problem area, it was a straightforward procedure to propose remedies for each problem viewed in isolation. But how is policy to be fashioned when we recognize all six energy problem areas? Solutions to one problem may exacerbate related problem areas while ameliorating still others.

Before surveying these six policy problem areas, however, it is necessary to devote some attention to two often overlooked aspects of policy formulation: time horizons and international relationships. Too often the phrase "public policy" is practically synonymous with the short-run domestic policy of a particular nation. In retrospect, it seems little short of ridiculous that major oil importing nations in Europe and North America persisted in regarding energy policy as a purely domestic issue right up to and even beyond the Arab oil embargo of 1973, despite the fact that their dependence upon imported oil had been steadily increasing for a number of years. Some European oil importers, for example, considered the major energy policy issues of the late 1960s and early 1970s to be confined largely to the degree of subsidization of domestic coal producers and the extent of taxation of other energy industries operating within their own borders. But some of the most important energy policy areas are primarily international in scope, such as importer policies to cope with OPEC, with oil supply interruptions, and with global environmental problems such as air pollution and the buildup of atmospheric carbon dioxide.

As to time horizons, it is characteristic of the practical programs used to implement all public policies, energy and nonenergy alike, that the focus is on short-run expediency at the expense of long-run program integrity. Combating and containing existing disequilibria always seems more urgent that the less dramatic tasks of preventing future disequilibria. Thus when short-run scarcities materialize, it is virtually certain that too much effort will be expended in devising short-run price control and rationing systems, and too little attention will be devoted to laying the foundations for a more appropriate balance between long-run supply and demand in the future. These weaknesses of preoccupation with the short run and with national rather than group objectives must be kept in mind in the ensuing survey of the interrelationships among the six policy problem areas discussed in the last six chapters.

Chapter 4 demonstrated that OPEC monopoly power, while variable in intensity, is quite real and that world oil prices are well above the level consistent with existing world oil reserves. As an offset to the welfare loss in the world crude oil market, OPEC's high prices tend to improve resource allocation in the markets where distortions exist, such as import supply uncertainty and research and development. Higher OPEC prices tend to encourage oil exploration in non-OPEC areas such as the United States, the North Sea, Canada, and Mexico. Consequently, the major importing countries may be much less dependent upon OPEC oil in the future than if OPEC had allowed the world price to remain at competitive levels. In addition, higher OPEC prices tend to encourage research and development on new energy sources, which could produce the breakthroughs that would provide abundant low-cost energy for the twenty-first century.

Conflicts and compatibilities are also apparent between U.S. pricing policies and other energy problem areas. The long-delayed removal of domestic price controls on crude oil and the still incompletely achieved price decontrol of natural gas tended to weaken OPEC's monopoly power, by increasing both the world price elasticity of demand and the price elasticity of supply from the competitive fringe. Crude oil price decontrol reduced the import supply uncertainty distortion as higher oil prices reduced overall consumption and increased domestic production. Since new energy forms must compete with domestic oil and gas, price decontrol will speed the development of new energy sources. On the negative side of the ledger, if the increased production of domestic energy does not occur under conditions that fully internalize externalities in energy production, the welfare loss from environmental externalities will be increased.

The existence of these conflicts and compatabilities precludes the meaningful formulation of simple quantitative goals for energy policy. Politicians in particular like to announce quantitative goals for energy policy because quantitative goals give an appearance of precision. Examples of such goals include "self-sufficiency" for U.S. energy production as espoused by the Nixon administration, and the Ford Foundation study's goal of limiting annual energy consumption to 100 quadrillion Btu by the year 2000.[1] Let us further generalize by contemplating the setting of a quantitative goal for each of the six energy problem areas. These could include: forcing OPEC prices down by $\$a$ per barrel per year, limiting SO_x emissions to b tons per year, reducing imports to c barrels per year, holding total energy consumption below d Btu per year, limiting domestic oil and gas price increases to e percent per year, and producing f barrels per year of synthetic oil.

How do we know if these goals are compatible? Is it possible to limit domestic oil and gas price increases to e percent per year and still meet the conservation, import supply security, and research and development targets? Even if the goals were mutually compatible, given assumptions about OPEC stability, world economic growth, and so forth, what happens when a critical assumption changes? Continuing disunity among OPEC members would assure that the goal of steady decreases in real OPEC prices would be achieved, but falling world oil prices would probably mean that conservation, import limitation, and R&D targets would not be met. How, then, does one assess the success or failure of an energy policy? Should one merely weigh all goals equally and compute a simple batting average?

Chapters 2 and 3 demonstrated that efficient energy allocation is really a pricing problem. Prices should reflect the equality of marginal social costs and benefits, not only at a point in time, but over time. Prices must be made to reflect the marginal social cost of production, which involves internalizing any externalities, correcting for the effects of monopoly, and incorporating the user costs owing to the scarcity of a nonrenewable resource. The important conclusion is that if this condition is met, resource allocation is efficient, regardless of the amount of domestic production, the quantity of total consumption, or the level of imports! Policies designed to yield efficient prices will, of course, result in specific quantities of domestic energy production and total energy demand, and a given level of imports, but these numbers are only statistical artifacts resulting from efficient pricing and not its cause. The advantage of focusing on efficient pricing as opposed to specific quantities is that policy makers are then forced to undergo the discipline of computing marginal social costs and asking to what extent these are approximated by market prices.

TOWARD A COMPREHENSIVE ENERGY POLICY

Given that an enlightened policy can overcome these contradictions through the efficient pricing of energy, the next question is how to implement it. Obviously, energy policy must necessarily proceed sequentially, focusing on one specific distortion at a time. This raises an important methodological question: In calculating the efficient pricing solution for a given distortion, should the resulting welfare effects of other distortions enter the analysis? One approach is to propose efficient pricing based solely on the distortion under consideration at the time. The second approach is to select an efficient price after including the direct welfare effects arising from other energy market distortions. Recall from Chapter 2 the example of an implacable distortion in market C while policy is aimed at correcting a distortion in market A. A second-best policy would be to select a price in market A that would maximize the welfare gain in the two markets. In essence, the first approach is to solve for the "best" solution while the second approach finds a "second-best" solution.

The appropriateness of these two alternative solutions ultimately hinges on what one assumes about the permanence of the other distortions. If policy will subsequently deal with these distortions, then a purely piecemeal approach to efficient pricing is appropriate. Since a given distortion will be eliminated, there is no reason to include welfare effects from it in dealing with some other policy problem. On the other hand, if certain distortions are implacable, subsequent policy initiatives will not remove them. Therefore, to the extent that other policy changes generate welfare effects associated with these distortions, these welfare effects should be allowed for in formulating an optimal pricing solution. Our approach in the remainder of this chapter is to outline a "best" set of policies. Of course, this simplifies the analysis, but more importantly, the student and policy analyst should always explore the best solution first, before reluctantly modifying it to account for implacable distortions. Too often, policy proceeds on the basis of "what is politically feasible" (i.e., assuming a host of implacable distortions) rather than asking what ought to be. Since "what is politically feasible" involves highly subjective judgments that are subject to change over time, we shall do well to avoid this type of speculation.

OPEC: A SHIFT FROM PASSIVE ACCEPTANCE

As illustrated in Chapter 4, even though world oil reserves will become less abundant in the 1990s, the prices extracted by OPEC are still well above that which would occur in a competitive world crude oil market. The world-wide welfare loss from the world's most successful cartel was estimated to exceed $80 billion in 1984.

In the long run, the best way to eliminate OPEC's monopoly power is for each importing nation to follow a rational and coherent energy policy that places highest priority on reliance upon non-OPEC sources and limits OPEC imports to unavoidable minimum volumes, which should decline over time. But such policies are expensive and require patient concentration on long-run goals. What can be done in a short-run time perspective? Even though short-run policy actions by consuming nations are not likely in themselves to result in the cartel's disintegration, OPEC's monopoly power to control prices can be attenuated substantially. Cartel unity is undermined through exploiting fundamental differences in interest among OPEC members. Certain countries have strong incentives to cut prices if not detected. Direct crude sales by government-owned companies allow the terms of such transactions to remain secret. With the international oil companies acting as vigorously price-competitive purchasers of OPEC oil, cartel solidarity will be weakened. Competitive bidding for import rights along the lines suggested by Professor Adelman fits into this category of policies that would exploit intercountry differences among OPEC members.

In addition, Chapter 4 showed that both the world price elasticity of demand for oil and supply elasticity from the competitive fringe nations were quite sensitive in determining OPEC's optimal price. The use of tariffs rather than import controls helps make OPEC's demand schedule more price-elastic. To go a novel step forward, if the major consuming nations were to uniformly raise tariffs to match OPEC price increases, the effect of such a policy would be to double the price elasticity of demand! On the elasticity of supply side, prices from non-OPEC sources must be allowed to rise to the level set by OPEC, as the supply response from the competitive fringe is an important check on the cartel's power. In addition, the long-run elasticity of supply from the competitive fringe is vital to checking OPEC power over the longer term. It is here that a vigorous R&D policy can lead to substantial welfare gains.

In the 1970s OPEC was favored by a host of beneficial external circumstances, which various cartel members exploited mercilessly. The 1980s have been less congenial to cartel prosperity, largely because of its own previous pricing excesses, which cut world oil consumption and increased non-OPEC production. Thus during the 1970s the cartel's members were its own worst enemies. By the mid-1980s this lesson had been learned and renewed attempts at effective collusion were being undertaken. The economic incentives for collusion have always been quite compelling. Nevertheless, OPEC's monopoly power can be further attenuated, resulting in additional reductions in real oil prices. But this will require a new posture from the consuming nations, relying less upon supplications to foreign potentates and more on policies recognizing long-term economic realities.

METHODS OF AMELIORATING
THE ENERGY/ENVIRONMENTAL
CONFLICT

Chapter 5 underscored the strong relationship between energy use and air pollution, and the weaker links with water pollution and with thermal pollution. Some may argue that energy development must take precedence over environmental controls or vice versa. This is a gross oversimplification, which overlooks the fact both are pricing problems. If energy sources are priced properly, the appropriate trade-off between the two can be achieved. The key to preserving a livable environment and expanding energy supplies lies in a careful cost-benefit analysis of the pollutants associated with each specific fuel. The price of that fuel must be made to include not only the private costs of producing the fuel but also the costs borne externally if the price is to truly reflect marginal social costs. Externalities can be internalized in the price of a fuel through either pollution standards or taxes. While there are situations where pollution taxes are inappropriate, we feel that in many areas taxes could supplant pollution standards and lead to increased welfare. Too often quantitative pollution standards are set with little or no regard for the marginal damages created by the last unit of pollution or the marginal cost of controlling it. By focusing on taxes, one must necessarily ask what tax rate equilibrates marginal damages with marginal control costs.

Still another difficulty arises due to the uncertainty about present and future government environmental regulations. These are particularly serious in their impact on the development of synthetic fuels from coal and shale oil. A sensible policy would be for EPA officials to agree initially with synthetic fuel developers on acceptable operating procedures, which would remain in effect for a sufficiently long period, perhaps 20 to 25 years. Even though these standards might not be optimal for such a long period, they would eliminate the crucial uncertainty of having to meet much more stringent standards in the future. Particularly in the development of new fuel sources, environmental policies that reduce uncertainty can improve R&D performance.

A common difficulty present in environmental policy formulation has been excessive stress on short-run programs aimed at achieving quick results, to the detriment of attaining long-run goals. A related example is the very long-run problem of carbon dioxide buildup in the atmosphere. In the short run, combustion reactions that yield carbon dioxide are regarded as environmentally benign, since carbon dioxide in itself does not give rise to the sort of pollution problems that are associated with carbon monoxide or sulfur and nitrogen oxides. Hence measures are adopted, such as catalytic converters on automobile engine exhaust systems, which increase carbon dioxide emission. But in the long run the climatic changes brought on by increasing concentrations of atmospheric carbon dioxide may cause intense social and economic disruption on a global scale. The problem is both long-run and international in scope—precisely the sort of policy issue that conventional approaches are poorly qualified to deal with. It is, however, encouraging that at the scientific and technological level the carbon dioxide buildup phenomenon is receiving cooperative research efforts on an international scale previously unparalleled.

SUGGESTED APPROACHES TO THE PROBLEM OF COPING WITH OIL IMPORT INTERRUPTIONS

Chapter 6 illustrated that the national security problem is nothing more than a standard externality problem. Again the starting point for policy analysis must be a careful cost-benefit analysis involving at least four steps. First, the marginal damage function must be quantified. Second, policy makers must identify the policy set of security-enhancing measures that lead to the overall minimization of the sum of damage costs, control or security costs, and administrative costs. A third step is to implement the provision of these security-enhancing measures at their socially optimal levels. A fourth step involves translating the implicit security premium attachable to secure domestic and foreign oil supplies into market prices that internalize the external security premium.

To date, considerable progress has been made on steps one and two. Knowledge about the marginal damage function and identification of the Strategic Petroleum Reserve as a low-cost security-enhancing device are heartening. Progress on steps 3 and 4 is less encouraging. Despite analysis supporting at least a 750 million barrel SPR, the outlook in the mid-1980s was that it would be scaled back to 500 million barrels or roughly 100 days' supply of imports. There is the additional question of how and when withdrawals from the SPR will proceed.

While international oil-sharing agreements are theoretically in place among nations participating in the International Energy Agency, it is not obvious how they would in fact operate. It must constantly be realized, however, that oil import interruption is a problem common to all importers, and policies that appear to be optimal for one importer in isolation will not prove optimal in practice, since no country is in fact isolated from all other importers. A cooperative framework must be developed within which free trade among importers takes place on the basis of prices that adequately internalize the external costs associated with insecure sources of imported oil. Since international cooperation in policy matters is both crucial and difficult, the formulation of an optimal program among the importing countries will be a matter of extreme difficulty.

Even if governmental authorities attain the optimal level of national security through the provision of these emergency supply and conservation policies, there remains the fourth problem—a distortion in the market for crude oil. Assuming domestic oil sources are allowed to compete with foreign imports subject to embargo, the two prices will be equivalent. Yet the latter includes a risk premium against which authorities have had to purchase security. In effect, the true social costs of the nonsecure oil are not fully reflected in its market price. To correct for this distortion, a tariff equivalent to the security premium should be attached to the nonsecure imports. Additionally, a tariff policy by the United States helps to increase the demand elasticity facing OPEC and thereby to attenuate price increases.

POLICIES TO PROMOTE CONSERVATION

The term energy conservation means many different things to different people. To many, energy conservation is simply using less energy per dollar of GNP. In the 1970s, the concern was that there were only limited possibilities to substitute energy for nonenergy inputs. Therefore, reductions in energy supplies would, according to this view, result in more or less proportional reductions in GNP. The experience of the 1980s puts such fears to rest. The corresponding reductions in energy-GNP ratios and the substitution from oil to other energy forms in the 1980s has been impressive.

Today, the conservation issue centers not on the feasibility of reducing energy consumption but rather on the criteria one should use to determine whether energy consumption and production are occurring at the economically optimal rate. To an economist, conservation on the demand side of the market occurs when the marginal social value equals the marginal social cost. This implies that the prices of energy include their full social costs, including any external costs. Nonprice methods of energy allocation generally behave poorly in allocating energy to its highest valued uses. Furthermore, such policies, adopted during short-run emergencies, frequently end up as long-term allocation devices. The experience of the 1970s counsels emphatically against nonprice allocation schemes despite their attribute of avoiding large scale income redistribution. Unfortunately, these are lessons soon forgotten, particularly in the face of an impending embargo.

When conservation criteria are applied to domestic oil production, it is apparent that in the absence of any public intervention, a serious market failure would exist. State prorationing laws have sought to deal with the symptoms of the market failure—excessive drilling and supernormal production rates. Instead, the economically efficient solution requires that an oil field be treated as a single economic unit and produced so as to maximize fieldwide production. Unitization rarely occurs voluntarily, and compulsory unitization laws fail to reach a large portion of U.S. production.

GOVERNMENTAL PRICE CONTROLS AND TAX POLICIES

During the period when oil and gas prices were controlled at low levels, these price controls occasioned a loss in U.S. economic welfare second only to the welfare losses imposed by the OPEC price hikes themselves. These price controls led to a welfare loss from overconsumption by artificially lowering the prices of oil and gas. At the same time, price controls on domestic production restricted domestic output below the socially optimal level.

Deregulation of crude oil prices in 1981 and of many categories of gas prices in 1985 considerably reduced welfare losses in these and in other related markets. The elimination of price controls on oil definitely increased the price elasticity for OPEC's oil exports. Under price controls, every increase of $1 per barrel charged by OPEC increased the average oil price paid in the U.S. by only about $.50. After deregulation, every $1 price increase by OPEC increased U.S. prices by the same dollar amount. Price decontrol of oil and gas will lead over time to greater discoveries and production by competitive fringe producers, further undermining OPEC. Increased domestic production will likewise reduce the dependence of the U.S. on nonsecure oil sources and reduce national security costs. Since all fuels, both conventional and exotic, must compete against oil and gas, the elimination of low oil and gas price ceilings will enable the more rapid development of new energy forms.

Notwithstanding these achievements, the legacy of these earlier policies is the Windfall Profit Tax and continued price controls on certain categories of natural gas. While the Windfall Profit Tax is scheduled to be phased out beginning in 1991, it remains unclear whether such a phaseout will indeed occur. In the interim, secure domestic oil commands a lower net price than oil from the Middle East.

ENERGY RESEARCH AND DEVELOPMENT

It is time to take a long look down the road into the twenty-first century, when oil and gas supplies will have become even more expensive. Our decisions now will determine whether abundant new energy sources will be available at lower prices. Chapter 9 outlined a number of promising new technologies, but their cost and availability will all require substantial technical breakthroughs. The fact that the successful innovator seldom appropriates the full social benefits from his innovation means that in the absence of government expenditure the private sector will underinvest in R&D. Obviously, government can support a variety of research modes, from broadly fundamental to narrowly applied, and can range from support of a variety of technologies to support of only one technology.

We visualize the government as being able to spawn new energy industries through a system of competitive bids at a very low cost to the taxpayer. For energy technologies that appear reasonably close to becoming economic, the government could agree to guarantee the price received by producers of the new energy form. Let us assume initially that five firms might receive such a price guarantee. To use synthetic gas as an example, firms would submit bids for the minimum price guarantee necessary to allow them to build a synthetic gas plant of specified capacity. Suppose it were decided that initially five separate producers should begin production in the industry. The fifth from the lowest bid would then become the guaranteed price for all five producers. On the other hand, if there were a big price differential between the fourth and fifth lowest bids, authorities might decide to begin with only four producers, using the bid of the fourth firm as the guarantee price.

This approach of founding new energy industries has three prominent advantages. First, the firm has the incentive to minimize costs and make the technology commercial. Second, the cost to the taxpayer is only the difference between the guarantee price and existing market prices. Third, establishing a number of initial producers fosters a competitive market structure and the use of diverse technologies.

One should anticipate that technological change will result in major cost reductions in some of the new energy markets and not in others. Once the cost falls below existing market prices, new firms will enter and existing firms will expand capacity without the necessity of any guarantees. For other new energy industries, the cost breakthroughs may never be significant enough to lower costs to be competitive with existing fuels, and the industry will terminate with the price guarantees after, say, a twenty-year period.

To recapitulate, through a sealed-bid minimum guarantee price, a number of promising infant industries utilizing new energy technologies would enter the market. The size of these infant industries would of course vary depending on a number of factors, including the price differential between existing fuels and the bid prices. Once they were established, the only government assistance would come for the plants initially granted the price guarantee, and even these could expire after, say, a twenty-year period. Thus we are not envisioning a huge system to subsidize high-cost energy production just because it originates from nonconventional sources. An additional element in the bidding process is that environmental procedures for the life of the plant must be stipulated to the bidders in advance, eliminating environmental uncertainties. In principle, the creators of the Synthetic Fuels Corporation visualized an agenda similar to that outlined here.

It must be admitted that it is easier to spawn new energy industries during a period of rising real energy prices than during a decline. Thus the efforts first undertaken during the Carter administration should have been more vigorously pursued during Reagan's first administration. The reverse happened: what little momentum had been previously achieved was allowed to be completely dissipated. Renewed efforts are now needed to offset the additional years lost to inaction.

LESSONS LEARNED FROM THE PAST

The principal lesson to be learned from past governmental policies in energy markets is that they are frequently misdirected, without a clear rationale or well-defined purpose. Perhaps this is the necessary result of injecting technically and economically complicated energy issues into the political arena, which functions on the basis of compromise rather than technical analysis. Whatever the explanation, on balance regulation has done little to solve the energy crisis. Nor has this regulation been costless. The budget of the Department of Energy in 1984 exceeded $12 billion—a good portion of which produces only minor social benefits. In addition, one must include the resource costs devoted by the private sector to complying with these regulations. In sum, it would not be surprising if $10 to $20 billion of resources were devoted to either ineffectual or counterproductive regulation.

It does not follow from this, however, that government has no role to play; rather it must be more selective. Chapter 2 illustrated that in situations with serious market failures due to externalities, public goods, monopoly, and indivisibilities, government policies can improve resource allocation, providing the cost of the regulation is less than the resulting welfare gain. Following this criterion, we feel government energy policy has an important role to play in dealing with the environment, national security, the limitation of OPEC's monopoly power, conservation in oil and gas production, and R&D on new energy forms. In these areas government policy can have and in some cases is already having a quite positive influence.

POSTSCRIPT: POLITICAL CONSTRAINTS ON ECONOMIC POLICIES IN THE ENERGY ARENA

While this book is primarily concerned with the economic analysis of energy policy issues, it is only fair to warn the student that where public policies are concerned, politicians rather than economists have the last word. Although public bodies may invite input from both scientists and economists, the final product of political deliberations may be both unscientific and uneconomic. The professional politicians who preside over the inevitable compromises respond pragmatically to the balance of pressures and must in effect act charitably toward the illusions of those in power. (One hesitates to characterize the politician who, when informed that his proposal violated the second law of thermodynamics, ordered his legislative assistant to see what could be done about repealing "Section II of the Thermodynamics Act.")

Although democratic processes are absolutely necessary to maximize the likelihood of the retention of personal freedoms, they are not always conducive to achieving purely economic goals like securing the most efficient development of highly complex new energy technologies. The reason is clear: political freedom includes the freedom to waste. This fact must simply be faced. Economists and others interested in output and efficiency cannot afford to dissipate their efforts in mere condemnation. They must present facts and arguments and attempt in every way to influence policy decisions in the interest of objectivity, but in the end they must realize that while political decisions may sometimes seem to be made in an intellectual vacuum, a technical vacuum, an economic vacuum, and perhaps even an ethical vacuum, they are never made in a political vacuum.

1. Explain why, even though OPEC's marginal social cost of oil is far less than the market price, for welfare calculations within the consuming countries the relevant marginal social cost of oil equals the OPEC price, plus any national security externalities.

2. Show graphically the welfare effects accruing to the United States of a $5 per barrel reduction in OPEC's price. Measure the welfare effects in the crude oil market, national security, and R&D.

3. In performing applied welfare analysis on externalities, what in your opinion is the most important thing to measure?

4. Now assume OPEC collapses and world prices fall to $5 per barrel. For the U.S. economy operating under a tariff, show the welfare gains in the crude oil market resulting from the price decline. Show

the welfare loss resulting from increased dependence on OPEC oil. How should the tariff level be adjusted to promote optimal welfare?

5. Now assuming the price declines and U.S. import controls are used instead of tariffs, show the effect on OPEC's demand schedule. Draw the additional welfare loss. Furthermore, using Figure 8.1, show how state regulatory agencies through prorationing might raise prices. Describe the welfare loss.

6. Assuming a given conservation target, show how the tax receipts vary with the price elasticity of demand.

7. It can be argued that old gas fields with constant marginal costs of production should not be deregulated, since higher prices will not increase production. If these prices are not deregulated, is there an efficiency loss? Can you devise a tax that would promote economic efficiency and avoid windfall profits to the producers of these fields?

8. List the priority you place on dealing with the six energy problem areas outlined here.

9. Can you think of other energy problem areas that are potentially more important than some of these six?

Note 1. Energy Policy Project of the Ford Foundation, *A Time to Choose* (Cambridge, Mass.: Ballinger, 1974).

BIBLIOGRAPHIC ITEMS

Chapter 1. The Dimensions of the Energy Problem

1. Sam Schurr and Bruce Netschert, *Energy in the American Economy, 1850–1975* (Baltimore: Johns Hopkins Press, 1960).

2. Joel Darmstadter, Hans Landsberg, Herbert Morton, and Michael Coda, *Energy Today and Tomorrow: Living With Uncertainty* (Englewood Cliffs, N.J.: Prentice-Hall, 1983).

3. L. C. Ruedisili and M. W. Firebaugh, editors, *Perspectives on Energy: Issues, Ideas, and Environmental Dilemmas* (New York: Oxford University Press, 1982).

Chapter 2. Static Criteria for Efficient Energy Resource Allocation

1. Arnold E. Harberger, "*Three Basic Postulates of Applied Welfare Analysis,*" *Journal of Economic Literature*, September 1971.

2. R. G. Lipsey and K. Lancaster, "The General Theory of Second Best," *Review of Economic Studies*, 1956–1957.

3. R. E. Just, D. L. Hueth, and Andrew Schmitz, *Applied Welfare Economics and Public Policy* (Englewood Cliffs, N.J.: Prentice-Hall, 1982).

Chapter 3. Criteria for Efficient Dynamic Resource Allocation

1. Harold Hotelling, "The Economics of Exhaustible Resources," *Journal of Political Economy*, April 1931.

2. L. C. Gray, "Rent Under the Assumption of Exhaustibility," *Quarterly Journal of Economics*, May 1914.

3. P. S. Dasgupta and G. M. Heal, *Economic Theory and Exhaustible Resources* (Cambridge, Mass.: Cambridge University Press, 1979).

Chapter 4. OPEC Behavior and World Oil Prices

1. Morris A. Adelman, *The World Oil Market* (Baltimore: Johns Hopkins Press, 1972).

2. Raymond Vernon, editor, *The Oil Crisis* (New York: Norton, 1976).

3. J. M. Griffin and D. J. Teece, editors, *OPEC Behavior and World Oil Prices* (London: George Allen & Unwin, 1982).

Chapter 5. Environmental Issues in Energy Development

1. John M. Fowler, *Energy and the Environment* (New York: McGraw-Hill, 1975).

2. E. S. Mills, *The Economics of Environmental Quality* (New York: Norton, 1978).

3. W. A. Nierenberg, editor, *Changing Climate* (Washington: National Academy Press, 1983).

4. Robert H. Boyle, *Acid Rain* (New York: Nick Lyons Books, 1983).

5. G. T. Miller, Jr., *Energy and Environment: The Four Energy Crises* (Belmont, Calif.: Wadsworth, 1980).

Chapter 6. Coping With Oil Supply Disruptions

1. Douglas Bohi and Milton Russell, *Limiting Oil Imports: An Economic History and Analysis* (Baltimore: Johns Hopkins Press, 1978).

2. D. A. Deese and J. S. Nye, editors, *Energy and Security* (Cambridge, Mass.: Ballinger, 1981).

3. J. Plummer, editor, *Energy Vulnerability* (Cambridge, Mass.: Ballinger, 1982).

Chapter 7. Conservation

1. James M. Griffin, *Energy Conservation in the OECD: 1980–2000* (Cambridge, Mass.: Ballinger, 1979).

2. D. R. Bohi, *Analyzing Demand Behavior: A Study of Energy Elasticities* (Baltimore: Johns Hopkins Press, 1981).

3. Stephen L. MacDonald, *Petroleum Conservation in the United States: An Economic Analysis* (Baltimore: Johns Hopkins Press, 1971).

Chapter 8. Federal Taxation and Price Regulation of Energy Production

1. E. A. Copp, *Regulating Competition in Oil* (College Station, Texas: Texas A&M University Press, 1976).

2. Paul W. MacAvoy, *Price Formation in Natural Gas Fields* (New Haven: Yale University Press, 1962).

3. Joseph P. Kalt, *The Economics and Politics of Oil Price Regulation* (Cambridge, Mass.: MIT Press, 1981).

Chapter 9. Energy Sources for the Twenty-First Century

1. S. Herman and L. Cannon, *Energy Futures* (New York: Inform, 1976).

2. Max Fogiel, editor, *Modern Energy Technology* (New York: Research and Education Association, 1981).

3. S. Penner and L. Icerman, *Energy: Demand, Resources, Impact, Technology, and Prices* (Reading, Mass.: Addison-Wesley, 1974, 1975, and 1977 [3 volumes]).

Chapter 10. Suggested Policy Directions

1. R. Kalter and W. Vogely, editors, *Energy Supply and Government Policy* (Ithaca, New York: Cornell University Press, 1976).

2. Ford Foundation and Resources for the Future, *Energy: The Next Twenty Years—An Overview* (Cambridge, Mass.: Ballinger, 1979).

3. Paul W. MacAvoy, *Energy Policy: An Economic Analysis* (New York: Norton, 1983).

INDEX

Canada *(continued)*
    energy prices in, 250
    fuel mix used in, 255, 257
    imports as percent of oil requirements, 215
    oil production of, 14
    tar sands, 153, 342, 343
Carbon, role in air pollution, 175
Carbon cycle, 183
Carbon dioxide
    atmospheric buildup, 180–184, 375–376
    role in air pollution, 173, 175
Carbon monoxide
    emission levels, 178
    role in air pollution, 173, 177
Carter administration, energy policy of, 123, 292, 368, 380
Cathedral Bluffs shale oil project, 345
Cereal grains, use for fuel production, 354
Chemical technology as cause of pollution, 167
China, coal reserves of, 25
Chlorofluorocarbons, 180
Christensen, L., 251
Cities Service Company, share of natural gas market, 318
Clean Air Act of 1967
    air quality regions, 209
    nondegredation doctrine, 211
    1977 amendments, 210
Coal
    air pollution from, 170, 192
    decline in use of, 255–256
    for electricity generation, 25, 26
    environmental disadvantages of, 26
    gasification of, 194, 341, 345–348
    industrial role of, 3, 25–26, 250, 255
    liquefaction of, 194, 341, 345–348
    metallurgical use of, 12
    pricing of, 267
    replacement of wood by, 3
    reserves of, 25
    residential use of, 26, 255
    share in energy consumption, 6–10, 25, 26, 255–256
    sulfur removal from, 346
    synthetic fuels from, 26, 194, 339, 340, 345–348
Coal Mine Health and Safety Law of 1969, 187
Coal mining
    in Elizabethan England, 3
    environmental impact of, 26, 188, 192
    hazards of, 187
Cobb-Douglas production processes, 19
Coda, M. J., 254
Cold Lake tar sands, 342
Colony shale oil project, 344–345
Combustion reactions
    incomplete, 172, 175
    inefficient, 172, 175
    role in air pollution, 172
Communism, Arab opposition to, 157
Communist bloc countries. *See also* China; Soviet Union
    coal reserves of, 25
    energy consumption patterns of, 6–9
    natural gas reserves of, 25
    oil production in, 148
    proved oil reserves, 23
Competition. *See also* Monopolies
    in oil and gas industries, 317–327
    in research and development, 326–327
    theoretical bases for, 37–39, 78–79
Competitive equilibrium, 35
Competitive fringe (of non-OPEC oil producers), oil supply from, 137–141, 151–153
Conservation movement of the nineteenth century, 167
Conservation of energy resources
    definitions of, 245–246
    feasibility of, 246–257
    fuel efficiency standards for, 265–266
    interfuel substitutions for, 252–257
    in oil. *See* Conservation of oil
    public exhortation as means of, 264–265
    rationale for, 245–246, 257–259
    rationing as means of, 262–264, 377
    taxes on energy-consuming equipment as means of, 268–269
    taxes on fuels, 266–268
Conservation of oil
    drain OPEC first policy for, 230–231
    and government pricing policies, 377
    production techniques for, 270–279
    prorationing for, 276–279, 285, 322–323
    as response to embargoes, 229–230
    and shut-in oil supplies, 220
    state regulation agencies for, 218–219, 377–378
    unitization for, 272–277, 320
Consumer surplus in welfare analysis, 56–58
Consumers
    per capita expenditure of energy, 308
    price controls as protection for, 308–310, 312–313
Contracts, long-term, with foreign oil suppliers, 231–232
Conversion efficiencies of energy sources, 6
    of coal to synthetic fuels, 26
    improvement of, 324
    of natural gas to liquid fuel, 25
    of nuclear fission reactors, 357
    and thermal pollution, 171
Cool water coal gasification project, 345
Cost-benefit analysis. *See* Welfare analysis

imports, percent of oil requirements, 215

market share of OPEC oil exports, 160

Getty Oil Company, 319

Geysers geothermal field, California, 363

Glacial melt, role in changing climate
alpine and continental glaciers, 182
ice caps, 181
west Antarctic ice shelf, 182

Government revenues in welfare analysis, 57–58

Government role in energy markets. *See also* Federal Power Commission; Price controls; Subsidies
as cause of market failures, 40, 89, 259–261, 263–264
offshore leasing by, 317, 320–321
role in development of new energy sources, 366–368, 379–380
welfare analysis as determinant of. *See* Welfare analysis

Great Plains synthetic gas project, 347

Greenhouse effect, 180

Greenhouse gases, 180

Gross domestic production (GDP) per capita, and energy consumption, 248–252, 256–257

Group security of oil supply, 221

GSI service company, innovation activity of, 327

Gulf Oil Company
coal liquefaction process of, 347
offshore leasing of, 321
share of natural gas market, 318
merger with Chevron, 319

Harberger, Arnold, 61–62

Health hazards
of air pollution, 170–171, 176–177
of coal mining, 187
of radiation, 189–190, 193

Heat content measurements of fuel. *See* British thermal units

Heat of combustion, 172

Heating fuel, prices of, by country, 250

Heavy oil, California, 342–343

Hogan, William, 18

Horwich, George, 236

Hotelling Harold, 74, 78, 337

Human muscle, as energy resource, 2

Hybrid model of OPEC cartel, 139–143

Hydrocarbons
chemical nature of, 178
role in air pollution emissions, 170–171, 178

Hydroelectric power, 354–355
Btu measurements of, 5
environmental effects of, 192–193
share in U.S. energy consumption, 10
share in world electric power

consumption, 9, 11, 27

Hydrogen
content in fuels, 346
costs of utilizing, 365–366
uses for energy production, 365

Import controls on oil, 218–221, 238–242, 285, 374, 377

Import tickets for U.S. oil refiners, 219–220

Incinerator emissions, tax on, 207

Income distributional effects of price controls, 308–313
in welfare analysis of energy market, 56–60

Income tax, foreign, as tax deduction, 108–110

Indifference curves in resource allocation analysis, 35–37

Indonesia. *See also* Dutch East Indies
economic characteristics of, 143
oil producing history of, 13, 14
role in OPEC of, 98, 111, 132, 133

Industrial processing as source of air pollution, 177

Industrial revolution, impact on energy consumption of, 3

Inflation
effects of, in resource allocation, 82–83, 330
rates, 1973–75: 120, 308

Interest rates
in resource allocation analysis, 69, 83, 87–91
and social rate of discount, 87–91

Interfuel substitutions, 252–256

Internal combustion engine, 5
as cause of smog, 171

International commodity agreements, 283

International Energy Agency (IEA), 163, 232–233, 376

Investment
of OPEC oil profits, 100–102
in research and development. *See* Research and development activities

Iran
nationalization of oil industry by, 108
oil producing history of, 14
political instabilities in, 215
pricing policies of, 122–123
role in OPEC of, 120–121, 122–124
Soviet strategy on, 31

Iran-Iraq war, 124, 158, 215, 235–236

Iraq
nationalization of oil industry by, 101
price cutting to gain greater OPEC market share, 122
role in OPEC of, 98, 100, 111, 133, 155, 156–158

Ireland
energy fuel mix, 257

Ireland *(continued)*
  energy/gross domestic product ratio,
    249
Israel, role of, in energy crisis. *See* Arab-
    Israeli conflict
Italy
  energy/gross domestic product ratio,
    249–251
  fuel mix in, 255
  fuel prices in, 250
  imports as percent of oil requirements,
    215
  share of OPEC exports consumed by,
    160

Jailbreak reactor simile, 358
Japan
  energy consumption patterns of, 6–10
  energy/gross domestic product ratio,
    249–251
  fuel prices in, 250
  oil importation by, 14, 15, 30, 160, 215
Jevons, W. S., 84, 85
Johany, A. D., 98, 99
Jorgensen, D., 251

Kerosene, use for lighting, 3, 4, 9
Kilowatt hours, and heat content
    measurement, 5
Kissinger, H. A., 96
Kneese, Allan, 212
Kuwait
  economic characteristics of, 141, 142
  oil production from British Petroleum,
    109
  role in OPEC of, 98, 111, 122, 133, 155–
    157

Labor theory of value and Btu theory of
    value, 259
Land erosion from strip mining, 188
Landis report on government regulatory
    agencies, 330
Landsberg, H. H., 254
Lardarello geothermal field, Italy, 364
Lave, Lester, 252
Libya. *See also* Africa
  economic characteristics of, 141–142
  oil production of, 14, 98, 133
  price increase forced by, 112, 113, 117,
    118
  role in OPEC of, 155–157
Lighting, 3, 4, 9
Livestock, use of, for motive power, 4
Locational choice for energy industry
    facilities, 201–202
Long-run average cost function (LRAC)
  market distortions from, 43–44
Louisiana
  offshore wells of, 317
Lubricants, use of petroleum for, 3, 11

Manne, A. S., 18
Marathon Oil Company, Yates field, 234
Marginal control cost (MCC)
  applied to welfare analysis of pollution
    control problems, 196–206
  uncertainties associated with, 202–205
Marginal cost (MC)
  applications in OPEC pricing policies,
    104, 115–117, 128–131, 137–141
  in resource allocation analysis, 37–39,
    70–72, 85–86
  in welfare analysis, 197, 201–202
Marginal damage function (MDF)
    applications
  in analysis of oil import disruptions,
    223–228, 376
  to national security problems, 223
  to oil conservation issues, 230
  to pollution control problems, 196–208
Marginal efficiency of investment
    schedule applied to resource
    allocation analysis, 88, 101
Marginal rate of substitution (MRS) in
    resource allocation analysis, 38–39,
    46–49
Marginal rate of transformation (MRT) in
    resource allocation analysis, 37–39
Marginal revenue (MR) schedule applied
    to OPEC oil production, 128–131,
    137–141
  in resource allocation analysis, 71–72,
    78–79
Marginal security cost (MSC) function
    applied to problem of security of U.S.
    oil imports, 223–228
Marginal social cost and benefit schedules
    applied to energy production and
    pricing, 46, 53, 246, 372, 377. *See also*
    Welfare analysis
Marginal utility applied to resource
    allocation, 35
Marine sediments and carbon dioxide
    concentrations, 183
Market economy
  private versus social costs of production
    of energy in, 39–40
  role in solution to oil crisis, 378
Market failures in resource allocation
  decreasing cost production as cause of,
    44–45
  external causes of, 40–42
  monopolies and oligopolies as cause of,
    43–44
  public goods as cause of, 42
  as rationale for conservation policies,
    259–260
  social rate of discount as source of, 87–
    91
  welfare analysis of. *See* Welfare analysis
Marx, Karl, labor theory of value, 259
Metal refining, pollution from, 170

A 6
B 7
C 8
D 9
E 0
F 1
G 2
H 3
I 4
J 5